Deterring Terrorism

Deterring Terrorism

THEORY AND PRACTICE

Edited by Andreas Wenger and Alex Wilner

Stanford Security Studies
An Imprint of Stanford University Press
Stanford, California

Stanford University Press
Stanford, California

Special discounts for bulk quantities of Stanford Security Studies are available to corporations, professional associations, and other organizations. For details and discount information, contact the special sales department of Stanford University Press. Tel: (650) 736-1782, Fax: (650) 736-1784

Printed in the United States of America on acid-free, archival-quality paper

Library of Congress Cataloging-in-Publication Data

Deterring terrorism : theory and practice / edited by Andreas Wenger and Alex Wilner.
     pages   cm
     Includes bibliographical references and index.
     ISBN 978-0-8047-8248-7 (cloth : alk. paper)—ISBN 978-0-8047-8249-4 (pbk. : alk. paper)
   1. Terrorism—Prevention. 2. Deterrence (Strategy) I. Wenger, Andreas, editor of compilation. II. Wilner, Alex, 1979– editor of compilation.
     HV6431.D4784   2012
     363.325'17—dc23   2012009555

Typeset by Westchester Book Group in 10/14 Minion

CONTENTS

DETERRING WMD TERRORISM

EMPIRICAL EVALUATIONS

CONCLUSION

FOREWORD

Thomas C. Schelling

What is impressive is not how complicated the idea of deterrence
has become, and how carefully it has been refined and developed,
but how slow the process has been, how vague the concepts still
are, and how inelegant the current theory of deterrence is.

—Thomas C. Schelling, *The Strategy of Conflict*

DURING THE COLD WAR, the U.S. government was scandalously slow to learn, or at least to put into operation, the rudiments of deterrence. We must hope that learning how to deter terrorists may go more smoothly and more rapidly. I cannot tell just when that learning may have started; there is no obvious benchmark like Hiroshima, and there was no Pearl Harbor–like stimulus before 9/11. The comparison of progress post-Hiroshima and, say, post-9/11, is not very satisfying: the earlier problem was comparatively elementary, almost simplistic, compared with the chiaroscuro mess these authors have to deal with.

Furthermore, the post-Hiroshima era was not a history of successful deterrence. The North Koreans were not deterred in 1950. There is some hint that the North Koreans or their Soviet mentors took seriously a U.S. diplomatic statement that seemed to leave Korea out of the declared U.S. area of responsibility; still, they knew they were facing U.S. nuclear weapons. The People's Republic of China, that same year, was not deterred. North Vietnam was not. Egypt and Syria risked Israeli weapons in 1973. Argentina must not have bothered to consider British weapons in its ambitious campaign to recover the Falklands. Saddam Hussein was not afraid in 1991. Deterrence does not come without effort. Still, the one transcendent confrontation, between the USSR and the United States, or the Warsaw Pact and NATO, was a success (for both sides!). "Mutual deterrence" worked, and I would say quite comfortably after 1962. But mutuality was unique to that particular confrontation, until India and Pakistan entered such a relationship in the 1990s.

But what a simple thing that was, that bilateral mutual relationship! Just two parties, fully identified, sophisticated and "rational," fully reciprocal, with nothing at stake worth a war, no real territorial threats, at least after 1962, no great technological secrets, good diplomatic communication, especially after the "hotline" of 1963.

The present situation is vastly more unfamiliar, uncertain, complicated. Multiple adversaries, multiple target nations, uncertain or unknown "addresses," multiple motives and motives in dispute, poor or nonexistent communications, some hostilities domestic, some transnational, no collaboration on anything like mutual deterrence, no confidence in any taboo (biological, nuclear), no confidence in "rationality," multiple vulnerabilities in population targets, potential financial and industrial targets, and people vulnerable to being terrified out of all proportion to actual experienced terrorist actions. And behind it all the possibility of nuclear or biological attacks on a scale to eclipse anything yet experienced. Whether any terrorist organization has recruited, or could recruit, the scientists and technicians required for any sort of nuclear enterprise may be dubious but not out of the question.

The chapters presented here cite a substantial literature that delves deeply into the study of deterrence and the study of terrorism. Their authors were under no obligation to coordinate or come to agreement. They did together undergo two days of intense presentation and conversation in the agreeable environment of Zurich, Switzerland, and to a greater or lesser extent revised their contributions. But you will find disagreement—not expressed disagreement, but presentations that at some points are alternative or even contradictory. You have to make up your own mind. It was my privilege not only to participate in the conference at the ETH Zurich but to review the final manuscript, not as editor but as preparation for this foreword. I can assure you this is a challenging collection, one especially valuable for its variety.

ACKNOWLEDGMENTS

THANKS ARE DUE TO Geoffrey Burn at Stanford University Press for his guidance in preparing this volume. We also give thanks to Thomas Schelling and to all our contributing authors for their patience and dedication to this project. We could not have done any of this without you. We are indebted to the thoughtful reviews and useful comments and suggestions offered by our anonymous reviewers. And finally, we would like to acknowledge the support we received from our friends and colleagues at the Center for Security Studies in Zurich, Switzerland, and to thank the ETH Zurich (the Swiss Federal Institute of Technology Zurich) for supporting our 2009 conference, which was the very genesis for this book.

NOTES ON CONTRIBUTORS

Editors

Andreas Wenger is professor of Swiss and international security policy at the ETH Zurich and director of the Center for Security Studies at ETH Zurich (Swiss Federal Institute of Technology Zurich). He is the author/coeditor of several books, including *Bioterrorism: Confronting a Complex Threat* (Lynne Rienner, 2007), *How States Fight Terrorism: Policy Dynamics in the West* (Lynne Rienner, 2006), *Transforming NATO in the Cold War: Challenges Beyond Deterrence in the 1960s* (Routledge, 2006), *War Plans and Alliances in the Cold War: Threat Perceptions in the East and West* (Routledge, 2006), *Living with Peril: Eisenhower, Kennedy, and Nuclear Weapons* (Rowman & Littlefield, 1997). He also has published articles in *Cold War History*, the *Journal of Cold War Studies*, *Vierteljahrshefte für Zeitgeschichte*, the *Presidential Studies Quarterly*, and other journals.

Alex Wilner is Senior Fellow at the Center for Security Studies at the ETH Zurich. His research on deterring terrorism has been awarded a number of scholarships and grants, including those awarded by the Canadian Department of National Defence, the Social Sciences and Humanities Research Council of Canada (SSHRC), and the Transatlantic Post-Doc Fellowship for International Relations and Security (TAPIR). Dr. Wilner's work has been published in the *Journal of Strategic Studies*, *Studies in Conflict and Terrorism*, the *Israel Journal of Foreign Affairs*, *Perspectives on Terrorism*, the *Canadian Military Journal*, *Comparative Strategy*, and elsewhere. His 2011 article "Deterring the Undeterrable: Coercion, Denial, and Delegitimization in Counterterrorism" received the 2010 Amos Perlmutter Prize from the *Journal of Strategic Studies*.

Contributing Authors

Shmuel Bar is Director of Studies at the Institute of Policy and Strategy in Herzliya, Israel. Dr. Bar served for thirty years in the Israeli government, first in the IDF Intelligence and then in the Office of the Prime Minister. He has published extensively on issues relating to the Middle East, the Jihadi-Salafi movement, and global and regional terrorism and is author, most recently, of *Warrant for Terror: Contemporary Fatwas and the Duty of Jihad* (Rowman & Littlefield, 2006). He was adjunct Senior Fellow at the Hudson Institute, a Distinguished Koret Visiting Fellow at the Hoover Institution at Stanford University (2007), and is founder and CEO of IntuView Ltd., a software company dealing in text mining and hermeneutic summarization of texts in Arabic, Urdu, and other languages.

Wyn Q. Bowen is Professor of Non-Proliferation and International Security and Director of the Centre for Science and Security Studies in the Department of War Studies at King's College London. From September 2005 until August 2007 he was Professor of International Security in the Defence Studies Department at King's College based at the UK Joint Services Command and Staff College, where he was also Director of Research (2002–7). Prior to joining King's College London he spent two years as a Senior Research Associate of the Center for Nonproliferation Studies, Monterey Institute of International Studies California (1995–97). He has written widely on proliferation issues.

Michael D. Cohen received his PhD (Department of Political Science) from the University of British Columbia, Canada in 2012. His dissertation examines the relationship between nuclear proliferation, war, and time. His research has been funded by numerous UBC fellowships, the Simons Foundation, and the Lyndon Baines Johnson Foundation.

Martha Crenshaw is a Senior Fellow at the Center for International Security and Cooperation (CISAC) and the Freeman Spogli Institute for International Studies, as well as Professor of Political Science by courtesy, at Stanford University. She is also Professor of Government Emerita at Wesleyan University, where she taught from 1974 to 2007. *Explaining Terrorism*, a collection of her published work since 1972, was published by Routledge in 2011.

Paul K. Davis is a senior principal researcher at the RAND Corporation and a professor of policy analysis in the Pardee RAND Graduate School. His most recent publications include *Developing Resource-Informed Strategic Assessments and Recommendations* (RAND, 2008) and *Social Science for Counterterrorism: Putting the Pieces Together* (RAND, 2009), and *Looming Discontinuities in U.S. Military Strategy and Defense Planning* (RAND Occasional Paper, 2011).

Frank Harvey is Professor of International Relations at Dalhousie University, Canada. His most recent books include *Explaining the Iraq War: Counterfactual Theory, Logic and Evidence* (Cambridge University Press, 2011), *The Homeland Security Dilemma: Fear, Failure and the Future of American Insecurity* (Routledge, 2008), and *Smoke and Mirrors: Globalized Terrorism and the Illusion of Multilateral Security* (University of Toronto Press, 2004). Dr. Harvey was a NATO Research Fellow (1998–2000), was former director of the Centre for Foreign Policy Studies at Dalhousie, and held the 2007 J. William Fulbright Visiting Research Chair in Canadian Studies (SUNY, Plattsburgh, New York).

Brian Michael Jenkins is a senior adviser to the president of the RAND Corporation. In 1972, he initiated RAND's research on terrorism and has since become one of the world's leading authorities on political violence and sophisticated crime. A former captain in the elite Green Berets, he served in the Dominican Republic during the American intervention and later in Vietnam. In 1996, President Clinton appointed Jenkins to be a member of the White House Commission on Aviation Safety and Security. His latest books are *The Long Shadow of 9/11: America's Response to Terrorism* (RAND, 2011) and *Will Terrorists Go Nuclear?* (Prometheus Books, 2008).

Jeffrey W. Knopf is a senior lecturer at the Naval Postgraduate School, Monterey, California. He has an edited volume on *Security Assurances and Nuclear Nonproliferation* forthcoming from Stanford University Press and is the author of *Domestic Society and International Cooperation: The Impact of Protest on US Arms Control Policy* (Cambridge University Press, 1998). Dr. Knopf also previously served as the editor of *The Nonproliferation Review*. His article "The Fourth Wave in Deterrence Research" received the Bernard Brodie Prize for the best paper published in *Contemporary Security Policy* in 2010.

Jasper Pandza is a PhD student at the Centre for Science and Security Studies in the Department of War Studies at King's College London. He is also a Research Analyst in the Non-Proliferation and Disarmament Programme at the International Institute for Strategic Studies, where he conducts research on nuclear and radiological security issues. He holds a BSc in Physics and an MA in Science and Security.

David Romano holds the Thomas G. Strong Chair in Middle East Politics at Missouri State University. His work has appeared in journals such as *International Affairs*, the *Oxford Journal of Refugee Studies*, *Third World Quarterly*, and *Ethnopolitics*, and he is also the author of *The Kurdish Nationalist Movement* (Cambridge University Press, 2006). Dr. Romano writes a weekly political column for *Rudaw*, an Iraqi Kurdish newspaper, and has spent several years living and/or conducting field research in Turkey, Iraq, Iran, Syria, and Israel/Palestine.

Thomas C. Schelling received his PhD from Harvard University (1951), was on the faculty of Yale University (1953–57), Harvard (1958–90), and the University of Maryland

(1990–2005). He was with the Marshall Plan in Denmark (1948–49) and Paris (1949–50), the White House Foreign Policy Staff (1950–51), and the Executive Office of the President (foreign aid programs, 1951–53). His books include *The Strategy of Conflict* (1960), *Arms and Influence* (1966), *Micromotives and Macrobehavior* (1978), *Choice and Consequence* (1984), and *Strategies of Commitment and Other Essays* (2006). He has been elected to the National Academy of Sciences and received the National Academy of Sciences Award for Behavioral Research Relevant to the Prevention of Nuclear War. In 2005 he was awarded, together with Robert Aumann, the Bank of Sweden Prize in Economic Sciences in Memory of Alfred Nobel.

James M. Smith is Director of the United States Air Force Institute for National Security Studies and Professor of Military and Strategic Studies at the United States Air Force Academy. His related publications include *The Terrorism Threat and US Government Response* (INSS, 2001); "A Strategic Response to Terrorism" in *After 9/11: Terrorism and Crime in a Globalised World* (Centre for Conflict Studies / Centre for Foreign Policy Studies, 2005); "Japan and Aum Shinrikyo" in *Countering Terrorism and Insurgency in the 21st Century* (Praeger, 2007); and "Terrorism and Deterrence by Denial" in *Terrorism and Homeland Security* (Taylor and Francis, 2008). Dr. Smith also teaches courses on terrorism at the Josef Korbel School of International Studies, Denver University, and at the George H. W. Bush School of Government and Public Service, Texas A&M University.

Janice Gross Stein is the Belzberg Professor of Conflict Management in the Department of Political Science and the Director of the Munk School of Global Affairs at the University of Toronto, Canada. She is a Fellow of the Royal Society of Canada, and a member of the Orders of Canada and of Ontario. Dr. Stein is coeditor with Michael Barnett of *Sacrificial Aid: Faith and Humanitarianism* (Oxford University Press, 2012); with Peter Gourevitch and David Lake of *Credibility and Non-Governmental Organisations in a Globalizing World* (Cambridge University Press, 2012); and *Diplomacy in the Digital Age* (McClelland and Stewart, 2011).

Fred Wehling is Director of Educational Programs at the James Martin Center for Nonproliferation Studies and Associate Professor and Program Chair for Nonproliferation and Terrorism Studies in the Graduate School of International Policy and Management at the Monterey Institute of International Studies. Before joining the Monterey Institute, Dr. Wehling was a consultant at RAND, Coordinator of Policy Research for the University of California's Institute on Global Conflict and Cooperation (IGCC), and a researcher at the Cooperative Monitoring Center (CMC) at Sandia National Laboratories. He is a contributor to *The Four Faces of Nuclear Terrorism* (Routledge, 2005), coauthor of *World Politics in a New Era*, 3rd ed. (Thomson Wadsworth, 2003), and author of various other books, articles, and reports.

INTRODUCTION

LINKING DETERRENCE TO TERRORISM
Promises and Pitfalls

Alex Wilner and Andreas Wenger

CAN TERRORISM BE DETERRED? Despite the subject's overwhelming practical importance, deterrence theory has yet to be systematically applied to counter-terrorism. For the most part, the literature evaluating deterring terrorism is innovative but sparse. A critical mass has by no means been reached, nor has a concrete research agenda been identified. These deficiencies need to be remedied. Applying the logic of deterrence to terrorism will not only prove an interesting theoretical enterprise, but it might also reveal more pragmatic strategies for confronting and containing the threat of terrorism. What we need today is a better appreciation for the theory and practice of deterring terrorism.

Much of the debate on deterring terrorism has been driven by reactions to the policy responses following 9/11. With al Qaeda's attack on the United States, the immediate thrust of state policy was built around the assumption that terrorist organizations like al Qaeda were altogether undeterrable. The 9/11 attacks corroborated arguments that terrorists were irrational and that religiously motivated terrorism in particular could not be deterred. The strategic response of the United States was a global "War on Terror," a marshaling of preventive capabilities, a reliance on the use of preemptive force in international relations, and a strategy of eradicating al Qaeda and its supporters. The global conflict with al Qaeda necessarily formed the contextual backdrop against which the emerging research on deterring terrorism developed.

Eventually, however, the accepted premise that terrorists were irrational and that deterring terrorism was not possible was critically questioned. Terrorists were more properly described as "rational fanatics."[1] Though individual members may embrace extremist views, the organizations they form none-theless establish practical priorities and use violence to achieve a variety of strategic, territorial, and political goals.[2] Consequently, the logic of deterrence is relevant when thinking about combating terrorism.

Nevertheless, focusing on al Qaeda has led to other theoretical and practical concerns. Al Qaeda's demise, for instance, may be a worthy goal, but it also negates the feasibility of applying deterrence in practice. That the United States and its allies have sought to destroy al Qaeda and have purposefully targeted and killed many of its top leaders, including Osama bin Laden, creates a deterrent dilemma. Deterrence is a bargaining tactic that emphasizes the use of threats to manipulate an adversary's behavior and hinges on offering an adversary a way out. If al Qaeda rightly assumes that the United States is seeking its eventual annihilation, it will have little reason to believe that an alternative deterrent relationship, in which it is allowed to survive, is ever possible. And yet, terrorist groups are complex and intricate organizations. In thinking about deterrence, disaggregating the terrorist organization into its parts and processes reveals the peripheral actors and specific individuals against which deterrence might be applied. If so, even in al Qaeda's case, where destruction is a primary strategic goal, deterrence theory remains relevant.

Finally, any study of deterring terrorism should avoid too narrowly focusing on al Qaeda. The differences between terrorist groups are important. Disparate goals and diverging terrorist motivations—whether nationally, ideologically, or religiously rooted—determine whether and how deterrence can be applied to any particular case. The contours of a deterrent strategy are therefore partially determined by the type and nature of the terrorist organization in question, its distinctive goals, assets, activities, and areas of operation, and on the specific actors and processes inherent to it. Importantly, this book is about deterring terrorism, writ large, and looks beyond al Qaeda and 9/11 in order to identify the circumstances and cases in which deterrence is feasible.

Many of these initial quandaries reveal how an application and evaluation of deterring terrorism might properly begin. However, under all circumstances, deterrence, when applied to terrorism, is but one part of a much broader counterterrorism strategy that includes both offensive and defensive tactics. The simultaneous application of deterrence and other more traditional counterterrorism approaches necessarily blurs the line between offense, defense, and deterrence, creating theoretical, practical, and methodological challenges in how we think about and apply deterrence theory to terrorism.

FOUR WAVES OF DETERRENCE RESEARCH

During the Cold War, Thomas Schelling reminds us in his foreword, the evolution, development, and maturation of deterrence theory proved a slow and deliberate process. The growth and refinement of core concepts of deterrence took many decades and were the result of "three waves" of deterrence research.[3] The process began in earnest in a preliminary, first wave of research that followed quickly after the end of the Second World War. Early theorists were responding specifically to the development of nuclear weapons and their effect on the study and practice of warfare more broadly.[4] While these early deterrence theorists established the conceptual groundwork for the approaches that were to be developed a decade later, their immediate theoretical and political influence on the theory and practice of international relations was more limited. It was not until the USSR eventual emerged as a capable nuclear power that policymakers and academics were united in one common goal: avoiding any and all nuclear conflicts.

In the second wave of research that emerged as a reaction to these shifting international priorities, deterrence theory provided strategists with an abstract framework with which to manage the nuclear rivalry. This wave of deterrence research was marked by scientific modeling and the application of game theory methodology to deterrent relations. Many of the core theoretical deterrent concepts that remain in use today are products of this second wave of research. In a relatively short burst of theoretical creativity, deterrence theory developed into a nuanced area of study.[5] Herein, the theoretical prerequisites of deterrence—*commitment, communication, capability, credibility, and resolve*—were identified and fleshed out, and the theoretical foundations of deterrence were established.[6] Deterrence, or "inducing an adversary . . . *not* to do something," was differentiated from "compellence," or inducing another "*to do* something" it might not otherwise have done.[7] *Deterrence by punishment*, which manipulates behavior through the application of threats, was subdivided from *deterrence by denial*, which functions by reducing the perceived benefits an adversary expects to collect.[8] Both processes address an actor's cost-benefit calculus but approach it from different ends; punishment adds costs, while denial takes away benefits.

Given the characteristic similarities shared by the United States and the USSR and their alliance partnerships, the scope conditions of the deterrence concepts developed during this second wave of research were respectively narrow. Elementally, traditional deterrence theory referenced the bipolar setting of the era, applied most specifically to nuclear conflict, was oriented toward preserving the international status quo, and sought to inform the behavior of mutually rational and unitary state actors.

In time, the theoretical and deductive enterprise of the second wave gave way to the empirically driven third wave of deterrence research. Emerging during the 1970s, the third wave was primarily geared toward evaluating and testing the concepts, models, causal links, and theories that had been previously proposed.[9] By means of both qualitative and quantitative methodology, a substantial research agenda emerged. Deterrence success and failure, it was illustrated, were based not only on an actor's commitment and/or resolve but could also be dictated by the type and nature of the interests at stake and by the costs associated with acquiescing to a threat.[10] And while in theory a deterrent was deemed effective when the expected utility of pursuing a given action was less than the expected costs of enduring a punishment, utility itself, it was found, could be measured differently by varied, though equally rational, actors.[11]

Likewise, threats and denial strategies were offset by the deterrent/compellent value of positive inducements and rewards, which second-wave theories neglected to properly address.[12] The third wave also tackled some of the psychological processes inherent to deterrent relations, illustrating how individual cognitive characteristics, fear, pressure, fatigue, and other human traits and organizational constraints influenced the manner in which calculations were made and decisions taken.[13] An actor's assessment of costs, benefits, and probabilities could also be influenced by misperceptions and failures to accurately or systematically interpret an adversary's views, intentions, and positions.[14] And culture, values, historical development, and other social and political characteristics were also thought to influence how deterrence could be applied in practice.[15] In culmination, the third wave provided a more nuanced interpretation of the limitations, scopes, and boundaries associated with applying deterrence theory in practice.

Today, we are in the midst of a "fourth wave" of deterrence research,[16] which emerged at the end of the Cold War as a result of the collapse of the USSR. The focus of this research is directed toward mapping the contours of deterrence theory against a backdrop of novel and often asymmetric threats, from "rogue" states capable of producing and proliferating weapons of mass destruction to non-state actors like cyber warriors, pirates, and terrorist organizations.[17] As part of the fourth wave of deterrence research, this edited volume aims to evaluate the theoretical and practical challenges involved in deterring terrorism in particular. Today, as in the early phases of the Cold War, the theory and practice of deterring terrorism remain in their mere infancy. Core concepts of deterring terrorism are only now being developed, and very few studies have taken empirical steps to test and refine theoretical propositions.[18] This volume addresses both these areas, offering insight on the theory and practice of deterring terrorism while highlighting empirical evaluations of the subject.

DETERRING TERRORISM: THEORY, PRACTICE, AND EMPIRICISM

The research presented here is based on findings generated during a conference organized by the Center for Security Studies (CSS), held in November 2009 at the ETH Zurich (Swiss Federal Institute of Technology) in Switzerland. The Zurich gathering was the first of its kind to bring terrorism experts and deterrence experts together to discuss the common theme of deterring terrorism.

This volume, like the conference itself, investigates two broad themes. The first is theoretical in nature: Can the traditional tenets of deterrence theory be applied to counterterrorism? What theoretical boundaries need to be expanded, and what core concepts need to be refined or developed? How can we circumvent the incompatibility between destroying an organization and deterring an organization? And how do structural complexity and asymmetries in power, organization, capability, and resolve inform deterrent relationships between states and terrorist organizations? The second broad theme is practical in nature: What role does deterrence have within a dynamic counterterrorism strategy? Are some terrorist organizations more predisposed than others to deterrence, and if so, why? More specifically, what particular elements within terrorist networks and what stages within the terrorism process are most susceptible to deterrence and compellence? How can we distinguish between deterrent measures and traditional offensive and defensive counterterrorism measures? And how are we to establish metrics for measuring the success and failure of our counterterrorism deterrent policies and strategies?

The book is organized in three parts. The first section evaluates the theoretical and practical promises and pitfalls of linking deterrence theory to conventional terrorism. It begins from the consensus view emerging from fourth-wave scholarship that while deterrence may contribute to the management of terrorist threats (and should not so easily be discarded), actual applications of deterrence to counterterrorism will be more limited in scope. In thinking about deterring terrorism, absolute deterrence success—an imperative goal during the Cold War—is replaced by marginal success. Deterring all terrorism may not be possible, but deterring some terrorism may be sufficient. The conceptual difference is important. The conditions and structural context that were associated with deterring the Soviet Union, for instance, are radically different from those associated with deterring conventional terrorism. Traditional deterrence practice, especially during the Cold War, was based on the avoidance of all wars—particularly those that risked a nuclear exchange. In counterterrorism, on the other hand, deterrence is based on influencing adversarial behavior at the fringes, so that applications of deterrence in theory and practice allow room for some acts of political violence to occur even within an ongoing deterrent relationship. From this starting position, the chapters in the first section investigate both the theory and practice of deterring terrorism.

From a theoretical point of view, these chapters illustrate how traditional deterrence theory may be too narrow in scope to serve as a single, unifying theory for counterterrorism and investigate the benefits and unintended trade-offs of broadening the logic and meaning of deterrence. From a practical point of view, the chapters suggest that while in theory deterrence can be applied to counterterrorism, doing so in practice may be especially challenging because of the difficulties associated with properly building, defining, communicating, and situating deterrent threats within the context of an ongoing counterterrorism campaign.

In the second section of the book, the focus in particular is on deterring terrorism employing chemical, biological, radiological, and nuclear (CBRN) weapons—collectively referred to as weapons of mass destruction (WMD). An especially worrying trend that has emerged from the end of the Cold War has been the confluence between the growth of transnational terrorist organizations and the continued proliferation of WMD technology, know-how, and weaponry. These chapters explore the various strategies that might help deter the terrorist acquisition and use of WMD. This focus is especially pertinent given recent decisions in the United States to adopt a strategy of deterring WMD terrorism. Closer analysis, however, illustrates that significant strategic ambiguities remain and that little consideration has been placed on gauging how deterring WMD terrorism might work in practice. Successfully applying deterrence to WMD terrorism may depend on how terrorist groups themselves think about the practicality of acquiring WMD materials and the utility of using such weapons. Herein, a strategy that relies on deterrence by denial offers persuasive contributions to more traditional approaches that are primarily based on deterrence by punishment.

In the third section of the book, several empirical evaluations of deterring terrorism are put forward. To date, qualitative and quantitative research on the subject of deterring terrorism has been near nonexistent.[19] Despite the fact that testing and assessing theoretical propositions require robust empirical research—as third-wave scholars have shown—very few authors have tested deterring terrorism against specific historical events or case studies. The chapters in this section offer a cross-selection of empirical research on the subject of deterring terrorism, relying on both comparative case studies of various terrorist groups and state facilitators and on more tailored evaluations of specific campaigns of terrorism. In so doing, the third section of this volume offers insight on how the theory of deterrence actually applies in practice. It derives regional, local, and historical lessons for deterring terrorism, develops policy recommendations for countering terrorism more broadly, and addresses some of the traditional methodological concerns involved in testing deterrence theory.

A ROADMAP TO THE VOLUME

Deterring Conventional Terrorism

The volume is composed of twelve chapters, four in each of the three thematic sections. In Chapter 1, Jeffrey Knopf offers a broad overview of the literature on deterring terrorism, laying down the theoretical and analytical groundwork upon which subsequent chapters are rooted. Knopf situates research on deterring terrorism into the broader fourth wave. He then illustrates that despite public reservations concerning the feasibility of deterring terrorism, there is general consensus within the literature that the logic of deterrence "remains relevant in dealing with terrorism," and that while it is "unlikely to be 100 percent effective," the emphasis is on improving results "at the margins" rather than on achieving perfection. In Chapter 2, Janice Gross Stein suggests that while deterring terrorism is "not impossible in theory," doing so in practice is "exceedingly difficult." Deterring terrorism is possible under certain conditions, Stein explains, but the "abstract formulation" of deterrence theory "is deceptively simple," such that applications of deterrence in practice are far more problematic than is conventionally accepted. She suggests that applying deterrence theory to counterterrorism requires that we think about deterrence as a broader political strategy of influence that not only takes into consideration our own behavioral limitations in combating terrorism but also explores the role promises and positive inducements (and not only threats) have in shaping our deterrent relationships with adversaries.

In Chapter 3, Paul Davis argues that classic deterrence theory, with its emphasis on punishment, is "not an appropriate focal point" for thinking about deterring terrorism. Instead, Davis places impetus on "influence," a concept that goes well beyond threats of punishment to incorporate all varieties of instruments in affecting behavior. He then offers a number of conceptual models depicting terrorist decision making and (group and individual) motivation for participating in terrorism to further pinpoint which elements, actors, and processes within each model might be most susceptible to influencing strategies. In Chapter 4, Frank Harvey and Alex Wilner investigate the theoretical prerequisites for deterrence and compellence success and examine the dilemmas and limitations associated with deterring terrorism in practice. Their focus is on "counter-coercion": an opponent's ability to "interfere with and diminish" a defender's coercive strategy in ways that alters that defender's behavior. Terrorist organizations, they argue, retain "enormous counter-coercion potential" that can diminish and undermine a state's preferred deterrent or compellent strategy. Terrorists do so, Harvey and Wilner propose, through both active and passive counter-coercion.

Deterring WMD Terrorism

Chapters 5 through 8 mark the volume's shift in focus from assessing the theoretical and practical assumptions involved in deterring terrorism in general to evaluating the prospects for deterring WMD terrorism more specifically. In Chapter 5, Brian Michael Jenkins speculates on how terrorist organizations might interpret the utility and risk of acquiring and using nuclear weapons. Jenkins suggests that understanding how terrorists think about nuclear weapons will help states decide how best to further reduce the likelihood that they acquire and use them. In Chapter 6, Martha Crenshaw reviews the U.S. policy and strategy of deterring al Qaeda's use of nuclear weapons. As it now stands, the primary intent of U.S. policy is to deter nuclear terrorism "through threats of retaliation." In a detailed overview of the steps taken by the George W.

Bush and Barack Obama administrations, Crenshaw demonstrates that while Washington has taken strides to formulate a deterrent strategy that specifically targets al Qaeda's use of nuclear weapons, the very idea of deterrence is not yet "integrated into an overall strategic conception that is logically coherent in relating ends to means." Establishing a deterrent policy on paper is one thing; putting U.S. deterrent policy into practice is quite another.

In Chapter 7, James Smith develops a framework for deterring WMD terrorism that relies on the application of deterrence by denial. For Smith, deterrence by denial "targets the adversary strategy" and operates through a "counter-strategy aimed at denying the adversary strategic success." He suggests that denial has gained a degree of importance in deterring terrorism and offers a comprehensive framework that includes the denial of opportunity, capability, strategy, and legitimacy. In Chapter 8, Wyn Bowen and Jasper Pandza assess how deterrence by denial can be applied to counter radiological terrorism. The authors begin by illustrating the wide range of potential attack scenarios involving radiological materials and assess the likely consequences of a terrorist attack using a radiological dispersion device (RDD), or "dirty bomb." Contrary to public perceptions, they suggest that RDD attacks "would cause very few, if any, casualties due to radiation," but would have major and lasting psychological, social, and economic effects. With this backdrop, the authors explore how deterrence by denial might inform efforts to counter radiological threats.

Empirical Evaluations of Deterring Terrorism

The remaining four chapters present empirical evaluations of deterring terrorism, testing some of the propositions, frameworks, and theories developed in the previous eight chapters against particular case studies. In Chapter 9, Shmuel Bar offers a case study evaluation of Israeli deterrence vis-à-vis the Palestinian organizations Hamas and Fatah over the past decade. Differentiating between strategic and tactical deterrence, he suggests that Israel has retained strategic deterrence in relation to its state adversaries (as a result of their "perception" of Israel's military capabilities) but only occasionally achieved tactical deterrence with terrorist adversaries (as a result of Israel's "day-to-day" use of its counterterrorism capabilities). Bar concludes that Israel was able to achieve "a degree of intermittent deterrence against Palestinian terrorists," but that success was generally limited to the few historical periods where terrorist leaders were in control of the violence "orchestrated by their followers" and the occasions where Israel "properly and credibly communicated" deterrent threats. In Chapter 10, David Romano offers a comparative analysis of two case studies of deterring political violence: Turkish and Iranian efforts to deter/compel Kurdish insurgent groups. In a detailed historical assessment of both cases, Romano offers insight as to the role deterrence, compellence, positive inducements, and other forms of persuasion have had on informing both Turkish and Iranian policy vis-à-vis violent Kurdish non-state actors. Deterrent success was the result of applying the right balance of threats and promises.

In Chapter 11, Michael Cohen investigates the deterrence of state sponsorship of conventional terrorism. In a comparative analysis of Iran and Libya, he highlights the factors involved in deterring and compelling these states from facilitating and actively supporting terrorist activity. Cohen argues that retarding the "growth of existing terrorist groups" and impeding "the birth of new ones" will require investigating why some states forgo the sponsorship of terrorism while others do not and gaining a deeper understanding of the "cross-national variation" in the cessation of state sponsorship. Finally, in Chapter 12, Fred Wehling investigates a case of CBRN terrorism, drawing lessons for deterring terrorism from the campaign of chlorine-enhanced bombings by al Qaeda in Iraq (AQI) in 2006–7. AQI's chlorine campaign, writes Wehling, "offers a rare opportunity to study deterrence theory when terrorists demonstrate both a clear motivation and capability to use CBRN." After illustrating how the Coalition (and Iraqi) strategy was carried out, Wehling judges its deterrent and compellent effect on AQI's behavior.

In the Conclusion, we, as editors of the volume, highlight some of the more pertinent conclusions derived from the chapters. We emphasize the unresolved issues and theoretical, practical, and methodological dilemmas associated with deterring terrorism. By drawing out the theoretical and practical implications of the overall analysis, we offer insight on where the study of deterring terrorism is heading and suggest avenues for further research.

FINAL THOUGHTS

The goal of this edited volume in bringing these chapters together is to offer a comprehensive overview of the theory and practice of deterring terrorism. By combining theoretical research with empirical research, the book as a whole takes two important steps. First, it identifies how and where theories of deterrence apply to counterterrorism, shedding light on how traditional and less-traditional notions of deterrence can be applied to novel and asymmetric threats. Second, the book offers a preliminary assessment of these theoretical propositions, evaluating specific terrorist groups, conflicts, and events in light of the deterrence literature. The sum of these two processes is greater appreciation for how deterrence continues to resonate with and can be applied to emerging, twenty-first-century threats. And while deterrence is unlikely to become a policy panacea for terrorism, the processes involved in deterrence carry value for developing and applying effective counterterrorism policies that can help states contain and curtail the nature and ferocity of the terrorism challenge they face.

Deterring terrorism will prove a complicated endeavor, far more complex than deterring state adversaries. But both deterrent processes share the same inherent logic: manipulating an adversary's behavior in ways that suit one's preferences by applying a variety of coercive leverages against that adversary's assets, goals, and values. Deterring terrorism is possible, but difficult. With the right approach and under the right conditions, deterrence theory can help inform broader counterterrorism strategies in a way that allows states to better manage the threats they face.

NOTES

1. Ehud Sprinzak, "Rational Fanatics," *Foreign Policy*, No. 120 (September/October 2000); David Lake, "Rational Extremism: Understanding Terrorism in the Twenty-first Century," *Dialog IO* 1:1 (2002); Marc Sageman, *Understanding Terror Networks* (Philadelphia: University of Pennsylvania Press, 2004); John Horgan, *The Psychology of Terrorism* (New York: Routledge, 2005); Christopher Harmon, "The Myth of the Invincible Terrorist," *Policy Review* 142 (2007); Audrey Kurth Cronin, *How Terrorism Ends: Understanding the Decline and Demise of Terrorist Campaigns* (Princeton, NJ: Princeton University Press, 2009).

2. Martha Crenshaw, "An Organizational Approach to the Analysis of Political Terrorism," *Orbis* 29:3 (1985); Bruce Hoffman, *Inside Terrorism* (New York: Columbia University Press, 1998); Martha Crenshaw, "The Logic of Terrorism: Terrorist Behavior as a Product of Strategic Culture," in *Origins of Terrorism*, ed. Walter Reich (New York: Cambridge University Press, 1990); Richard Betts, "The Soft Underbelly of American Primacy: Tactical Advantages of Terror," *Political Science Quarterly* 117:1 (2002); Bruce Hoffman, "The Logic of Suicide Terrorism," *Atlantic Monthly* 291:5 (2003); Robert Pape, *Dying to Win: The Strategic Logic of Suicide Terrorism* (New York: Random House, 2005); Mia Bloom, *Dying to Kill: The Allure of Suicide Terrorism* (New York: Columbia University Press, 2005); Louise Richardson, *What Terrorists*

Want (New York: Random House, 2006); Robert Pape, "Suicide and Terrorism: What We've Learned Since 9/11," *Policy Analysis* No. 582 (2006); Fawaz Gerges, *Journey of the Jihadist: Inside Muslim Militancy* (Toronto: Harcourt, 2007). For work that critically investigates the strategic model of terrorism, see Scott Atran, "Mishandling Suicide Terrorism," *Washington Quarterly* 27:3 (2004); Max Abrahms, "Are Terrorists Really Rational? The Palestinian Example," *Orbis* 48:3 (2004); Scott Atran, "The Moral Logic and Growth of Suicide Terrorism," *Washington Quarterly* 29:2 (2006); Max Abrahms, "What Terrorists Really Want: Terrorist Motives and Counterterrorism Strategy," *International Security* 31:1 (2008); Assaf Moghadam, "Motives for Martyrdom: Al-Qaida, Salafi Jihad, and the Spread of Suicide Attacks," *International Security* 33:3 (2008/9).

3. Robert Jervis, "Deterrence Theory Revisited," *World Politics* 31:2 (1979); Lawrence Freedman, *Deterrence* (Malden, MA: Political Press, 2004), 21–25.

4. See the contributions offered in Bernard Brodie, ed., *The Absolute Weapon* (New York: Harcourt, Brace, 1946); Oskar Morgenstern, *The Question of National Defense* (New York: Random House, 1959).

5. For instance, *immediate deterrence*, which occurs when a challenger contemplates an attack such that a defender mounts a retaliatory threat, was differentiated from *general deterrence*, where adversaries utilize coercive threats "to regulate" their relations more broadly. *Direct deterrence*, preventing an attack on one's own territory, was separated from *extended deterrence*, deterring attacks on an allied party. And *countervalue targeting*, threatening societal and economic assets, was distinguished from *counterforce targeting*, threatening military capabilities. See Patrick Morgan, *Deterrence: A Conceptual Analysis* (Beverly Hills, CA: Sage Publications, 1977); Patrick Morgan, *Deterrence Now* (Cambridge: Cambridge University Press, 2003); Herman Kahn, *On Thermonuclear War* (Princeton, NJ: Princeton University Press, 1960); Bruce Russett, "The Calculus of Deterrence," *Journal of Conflict Resolution* 7:2 (1963); Paul Huth and Bruce Russett, "What Makes Deterrence Work? Cases from 1900 to 1980," *World Politics* 36:4 (1984).

6. William W. Kaufmann, "The Requirements of Deterrence," in *Military Policy and National Security*, ed. William Kaufmann (Princeton, NJ: Princeton University Press, 1956); Thomas Schelling, *The Strategy of Conflict* (Cambridge, MA: Harvard University Press, 1960); Herman Kahn, *On Escalation: Metaphors and Scenarios* (New York: Praeger, 1965).

7. Thomas Schelling, *Arms and Influence* (New Haven, CT: Yale University Press, 1966); Thomas Schelling, "Thinking About Nuclear Terrorism," *International Security* 6:4 (1982).

8. Glenn Snyder, *Deterrence and Defense: Toward a Theory of National Security* (Princeton, NJ: Princeton University Press, 1961); John Mearsheimer, *Conventional Deterrence* (Ithaca, NY: Cornell University Press, 1983); Jonathan Shimshoni, *Israel*

and Conventional Deterrence: Border Warfare from 1953 to 1970 (Ithaca, NY: Cornell University Press, 1988).

9. See, among others, Alexander George and Richard Smoke, *Deterrence in American Foreign Policy: Theory and Practice* (New York: Columbia University Press, 1974); Bruce Russett, "The Calculus of Deterrence," *Journal of Conflict Resolution* 7:2 (1963); Morgan, *Deterrence Now*; Glenn Snyder and Paul Diesing, *Conflict Among Nations* (Princeton, NJ: Princeton University Press, 1977).

10. George and Smoke, *Deterrence*; Huth and Russett, "What Makes Deterrence Work?"; Trevor Salmon, "Rationality and Politics: The Case of Strategic Theory," *British Journal of International Studies* 2:3 (1976); Gary Schuab, "Deterrence, Compellence, and Prospect Theory," *Political Psychology* 25:3 (2004).

11. Richard Ned Lebow, *Between Peace and War: The Nature of International Crisis* (Baltimore: Johns Hopkins University Press, 1981); Richard Ned Lebow and Janice Gross Stein, "Rational Deterrence Theory: I Think, Therefore I Deter," *World Politics* 41:2 (1989); Richard Ned Lebow and Janice Gross Stein, "Deterrence: The Elusive Dependent Variable," *World Politics* 42:3 (1990).

12. Paul Huth and Bruce Russett, "Testing Deterrence Theory: Rigor Makes a Difference," *World Politics* 42:4 (1990); Jervis, "Deterrence Theory Revisited"; Ted Hopf, *Peripheral Visions: Deterrence Theory and American Foreign Policy in the Third World, 1965–1990* (Ann Arbor: University of Michigan Press, 1994).

13. Ole Holsti, *Crisis, Escalation, War* (Montreal: McGill–Queen's University Press, 1972); John Steinbruner, "Beyond Rational Deterrence: The Struggle for New Conceptions," *World Politics* 28:2 (1976); Robert Jervis, Richard Ned Lebow, and Janice Gross Stein, *Psychology and Deterrence* (Baltimore: Johns Hopkins University Press, 1985); Christopher Achen and Duncan Snidal, "Rational Deterrence Theory and Comparative Case Studies," *World Politics* 41:2 (1989); Frank Harvey, "Rigor Mortis or Rigor, More Test: Necessity, Sufficiency, and Deterrence," *International Studies Quarterly* 42:4 (1998); Stephen Walt, "Rigor or Rigor Mortis, Rational Choice and Security Studies," *International Security* 23:4 (1999); Frank Harvey, "Practicing Coercion: Revisiting Successes and Failures Using Boolean Logic and Comparative Methods," *Journal of Conflict Resolution* 43:6 (1999); Jeffrey Berejikian, "A Cognitive Theory of Deterrence," *Journal of Peace Research* 39:2 (2002).

14. Robert Jervis, *Perception and Misperception in International Politics* (Princeton, NJ: Princeton University Press, 1976); Robert Jervis, "Deterrence and Perception," *International Security* 7:3 (1982/83); Kevin Woods and Mark Stout, "Saddam's Perceptions and Misperceptions: The Case of 'Desert Storm,'" *Journal of Strategic Studies* 33:1 (2010).

15. Keith Payne, *Deterrence in the Second Nuclear Age* (Lexington: University Press of Kentucky, 1996); Keith Payne, "The Fallacies of Cold War Deterrence and a New Direction," *Comparative Strategy* 22:5 (2003); Colin Gray, "The Reformation of Deterrence: Moving On," *Comparative Strategy* 22:5 (2003).

16. Jeffrey W. Knopf, "The Fourth Wave in Deterrence Research," *Contemporary Security Policy* 31:1 (2010).

17. Richard Harknett, "The Logic of Conventional Deterrence and the End of the Cold War," *Security Studies* 4:1 (1994); Frank Zagare and David Kilgour, *Perfect Deterrence* (Cambridge: Cambridge University Press, 2000); Robert L. Jervis, "The Confrontation Between Iraq and the US: Implications for the Theory and Practice of Deterrence," *European Journal of International Relations* 9:2 (2003); Freedman, *Deterrence*; Anne Sartori, *Deterrence by Diplomacy* (Princeton, NJ: Princeton University Press, 2005); Derek Smith, *Deterring America: Rogue States and the Proliferation of Weapons of Mass Destruction* (Cambridge: Cambridge University Press, 2006); James Lebovic, *Deterring International Terrorism and Rogue States: US National Security Policy After 9/11* (London: Routledge, 2007); M. Elaine Bunn, "Can Deterrence Be Tailored?" *Strategic Forum* 225 (2007); T. V. Paul, Patrick Morgan, and James Wirtz, eds., *Complex Deterrence: Strategy in the Global Age* (Chicago: University of Chicago Press, 2009); Martin Libicki, *Cyberdeterrence and Cyberwar* (Santa Monica, CA: RAND, 2009).

18. See, among others, Paul Davis and Brian Jenkins, *Deterrence and Influence in Counterterrorism: A Component in the War on al Qaeda* (Santa Monica, CA: RAND, 2002); Martha Crenshaw, "Coercive Diplomacy and the Response to Terrorism," in *The United States and Coercive Diplomacy*, ed. Robert Art and Patrick Cronin (Washington, DC: United States Institute of Peace, 2003); Wyn Bowen, "Deterrence and Asymmetry: Non-State Actors and Mass Casualty Terrorism," *Contemporary Security Policy* 25:1 (2004); Daniel Whiteneck, "Deterring Terrorists: Thoughts on a Framework," *Washington Quarterly* 28:3 (2005); David Auerswald, "Deterring Nonstate WMD Attacks," *Political Science Quarterly* 121:4 (2006); Ian Shapiro, *Containment: Rebuilding a Strategy Against Global Terror* (Princeton, NJ: Princeton University Press, 2007); Jeffrey W. Knopf, "Wrestling with Deterrence: Bush Administration Strategy After 9/11," *Contemporary Security Policy* 29:2 (2008); Lewis Dunn, "Influencing Terrorists' Acquisition and Use of Weapons of Mass Destruction" (paper presentation at NATO Defence College, Rome, Italy, August 5, 2008); Elbridge Colby, "Expanded Deterrence: Broadening the Threat of Retaliation," *Policy Review* 149 (2008); James Smith and Brent Talbot, "Terrorism and Deterrence by Denial," in *Terrorism and Homeland Security*, ed. Paul Viotti, Michael Opheim, and Nicholas Bowen (New York: CRC Press, 2008); Patrick Porter, "Long Wars and Long Telegrams: Containing Al–Qaeda," *International Affairs* 85:2 (2009); Janice Gross Stein, "Rational Deterrence Against 'Irrational' Adversaries? No Common Knowledge," in Paul, Morgan, and Wirtz, *Complex Deterrence*; Alex Wilner, "Deterring the Undeterrable: Coercion, Denial, and Delegitimization in Counterterrorism," *Journal of Strategic Studies* 34:1 (2011).

19. For the exceptions, see Robert Anthony, "Deterrence and the 9-11 Terrorists," Institute for Defense Analyses, May 2003; Robert Trager and Dessislava Zagorcheva,

"Deterring Terrorism: It Can Be Done," *International Security* 30:3 (2005/6); Gary Geipel, "Urban Terrorists in Continental Europe After 1970: Implications for Deterrence and Defeat of Violent Nonstate Actors," *Comparative Strategy* 26:5 (2007); Shmuel Bar, "Deterring Nonstate Terrorist Groups: The Case of Hizballah," *Comparative Strategy* 26:5 (2007); Amos Malka, "Israel and Asymmetrical Deterrence," *Comparative Strategy* 27:1 (2008); Shmuel Bar, "Deterring Terrorists: What Israel Has Learned," *Policy Review* 149 (2008); Alex Wilner, "Targeted Killings in Afghanistan: Measuring Coercion and Deterrence in Counterterrorism and Counterinsurgency," *Studies in Conflict and Terrorism* 33:4 (2010).

DETERRING TERRORISM

1 TERRORISM AND THE FOURTH WAVE IN DETERRENCE RESEARCH

Jeffrey W. Knopf

PRIOR TO 9/11, there was little research on deterring terrorism.[1] Some terrorism specialists expressed skepticism about using a deterrence framework to combat terrorism,[2] but most terrorism researchers did not examine this strategy in detail. Deterrence researchers in the field of security studies, meanwhile, focused on the strategy's uses in relation to interstate conflict, especially at the nuclear level, and generally ignored terrorism by non-state actors.

This changed after the September 11 attacks. A conventional wisdom quickly emerged that deterrence would prove irrelevant against groups like al Qaeda. Skeptics expressed doubt that deterrent threats would sway either individual terrorists, who are willing to commit suicide for their cause, or terrorist organizations, who "lack a return address" against which to retaliate. Ironically, as the prospects for deterring terrorism started to appear more daunting, scholars began seeking to adapt deterrence to meet the new challenge. The result has been a sizable body of new research on deterring terrorism.[3]

Elsewhere, building on earlier work by Robert Jervis that identified three waves in deterrence research,[4] I have described the recent research on deterring terrorism as being part of a broader fourth wave in deterrence research.[5] The fourth wave includes reflections on the appropriate role of deterrence in general after the Cold War and research on the prospects for deterring rogue states armed with weapons of mass destruction (WMD). Research on deterring terrorism, however, constitutes the largest and most original part of the fourth wave, and it will be the focus of this chapter. The goal of this chapter is to provide a classic literature review. It summarizes the key developments in the literature, identifies the main points of consensus and remaining disagreement, and draws attention to the most important gaps and problems in the recent research.

The most important point on which there is a near consensus in the literature is that deterrence remains relevant in dealing with terrorism. But given the many challenges involved, scholars also agree that the strategy is unlikely to be 100 percent effective. Current research on deterring terrorism therefore focuses on improving results at the margins, not on achieving perfection.

Three approaches to deterring terrorism have received the most supportive commentary. The first approach involves deterrence that is indirect in nature, intended to pressure third parties who facilitate terrorism rather than terrorist operatives themselves. The second approach reflects a return to Glenn Snyder's old concept of "deterrence by denial."[6] The third approach, consistent with a general trend in the fourth wave toward broadening the concept of deterrence, explores sources of deterrence that are nonmilitary in nature, such as "deterrence by delegitimization."[7] The area of greatest debate concerns traditional notions of deterrence by punishment, in particular the efficacy of threatening retaliation against the communities that terrorists claim to represent. Because there is considerable disagreement about the likely effects of seeking to deter terrorism through threats of societal punishment, classic punishment approaches have not been endorsed and elaborated in the literature as widely as the other three approaches listed above.

The rest of this chapter proceeds as follows: It first reviews literature that focuses on conventional terrorism. This section summarizes indirect, denial, and punishment approaches. The chapter then reviews literature that focuses explicitly on WMD terrorism. This discussion summarizes the most innovative of the nonmilitary approaches, which involves seeking to delegitimize and thereby ensure a public backlash against WMD terrorism; this section also highlights dilemmas involved in trying to hold states accountable as potential sources of nuclear materials. The chapter concludes by identifying a need for more empirical research and calling attention to possible trade-offs involved in the various proposals for deterring terrorism.

DETERRING CONVENTIONAL TERRORISM

The suggestions in the fourth wave for deterring conventional (that is, non-WMD) terrorism are organized below into indirect, denial, and punishment approaches, respectively. Delegitimization approaches are not addressed here because they have been proposed mainly in connection with threats of nuclear terrorism. Suggestions for deterring WMD terrorism are dealt with separately in the next section.

Indirect Deterrence

Most of the core ideas for how to apply deterrence to terrorism appeared fairly soon after 9/11. A short book published in 2002 by Paul Davis and Brian Jenkins of RAND was especially influential. Their key insight involved disaggregating a terrorist network into its component elements. Although the suicide terrorist who has hijacked an airplane is almost certainly beyond the reach of deterrence, other actors involved in terrorism might not be. As Davis and Jenkins put it:

> It is a mistake to think of influencing al Qaeda as though it were a single entity; rather, the targets of U.S. influence are the many elements of the al Qaeda *system*, which comprises leaders, lieutenants, financiers, logisticians and other facilitators, foot soldiers, recruiters, supporting population segments, and religious or otherwise ideological figures. A particular leader may not be easily deterrable, but other elements of the system (e.g., state supporters or wealthy financiers living the good life while supporting al Qaeda in the shadows) may be.[8]

Thinking of al Qaeda as a system opens the door to deterrence by punishment. The various supporters and enablers of terrorism who are not eager to sacrifice their own lives for the cause can be threatened with retaliation for their role in facilitating terrorist operations. The threatened response need not be lethal, but could, depending on the actor, involve financial sanctions or imprisonment.

This approach is a good example of what Alexander George has described as "indirect deterrence."[9] Traditionally, deterrent threats have been aimed directly at a potential attacker. Indirect deterrence, in contrast, is not aimed at attackers themselves, but at third parties whose actions could affect the likelihood that a potential attacker can or will carry out an assault. The likely need to pursue deterrence indirectly in countering terrorism was a major theme in a study conducted for the National Academy of Sciences soon after 9/11 and has been echoed in much of the subsequent research.[10]

The indirect approach has an important implication. Just because a terrorist organization is a non-state actor, this does not mean states are irrelevant to deterrent calculations. If a terrorist group relies upon or benefits from some form of state assistance, then the state in question can be threatened with consequences if it does not cease providing support. Wyn Bowen has pointed out that threats to take action against state sponsors may be more a matter of "compellence" than deterrence.[11] If a state is already supporting a terrorist group, the purpose of the threat is to get it to stop an activity already under way (compellence) rather than to prevent initiation of that activity (deterrence). The same logic applies to private supporters of terrorism as well. Since the conventional wisdom holds that compellence is harder to achieve than deterrence, Bowen cautions that it may be difficult to successfully coerce state sponsors to abandon their support for terrorism (though he concludes that it is still worth trying).

In addition, even failed compellence (for example, efforts after 9/11 to coerce the Taliban in Afghanistan to turn Osama bin Laden over to the United States) can have deterrent benefits if there is appropriate follow-up. In such cases, effective action to remove an offending regime from power (for example, the subsequent invasion of Afghanistan and removal of the Taliban government) can exercise a deterrent effect on other states.[12] However, in efforts to deter other non-state actors rather than state sponsors, the fate of al Qaeda is more relevant. Elbridge Colby concludes that "deterrence requires that the United States take every step to destroy al Qaeda in order for our deterrent against terrorists to be credible."[13]

This goal of destroying al Qaeda creates complications because, as Davis and Jenkins put it, "deterrence and eradication do not fit together easily."[14] This reflects a famous observation by Thomas Schelling that deterrent threats only work if they are paired with an assurance that the threat will not be implemented if the other side complies.[15] The U.S. intention to go after al Qaeda whether or not al Qaeda launches further attacks means there can be no U.S. promise to let the organization survive if it refrains from future terrorism. Without such an assurance, using deterrence by punishment against al Qaeda central is not possible. As noted above, though, threats of punishment might nonetheless work against elements of the network that enables al Qaeda. It is important to recognize that this will make assurances a necessity: to threaten private financiers or state sponsors with punishment if they support terrorism also requires promising to leave them be if they desist from aiding al Qaeda.

This insight is the basis for a proposal that in effect applies indirect deterrence to terrorist organizations rather than state or individual facilitators. Robert Trager and Dessislava Zagorcheva focus on deterring terrorist groups that are not affiliated with al Qaeda from allying with it.[16] Some groups that share al Qaeda's ideology might be more concerned with local political struggles than with bin Laden's vision of global jihad. If so, Trager and Zagorcheva argue, their local goals can be held at risk. If the United States is willing to indicate that it will refrain from acting against local groups as long as they forgo assisting al Qaeda, it might deter them from doing so by threatening to intervene in their local struggles if they *do* assist al Qaeda. Trager and Zagorcheva's proposal is a logical extension of the indirect deterrence approach. Instead of focusing on deterring elements of al Qaeda's existing network, however, it seeks to prevent al Qaeda from expanding its reach. This analysis has an important policy implication. It suggests that former U.S. president George W. Bush made a mistake in declaring "a global war on terror." By suggesting the United States would go on the offensive against all terrorist groups in all regions, it gave them each an incentive to join together as allies facing a common threat. Trager and Zagorcheva also support their analysis with a case study of contrasting approaches utilized against two different insurgencies in the Philippines, making their article one of the few fourth-wave studies to actually test its theoretical ideas against empirical evidence.

Deterrence by Denial

The fact that many analysts do not see a viable way to use deterrence by punishment directly against al Qaeda has led much of the recent literature to focus instead on deterrence by denial. Davis and Jenkins identified two approaches, subsequently developed more fully by others, that fit this mode of deterrence. The first involves increasing the probability that individual attacks will fail. Davis and Jenkins observed that "even hardened terrorists dislike operational risk and may be deterred by uncertainty and risk." This means that homeland security measures and other steps taken to reduce the chances that terrorists can carry out spectacular attacks have deterrent effects. Terrorists "may be willing to risk or give their lives, but not in futile attacks. Thus, better defensive measures can help to deter or deflect, even if they are decidedly imperfect."[17] Indeed, even before the Davis and Jenkins study appeared, a study conducted by Lawrence Livermore National Laboratory had also proposed that increasing the chances of operational failure could deter some terrorist attacks,[18] and many subsequent studies have echoed this conclusion. Robert Anthony has provided empirical backing to the notion that anything that reduces the estimated probability of operational success could deter some behavior. Anthony notes that the 9/11 hijackers took multiple test trips on the same flights they later hijacked because they wanted to convince themselves that they would not be stopped before boarding on the day of the attacks. This suggests that successfully identifying and arresting one or more of the hijackers before 9/11 might have deterred the entire plot by increasing the perceived risk of failure.[19]

As a second observation consistent with denial, Davis and Jenkins stressed the importance of illustrating that even successful terrorist attacks will not produce larger-scale effects on the United States. More recent work has come to see bolstering societal resilience as especially important.[20] When a society can demonstrate the ability to withstand terrorism, it sends a message that using this tactic will not enable terrorist organizations to achieve their goals. Although Davis and Jenkins did not use the punishment and denial terminology in their work, other studies have invoked the distinction and argued that both approaches will be necessary to deter terrorism.[21] Several analyses especially emphasize the second type of denial strategy discussed by Davis and Jenkins. They attach particular importance to showing that even successful attacks will not advance terrorists' overarching political goals. A report by a Student Task Force at the U.S. National War College (NWC) stressed that one way to deter terror groups is to ensure that there is "doubt placed in the terrorist's mind that even if acts of terrorism are successfully carried out, the overall aims may not be achieved."[22] Some influential senior scholars have endorsed this idea as well, using it as a central argument to explain why they reject the premise that terrorism is undeterrable. Colin Gray, for example, claims that, despite the grandiosity of its objectives, al Qaeda "functions strategically" in trying to use its suicide attacks to advance those objectives. As a result, "it can be deterred by the fact and expectation of strategic failure."[23]

A helpful framework for identifying different ways to use deterrence by denial against terrorism has been developed by James Smith and Brent Talbot.[24] They observe that denial strategies can be implemented at the tactical, operational, and strategic levels. Efforts to improve homeland defenses and increase operational risk produce tactical deterrence. Smith and Talbot refer to this as "denial of opportunity." At the operational level, the goal is "denial of capability"—restricting access to resources terrorists require to conduct an ongoing campaign of attacks. Here, denial and punishment work in synergy. The indirect approach that threatens retaliation against third-party enablers can contribute to a direct version of denial by preventing terrorist organizations from getting the resources they need, such as money, weapons materials, and safe havens. Finally, at the strategic level, deterrence by denial involves the approach emphasized by the NWC Student Task Force, Gray, and others. Strategic deterrence by denial entails the "denial of objectives"—showing that terrorism will ultimately fail to help terrorist groups achieve their end goals.

An analysis by Lee Dutter and Ofira Seliktar suggests the strategic level is the most important one. As long as terrorists believe there is a chance of success in achieving their fundamental goals eventually, the risk of tactical or operational failure might not be sufficient to deter them from trying to launch further attacks.[25] Other analysts who see promise in deterrence by denial at the strategic level argue that it is especially important to avoid public and governmental overreaction to terrorism, since manipulation of fear among the public or government officials is what enables terrorists to achieve their objectives.[26] The potential sticking point in this approach is that avoiding overreaction can be difficult, because elected officials generally feel public pressure to take dramatic, visible measures to minimize the terrorist threat in the short term.[27]

Another approach, which overlaps with denial strategies, has been proposed by Doron Almog, who adapts the Israeli notion of "cumulative deterrence" to counterterrorism.[28] Israeli strategists believe their country achieved deterrence against the Arab front-line states by repeatedly defeating them in a series of military confrontations. Although each war represented a deterrence failure in the short term, successive Israeli victories eventually convinced Arab states that they could not defeat Israel militarily. Deterrence was the cumulative result. Almog argues that a combination of successfully interdicting some terrorists, retaliating for those attacks that do occur, and demonstrating long-term patience could work similarly to establish cumulative deterrence against terrorism. Almog's suggestion is similar to the idea of strategic deterrence by denial, in that it involves convincing terrorists over time that they will not prevail. It differs, however, because his emphasis on effective retaliation means that Almog puts more weight on punishment than on denial. Whether or not cumulative deterrence offers a useful framework for preventing terrorism depends, then, on whether punishing forms of retaliation would add a significant increment of deterrence to the indirect and denial approaches outlined so far.

Deterrence by Punishment

The question of whether threats of retaliation could be effective as a direct deterrent against terrorism is an obvious one. This is the issue on which there is the greatest disagreement in the literature. Some analysts believe that threats analogous to the Cold War threat of massive retaliation are necessary to establish deterrence, while others strongly criticize the idea of seeking to deter terrorism in this way. This dilemma arises in discussions of both conventional and WMD terrorism, with the important difference that only in the latter case is there ever consideration of a nuclear response. Punishment scenarios for WMD terrorism are discussed separately below, while this section considers proposals for direct deterrence by punishment as a response to terrorism in general. Here, debate centers on whether or not it is a good idea to threaten retaliation against the families of terrorists or the larger communities from which they originate.

Among those who advocate threatening such forms of retaliation are several Israeli analysts who have drawn conclusions from their own country's experience as a target of terrorism. Gerald Steinberg wrote one of the first articles published after 9/11 that contended that terrorism could be deterred. In it, he deliberately invoked the notion of massive retaliation. He argued that "it is important to identify high-value targets, including family and supporters, that will cause even the most radical leaders to weigh the costs and benefits of their actions." Steinberg added that responses might have to appear "excessive" or "disproportionate" in order to make the costs great enough to deter further terrorism.[29] Ariel Merari, Shmuel Bar, and Amos Malka have made similar arguments, stressing that the defender needs to cultivate an image of being "willing to go 'all the way'" or "go crazy."[30] According to Bar, the most important factor is not the severity of the response, but rather its certainty. Bar believes that deterrence erodes quickly, leading him to conclude that repeated counterstrikes are necessary to continuously establish temporary periods of deterrence against terrorist adversaries.[31] In a similar vein, Uri Fisher suggests that only harsh reprisals, including threats to kill family members, can deter terrorism, but he worries that U.S. liberal values will prevent the United States from ever implementing this type of deterrent policy.[32] This concern seems overstated, given that reported civilian casualties have not caused the United States to halt its use of air strikes and drone attacks in Afghanistan, Pakistan, and elsewhere.

Others question whether deterrence should be sought by threatening collective punishment. The objections are partly normative in nature, as retaliation would be directed against people who do not necessarily support terrorism and at least some of whom are innocent bystanders. Many studies also cite practical reasons for not relying on threats to punish families and communities. Davis and Jenkins contend that indiscriminate retaliation would diminish the moral legitimacy of U.S. efforts, which could reduce international support for and cooperation with the U.S. campaign against terror.[33] Returning to the Israeli example, Jonathan Schachter contends that collective punishment has been ineffective because community members direct their anger at Israel after reprisals rather than hold terror groups accountable for provoking those reprisals.[34]

The biggest problem, according to most analysts, is that targeting families or broader populations is more likely to increase support for al Qaeda or other terrorist groups than to decrease it.[35] Indeed, groups often use terrorism with the intent of provoking an excessive government reaction in order to prove their claims that the government in question is brutal and/or oppressive. Hence, it is important not to fall into the terrorists' trap by reacting in a heavy-handed manner that terrorists not only expect but also desire.[36] There are good reasons, then, to be wary of retaliating against family members or societal targets. However, practicing deterrence by denial (rather than punishment) with respect to these actors is still important. For example, the NWC Student Task Force points to the need to make sure families do not gain financially if a family member conducts an act of terrorism.[37] This will help deter individuals who may be recruited with promises of financial reward.

It is also important to recognize that large-scale military retaliation is not the only possible way to implement a direct punishment strategy. Some propose a narrower focus. They suggest that targeted killings of mid-level terrorist operatives could have a deterrent effect by increasing the personal risks for those who plan and prepare terrorist attacks but do not themselves conduct them. In one of the handful of fourth-wave studies based on systematic empirical research, Alex Wilner found that targeting killings in Afghanistan did not reduce the rate of terrorism, but did shift it toward lower-value targets and less-effective forms of attack.[38] It is difficult to tell from the data, however, to what extent this shift arose from terrorist operatives being deterred from certain attacks out of fear for their personal safety versus terrorist capabilities being degraded by the loss of key personnel.

Others speculate that lethal forms of punishment might not be the most effective form of deterrence. Brad Roberts suggests that for terrorist foot soldiers who want to die for the cause, the threat to arrest and imprison them may be a greater deterrent than the threat to kill them.[39] The NWC Student Task Force also envisions the threat of life in prison as a possible deterrent. The group's report argues that "if captured, the terrorist's fate must be worse than a martyr's death. . . . A terrorist may be willing to die for his cause but be unwilling to spend the rest of his life in the unglamorous, isolated, largely forgotten role of a prisoner."[40]

Of especial relevance to punishment approaches, most fourth-wave studies also recognize that any form of deterrence, including against terrorism, results from an adversary's comparison of the expected utility of attacking versus that of not attacking. Bolstering deterrence therefore requires improving the attractiveness of alternatives to terrorism. Bruno Frey observes, for example, that increasing opportunities for peaceful political participation and for membership in civil society organizations might reduce the incentives disaffected individuals have to press their cause through terrorism.[41] As noted above, though, some studies exclusively emphasize the need for greater toughness. These studies tend to be wary of any efforts to create positive alternatives out of fear that these strategies will convey an image of weakness. This issue needs to be addressed with more systematic empirical research. Based on existing deterrence theory, however, there are strong logical grounds for expecting that deterrence will be more effective when it is paired with efforts to improve available alternatives to terrorism.

The Need for Realistic Expectations

Given the widespread expressions of skepticism after 9/11 about the ability to deter terrorism, my initial work on the fourth wave stressed the scholarly consensus that deterrence remains viable. In some of the most recent work, however, including some of the subsequent chapters in this volume, the pendulum has begun to swing back toward stressing the difficulties of deterring terrorism. Work from a social constructivist perspective is an example.[42] If one views deterrence as a social construct, its success depends in part on the parties in a deterrence relationship sharing certain understandings, such as the legitimacy of "red lines" and the punishments threatened for crossing them. Such shared understandings existed in the Cold War because the United States and the Soviet Union agreed about the danger of nuclear war and communicated directly about how to avoid it. Similar common understandings may not exist between Western governments and global terrorist organizations, as the two parties do not share beliefs about what is or is not morally acceptable and have little or no direct communication. This makes it harder to erect a stable deterrence relationship.

Even though new doubts are being raised about deterring terrorism, none of the newest scholarship explicitly declares it impossible. Hence, it still makes sense to seek whatever leverage one can from the strategy. Although deterring all terrorism will likely not be possible, it is still better to deter some terrorism than to deter none. Hence, seeking ways to improve results at the margins remains important, but a realistic understanding of the limits of deterrence is also necessary.

DETERRING WMD TERRORISM

In addition to research on deterring terrorism in general, another strand of the literature focuses on the specific problem of deterring terrorism involving weapons of mass destruction, and especially nuclear weapons. The majority of analysts assume that if groups such as al Qaeda manage to acquire a nuclear device, they will use it. Hence, most studies focus on how to deter third parties from assisting terrorist groups in obtaining weapons of mass destruction. There are, however, some analysts who think it might also be possible to directly deter terrorist groups from using such weapons.

Threatening Societal Targets

Similar to the analysts discussed above who favor applying direct deterrence by punishment against conventional forms of terrorism, some scholars propose threatening to respond to WMD terrorism with counterstrikes against population and infrastructure targets. Daniel Whiteneck, Elbridge Colby, and Paul Kapur all argue for the need to threaten retaliation against societal targets in response to a WMD attack.[43] Kapur makes it clear that the U.S. retaliation need not be nuclear and indicates that he considers threats against society legitimate only in the case of nuclear terrorism. Colby goes even further, suggesting that retaliation does not even have to be based on a military response, and he would likewise limit counter-society targeting only to "catastrophic" WMD terrorism (including biological and nuclear attacks). The three authors vary somewhat in the targets they propose holding at risk. Whiteneck lists family members, religious schools, and public infrastructure, while Colby adds food and housing as potential targets. Kapur proposes more broadly that both the population and territory with which terrorist groups identify could be threatened.[44]

Colby differs from others who advocate punishing community members in that he frames the response entirely as an effort at indirect rather than direct deterrence. He does not believe that targeting other members of the community for retaliation will cause terrorist leaders to hesitate. Instead, he envisions that threats against those who support or passively allow terrorist activities will pressure those actors to take steps to prevent members of a terrorist group living in their midst from carrying out a WMD attack.[45]

It is noteworthy that even scholars who advocate counter-society targeting do not generally call for responding to WMD terrorism with nuclear retaliation against non-state actors (though state sponsors, discussed below, are a somewhat different story). The U.S. Defense Department even commissioned a team at West Point's Combating Terrorism Center to study whether there is a role for nuclear weapons in deterring terrorist organizations. The study team firmly recommended against any use of nuclear threats. Not only might such threats increase general sympathy for al Qaeda, the study concluded, but they could also sway Muslim opinion toward greater support for al Qaeda acquiring or even using nuclear weapons.[46]

Deterrence by Popular Backlash

Proposals to seek deterrence through threats against society are not the main thrust of suggestions for how to deter WMD terrorism. This is primarily because all the arguments against punishing community members for acts of terrorism in general also apply in the case of WMD attacks more specifically. But not all analysts have given up on direct forms of deterrence. Instead, several have identified a possible alternative to large-scale military retaliation. They note that, for al Qaeda at least, sympathy and support among Muslims is an important center of gravity. If al Qaeda leaders came to expect that key Muslim audiences would react negatively to new attacks, this could serve as a source of restraint on terrorist behavior.[47] Lewis Dunn has explicitly connected this insight to a proposed path for deterring nuclear terrorism. He contends that "nuclear use does have the potential of provoking revulsion among the very communities that bin Laden is seeking to rally." This makes it important "to shape perceptions among al Qaeda leaders of the possibility that nuclear or biological weapons use could backfire, alienating . . . the wider Islamic community."[48]

To increase the chances of such a backlash, analysts call for putting forward or eliciting challenges that could discredit the ideological justifications terrorists invoke for WMD acquisition and/or use. According to Dunn, one way to do this is to encourage declarations by Islamic clerics and other respected Muslim leaders that indiscriminate killing, as would result from WMD use, is illegitimate.[49] Brad Roberts adds that groups affiliated with al Qaeda could also exert pressure against WMD use if they expect local reactions in the areas where they operate would be negative.[50] In short, if al Qaeda's leaders come to anticipate that WMD use would hurt their cause, this might dissuade them from such a course.

The study by the Combating Terrorism Center endorses this approach, labeling it "deterrence by counter-narrative."[51] Wilner uses an alternative term, "deterrence by delegitimization," which he defines as "targeting what terrorists believe."[52] Whichever label is used, it is not clear that this approach represents an alternative to punishment and denial as a way to produce deterrence; it seems rather to be a particular way of blending the two. It would deny a terrorist organization the benefit of gaining approval and support while also imposing the punitive cost of increased criticism and loss of support.

As with some of the other proposals discussed above, effective implementation of deterrence by delegitimization will be challenging. Adam Garfinkle observes that it is difficult for non-Muslims to influence relations among Muslims.[53] But this is not a reason to reject this approach out of hand. Rather, it points to the need for additional thinking and, if possible, empirical research about how to implement a counter-narrative strategy successfully.

This proposed approach highlights another way in which thinking about deterrence is becoming broader. This effort at deterrence would not rely on military reprisal, homeland defenses, or criminal justice measures. It instead represents an attempt to use information or discourse as a source of leverage.

Deterring Third-Party Assistance

Although, as the preceding subsections indicate, there are some suggestions for deterring terrorist groups directly, most of the research on deterring WMD terrorism emphasizes indirect deterrence. Despite the ideas noted above, it is hard to have confidence that a group that has obtained weapons of mass destruction can reliably be persuaded not to use them. Hence, the primary focus of deterring WMD terrorism has been on preventing terrorists from obtaining such weapons in the first place. With respect to nuclear weapons, though not necessarily chemical or biological agents, terrorist organizations will require outside assistance. They do not have the capacity to produce fissile materials on their own, so they will have to acquire these materials or an actual nuclear device from third parties. This creates an opening, and indeed an urgent necessity, to deter third parties from assisting or enabling terrorist acquisition of nuclear materials.

Existing proposals aim to forestall both deliberate transfers of nuclear materials and inadvertent leakages from poorly secured facilities. The suggestions generally involve threatening punishment against any actor that enables terrorists to obtain weapons of mass destruction. As Kapur points out, such efforts could also contribute to deterrence by denial by making it more difficult or more expensive for terrorist organizations to acquire nuclear materials.[54]

There is broad consensus over the basic approach to deterring WMD assistance to terrorists, but considerable debate about the details of implementing such a strategy and its overall effectiveness. One disagreement centers on an issue that was prominent in the debate over the 2003 Iraq War, namely the Bush administration's claim that a rogue state might give or sell weapons of mass destruction to terrorists in the belief it could keep its involvement secret. Most analysts discount the likelihood of deliberate state transfer. Among other considerations, they argue that uncertainty about whether a state could truly keep its role hidden would be a disincentive against taking the risk, especially given the sizable retaliation that might follow an act of WMD terrorism.[55] Some analysts, however, question whether uncertainty about avoiding detection would be sufficient to deter rogue states from supplying nuclear weapons or materials to terrorists. According to these analysts, if a state's leaders are highly risk acceptant, the thought that they might get away with a clandestine transfer might lead them to take the risk.[56]

Disagreements about the probability of deterring intentional WMD transfers or sales should not obscure a broader agreement, however, on the importance of making such deterrence as effective as possible. In addition, most analysts recognize that inadvertent leakage of nuclear, biological, and chemical weapons or materials is also possible and may be the more likely scenario. There have thus been a number of suggestions for how to strengthen deterrence of both deliberate and unintentional supply scenarios. Figuring out how to improve such deterrence involves questions of technical capabilities and declaratory strategy. Both are discussed below.

Nuclear Forensics

Efforts to deter states or subnational actors from enabling terrorist efforts to acquire a nuclear device will depend on the ability to determine the origin of nuclear materials used in a terrorist attack. Such attribution is partly a function of intelligence and police work, but it also has a significant technical component, known as nuclear forensics. Different facilities for making fissile materials vary in the mix of isotopes in the plutonium or highly enriched uranium they produce. In theory, analysis of isotopes in radioactive debris after a nuclear detonation could be matched against samples of fissile materials produced at various facilities to determine the source of the fissile material used in an attack.[57]

Early discussions of nuclear forensics assumed that simply establishing attribution capabilities would be enough to deter nuclear terrorism.[58] But subsequent studies identified several problems with this assumption. For starters, forensic investigation requires a comprehensive database of samples against which to match post-attack debris, and such a complete database does not exist at present.[59] Moreover, even if samples are available, it is difficult to pinpoint with certainty the source of materials used in an attack. And where definitive proof is lacking, Caitlin Talmadge suggests, political leaders will have difficulty lining up diplomatic support for military action.[60] Given the problems associated with nuclear attribution, attention has increasingly focused on how to maximize the deterrent benefits of nuclear forensics despite its limitations. One simple measure, recommended by several authors, is to increase the publicity given to nuclear attribution programs.[61] Calling greater attention to U.S. efforts and capabilities would increase the chances that others might fear being identified if their nuclear materials are used by terrorists.

Dilemmas of Declaratory Posture

Leveraging the deterrent potential of nuclear attribution also requires a declaratory strategy. Initial proposals held that the United States should communicate that any state will be held accountable if its nuclear materials are used in a terrorist attack. Based on an assumption that states would anticipate retaliation in a case of deliberate transfer, the goal in this case is to reduce the chances of unintentional leakage by putting pressure on all states to improve the security of their nuclear materials. This strategy seeks both to deter states from giving nuclear materials to terrorists and to compel them to minimize the chances that terrorists could acquire poorly secured materials. In this regard, Anders Corr has called for a "negligence doctrine" in which states whose nuclear materials are used by terrorists could be retaliated against if they had failed to take adequate steps to secure their materials.[62] Robert Gallucci has put forward a similar proposal, labeled "expanded deterrence," in which threats of punishment would be expanded beyond terrorists who carry out an attack to also cover any state whose materials were used in an attack.[63] Elbridge Colby has subsequently stretched the concept of "expanded deterrence" to cover private individuals complicit in WMD terrorism as well.[64]

Although many analysts suggest holding accountable any state that becomes a source of nuclear material, deciding on the retaliation has proven a thorny issue. Some analysts note that the U.S. response could be either nuclear or nonnuclear, but they do not specify when nuclear retaliation would be a must.[65] Others, in contrast, argue there are good reasons not to threaten nuclear strikes against certain states, like Russia and Pakistan, whose fissile materials might not be secure. Russia could launch extensive nuclear counterstrikes, and Pakistan is considered an ally, if an ambivalent one. The threat of retaliation could also reduce cooperation from such states in the aftermath of inadvertent leakage, as it would give them an incentive to cover up a loss of nuclear materials rather than come forward with information that could assist tracking those materials.[66] In cases of inadvertent leakage, nuclear retaliation could also be seen as excessive by the international community and lead to a loss of diplomatic support. For these reasons, Corr advocates threatening weaker states with a conventional invasion and regime change rather than nuclear retaliation.[67] In contrast, Whiteneck argues that it makes sense to leave the nuclear option on the table because U.S. conventional capabilities were stretched so thin by the wars in Afghanistan and Iraq that threatening occupation might lack credibility.[68] In a useful complement to this discussion, David Auerswald notes that dissuading WMD transfers as a result of nuclear leakages must also focus on transnational criminal organizations. That criminal groups are motivated by profit, rather than ideology, suggests they might be susceptible to threats of punishment. And by improving interdiction capabilities, states might deny criminals the benefits of smuggling WMD.[69]

As a result of the various dilemmas discussed above, the majority of analysts recommend a declaratory posture of calculated ambiguity.[70] Matthew Phillips, for example, advocates a "broadly scoped, operationally ambiguous declaratory policy," in which all retaliatory options are open but the exact nature of the military response is not specified.[71] And because of the inherent uncertainties in attribution, Phillips and others recommend that the United States declare it will not necessarily require definitive attribution before responding to an act of WMD terrorism.[72] Regardless of the variations in individual proposals, it is clear that analysts broadly agree about the importance of seeking indirect deterrence of WMD terrorism through measures to dissuade states and other actors from behavior that could assist terrorist groups in obtaining such weapons.

CONCLUSIONS

As part of a recent fourth wave in deterrence research, numerous scholars have been exploring the prospects for using deterrence to combat terrorism. Given how much skepticism has been expressed publicly about deterring terrorism, there is a surprising degree of consensus in the recent research that deterrence still has potential utility in dealing with threats from non-state actors. At the same time, few if any analysts believe it is possible to make deterrence foolproof. As a result, the primary focus has been on increasing the marginal effectiveness of deterrence as a way to reduce terrorism.

Three deterrent approaches have been widely supported in the literature. First, deterrence by denial has become a central feature of deterrence proposals (though many analysts would also retain a role for deterrence by punishment). Second, recent research has also emphasized an indirect approach that would use deterrence to dissuade third parties from providing assistance to terrorists. Third, there is interest in deterrence by delegitimization, which aims to convince al Qaeda that WMD terrorism would cause a backlash from within its intended support base. Such proposals are consistent with a broader trend in the fourth wave toward consideration of not just nonnuclear but even nonmilitary means as a basis for deterrence. One area of significant disagreement nonetheless remains: whether or not it would be appropriate and effective to threaten retaliation against the communities that terrorists stem from or identify with.

Overall, the fourth wave has made a persuasive case against giving up on deterrence, as many seemed inclined to do after 9/11, and has put forward a number of promising ideas for how to get some leverage from this strategy in combating terrorism. Nevertheless, the recent research on deterring terrorism also has weak points. Much of the literature consists of plausible suggestions, but in many cases the underlying theoretical logic has not been thoroughly developed, and the ideas have not been tested against empirical evidence. More empirical research is needed to assess which ideas have the greatest potential and how to implement them effectively.

Another area in which further analysis would be useful concerns possible trade-offs. Understandably, fourth-wave studies have focused on identifying possible ways to deter unwanted actions. Individual suggestions, however, can entail trade-offs with alternative ideas for how to achieve deterrence or with various other policy objectives. For example, researchers have shown awareness of possible trade-offs when it comes to threatening retaliation against states that are identified as a source of loose nuclear materials used in a terrorist attack. As discussed above, if a terrorist attack does occur, this deterrent posture could reduce cooperation in the aftermath if states fear the consequences of being blamed for not securing their nuclear materials.[73]

Other possible trade-offs have received less attention. An example is possible tensions between punishment and denial approaches. Some analysts believe that terrorism can be stopped in the long run by practicing deterrence by denial at the strategic level. If states and their populations demonstrate that they will not give in to terrorist demands and convince groups that terrorism will not help them achieve their strategic objectives, these groups should eventually stop using a tactic that fails to produce the political results they want. Such denial efforts at the strategic level, however, seem to preclude alternative suggestions for establishing deterrence by punishment. Because terror groups might be trying to elicit a heavy-handed response, a denial strategy could lead to a decision to refrain from significant military retaliation after attacks. To the extent that punitive retaliation could have deterrent effects, this would create a trade-off between denial and punishment strategies. Careful analysis is needed to try to determine which approach is more likely to be effective and under which circumstances.

Pursuing strategic deterrence by denial against terrorism also involves a trade-off with more proactive attempts to prevent terrorism. For the United States, part of a denial strategy could include showing that the nation will not abandon its commitments to civil liberties and the rule of law. But holding fast to these traditional values could mean not doing certain things that would increase the chances of preventing individual terrorist attacks. For example, warrantless surveillance, racial profiling, or the torture of suspected terrorists might lead to the discovery of a terrorist plot that could be stopped before it is carried out. Yet pursuing such extreme measures also involves a

second trade-off, with core democratic values. How to balance these competing values is not obvious. It is important to preserve civil liberties and signal
to terrorists that their use of violence will not provide results, but it is also
important to prevent future 9/11s. Individual academics should not be expected to resolve these strategic trade-offs. It is up to the public and its elected
representatives to decide how they want to balance competing values and
policy goals. Within the scholarly literature, however, there needs to be greater
recognition that such trade-offs exist. Future research could do more to identify the key trade-offs and to analyze them in ways that would facilitate informed public debate and discussion.

Although there are remaining weaknesses, the research since 9/11 on
deterring terrorism has been quite productive. It has helped convince policymakers that it is premature to abandon deterrence altogether; it has put forward a number of promising policy proposals; and it has encouraged thinking
in new ways about deterrence more generally. Deterrence strategy cannot and
should not be asked to carry the whole burden of responding to terrorism, but
it can still play a useful role. There is still work to be done, however. Important remaining tasks include identifying the most effective ways to utilize deterrence in counterterrorism, figuring out how best to implement it in practice, and coming to a more accurate understanding of the actual limitations
and downsides of deterrence.

NOTES

1. This chapter is partly based on Jeffrey W. Knopf, "The Fourth Wave in Deterrence Research," *Contemporary Security Policy* 31:1 (2010). I thank the journal editors
for permission to reuse material from that article here.

2. Helen Purkitt, "Dealing with Terrorism: Deterrence and the Search for an
Alternative Model," in *Conflict in World Society*, ed. Michael Banks (New York: St.
Martin's Press, 1984).

3. Growing concerns in the 1990s about WMD terrorism led to some important pre-9/11 studies of how to apply deterrence to the problem. See Michael Powers,
"Deterring Terrorism with CBRN Weapons: Developing a Conceptual Framework,"
Occasional Paper 2, Chemical and Biological Weapons Arms Control Institute
(2001).

4. Robert Jervis, "Deterrence Theory Revisited," *World Politics* 31:2 (1979).

5. Knopf, "Fourth Wave."

6. Glenn Snyder, "Deterrence by Denial and Punishment," Research Monograph
No. 1, Princeton University Center of International Studies (1959); Glenn Snyder,

Deterrence and Defense: Toward a Theory of National Security (Princeton, NJ: Princeton University Press, 1961).

7. Alex S. Wilner, "Deterring the Undeterrable: Coercion, Denial, and Delegitimization in Counterterrorism," *Journal of Strategic Studies* 34:1 (2011).

8. Paul Davis and Brian Michael Jenkins, *Deterrence and Influence in Counterterrorism: A Component in the War on al Qaeda* (Santa Monica, CA: RAND, 2002), xi, 13–16, emphasis in original.

9. Alexander George, "The Need for Influence Theory and Actor-Specific Behavioral Models of Adversaries," *Comparative Strategy* 22:5 (2003): 465.

10. National Research Council, *Discouraging Terrorism: Some Implications of 9/11*, ed. Neil Smelser and Faith Mitchell (Washington, DC: National Academies Press, 2002).

11. Wyn Q. Bowen, "Deterrence and Asymmetry: Non-State Actors and Mass Casualty Terrorism," *Contemporary Security Policy* 25:1 (2004): 58, 65, 67.

12. Davis and Jenkins, *Deterrence and Influence*, 19–20.

13. Elbridge Colby, "Restoring Deterrence," *Orbis* 51:3 (2007): 421; Davis and Jenkins, *Deterrence and Influence*, 10, 60.

14. Davis and Jenkins, *Deterrence and Influence*, 5.

15. Thomas Schelling, *Arms and Influence* (New Haven, CT: Yale University Press, 1966), 74.

16. Robert Trager and Dessislava Zagorcheva, "Deterring Terrorism: It Can Be Done," *International Security* 30:3 (2005/6).

17. Davis and Jenkins, *Deterrence and Influence*, xii, 15, 59.

18. C. Poppe et al., *Whither Deterrence? Final Report of the 2001 Futures Project* (Livermore, CA: Lawrence Livermore National Laboratory, 2002), 24.

19. Robert Anthony, "Deterrence and the 9-11 Terrorists," Institute for Defense Analyses, May 2003.

20. Esther Brimmer and Daniel S. Hamilton, "Introduction: Five Dimensions of Homeland and International Security," in *Five Dimensions of Homeland and International Security*, ed. Esther Brimmer (Washington, DC: Center for Transatlantic Relations, Johns Hopkins University, 2008), 3, 10.

21. Brad Roberts, "Deterring Terrorism: Terrorist Campaigns and Prolonged Wars of Mutual Coercion," in *Deterring Terrorism: Exploring Theory and Methods*, IDA Paper P-3717 (Alexandria, VA: Institute for Defense Analyses, August 2002, For Official Use Only); Gordon Drake, Warrick Paddon, and Daniel Ciechanowski, "Can We Deter Terrorists from Employing Weapons of Mass Destruction on the U.S. Homeland?" National Security Program Discussion Paper Series, John F. Kennedy School of Government, Cambridge, MA, 2003; Bowen, "Deterrence and Asymmetry"; David Auerswald, "Deterring Nonstate WMD Attacks," *Political Science Quarterly* 121:4 (2006/7); S. Paul Kapur, "Deterring Nuclear Terrorists," in *Complex Deterrence:*

Strategy in the Global Age, ed. T. V. Paul, Patrick M. Morgan, and James J. Wirtz (Chicago: University of Chicago Press, 2009).

22. Report by the National War College Student Task Force on Combating Terrorism, *Combating Terrorism in a Globalized World* (November 2002), 45, xxii.

23. Colin Gray, "Maintaining Effective Deterrence," Strategic Studies Institute, U.S. Army War College, Carlisle, PA, August 2003, viii, 28. For another example of a senior scholar who makes this point see Lawrence Freedman, *Deterrence* (Cambridge, UK: Polity Press, 2004), 123–24.

24. James Smith and Brent Talbot, "Terrorism and Deterrence by Denial," in *Terrorism and Homeland Security: Thinking Strategically About Policy*, ed. Paul Viotti, Michael Opheim, and Nicholas Bowen (Boca Raton, FL: CRC Press, 2008).

25. Lee Dutter and Ofira Seliktar, "To Martyr or Not to Martyr: Jihad Is the Question, What Policy Is the Answer?" *Studies in Conflict and Terrorism* 30:5 (2007): 435–36. Despite this observation, the authors (438) still see tactical deterrence by denial as likely to be the most feasible approach.

26. James Lebovic, *Deterring International Terrorism and Rogue States: US National Security Policy After 9/11* (London: Routledge, 2007), 182; Jeffrey W. Knopf, "Wrestling with Deterrence: Bush Administration Strategy After 9/11," *Contemporary Security Policy* 29:2 (2008): 256–57.

27. Joseph Lepgold, "Hypotheses on Vulnerability: Are Terrorists and Drug Dealers Coercable?" in *Strategic Coercion: Concepts and Cases*, ed. Lawrence Freedman (New York: Oxford University Press, 1998), 136, 145.

28. Doron Almog, "Cumulative Deterrence and the War on Terrorism," *Parameters* 34:4 (2004/5).

29. Gerald Steinberg, "Rediscovering Deterrence After September 11, 2001," *Jerusalem Letter/Viewpoints*, No. 467, Jerusalem Center for Public Affairs, December 2, 2001.

30. Ariel Merari, "Deterring Fear: Government Responses to Terrorist Attacks," *Harvard International Review* (2002): 29–30; Shmuel Bar, "Deterring Terrorists: What Israel Has Learned," *Policy Review* 149 (2008): 40, n. 6; Amos Malka, "Israel and Asymmetrical Deterrence," *Comparative Strategy* 27:1 (2008): 17.

31. Bar, "Deterring Terrorists," 42.

32. Uri Fisher, "Deterrence, Terrorism, and American Values," *Homeland Security Affairs* 3:1 (2007).

33. Davis and Jenkins, *Deterrence and Influence in Counterterrorism*, 27–28.

34. Jonathan Schachter, *The Eye of the Believer: Psychological Influences on Counter-Terrorism Policy-Making* (Santa Monica, CA: RAND, 2002), 113–15.

35. Bowen, "Deterrence and Asymmetry," 63; Auerswald, "Deterring Nonstate WMD Attacks," 551; Lebovic, *Deterring International Terrorism and Rogue States*, 126; Lewis Dunn, "Deterrence Today: Roles, Challenges, and Responses," *IFRI Proliferation*

Papers (2007): 24. For a contrary position, see Elbridge A. Colby, "Expanded Deterrence," *Policy Review* 149 (2008): 53. But Colby just asserts that retaliatory threats will do more to reduce than to provoke hostile behavior, without explaining how to keep threats against Muslim populations or religious symbols from working to al Qaeda's advantage.

36. Roberts, "Deterring Terrorism," IV-32; Auerswald, "Deterring Nonstate WMD Attacks," 548; Lebovic, *Deterring International Terrorism and Rogue States*, 125.

37. Report by the National War College Student Task Force on Combating Terrorism, 42.

38. Alex Wilner, "Targeted Killings in Afghanistan: Measuring Coercion and Deterrence in Counterterrorism and Counterinsurgency," *Studies in Conflict and Terrorism* 33:4 (2010).

39. Roberts, "Deterring Terrorism," IV-55.

40. Report by the National War College Student Task Force on Combating Terrorism, 44.

41. Bruno Frey, *Dealing with Terrorism—Stick or Carrot?* (Cheltenham, UK: Edward Elgar, 2004). Frey is one of the few fourth-wave analysts who rejects the use of deterrence against terrorism; he advocates reliance on positive incentives instead. While his proposal to improve the peaceful alternatives to terrorism makes sense, some of his other recommendations do not. For example, Frey proposes decentralizing society by dispersing government and population so as to reduce the number of high-value targets for terrorist attack. Whatever its theoretical merit, this is a practical nonstarter.

42. Emanuel Adler, "Complex Deterrence in the Asymmetric-Warfare Era," in Paul, Morgan, and Wirtz, *Complex Deterrence*.

43. Daniel Whiteneck, "Deterring Terrorists: Thoughts on a Framework," *Washington Quarterly* 28:3 (2005); Colby, "Expanded Deterrence"; Kapur, "Deterring Nuclear Terrorists."

44. Whiteneck, "Deterring Terrorists," 194, 196; Colby, "Expanded Deterrence," 49; Kapur, "Deterring Nuclear Terrorists," 117.

45. Colby, "Expanded Deterrence."

46. Scott Helfstein et al., "Terrorism, Deterrence and Nuclear Weapons," white paper prepared for the Secretary of Defense Task Force on DoD Nuclear Weapons Management (West Point, NY: Combating Terrorism Center, October 31, 2008), 3–5, 18–21.

47. Roberts, "Deterring Terrorism," IV-23–24; Michael Quinlan, "Deterrence and Deterrability," *Contemporary Security Policy* 25:1 (2004): 15–16. In an important forerunner to these suggestions from before 9/11, Joseph Lepgold noted that efforts to delegitimize terrorist methods or political objectives could have deterrent effects, but

he did not elaborate on how this might be done ("Hypotheses on Vulnerability," p. 144).

48. Lewis Dunn, "Can al Qaeda Be Deterred from Using Nuclear Weapons?" Occasional Paper 3, Center for the Study of Weapons of Mass Destruction (Washington, DC: National Defense University Press, 2005), 11, 2.

49. Dunn, "Can al Qaeda Be Deterred?" 24. See also Dunn, "Deterrence Today," 20–22.

50. Brad Roberts, "Deterrence and WMD Terrorism: Calibrating Its Potential Contributions to Risk Reduction," Institute for Defense Analyses, Alexandria, VA, June 2007, 18.

51. Helfstein et al., "Terrorism, Deterrence and Nuclear Weapons," 30.

52. Wilner, "Deterring the Undeterrable."

53. Adam Garfinkle, "Does Nuclear Deterrence Apply in the Age of Terrorism?" *Footnotes: The Newsletter of FPRI's Wachman Center* 14:10, Foreign Policy Research Institute, May 2009.

54. Kapur, "Deterring Nuclear Terrorists."

55. Robert Jervis, "The Confrontation Between Iraq and the US: Implications for the Theory and Practice of Deterrence," *European Journal of International Relations* 9:2 (2003): 332, n. 8; Jasen Castillo, "Nuclear Terrorism: Why Deterrence Still Matters," *Current History* 102:668 (2003): 429; Jeffrey Record, "Nuclear Deterrence, Preventive War, and Counterproliferation," *Policy Analysis* 519, Cato Institute (2004), 20; Whiteneck, "Deterring Terrorists," 192–93; Robin Frost, "Nuclear Terrorism After 9/11," *Adelphi Papers* 378 (Abingdon, UK: Routledge, 2005), 9, 64, 70; Robert Litwak, *Regime Change: U.S. Strategy Through the Prism of 9/11* (Baltimore: Johns Hopkins University Press, 2007), 304; Vera Zakem and Danielle Miller, "Stop or Else: Basic Concepts to Deter Violent Non-State Actors," in *Weapons of Mass Destruction and Terrorism*, ed. Russell Howard and James Forest (New York: McGraw-Hill: 2008), 351–52; Auerswald, "Deterring Nonstate WMD Attacks," 555; Knopf, "Wrestling with Deterrence," 250.

56. Gerard Alexander, "International Relations Theory Meets World Politics," in *Understanding the Bush Doctrine*, ed. Stanley A. Renshon and Peter Suedfeld (New York: Routledge, 2007), 49; Matthew Phillips, "Uncertain Justice for Nuclear Terror: Deterrence of Anonymous Attacks Through Attribution," *Orbis* 51:3 (2007): 439.

57. Michael Miller, "Nuclear Attribution as Deterrence," *Nonproliferation Review* 14:1 (2007).

58. Michael Levi, "Deterring Nuclear Terrorism," *Issues in Science and Technology* (Spring 2004); Graham Allison, "Nuclear Accountability," *Technology Review* (July 2005); Jay Davis, "The Grand Challenges of Counter-Terrorism," Center for Global Security Research, Lawrence Livermore National Laboratory, 2001; Jay Davis, "The Attribution of WMD Events," *Journal of Homeland Security* (April 2003).

59. Levi, "Deterring Nuclear Terrorism"; Robert Gallucci, "Averting Nuclear Catastrophe: Contemplating Extreme Responses to U.S. Vulnerability," *Annals of the American Academy of Political and Social Science* 607:1 (2006): 57–58; Miller, "Nuclear Attribution," 52, 54; Caitlin Talmadge, "Deterring a Nuclear 9/11," *Washington Quarterly* 30:2 (2007): 29.

60. Talmadge, "Deterring a Nuclear 9/11."

61. Miller, "Nuclear Attribution," 33, 52; Talmadge, "Deterring a Nuclear 9/11," 30–31; Kapur, "Deterring Nuclear Terrorists"; Michael Levi, *Deterring State Sponsorship of Nuclear Terrorism*, Council Special Report No. 39 (New York: Council on Foreign Relations, 2008), 27.

62. Anders Corr, "Deterrence of Nuclear Terrorism: A Negligence Doctrine," *Nonproliferation Review* 12:1 (2005).

63. To maximize cooperation in securing nuclear materials, Gallucci suggests that a threat "would remain even if the transfer were *not* authorized, but *only* if that government had failed to be fully cooperative in controlling its fissile material and weapons." Gallucci, "Averting." Gallucci published an earlier, slightly shorter version of the article in *Harvard International Review* 26:4 (2005); this and subsequent references are to the 2006 article in *Annals*, cited in n. 59.

64. Colby, "Expanded Deterrence."

65. Whiteneck, "Deterring Terrorists," 191–92, 198; Gallucci, "Averting," 57; Lewis Dunn, "Influencing Terrorists' Acquisition and Use of Weapons of Mass Destruction: Exploring a Possible Strategy," in *NATO and 21st Century Deterrence*, ed. Karl-Heinz Kamp and David Yost (Rome: NATO Defense College, 2009), 138.

66. For this reason, Michael Levi, an early proponent of deterrence by attribution, now recommends limiting threats of retaliation for nuclear transfer or leakage to North Korea and perhaps Iran. Levi, *Deterring State Sponsorship*. See also Evan Braden Montgomery, *Nuclear Terrorism: Assessing the Threat, Developing a Response* (Washington, DC: Center for Strategic and Budgetary Assessments, 2009), 91.

67. Corr, "Deterrence of Nuclear Terrorism," 136. This is also the recommendation of Fisher, "Deterrence, Terrorism and American Values," 6; and Knopf, "Wrestling with Deterrence," 255.

68. Whiteneck, "Deterring Terrorists," 191.

69. Auerswald proposes threatening their lives, their freedom, and/or their property and legitimate businesses. Auerswald, "Deterring Nonstate WMD Attacks," 557–59, 561, 565–67.

70. Gallucci, "Averting," 58; Litwak, *Regime Change*, 318; Colby, "Expanded Deterrence," 57.

71. Phillips, "Uncertain Justice," 442.

72. See also, for example, Levi, *Deterring State Sponsorship*, 18.

73. At a 2007 conference that discussed proposals for expanded deterrence, academics and Bush administration officials recognized that this is a critical trade-off, leading participants to recommend retaining the flexibility not to retaliate. See David Sanger and Thom Shanker, "Response to Nuclear Threats Hinges on Policy Debate," *New York Times*, May 8, 2007.

2 DETERRING TERRORISM, NOT TERRORISTS

Janice Gross Stein

THE THEORY AND PRACTICE OF DETERRING TERRORISM has been challenged by the growing incidence of suicide bombers who are prepared to sacrifice their life for the cause that they support. In its essence, deterrence theory builds on the assumption of a rational cost-benefit calculus by the challenger. When someone is prepared to sacrifice her life, to pay the ultimate cost, how can terrorists be deterred in theory or in practice?

This chapter proceeds in three parts. First, it examines and disputes the claim that terrorism is inherently undeterrable.[1] Deterrence of terrorism is exceedingly difficult in practice, but not impossible in theory. The second part of the chapter examines the limits of deterrence as theory and strategy. I turn to the analysis of the meaning of "rationality," focusing on the "common-sensical" understanding of rationality, and look at new research from neuroscience that speaks directly to the primacy of emotion in human decision making.[2] I then explore the structure of the international system as a third variable that affects the deterrence of terrorism. In a well-structured environment, where the players are known and the rules are embedded, meaning gradually becomes established and responses become routinized, learned over time. Under these conditions, the scope and practice of deterrence theory become easier to define, its language familiar and its meaning established. In a global system that is structurally complex and uncertain—not only larger numbers but new kinds of actors, changing power relationships, and unfamiliar challenges to the status quo—deterrence becomes far more problematic.[3] It becomes more difficult to define the scope conditions of the theory, and those who attempt deterrence find themselves increasingly in unfamiliar territory. What game theorists have called "common knowledge," and what others describe as a "common life world," is absent; the shared understandings of the world and common interpretation of the meaning of action are much less readily available. The absence of common knowledge in a complex and uncertain world compounds the problem of deterring terrorism.

In the concluding section of the chapter, I examine three "deterrence traps" and their relevance for the practice of deterrence. I do so against the background of a larger question of what outcome those who are "at war" with terrorism are willing to accept. What, in other words, constitutes deterrence success? And how do we understand deterrence in an age of terror?

CAN TERRORISM BE DETERRED?

Modern terrorists have been described as "rational fanatics." They are "rational" because the organizations they create have goals and priorities, can deploy assets in pursuit of goals, and can learn from failure. They are "fanatics" because they target and kill innocent civilians, increasingly by killing themselves. Terrorists seek to inflict terror on a population to demonstrate the weakness of its government, its inability to protect its citizens and guarantee their safety. They seek to separate the population from its government, and ultimately to destroy that government through undermining its legitimacy and support. The term "fanatic" also speaks to an unwavering commitment, to passionate identification with the cause, and to a willingness to sacrifice. Terrorism is, at some level, about the production of theater, a drama created between producer and audience.

Several arguments converge to claim that terrorism is undeterrable. Generally, these arguments do not distinguish clearly between individual terrorists who are willing to sacrifice their lives and the political organizations that organize, control, and manage the terrorists who engage in suicide attacks. The first argument is familiar and has been made largely in the context of jihadists who have sacrificed their lives in suicide bombings. Those who value death and martyrdom above life, argues Robert Pape, cannot be deterred. They are willing to die and so are not deterred by fear of any punishment. No imaginable punishment can be effective if people are prepared to die for their cause. Deterrence becomes impossible in a strategic culture that glorifies martyrdom.[4] It is precisely this kind of argument that led the Bush administration, reacting to the attacks against Washington and New York in 2001, to reject deterrence in theory as impossible and to move to the doctrine and practice of preemptive military action.

This argument is at its core cultural. Deterrence is impossible against those informed by a culture that considers death a lesser cost than dishonor. In this kind of cultural analysis, deterrence becomes no more than an imagined truth in a (Western) culturally idiosyncratic way.[5] The human mind is shaped not only by its capacity for rationality, but also by culture, which shapes strategic reasoning in ways that are outside the scope of deterrence. If this argument is interpreted literally, deterrence does become impossible. This problem of credibility is not new to deterrence theory. Schelling struggled with the problem of the credibility of the threat of nuclear retaliation during the Cold War in the context of extended deterrence.[6]

It is indeed logically difficult to conceive of a deterrence strategy that would work when people are willing to die, when they embrace death. But this argument ignores the distinction between individuals who carry out suicide actions and the leaders of the organizations that stand behind them. It ignores the difference between "terrorists" and "terrorism." Those who organize and send bombers to their death engage in a strategic calculus. Militant groups pursue positive goals on behalf of their constituencies; the individual may sacrifice life but does so in the service of a greater cause.[7] Waves of suicide bombings have waxed and waned, for example, as Palestinian leaders responded to the changing imperatives of Israel's negotiating strategies, to the prospects of a peace agreement, and to their domestic politics. Suicide attacks by "spoiler" organizations, for example, tend to increase when negotiations seem likely to succeed. Theories of deterrence should distinguish between transnational groups, which are likely to espouse a religious commitment or political ideology and operate across borders, and insurgent groups with local goals, embedded in a local population and seeking local political change. In practice, transnational groups should be far more difficult to deter than local insurgents, who are more vulnerable to their local population.

A second argument focuses on the leaders of terrorist organizations, rather than on the foot soldiers who execute the actions, and argues that the leadership is irrational, that it is largely insensitive to cost-benefit calculations.[8] What is the evidence? Some analysts reason back from the outcomes and conclude that only a small minority of terrorist groups have achieved their goals. Others argue that terrorist leaders usually resist political compromises and give priority to political survival. They have "protean" political goals that constantly change and can never be fully satisfied.[9] Therefore, they reason, leaders of terrorist groups must be irrational. This argument ignores the possibility that for many "terrorist" organizations, who tend to be the weaker parties in asymmetric conflicts, terrorism may be the only alternative that they have or the best among a bad set of options.

A third argument looks to organizational dynamics and claims that terrorist organizations do not respond primarily to strategic but instead to organizational imperatives that are outside the strategic calculus modeled by deterrence theorists.[10] Ordinary members of such groups, one argument goes, respond largely to the social solidarity they enjoy as part of the group. They can be best understood as "social solidarity maximizers," who attach much greater importance to the social benefits rather than to any political gains that the organization might achieve.[11] There is compelling evidence for social solidarity and the benefits of group membership for members of terrorist organizations, but members' motivation to join and remain may have little relation to leaders' strategic goals and their capacity to pursue these goals over time.

Leaders, however, do not and cannot remain immune from their members' needs and goals. Martha Crenshaw argues that when a group consists of social solidarity maximizers, the group and its leaders may have an innate compulsion to act to preserve the group's organizational integrity.[12] Particularly as movements face repression and go deeper underground, the social rewards of group membership tend to become more important than the strategic goals of the movement.

Organizational dynamics are clearly important within terrorist organizations, as they are within any organization. They are likely to matter more under some circumstances than under others, as leaders balance between organizational imperatives and political goals.[13] In the life cycle of a single organization, the relative salience of the two sets of goals is likely to vary as a function of the relationship between the government and the organization. Organizational imperatives are likely to be especially important when negotiations between governments and insurgent leaders seem likely to come to fruition, and therefore to imperil the survival of the organization, or when governments are successful in repressing and curtailing an organization's actions. It is important, therefore, in analyzing the theory and practice of deterrence against terrorism to model not only the political calculus, but also the organizational dynamics and the cultural imperatives under different situational constraints, and to estimate which is dominant at a particular moment.

A fourth argument suggests that because terrorists have no return address, deterrence is impossible. If a threat is issued and a terrorist strike nevertheless goes ahead, to maintain credibility a deterrer must inflict the threatened punishment. But it is often difficult to inflict punishment when organizations have no fixed address and no visible assets. This argument reflects the predominance of asymmetric conflict in the contemporary international system, and the necessity to adapt theories of deterrence developed in a very different, interstate world.

Terrorist activity is best conceived as a process over time, rather than as a single act of violence. To mount a large-scale attack, leaders must build an organization that can fulfill specific functional roles: financiers, logisticians, foot soldiers, along with an ideology and a supportive population. In the early stages of an organization's history, it tends to be fluid and nimble, with little in the way of assets; it can legitimately be said to have no return address. As it matures, however, it develops organizational structures, assets, personnel, and routines that are identifiable and often leave traces.

It is often the case that insurgent groups who attack civilian targets are embedded in a population from which they draw support and cover. They are vulnerable to punishment even when the sites of the attacking group are difficult to identify. Israel's retaliation against Hezbollah in 2006 inflicted significant damage on the population of southern Lebanon. Many rallied initially to the support of Hezbollah, but the leadership acknowledged that it was reluctant to expose the population to that kind of punishment again. In the wake of the war, widely regarded as a strategic defeat for Israel, the leaders of Hezbollah were nevertheless self-deterred, at least for a while. In this limited sense, Hezbollah had an address. Similarly, Hamas and Israel both limited and bounded the violence they inflicted on one another in the wake of Israel's attack in 2008.

The principal arguments that deterrence of terrorism is impossible are overdrawn. They claim too much. I argue that deterrence of terrorism may conceivably work, but under carefully specified and limited conditions, conditions that make deterrence difficult in practice even though it is plausible in theory. Theoretical specification of the calculus of the leadership of a "terrorist" organization should include organizational and cultural as well as political dynamics when considering the likely success of deterrent threats. Once we understand terrorism as theater, the performative significance of the act grows, and the attractiveness of the performance, the lure of the theater, is as much a function of organizational, political, and cultural dynamics as it is of a strategic calculus.

THE LIMITS OF DETERRENCE AS THEORY AND STRATEGY

Rational Choice

The theory of deterrence, unlike the practice, is elegant in its simplicity. Deterrence, as traditionally understood, does not involve the use of force, only the threat of force. If force has to be used, then deterrence has failed.[14] Theories of deterrence also explain when the strategy is likely to succeed.[15] But abstract formulations of the theory of deterrence are deceptively simple. Its scope conditions are, first and foremost, a rational adversary that can calculate the likely consequences of a challenge, and then calculate again in response to a credible threat. The explanatory power of the theory is deeply grounded in microeconomic theory, which assumes that people consistently maximize their expected utility. The internal logic is tight. An adversary will proceed with a challenge if and only if the estimated benefits exceed the likely costs. The theory of deterrence holds even when the strategy of deterrence fails, if the challenger calculated that the likely benefits of a challenge will exceed the expected costs. Even when the calculation is in error—through a misreading of the intentions or calculations of a defender—the theory does not fail, although the strategy does. The theory fails under tightly specified and extraordinarily limited conditions: if and only if a challenger calculates that the likely costs will exceed the expected benefits and proceeds nevertheless to act in ways that the defender does not want. Even here, there is an escape: a challenger that does not choose to maximize expected utility cannot be considered rational. A challenger that is not rational is outside the scope of the theory.

The theory of deterrence, in other words, is almost self-confirming in large part because of the microeconomic model of rationality. Almost all failures of deterrence are either the result of poor implementation of the strategy, or they are beyond its scope. This formulation of deterrence theory leaves out almost all the interesting problems. To demonstrate the self-confirming quality of the theory, I look at the poverty of the construction of rationality.

A commonsensical understanding of rationality is more relaxed than the formal microeconomic model that informs the theory of deterrence. Rational decision making refers to the processes people should use to choose. In a rational decision-making process, people should be logical and orderly. Their preferences should be ranked, at least intuitively, in such a way that if I prefer peace to all-out war, and I prefer all-out war to low-level insurgency, then I should prefer peace to insurgency. If I violate this requirement of "transitive" preferences, if I prefer insurgency to peace, then I am ruled out as a rational decision maker and therefore my calculus lies outside the scope of deterrence theory. Rational decision makers also need to "update" their estimates in response to new, reliable, and valid information that contains significant evidence. The reliability and validity of information is a threshold barrier that any piece of evidence should cross on its way into the decision-making process. Determining the trustworthiness of information, however, is difficult, and as we shall see, "rational" processes of information management are often swamped by the quick emotional processes and deep cognitive biases that political leaders use to interpret evidence.

So far this picture of a rational decision maker fits with a commonsense understanding of rationality. People who make important choices about the use of threats or force need to be logical, they need to be discriminating and open to evidence, and they need to be "coherent" and "consistent" in responding to logical arguments. The minimal, commonsensical requirements of rationality expect that policymakers can learn from history, that they can draw some propositions from the past and apply these propositions in an appropriate way to the future as they think about the likely consequences of the options they face.[16]

The evidence is now overwhelming that even these relaxed requirements— far less demanding than the formal requirements of deterrence theory—are rarely met in practice. There is by now abundant evidence that not only leaders of "terrorist" organizations but political decision makers, too, rarely meet these standards. The most important evidence of the limits to rationality comes from well-established work in psychology. New, and still tentative, research results in neuroscience are also challenging the most fundamental tenets of the rational model. Neuroscientists are now demonstrating the primacy of emotion in choice. What makes the work of both even more important is that the two tend to converge.

The Cognitive Revolution

Forty years ago, psychologists started a "cognitive revolution" as they rejected simple behaviorist models and looked again at the way people shaped the choices they made. They brought the "mind" back into psychology. Although this was not its purpose, the cognitive revolution can be understood largely as a commentary on the limits to rationality. Much of the work accepts rational choice as the default position and then demonstrates its boundaries. Research has now cumulated to show that people rarely conform to the expectations of the rational model.[17] The grounds for pessimism are twofold: the difficulty of making inferences as models of rational choice expect, and the limitations of the human mind.

Cognitive psychology has demonstrated important differences between the expectations of rational decision models and the processes of attribution, estimation, and judgment people frequently use. It explains these differences by the need for simple rules of information processing and judgment that are necessary to make sense of environments that are both uncertain and complex. People have a preference for simplicity and consistency and tend to systematically discount evidence that is inconsistent with their beliefs. There are, however, important individual differences. Drawing on a well-known distinction made by Isaiah Berlin, foreign policy experts were classified as "foxes" or "hedgehogs." Hedgehogs know "one big thing" extremely well and extend what they know into other domains of foreign policy analysis. Foxes, on the other hand, know many small things, are generally skeptical of grand overarching schemes, stitch together explanations with different threads of knowledge, and are skeptical of prediction in world politics.[18]

The evidence shows that the foxes do much better at short-term forecasting within their broad domain of expertise than do hedgehogs. The worst performers were hedgehogs who made long-term predictions, usually with considerable confidence. Hedgehogs are generally people with strong needs for structure and closure, who are most likely to discount and dismiss inconsistent evidence when it contradicts their preconceptions. The more knowledge hedgehogs have, the better equipped they are to defend against inconsistency. Foxes are skeptical of deductive approaches, more likely to qualify analogies by looking for disconfirming information, more open to competing arguments, more prone to synthesize arguments, more detached, and, not surprisingly, more likely to admit they were in error and move on. The hallmark of the foxes was their more balanced style of thinking about the world. Foxes had "a style of thought that elevates no thought above criticism."[19]

This evidence suggests that deterrence is context specific, and that the cognitive styles of would-be challengers matter. The same differentiated pattern should hold among leaders of insurgent and terrorist organizations. The axiomatic theory of deterrence does not capture these differences in cognitive styles, the variation across leaders who may be more like hedgehogs or foxes and consequently respond quite differently to a deterrent threat. In this way, as well as others that I will identify, context matters. Context is precisely what is absent from the theory of deterrence.

People are also poor estimators of probability. They depart systematically from what objective probability calculations would dictate in the estimates they make. "Human performance suffers," argues Philip Tetlock, "because we are, deep down, deterministic thinkers with an aversion to probabilistic strategies that accept the inevitability of error."[20] Especially relevant is the evidence that people are not neutral about risk. Prospect theorists posit an S-shaped value function with varying risks as a function of losses and gains. Loss is more painful than comparable gain is pleasant, and people prefer an immediate smaller gain rather than taking a chance on a larger longer-term reward.[21] People systematically overvalue losses relative to comparable gains.

The impact of loss aversion on deterrence is considerable. Leaders of terrorist organizations are likely to be risk-averse when things are going well and relatively risk-acceptant, more prone to authorize action, when things are going badly, when they think that they are likely to lose or have lost something that matters to them. They are likely to take greater risk to protect what they already have—the "endowment effect"—than to increase their gains. They are also likely to take greater risk to reverse losses, to recapture what they once held, than they would take to make new gains. And when they suffer a significant loss, they will be far slower to accommodate to these losses than they would be to incorporate gains. This modeling of risk propensity explains the paradox that terrorist actions are most likely either when negotiations seem likely to succeed—negotiations that would make the organization irrelevant—or when the organization is being pushed back, encircled, and driven underground. Here, the evidence from cognitive psychology converges with the arguments put forward by organizational theorists.

The need for simplicity and consistency, the impediments to probabilistic thinking, and the predisposition to loss aversion are often treated as deviations from rational models of deterrence. Rational choice remains the default, and these "deviations" are treated as limiting conditions. Yet, these "deviations" are so pervasive and so systematic that it is a mistake to consider rational models of deterrence as empirically valid. These patterns of choice need to be built into theories of deterrence as core assumptions, and systematically tested in different contexts. This is especially important to the development of theories of deterrence of terrorism where, as we have seen, situational effects matter, common knowledge is absent, communication across dramatically different belief systems is likely to be especially difficult, and the risk propensities of leaders of insurgency or terrorist organizations in an asymmetrical conflict are likely to be very different from those defending the status quo.

Emotion

Neuropsychology, drawing on research results of the last two decades, now rejects a separation between cognition and emotion as untenable. The one is embedded within the other. And by extension, rationality and emotion are interdependent, not opposite to one another.[22] Behavior is strongly influenced by finely tuned affective systems.[23] "When these [emotional] systems are damaged or perturbed by brain injury, stress, imbalance in neurotransmitters, or the 'heat of the moment,' the logical-deliberative system—even if completely intact, cannot regulate behavior appropriately."[24] Rationality, in short, presupposes and indeed requires emotion.

There is widespread consensus that the brain implements "automatic processes" that are faster than conscious deliberations with little or no awareness or feeling of effort.[25] These automatic processes are the default mode of brain operation, processes that evolved over time to assure survival and reproduction. Emotion is "first," because it is automatic and fast, and it plays a dominant role in shaping behavior. We know now that emotion operates in part below the threshold of conscious awareness.[26] Contrary to conventional wisdom, we generally feel *before* we think and, what is even more surprising, often act *before* we think. Not surprisingly, the conscious brain then interprets behavior that emerges from automatic, affective, processes as the outcome of cognitive deliberations.[27] This is a strong claim that gives many scholars pause. It is a claim that has profound implications for theories of deterrence.

The human brain tags virtually all objects and concepts, and these emotional tags come to mind automatically when these objects and concepts are evoked.[28] People trust their immediate emotional reactions and only correct them through a comparatively laborious cognitive process after the fact.[29] The well-known "ultimatum game," for example, highlights the computational, cognitive, and emotional elements at play in decision making. The game comes out of economics but has direct relevance to deterrence. One partner has access to a resource—ten dollars, vast oil wealth, highly sophisticated military technology—and can propose how the resource should be split. If the other party accepts the proposal, then the resource is divided as they have agreed. If the split is rejected, neither receives anything and the game is over or war breaks out.

Rationally, the second party should accept anything that she is offered, because anything is clearly better than nothing. And again, the first party, knowing that for the other anything is better than nothing, should rationally offer as little as possible. Contrary to what rational models would expect, offers of less than 20 percent of the total are generally rejected out of hand. Why? Perhaps those who rejected the offer were worried about their bargaining reputation for the next round, as rational deterrence theory says they should. But they responded the same way even when reputational effects were removed from consideration, when they were told that they would play the game only once. When asked why they rejected an offer that would give them something, people responded that the offer was humiliating, insulting, patently unfair. They responded quickly and intuitively to reject an offer that gave them something but humiliated them in the process. Their rejection was driven by a strong, negative, emotional response. In a series of games where subjects agreed to submit to functional magnetic resonance imaging (fMRI), the insula cortex that encodes pain and odor disgust was activated when subjects received an unfair offer.[30] That emotional response likely preceded conscious calculation and the decision to reject the offer. The heuristic of the "ultimatum game" has important consequences for signaling and negotiation in asymmetric conflicts and in the deterrence of terrorism. The emotional encoding of offers was more important than the microeconomic calculation of gain.

All emotions are either positive or negative, and many carry action tendencies.[31] Emotions are adaptive programs of action that have evolved over time to ensure survival and then reproduction. A useful way of thinking about emotion and cognition is to see affective processes as those that address the go/no-go questions, the questions that motivate approach-avoidance, while cognitive processes are those that answer true/false questions.[32] Choice, the central focus of theories of deterrence, clearly invokes both kinds of processes, but, other things being equal, emotional processes are the primary determinants of whether or not to go, to launch an action. Establishing truth claims about states of the world is usually not enough for people to make a choice. What matters to me, what I value, is an emotional as well as cognitive process, and is important in what I decide to do, whether I go, or I don't, whether I approach or I avoid. Whether or not I am treated fairly is an emotional as well as a cognitive judgment, and in this sense, emotion carries utility. Emotions are so important because they are carriers of value.

Emotional and cognitive processes can collaborate or compete.[33] At low levels of intensity, affect appears to play a largely "advisory" role; it provides information that informs cognitive processes. At intermediate levels of intensity, people begin to become conscious of conflict between cognitive and affective inputs and struggle for self-control. At high levels of intensity, affect can be so powerful that it short-circuits thought and moves to action. "While conscious control over emotions is weak, emotions can flood consciousness. This is so," neuroscientist Joseph LeDoux concludes, "because the wiring of the brain at this point in our evolutionary history is such that connections from the emotional systems to the cognitive systems are stronger than connections from the cognitive systems to the emotional systems."[34] Emotion precedes and can trump cognition. Only after the fact can people reflect on the choices that they have made.

The new field of "neuro-economics" is beginning to conceive utility as something one experiences subjectively, as lived experience.[35] Emotions play a critical role, for example, in forward-looking decision making. People only care about the delayed or uncertain consequences of their decisions to the extent that thinking about these consequences evokes affect.[36] In thinking about risk, people anticipate the consequences of different options, but focus on what is emotionally salient to them.

It is this sense of emotion as lived experience that must inform theories of deterrence in asymmetric conflict. The outcome of deterrence is likely much more affected by a "hot" emotional reaction to betrayal, disappointment, shame, or humiliation than it is by a "colder" calculus of capability and resolve. Sustained research on the impact of emotion can help unlock the paradoxes of "irrationality" that shape much of the logic of deterrence. These paradoxes are particularly important in theories of deterrence of terrorism, where leaders provoke military action to fuel humiliation, outraged honor, and anger, which then is turned against sitting governments, who lose legitimacy. Delegitimation, a classic objective of insurgency, is both a strategic and an emotional process. The impact of a threat cannot be assessed without understanding its emotional as well as cognitive consequences. And the need for social solidarity, an important dynamic within terrorist organizations, is primarily an emotional experience. Emotion runs throughout the story of terrorism, its purposes, and its prevention.

DETERRENCE AMID STRUCTURAL UNCERTAINTY

Different styles of decision making are associated with different cognitive styles and with different emotional states. Changes in the meaning, the explanation, and the understanding of threat have also been informed by the increasing complexity and diversity of the international environment. "Linear thinking ('big events must have big causes') has given way to a more subtle perspective that emphasizes the unintended consequences of increased complexity. We now understand . . . [threats] as the complex result of multiple consequences, which interact over time to produce a threat with devastating potential. . . . Consequences escalate as they jump from one system to another, deepening the sense of threat, breakdown, and loss of control."[37] Rather than linear models of causation, anchored by unitary actors making rational choices, contemporary theories are informed by analyses of complexity and epidemiology that focus on the "pathogens" that live within a system and explode once they cumulate and reach a critical mass. These kinds of threats are more difficult to see, more challenging to manage, and less amenable to the primitive notions of "control" that so informed theories of deterrence—and coercive diplomacy—anchored in the Cold War experience.

Deterrence is more difficult in a global environment that is increasingly diverse in its ecology. Challenges come from a broader range of sources, some clearly identifiable, others not, some familiar, others new. Deterrence has consequently become more complex and poses strategic and coordination problems of a different order of magnitude. As the complexity and interconnectedness of systems have grown, societies have grown more vulnerable to small threats that amplify through networks to cause large disruptions.

Given the structural uncertainty and complexity of today's global system, even hypervigilant leaders face daunting challenges in scanning and reading complex environments, where chains of connection are often unclear, until their effects are large enough to capture attention in a noisy and crowded world. The barriers to recognizing that a threat is looming are formidable. Large organizations develop standard routines to monitor what they are doing. These routines do not equip them particularly well to notice what they do not expect to see. Similarly, intelligence agencies working within existing frameworks are less sensitive to the network effects that they are not monitoring at the time. It is, of course, a nearly impossible task to monitor the multiple chains that are weaving below the surface. Only when they amplify do they become visible, and by then the "threat" has erupted. In a world that is tightly interconnected across multiple levels, in a gridlike structure that works very differently from the more familiar hierarchies, those that are monitoring for threshold effects have many more places to look and much more to watch. It should not be surprising that they miss a gathering storm. The complexity of organizations, their overloaded channels of communication, and pervasive cognitive biases in the interpretation of data are not new obstacles to the identification of a threat, but these challenges are greater by orders of magnitude in the more tightly coupled contemporary global system.

The routines of deterrence work best when the environment is relatively stable and the challenges are familiar. They work far less well in a changing global system that throws up the "unknowable" and the "unimaginable." The operations of clandestine networks bent on attacking civilians, the detonation of a dirty bomb or a biological weapon, the destruction of critical infrastructure, and the chain reactions of high-risk technologies that escalate through tightly coupled systems are all challenges that reflect a global system that is evolving, that has no clear, well-defined structure.

Deterrence and Strategic Cultures

To deter terrorism, a deeper understanding of the culture that shapes strategic choices is important. The strategic culture of those who engage in asymmetric warfare is certainly culturally predicated. For most, suicide bombing is a tactic of warfare within a larger cultural context. Death to avenge dishonor or humiliation, to expel the occupier, or to reclaim lost glory is a postulate that springs from a distinct cultural tradition. It is important to understand that the success of deterrence is culturally contingent, as it is contingent on the emotional reactions and cognitive styles of leaders, and on organizational dynamics.

What this cultural interpretation of deterrence does is force a reexamination of the familiar culture of deterrence that focuses on avoiding death as the ultimate cost. It suggests that great attention be paid to the avoidance of humiliation and shame, especially in those cultures where honor and status matter a great deal. Strategy needs to be informed by the realization that deterrent threats and demonstrations of resolve can provoke deep emotional reactions when they violate cultural norms, that they can then provoke rather than restrain violence if adversaries are humiliated. Options need to be framed to avoid deliberate or inadvertent humiliation and dishonor and to provide recognition and status. This is not a new concern, but central to effective strategy, as scholars argued decades ago.[38]

DETERRING TERRORISM: DILEMMAS AND TRAPS

I have identified three sets of conditions that constrain deterrence of terrorism as a theory and as a strategy. The first is robust evidence, evidence that now converges from experimental psychology, from field studies of foreign policy experts, and from early research in neuroscience, that it is an error to model rational choice as the default position and treat departures from rationality as deviant. The default position is "hot" emotional decision making that precedes reflection and analysis.

There is also variation in strategic cultures that creates different value frames, and these are important when thinking about the utility of deterrence. Leaders who come from cultures of honor and have a strong sense of grievance are especially likely to escalate in response to deterrent threats. Here the use of deterrence alone, without accompanying strategies that signal respect and recognition and provide positive incentives to address historic grievance, is likely to fail. When leaders from honor cultures are the objects of deterrence, the risks of deterrence multiply. Emotional content, cognitive styles, and culture are mutually reinforcing.

Third, structural uncertainty and complexity in the contemporary global system complicates even further the calculus of deterrence. Networks like al Qaeda and militias that operate independently of—or against—their own governments are far more difficult to deter because they deliberately seek to provoke and escalate violence. These three factors, when they are mutually reinforcing, work together to deepen the challenges to threat-based strategies and generate what I call "deterrence traps."

Theories of deterrence assume that a would-be challenger seeks to avoid costly, violent punishment. Yet often, in asymmetric warfare, the weaker party deliberately uses low-intensity warfare in a grinding strategy of attrition in order to provoke escalation by the stronger. The purpose of low-intensity warfare is to force the enemy to escalate so that the weaker "wins" a political victory. The genius of asymmetric warfare, when it is well done, is to eliminate anything but poor choices for the stronger party. It is difficult to deter military action when those who challenge hope for coercion, so that the conflict escalates and people turn against the perpetrators of violence. Yet failing to respond is not an option when bombs are exploding in the streets, in schools, and in the markets. Damned if you do respond, damned if you don't.[39]

Since asymmetric warfare requires far fewer resources than conventional warfare, it can be sustained over long periods of time. It relies on easily available technology—the construction of bombs and rockets is not demanding—which is widely available and simple to use. And it inflicts serious damage on far more expensive military assets and on civilians and domestic infrastructure, which in turn provokes widespread public anger and frustration. When leaders resort to escalation because they cannot be seen by their publics to do nothing and because they fear that their deterrent reputation will be weakened, insurgents waging asymmetric warfare achieve their political objectives and are emboldened. Deterrence quickly becomes a value rather than a strategy for "defenders" who continue to escalate to preserve their deterrent reputations. Deterrence then becomes part of the problem rather than part of the solution.

The "deterrer's dilemma" is exacerbated by the unwillingness of developed democratic societies both to sustain casualties and to kill others.[40] Demographics in the developed world work to decrease the tolerance for enduring casualties, and the growing acceptance of international humanitarian law and international criminal law, and the moral sanctions that follow the open breach of either, constrain the kinds of strategies that can be used in the field. The UN's 2009 Goldstone Report, for example, which criticized both Israel and Hamas, gave no weight to those who would argue that when insurgents embed themselves within civilian populations, the use of force is nevertheless legitimate. The legality of drone attacks against militants along the Afghan-Pakistan border and targeted assassinations have yet to be tested in international criminal cases, but their status is at best uncertain.

Finally, self-deterrence favors the status quo, a consequence not lost on those who resort to terror to advance their political purposes. Theories of deterrence distinguish between deterrence by punishment and deterrence by denial. Denial of targets to organizations that use terror is an effective strategy but extraordinarily difficult to accomplish. Deterrence of terrorist organizations through the *threat* of punishment, as I have argued, is much more difficult than it is between states. Only after punishment has been inflicted, after innocent civilians have been killed, do both parties to a conflict sometimes self-deter for a period of time. The challenger is reluctant, for a while, to provoke punishment, and the deterrer is loath to pay the political, legal, and moral costs of inflicting punishment on the communities of innocent civilians in which terrorists live. Self-deterrence of this kind is, of course, inherently beneficial to the status quo power and, therefore, unstable and unlikely to endure. Unstable self-deterrence is hardly an optimal outcome, but it can be useful, particularly in local contexts, if it opens space for negotiation.

CONCLUSION

The difficulties of deterring terrorism and the traps that the practice of deterrence creates raise a fundamental question. Deterrence is an inherently conservative strategy; it seeks to conserve and protect the status quo against unwanted challenge. It is an inappropriate strategy when the objective is the destruction of an adversary, its eradication, its elimination. It is appropriate only if those who use it are prepared to live with their adversaries, as long as they do not resort to acts of force against civilians that are designed to terrorize a population. Yet leaders speak frequently, for example, of destroying al Qaeda, of running it to ground, of a war against terror. If leaders mean what they say, there is a poor fit between the objective and the strategy. Deterrence is either misunderstood or misused.

If political leaders are willing to live with an al Qaeda that refrains from the use of force against civilians—as unlikely as that seems at this moment—or with a Taliban that abjures the killing of civilians, then the appropriate sequencing of threats and promises matters. Traditionally, scholars have argued that a demonstration of resolve at the beginning is important to establish the political terrain for subsequent negotiation. The evidence I have reviewed suggests that deterrence should, subject to variation in leader types and cultures, be accompanied with positive inducements at the outset to reduce the "hot" emotional sting and lower the temperature, especially in uncertain and complex environments. Lowering the temperature becomes even more important when uncertainty and complexity reduce the stocks of common knowledge.

Just as we understand terrorism as a political strategy, born of anger, shame, isolation, or alienation and designed to delegitimize governments or leaders by alienating and frightening their populations, so we need to think theoretically about the deterrence of terrorism as a political strategy of influence, emotionally resonant when it is used, and implemented through a conversation that moves across cultures with different values and different needs.

In a complex and uncertain global system, characterized by sharp asymmetries, we need to think beyond deterrence to broader strategies of influence. Leaders need to go beyond the logic of deterrence to think more broadly about what they can and cannot accept, about promises as well as threats, about positive as well as negative inducements. Strategy must reach beyond the militants and the militias to create political alternatives and deepen the legitimacy of those the militants challenge. These are formidable challenges both to the theory of deterrence and to its practice.

NOTES

1. Terrorism is a strategy of political theater, inflicting punishment on innocent civilians who are not directly involved in a conflict, to delegitimize leaders or governments by alienating and frightening their populations. It can best be understood as a process over time, as political strategy in asymmetrical conflict.

2. It is this cumulating research that led Thomas Schelling to call game theoretic models of deterrence "heuristics," which, at best, set normative standards that can never be met. Thomas Schelling, presentation at the Munk School of Global Affairs at the University of Toronto, February 17, 2007.

3. Neil Harrison, *Complexity in World Politics: Concepts and Methods of a New Paradigm* (Albany: State University of New York Press, 2006); Robert Jervis, *System Effects: Complexity in Political and Social Life* (Princeton, NJ: Princeton University Press, 1997).

4. Robert Pape, *Dying to Win: The Strategic Logic of Suicide Terrorism* (New York: Random House, 2005); and Ivan Arreguín-Toft, "How Do the Weak Deter the Strong?" in *Complex Deterrence: Strategy in the Global Age*, ed. T. V. Paul, Patrick Morgan, and James Wirtz (Chicago: University of Chicago Press, 2009).

5. Adam Garfinkle, *Culture and Deterrence* (Washington, DC: Foreign Policy Research Institute, 2006).

6. A threat to retaliate with nuclear weapons in response to an attack against an ally was not believable if that meant, in turn, that one's homeland would be obliterated in response. To escape this paradox, Schelling recommended a "rational strategy of irrationality," where leaders deliberately threaten irrational consequences and then, in order to be credible, give up their capacity to prevent their own irrational action. Thomas Schelling, *Arms and Influence* (New Haven, CT: Yale University Press, 1966).

7. S. Paul Kapur, "Deterring Nuclear Terrorists," in Paul, Morgan, and Wirtz, *Complex Deterrence*; Monica Duffy Toft, "Getting Religion? The Puzzling Case of Islam and Civil War," *International Security* 31:4 (2007): 97–131.

8. Max Abrahms, "What Terrorists Really Want: Terrorist Motives and Counterterrorism Strategy," *International Security* 32:4 (2008): 78–105.

9. Jessica Stern, "The 'Protean' Enemy," *Foreign Affairs* 82:4 (2003).

10. David Rapoport, ed., *Inside Terrorist Organizations* (London: Frank Cass, 2001).

11. Abrahms, "What Terrorists Really Want," 101.

12. Martha Crenshaw, "An Organizational Approach to the Analysis of Political Terrorism," *Orbis* 29:3 (1985): 465–89; Martha Crenshaw, "Decisions to Use Terrorism: Psychological Constraints on Instrumental Reasoning," in *Social Movements and Violence: Participation in Underground Organizations*, ed. Donatella della Porta (Greenwich, CT: JAI Press, 1992): 29–42.

13. Gordon McCormick, "Terrorist Decision Making," *Annual Review of Political Science* 6 (2003).

14. This consensual understanding of deterrence has been challenged by those who argue that deterrence is "cumulative" over time; force can be used, repeatedly, until leaders understand that the price of continuing to strike civilians is too high and refrain from action. The concept of "cumulative deterrence" so badly violates the fundamental meaning of deterrence that it loses any analytical value. That kind of strategy is better described as—war. For a summary and critique of the literature on "cumulative deterrence," see Jeffrey W. Knopf, "The Fourth Wave in Deterrence Research," *Contemporary Security Policy* 31:1 (2010).

15. The rational calculations of a would-be "challenger" to change the status quo could be changed by a credible threat that raises the costs of that kind of action. To be credible, a threat must be reinforced by the capabilities to implement the threat of retaliation and firm resolve to do so. See, among others, Alexander George and Richard Smoke, *Deterrence in American Foreign Policy* (New York: Columbia University Press, 1974); Paul Huth and Bruce Russett, "Testing Deterrence Theory: Rigor Makes a Difference," *World Politics* 42:4 (1990): 466–501; Richard Lebow and Janice Gross Stein, "Beyond Deterrence," *Journal of Social Issues* 43:4 (1987): 5–71; Richard Lebow and Janice Gross Stein, "Rational Deterrence Theory: I Think, Therefore I Deter," *World Politics* 4:21 (1989): 208–34; Richard Lebow and Janice Gross Stein, "Deterrence: The Elusive Dependent Variable," *World Politics* 42:3 (1990): 336–69.

16. Robert Jervis, *Perception and Misperception in International Politics* (Princeton, NJ: Princeton University Press, 1976); Philip Tetlock, "Social Psychology and World Politics," in *Handbook of Social Psychology*, ed. D. T. Gilbert et al. (New York: McGraw-Hill, 1998); Philip Tetlock, *Expert Political Judgment: How Good Is It? How Can We Know?* (Princeton, NJ: Princeton University Press, 2005); Philip Tetlock and George Breslauer, eds., *Learning in U.S. and Soviet Foreign Policy* (Boulder, CO: Westview, 1991); Yaacov Vertzberger, *The World in Their Minds* (Stanford, CA: Stanford University Press, 1990).

17. Robyn Dawes, "Behavioral Decision Making and Judgment," in Gilbert et al., *Handbook of Social Psychology*, 497–548; William Goldstein and Robin Hogarth, eds., *Judgment and Decision Making: An Interdisciplinary Reader* (Cambridge: Cambridge

University Press, 1996); Daniel Kahneman, Paul Slovic, and Amos Tversky, eds., *Judgment Under Uncertainty: Heuristics and Biases* (New York: Cambridge University Press, 1982).

18. Isaiah Berlin, "The Hedgehog and the Fox," in *The Proper Study of Mankind* (New York: Farrar, Straus and Giroux, 1997): 436–98; Tetlock, *Expert Political Judgment*, 73–75; Arie Kruglanski and Donna Webster, "Motivated Closing of the Mind: 'Seizing' and 'Freezing,'" *Psychological Review* 103:2 (1996): 263–68.

19. Tetlock, *Expert Political Judgment*, 88, 118.

20. Ibid., 40.

21. Daniel Kahneman and Amos Tversky, eds. *Choices, Values, and Frames* (Cambridge: Cambridge University Press, 2000): "Prospect Theory: An Analysis of Decision Under Risk," *Econometrica* 47:2 (1979); "Advances in Prospect Theory: Cumulative Representation of Uncertainty," *Journal of Risk and Uncertainty* 5:4 (1992): 297–323.

22. Antonio Damasio, *Descartes' Error: Emotion, Reason, and the Human Brain* (New York: Putnam, 1994).

23. Joseph LeDoux, *The Emotional Brain: The Mysterious Underpinnings of Emotional Life* (New York: Simon & Schuster, 1996); Jaak Panksepp, *Affective Neuroscience* (Oxford: Oxford University Press, 1998); Edmund Rolls, *The Brain and Emotion* (New York: Oxford University Press, 1999).

24. Colin Camerer, George Loewenstein, and Drazen Prelec, "Neuroeconomics: How Neuroscience Can Inform Economics," *Journal of Economic Literature* 43:1 (2005): 9–64.

25. John Bargh et al., "The Automatic Evaluation Effect: Unconditional Automatic Attitude Activation with a Pronunciation Task," *Journal of Experimental Social Psychology* 32:1 (1996): 104–28; John Bargh and Tanya Chartrand, "The Unbearable Automacity of Being," *American Psychologist* 54:7 (1999): 462–79.

26. LeDoux, *Emotional Brain*; Piotr Winkielman and Kent C. Berridge, "Unconscious Emotion," *Current Directions in Psychological Science* 13:3 (2004): 120–23.

27. Camerer, Loewenstein, and Prelec, "Neuroeconomics," 26.

28. Bargh et al., "Automatic Evaluation Effect"; Jan de Houwer, Dirk Hermans, and Paul Eelen, "Affective and Identity Priming with Episodically Associated Stimuli," *Cognition and Emotion* 12:2 (1998): 145–69.

29. Daniel Gilbert and Michael Gill, "The Momentary Realist," *Psychological Science* 11:5 (2000): 394–98.

30. Alan Sanfey et al., "The Neural Basis of Economic Decision-Making in the Ultimatum Game," *Science* 300:5626 (2003):1755–65.

31. Nico Frijda, "The Laws of Emotion," *American Psychologist* 43:5 (1988): 349–58; Leonard Berkowitz, "Anger," in *Handbook of Cognition and Emotion*, ed. Tim Dalgleish and Mick Power (New York: Wiley, 1999): 411–28.

32. Robert Zajonc, "Feeling and Thinking: Preferences Need No Inferences," *American Psychologist* 35:2 (1980): 151–75; Robert Zajonc, "On the Primacy of Affect," *American Psychologist* 39:2 (1984): 117–23; Robert Zajonc, "Emotions," in Gilbert et al., *Handbook of Social Psychology*, 591–632; Camerer, Loewenstein, and Prelec, "Neuro-economics," 18.

33. George Loewenstein, "Out of Control: Visceral Influences on Behavior," *Organizational Behavior and Human Decision Processes* 65:3 (1996): 272–92; George Loewenstein and Jennifer Lerner, "The Role of Affect in Decision Making," in *Handbook of Affective Sciences*, ed. Richard Davidson et al. (Oxford: Oxford University Press, 2003): 619–42.

34. LeDoux, *Emotional Brain*.

35. Daniel Kahneman and Alan Krueger, "Developments in the Measurement of Subjective Well-Being," *Journal of Economic Perspectives* 20:1 (2006): 3–24.

36. Thomas Cottle and Stephen Klineberg, *The Present of Things Future* (New York: Free Press, 1974).

37. Arjen Boin, Paul 't Hart, Eric Stern, and Bengt Sundelius, *The Politics of Crisis Management: Public Leadership Under Pressure* (Cambridge: Cambridge University Press, 2005), 5.

38. George and Smoke, *Deterrence*; Richard Lebow and Janice Gross Stein, *We All Lost the Cold War* (Princeton, NJ: Princeton University Press, 1994).

39. Emanuel Adler, "Complex Deterrence in the Asymmetrical Warfare Era," in Paul, Morgan, and Wirtz, *Complex Deterrence*.

40. Ivan Arreguín-Toft, *How the Weak Win Wars: A Theory of Asymmetric Conflict* (New York: Cambridge University Press, 2005).

3 TOWARD AN ANALYTIC BASIS FOR INFLUENCE STRATEGY IN COUNTERTERRORISM

Paul K. Davis

THIS CHAPTER discusses terrorism-related deterrence and influence analytically, building on a 2002 monograph (Davis-Jenkins),[1] a recent review of the social science literature relevant to counterterrorism (Davis-Cragin),[2] and a recent paper.[3] The approach taken is to use conceptual modeling as a way to think about how to influence adversaries. Section two of the chapter summarizes earlier work. Section three sketches a system model that motivates both section four, which identifies factors that cause individuals to become terrorists and cause public support for terrorist organizations, and section five, which discusses factors affecting the decisions and behavior of terrorist organizations. This analytic decomposition into factors facilitates structured discussion of strategy.

PAST WORK ON DETERRENCE AND INFLUENCE
MORE GENERALLY

As discussed in the Davis-Jenkins monograph, the dominant Cold War interpretation of deterrence is largely irrelevant for dealing with al Qaeda as an entity or with al Qaeda leadership more specifically. That classic deterrence concept promised extreme punishment in the event of certain actions *and* withholding that punishment in the absence of the actions. However, the United States is determined to destroy al Qaeda and hunt down its lead-

---

This chapter is reprinted with permission from the RAND Corporation, from Paul K. Davis, *Simple Models to Explore Deterrence and More General Influence in the War with al-Qaeda* (Santa Monica, CA: RAND, 2010).

ers *in any case.* The United States is not about to ease up if al Qaeda merely promises to forgo further attacks. To make things worse, the rationality of al Qaeda leaders is quite different from that of Cold War leaders. True believers such as Osama bin Laden and Ayman al-Zawahiri would accept a martyr's death rather than bend. Classic deterrence theory (that is, deterrence by threat of punishment), then, is not an appropriate focal point for strategy. After reaching this gloomy conclusion in 2002, we found it necessary to redefine the problem and emphasize two points: decomposition and influence.

In terms of decomposition, the most important point was that al Qaeda is not a single entity but rather a system with many components, as illustrated by Figure 3.1. Al Qaeda's top leaders are different from its lieutenants, foot soldiers, logisticians, financiers, religious supporters, and so on. Some of those elements might well be subject to deterrence. The value of decomposing the system was soon recognized in U.S. strategy for combating terrorism[4] and is now part of the mainstream view of seeing al Qaeda as a number of somewhat overlapping networks.[5]

Our other major theme was to reconceive the "non-kinetic" challenge as one of *influence* rather than classic punishment-based deterrence (see Figure 3.2). The spectrum of influences includes deterrence by threat of punishment and

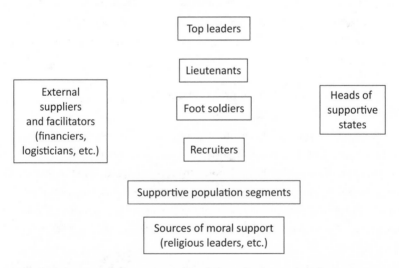

Figure 3.1. Seeing al Qaeda as a system, not an entity. Reprinted with permission from RAND Corporation, from Davis, Paul K., *Simple Models to Explore Deterrence and More General Influence in the War with al-Qaeda.* Santa Monica, CA: RAND Corporation, 2010.

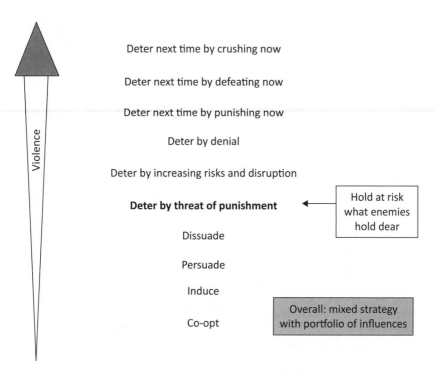

Figure 3.2. A spectrum of influences that includes classic deterrence. Reprinted with permission from RAND Corporation, from Davis, Paul K., *Simple Models to Explore Deterrence and More General Influence in the War with al-Qaeda*. Santa Monica, CA: RAND Corporation, 2010.

many others as well. The intent was to include all versions of deterrence (for example, deterrence by denial and deterrence of future actions by punishment for recent actions) and to include other relevant instruments of coercive and non-coercive diplomacy. There were precedents in the classic literature for this approach, as Jeffrey Knopf's chapter in this volume illustrates.[6]

This broader concept of influence effectively increases the battle space in which planning can operate. It even recognizes that some elements of organizations using terrorism eventually rejoin society and become part of political processes. That is, even if figures such as bin Laden and al-Zawahiri are "beyond the pale," that will not be the case for everyone associated with or supporting al Qaeda.

Having "increased the battle space," what more can be done to think analytically about influence?

MODELING DECISION MAKING AS A WAY TO THINK ABOUT INFLUENCE

If influence is ultimately about affecting behavior of others, then it makes sense to construct models of decision making to help us do so. As a group, the models should neither stereotype the adversary as irrational, nor assume the economist's version of rational-analytic thinking. One approach that avoids these errors is *synthetic cognitive modeling*: "synthetic" because it draws upon diverse factors affecting decision making, and "cognitive" because it attempts to reflect the factors at work in a real human's mind (although not the often-tortuous process of reaching a judgment).[7]

The author's work on such matters began in development of the 1980s-era RAND Strategy Assessment System (RSAS), which could be run as an automated computer simulation or with human teams making many of the important decisions. The system's Red, Blue, and Green "agents" were computer models of decision making for the Soviet Union and Warsaw Pact, the United States and NATO, and numerous other individual countries.[8] Three lessons from this research are worth reviewing here.

Use Alternative Models to Open Minds

The first lesson was the importance of developing *alternative* models to reflect uncertainties about the mind-set being represented. In an actual real-world crisis of significant duration we should expect to see a mix of behaviors rather than a single behavior represented by any given model. That was so also for U.S. and third-country leaders, so we had a variety of Blue and Green models. Anyone doubting the value of this approach might wish to review the later literature on the Cuban Missile Crisis, which conveys a sense of decision making that was anything but single-minded and consistent.[9]

Focus on "Real" Factors, Rather Than Just Math Calculations

A second lesson was that reducing discussion of deterrence and first-strike stability to mathematical calculations about nuclear weapon exchange ratios was seriously misleading. The *real* issues stimulating actual human beings to initiate nuclear war might include fear, desperation, honor, a sense of ultimate duty, or "dangerous ideas."[10] In the context of the struggle with al Qaeda, uncertainty and "dangerous ideas" also abound. These are part and parcel of the religious extremism that characterizes much of the al Qaeda rant, especially the claim that God demands violent jihad and that the rewards of martyrdom will be glorious. It is hardly unique to jihadis to be willing to die in direct defense of one's country, people, or cause, but it is especially troublesome when the exhortation is for indiscriminate offensive violence and martyrdom to be rewarded handsomely (as distinct from death bringing a vague eternal peace). So also it is troublesome when narrow actions by nations are seen as actions against the entire Muslim people and when moderate Muslims are regarded as apostates.

Use Simple Models

The third lesson was that the most important insights gained from decision modeling could be obtained with *simple* models, which could be reduced to figures, tables, and a story.[11] Recent work extended research on decision making and decision modeling in ways relevant to counterterrorism.[12] It reviewed literature bearing on decision science, including the contrasts between the rational-analytic and naturalistic (intuitive) approaches.[13] It and a subsequent report suggested approaches to decision support that drew on both strands of work and considered the strengths, weaknesses, and preferences of decision makers being served.[14] One conclusion was that decision makers are doing well if they are "merely" able to identify appropriate options and characterize those options for their best-estimate, best-case, and worst-case outcomes. Further, and relevant to this chapter, the potential errors of flawed decision making can often be understood in terms of the same model, but with different assessments of and weightings of those various outcomes.

To be sure, it is a stretch to use models of decision making to represent individuals "as though" they consider the various factors simultaneously as they make decisions. It is nonetheless useful to do so. What follows makes the further stretch of assuming that organizations or other groups act as though they make collective decisions using similar aggregate factors. This is a simplification, but one that we all make when talking as though the government, the public, a terrorist organization, and a foreign public are entities. Some of the dangers of doing so can be avoided by focusing on "factors" at work, and on alternative models, rather than on predicting ultimate decisions or behaviors.

A SYSTEM VIEW OF THE PROBLEM

In contemplating how influence can be brought to bear on al Qaeda it is useful to begin with a picture of a system model such as Figure 3.3.[15] Reading left to right, support for terrorism (both willingness to join in terrorism and public

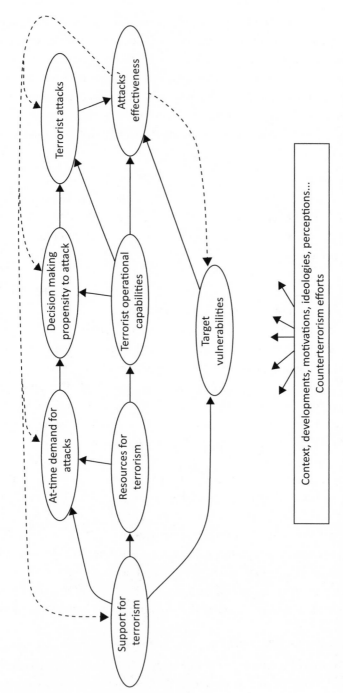

Figure 3.3. A system view of the problem. Reprinted with permission from RAND Corporation, from Davis, Paul K., *Simple Models to Explore Deterrence and More General Influence in the War with al-Qaeda*. Santa Monica, CA: RAND Corporation, 2010.

support of terrorism) contributes to the terrorist organization and its resources. That leads to the organization having operational capabilities. Support also contributes to demand calling for action. The terrorist organization creates a good deal of its own demand as well—not only by terrorist senior leaders, but also by hotheads eager for action even when ill-advised. Given capabilities and demand, there will be decisions to attack. The effectiveness of the attacks will depend upon the targets' vulnerabilities (increased by supporters who point out vulnerabilities or infiltrate targets) and counterterrorism activities. If the attacks are successful, they may increase support for terrorism generally; but they may instead trigger backlash. Further, the attacks may cause targets to be hardened further, they may weaken the ability to defend (for example, by weakening defensive structures and killing security people), or both.

The system, then, is dynamic, with considerable feedback and some conflicting influences. What matters to the chapter's story is that the nodes "support for terrorism" and "decision making" are natural focal points for influence-related counterterrorism. If we know the factors leading to people becoming terrorists, support for terrorism, and terrorist decisions to attack, then we may know targets for influence efforts.

MOTIVATION OF TERRORISTS AND THEIR SUPPORTERS

To identify the relevant factors, the following draws largely from a recent interdisciplinary review of the social-science literature (Davis-Cragin) and shows conceptual models of how different factors influence terrorism: so-called root-cause factors, factors in individual motivation, and factors in public support. These models are in the form of "factor trees," which lay out the factors affecting a phenomenon and may also indicate first-order combining relations by "ands" (all factors are necessary) or "ors" (combinations are sufficient).[16]

Root Causes

Figure 3.4 is a modest adaptation (mentioning intolerance) of a factor tree for root causes, based on a literature review by Darcy Noricks.[17] The root-cause factors can be seen as creating the environment in which terrorism may flourish. Efforts to reduce the root-cause factors by influence will, in most cases, be uphill and long-term in nature. Moreover, it is far easier to influence things negatively (that is, making things worse) than positively. Looking at

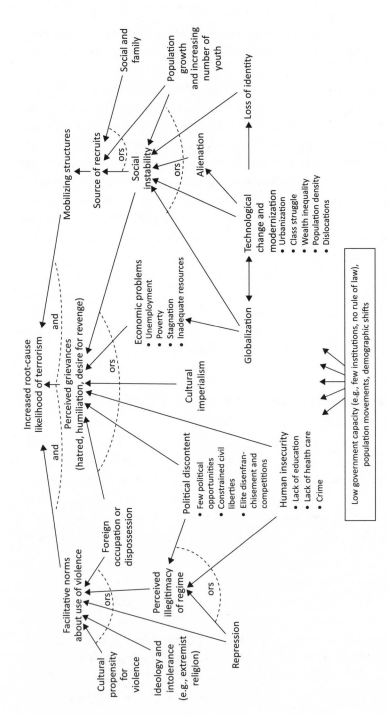

Figure 3.4. Root causes of terrorism. Reprinted with permission from RAND Corporation, from Davis, Paul K., *Simple Models to Explore Deterrence and More General Influence in the War with al-Qaeda*. Santa Monica, CA: RAND Corporation, 2010.

the leftmost node: the United States surely does not want to be perceived as a foreign occupier; nor does it want to be seen as propping up an illegitimate regime or as opposed to a region's dominant religion. It is one thing to express these cautions, but quite another to honor them amid the complexities of real-world foreign and domestic policy debates. Both President George W. Bush and President Barack Obama have sought to do so—studiously avoiding identifying Islamists as the threat (even extremist jihadis), and instead referring more vaguely to a global war on terrorism or to a war with al Qaeda specifically. A controversial factor that is too often omitted is also in the left branch. It relates to the kind of intolerance that is often associated with a combination of fundamentalism and isolation but that may arise in other ways as well (even if those other ways claim ties to religion, as with the Ku Klux Klan, right-wing militias, and homophobic groups). The importance of this factor was highlighted in the original Davis-Jenkins monograph.

Individual Motivations

The next place we may look for targets-of-influence efforts is the factors contributing to the motivations of individuals as they become terrorists. In many cases, there is no single decision to become a terrorist, but rather a process in which such radicalization occurs.[18] Analytically, however, we may see what happens "as if" there had been a decision. Figure 3.5 shows a factor tree based on a literature review by Todd Helmus.[19] Starting at the left, Helmus emphasizes the critical role in the radicalization process of mobilizing groups, which may be either bottom-up as emphasized by Marc Sageman, more top-down as Bruce Hoffman notes, or both. Next we see "real and perceived rewards," which range from financial incentives to fervently accepted visions of paradise with seventy-two virgins and to more high-minded but grandiose visions.[20] Continuing, the third branch refers to the "felt need" to respond to grievances of various kinds, whether collective or personal. As indicated at the next level down, the collective concern may be felt as a positive *duty* to defend. The last branch (passion for change) is related to the branch on grievances but may have a different emotional connotation, as in a passionate desire to recreate the fabled ideal caliphate.

If various factors can be identified that encourage individual terrorism, so also factors can be identified that encourage individuals to disengage.[21] Recently, two major sources have emerged on this topic. The first of these is an edited volume with case histories. The second is a summary account of John

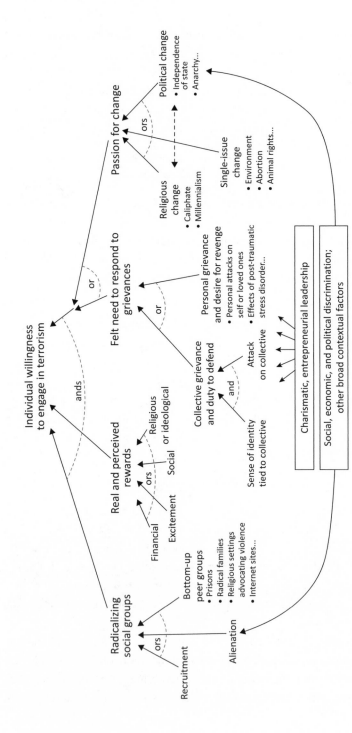

Figure 3.5. Factors for individual motivation. Reprinted with permission from RAND Corporation, from Davis, Paul K., *Simple Models to Explore Deterrence and More General Influence in the War with al-Qaeda*. Santa Monica, CA: RAND Corporation, 2010.

Horgan's thinking, based on interviewing current and "retired" terrorists. One important observation is that disengagement often occurs without deradicalization.

Public Support

Perhaps the most obvious focus for an influence campaign is the public support for terrorism. That has often been powerful—both in feeding the rise of a terrorist organization and in contributing to its decline.[22] How much and what kind of public support is necessary is a complicated matter.[23] The issue is also front and center in the U.S. counterinsurgency manual associated with General David Petraeus and General James Amos.[24] Let us discuss direct and indirect support separately.

Direct Support

State support is a natural focus for deterrence and other influence actions. Deterring state support of terrorism looms large in the minds of Indian, Israeli, Afghan, and Iraqi officials. The United States made it clear soon after 9/11 that it would not tolerate state support of al Qaeda. It then followed up by invading Afghanistan and displacing the Taliban. Subsequently, the United States invaded Iraq—due substantially to worries that at some point Saddam Hussein would cooperate significantly with al Qaeda, perhaps even to the extent of making weapons of mass destruction available.[25] Had the invasion of Iraq and its aftermath been successful, one consequence expected would have been increased credibility for the Bush administration's preemptive strategy (actually a strategy of preventive war).

Direct support by a non-state organization is likely also to be deterrable, so long as that non-state actor is targetable. Even the Taliban, if it regained power in Afghanistan, might well be very cautious. Direct support by individuals (for example, financiers, logisticians, security personnel) is certainly subject to traditional deterrence, as well as other influences. This is especially true if they are not truly devoted to the cause or if they have family, friends, income, or status that can be held at risk or deprived of what they value highly.

Indirect Support

Indirect public support may take a variety of forms. A population may, for example, be the source of recruits, finances and goods, or covert shelter. Even if the public merely turns a blind eye to the presence of al Qaeda members or affiliates, that may be enough. Conversely, if the public turns against al Qaeda, there may be huge improvements in intelligence—for example, in tips to the police or security forces, and in responses to reward offers. This is likely to be especially significant if the terrorists or direct supporters are easily distinguishable, as are foreign fighters that have moved into other countries. So also it is not necessarily easy for terrorists and their sympathizers to hide their activities from neighbors in dense communities. It is perhaps easier in places such as Britain, France, or Germany, which have large populations of immigrants and disaffected second-generation children that have freedom and mobility. Even there, however, terrorist plots are frequently uncovered in significant measure due to tips to police.

A Factor Tree for Public Support

If public support matters, then what are the factors contributing to it? Figure 3.6 is a factor tree based on Christopher Paul's work[26] (my colleagues and I published a new study on this subject in 2011; it sharpens and enriches the theory and draws upon new empirical data). Viewing the factors, one may think of influence efforts to mitigate the population's sense of need to resist, to reduce its respect for and identification with the terrorist group (that is, to undercut the sense that the group is leading an important movement), and to reduce social pressures and incentives to support the terrorism. That may include reducing the terrorists' opportunities to intimidate the population. The thickened arrow in Figure 3.6 indicates the particular importance of "identification." One reason for that emphasis is that sometimes terrorist organizations provide crucial group services, while the relevant governments do not. Indeed, they are not perceived as "terrorist organizations," but rather political organizations that, yes, sometimes use terrorism as a tactic.

A Composite View

Looking across the previous sections, it is possible to put together a composite view that tells a story, as in Figure 3.7.[27] Figure 3.7 asserts that—to a first approximation—the propensity to join in or support terrorism depends on (from left to right): (1) an underlying cause or activity that is deemed attractive; (2) the perceived legitimacy of terrorism; (3) the de facto perceived acceptability of costs and risk; and (4) the existence of mobilizing groups providing mechanisms for that support.

This factor tree (enriched in our 2011 work) explains that those supporting terrorism are often motivated by what they see as positives (for example,

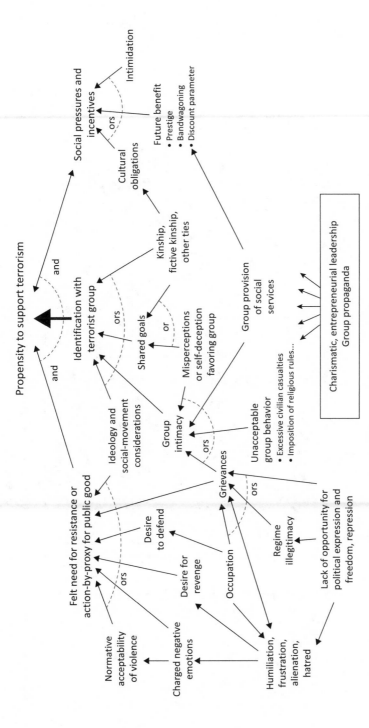

Figure 3.6. Factors underlying public support. Reprinted with permission from RAND Corporation, from Davis, Paul K., *Simple Models to Explore Deterrence and More General Influence in the War with al-Qaeda.* Santa Monica, CA: RAND Corporation, 2010.

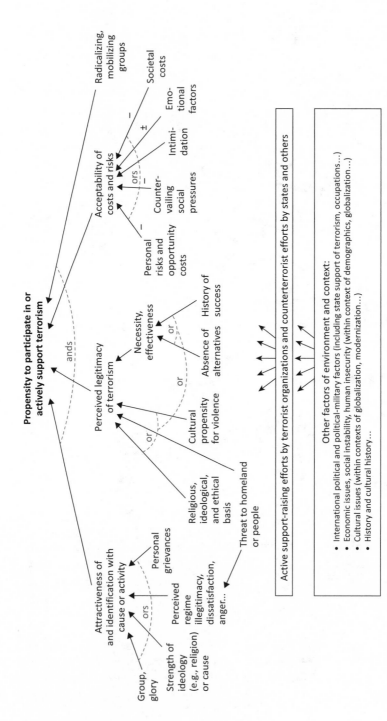

Figure 3.7. A composite view. Reprinted with permission from RAND Corporation, from Davis, Paul K., *Simple Models to Explore Deterrence and More General Influence in the War with al-Qaeda.* Santa Monica, CA: RAND Corporation, 2010.

the need to act against oppression, or in support of one's religion that is seen as under attack) and necessity. That is, by and large, people do not engage in or support terrorism *because* they favor attacks on civilians, but because they see it as either necessary (no alternatives), natural (violence is merely part of everyday life), a tolerable aspect of exciting activity (that is, being a "warrior"), or as part of a religious duty. As for calculations, the tree's depiction asserts that it is more a matter of there being strong pressures or desires to act at a time when the costs and risks are perceived as tolerable (or not much thought about). That is, there may be no conscious and informed balancing of benefits and costs. Those disengaging or withdrawing support may be doing so in part because the costs and risks have become more prominent in their thinking. Those costs and risks may be personal, societal, or related to the cause itself.

At this point it seems useful to collect some observations in each of several groups, drawing both on Figure 3.7 and the earlier discussions.

Motivations

Motivations can vary a great deal.[28] The attractiveness of the cause may, for example, have a great deal to do with extremist religion . . . or very little at all. As indicated in Figure 3.7, alternative mechanisms, and which mechanisms apply, may vary with neighborhood and point in history, not merely country. Also, Figure 3.7 applies at a slice in time and should not be construed to mean that cause proceeds neatly left to right. For example, al Qaeda recruits may join for the opportunity to join relatives or friends in exciting activities. In the course of being indoctrinated, however, they may pick up the strong religious views seen as necessary to become part of the organization. They may believe fervently even if they have given religion no thought at all before becoming involved. They may also lose their religious fervency if they disengage.

Others, in contrast, may have started with strong religious leanings and heeded what they felt as the clarion call of jihad from local religious authorities. The saddest version of this is perhaps when poor and ignorant schoolchildren are recruited in this way by religious leaders in the infamous madrasas. Lest we underestimate the power of religious extremism, perhaps treating it as mere pap fed to foot soldiers, we should remember that bin Laden and al-Zawahiri were strongly influenced by religion from their early years.[29] So also, Umar Farouk Abdulmutallab (the "Christmas Day bomber") was driven by religious convictions developed abroad rather than in his native Nigeria.[30]

One consequence of there being very different motivations is that influence campaigns need to be targeted, with different messages for different targets within a population.[31]

Many of the factors are subject to change. Terrorists may become more or less enthralled with a cause over time; they may be more or less convinced of terrorism's necessity; and, certainly, they can become more or less viscerally aware of costs and risks. And, of course, the ubiquity and effectiveness of the radicalizing, mobilizing groups can rise and fall dramatically as counter-terrorism activities take their toll. Some factors are crosscutting. For example, if a threat to the homeland or people is perceived, it affects both motivation and a sense of legitimacy. This sense of threat has sometimes been much underestimated.[32]

Although juxtaposing factors in a tree is helpful for understanding the phenomenon, many important factors are so crosscutting as to be best shown as the bottom, as affecting "everything." Some of these are the charisma of leaders; others are "exogenous" to the narrow terrorism-counterterrorism problem, as when wars or economic shocks occur for their own reasons. Taken as a whole, then, this section lays out a way of identifying targets for an influence campaign, and doing so systematically. However, the influencing itself remains very difficult. It is also seriously complicated by the potential—sometimes the near certainty—of unwanted side effects counter to those intended.

AFFECTING TERRORIST SYSTEMS

Let us next turn to modeling the decision making and behavior of terrorists. Figure 3.8 uses a factor tree adapted from a body of work by Brian Jackson to depict the considerations that enter into the decision of a terrorist organization about whether to go ahead with a particular operation.[33] The figure assumes that the organization exists and that it has strategic objectives, which are not at issue. The depiction conveys the imagery of the rational-analytic perspective but can allow for many aspects of more-limited rationality. For example, the reader should imagine the word "perceived" as a modifier for almost everything in the figure. Also, Jackson refers to sufficiency of information. The "sufficiency" may be misestimated, and the quality of the information may turn out to be poor. The model also includes concepts such as "group risk tolerance," which may be interpreted with a utility function comfortable to rational-actor modeling, or may include subjective and

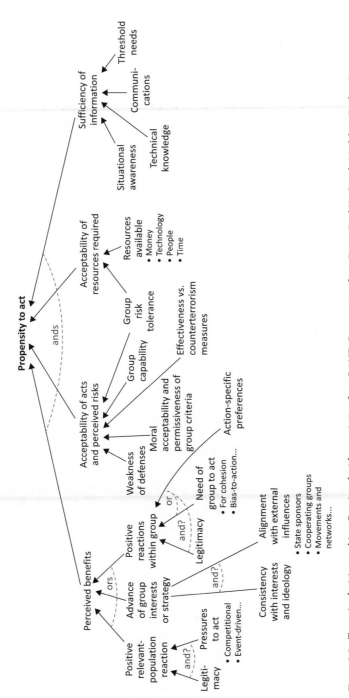

Figure 3.8. Terrorist decision making. Reprinted with permission from RAND Corporation, from Davis, Paul K., *Simple Models to Explore Deterrence and More General Influence in the War with al-Qaeda*. Santa Monica, CA: RAND Corporation, 2010.

circumstance-dependence heuristics. For the purposes of this chapter, the following points are germane:[34]

- The benefits may be judged not through the lens of a single all-powerful leader, but with consideration paid to perceived benefits to the relevant public audience and the terrorist organization as a whole. Does the proposed action advance the strategy of the organization and/or the desires of the group itself? Some members of the group are likely to be more eager for action than others.
- The assessment of risks depends on the defenses (broadly construed to include counterterrorism activities as well as immediate target hardening), the group's thinking about risks, *and* the capabilities of the group itself (for example, whether it has the requisite materials, talent, and opportunity).
- The "cost" of the cost-benefit calculation is not merely about financial expense, but about the likely expenditure of technology, people, and time. Although al Qaeda has a long waiting line of would-be recruits, it has many fewer capable and accomplished leaders and also many fewer specialists in skills such as bomb making and penetration of security systems.
- In this connection, there is a good deal of rationality to how terrorist organizations use suicide bombers, the competent ones being special resources to be used against hard targets.[35]

Modeling Decisions at Different Levels

While Figure 3.8 is an overview of terrorist decision making from a top-down perspective, primarily about particular operations, it is useful to think about deterrent and other influences at different levels of issue, organization, and operation. The traditional distinctions are among strategic, operational, and tactical levels. These distinctions are no longer as neat as they were in past centuries because the actions of even an individual can have horrific consequences, but they remain useful for our purposes.

Figure 3.9 shows an alternative way to decompose the risk factors appearing in Figure 3.8. It distinguishes among operational risks, the risk of negative effects internal to the organization (for example, dissension due either to ideological disagreements or some members fearing retaliatory consequences for families and community), and the risk that the strategic consequences of an attack will be negative even if the operation is a success operationally ("strategic

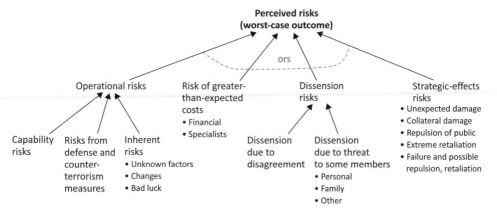

Figure 3.9. Decomposing risks to assess worst-case outcome. Reprinted with permission from RAND Corporation, from Davis, Paul K., *Simple Models to Explore Deterrence and More General Influence in the War with al-Qaeda*. Santa Monica, CA: RAND Corporation, 2010.

effects risk"). For example, there may be more casualties than intended or more casualties to Muslims than intended. The public reaction, including that of al Qaeda supporters, may be one of shock and horror rather than one of acclaim. There may be extraordinary retaliation by local states, the United States, or both—even to include what amounts to collective punishment.

Some general statements are possible, based on empirical evidence as well as common sense:

- Those executing attacks may be deterred from particular attacks by operational risks—even if they are committed to the cause and willing to sacrifice their lives.
- If enough specific attacks are deterred over time, the net effect may be as though deterrence had worked at a higher level (as discussed by Shmuel Bar in another chapter of this volume). It would not be proper to interpret that as "deterring further attack on the United States" if efforts continued apace to find a workable plan, but it would be accurate to refer to "deterring further attacks so far." That would hardly be nothing. Would al Qaeda be increasingly discouraged and reduce effort?—in which case *cumulative* deterrence would be working;[36] would the United States become more apathetic and sloppy, or both? If time is on our side with the al Qaeda movement fading, then even temporary deterrence is effective deterrence.

It is also possible to make observations rooted in specific cases and empirical sources of information. For example:

- Senior leadership sometimes argues against certain kinds of attacks because it fears back-reactions from the public, as in the aftermath of the 2003 Riyadh attack, which killed numerous Muslims rather than westerners. Likewise, the public beheadings ordered by Abu Musab al-Zarqawi were seen by Ayman al-Zawahiri as counterproductive: it was "better to kill the captives by bullet."[37]
- Those planning specific operations often do not like risks. They may proceed with an operation known to be risky, but they would prefer not to do so even if this means delay, diversion, or abandonment of a mission.[38]
- Individual terrorists can sometimes be deterred or dissuaded by knowledge that participation would bring severe harm to their families. Examples of this are described by Israeli authorities who have systematically interviewed large numbers of terrorist and would-be terrorists.[39]
- In other domains such as drug smuggling, the deterrent effect is a nonlinear function of perceived risk. Indeed, that has been empirically demonstrated.[40]

Unfortunately, it is easy to come up with counterexamples, such as that some attacks may be deemed "successful" even if foiled, as when the terrorists at least demonstrate the ability to penetrate anywhere in a country. Nonetheless, partial success will generally be better than none.

WALKING THROUGH SOME EXAMPLES WITH ALTERNATIVE MODELS

Another way to "see" the potential value of broader forms of deterrence is to use relatively simple decision models. Let us now walk through some examples contrasting the assessment of options that might be reached by senior leadership of al Qaeda according to two models. The models may represent different mind-sets at work at one time or another because of then-recent developments, our uncertainty as to how "al Qaeda" reasons, or some combination. Such models can open our minds as to how the adversary leadership may reason.

Each model assesses the option for its expected outcome, its best-case outcome, its worst-case outcome, and confidence that the worst-case outcome really is as bad as it could plausibly be. Scores of 0 to 10 are assigned to each assessment, corresponding to the range of very poor, poor, marginal, good, and very good. The models differ in their individual assessments and how they combine them to reach a net judgment. Model 1 is more willing to take risks. Model 2 is *somewhat* less willing to take risks and tends to see more risks than Model 1—whether by worrying about the unknown or worrying about whether the consequences of "success" will be more negative than expected.

The hypothetical assessments for Models 1 and 2 are given in Table 3.1 and Table 3.2. The first attack proposal shown corresponds to the September 11 attack, perhaps as assessed relatively soon before the attack. Al Qaeda having studied the plans and discussed issues with team leaders along the way, and having had no serious problems in preparing the attack, Model 1 rates the option highly. After all, the individual assessments assert that the attack will probably be quite successful; *could be* spectacularly successful; and is very unlikely to be a failure because even if three of the airplanes fail, and the other airplane merely causes serious damage to its target, the overall effect will still be dramatic—a daring strike into the U.S. homeland. Model 1 regards anything less successful than that as implausible, as indicated by "high" in the confidence column.

Now let us consider Model 2's assessment of the same option: it is inherently less confident because it worries about "unknown unknowns," and it gives more weight to the downside possibility than will Model 1. In shorthand, it is more cautious. In this case, even Model 2's assessment is "marginal"—

Table 3.1. Model 1's assessments of possible attacks at different times

Proposed attack	Best-estimate outcome	Best-case outcome (upside potential)	Worst-case outcome (downside risk)	Confidence in assessments	Model 1's net assessment
9/11 attack	7	10	5	High	9
Cyanide attack on subway system	5	10	5	Moderate	7
Nuclear attack on a city	10	10	5 (backlash)	Medium	8

NOTE: Scores are from 0 to 10, with 0 being very bad, 5 being marginal, and 10 being very good.

SOURCE: Reprinted with permission from RAND Corporation, from Davis, Paul K., *Simple Models to Explore Deterrence and More General Influence in the War with al-Qaeda.* Santa Monica, CA: RAND Corporation, 2010.

Table 3.2. Model 2's assessments of possible attacks at different times

Proposed attack	Best-estimate outcome	Best-case outcome (upside potential)	Worst-case outcome (downside risk)	Confidence in assessments	Model 2's net assessment
9/11 attack	5	10	5	High	5
Cyanide attack on subway system	7	10	3	Low	3
Nuclear attack on a city	10	10	0 (extreme backlash / retaliation)	Low	1

NOTE: Scores are from 0 to 10, with 0 being very bad, 5 being marginal, and 10 being very good. This assumes that even Model 2 has been convinced previously that attacking the U.S. homeland is necessary.

SOURCE: Reprinted with permission from RAND Corporation, from Davis, Paul K., *Simple Models to Explore Deterrence and More General Influence in the War with al-Qaeda*. Santa Monica, CA: RAND Corporation, 2010.

inclined to action, perhaps, but just barely. If unanticipated problems began to arise, Model 2 would tilt to a negative assessment.

In this hypothetical use of models, then, *either* model of al Qaeda senior leadership would have gone ahead with the 9/11 attack. Both models attempt to reflect the extreme ambition and ruthlessness of actual al Qaeda leadership; both models are seeing the same "facts" (for example, success in training runs, and the absence of strong warning signals); and both models are the same with respect to relatively objective matters such as estimating potential damage if an airplane hits its target.

The next row of the tables contemplates a cyanide attack on the New York subway system. The best-estimate outcome is not as high as with 9/11 because chemical weapons are less powerful and because of technical uncertainties, but the upside potential is very strong, and the worst-case outcome seems at least marginal from a direct-effect perspective (for example, deaths caused and disruption achieved), meriting a 5. In this case, however, the information available for the assessment is poor, because the security system is not fully understood and there are technical uncertainties about how well the gas would disperse and about whether there are damage-limitation mechanisms in place. Further, a downside-assessment should perhaps recognize the possibility of extreme negative reactions by the entire Muslim world. Perhaps the United States would have an extreme reaction—even more than immediately after 9/11 with the invasion of Afghanistan. It might flail out indiscriminately and inflame anti-American attitudes (which would be good from the al Qaeda perspective), but perhaps it would make no such mistakes, and the Muslim world—including many segments traditionally supportive of al Qaeda—would become strongly antagonistic. In this case, then, Models 1 and 2 see things quite differently. Model 1 favors the attack; Model 2 does not.

In fact, it has been reported that a cyanide attack was indeed planned for January 2003, but called off for reasons unknown, apparently by al-Zawahiri himself.[41] Perhaps the actual reasoning of al Qaeda leadership was less about risk than about the perceived need to do something *more* spectacular. The incident, then, suggests that we may need additional models if we are to contemplate the potential range of thinking among al Qaeda leadership.

The bottom row contemplates a nuclear bomb being set off in an American city. In this case, Models 1 and 2 are even more at odds—even if attack preparations and technical considerations are favorable. The primary reason is that Model 2 has more imagination (Model 1 might call it paranoia) about the ultimate consequences of "success." Model 2 asks whether the United States and its allies might respond by collective punishment of the Muslim world—perhaps with nuclear weapons or with the unleashing of some sinister disease that would be devastating in the region. Model 2 is less sanguine than Model 1 about the wisdom of an apocalypse or about the certainty with which God will protect against its happening. Model 2 may also be convinced that the anger against al Qaeda due to the attack might be extreme and general, including in the Muslim world.

The same uncertainties could have been discussed without mentioning the word "model," but using models adds structure and a degree of consistency and coherence. The essential feature is giving alternative constructs serious weight rather than focusing on the alleged best-estimate construct. An "analytic doctrine" that called for creating alternative models as part of assessment, and developing strategy to honor all the possibilities, might prove fruitful. Although governments have tried for many years to include dissenting opinions in decision processes, results have not typically been good, in part because the dissenters are either stigmatized or treated as merely performing a pro forma duty (both aspects of what the author has called the "tyranny of the best estimate"). The suggested analytic doctrine would deemphasize the controversy itself and instead emphasize that responsible planning should hedge against error.

CONCLUSIONS: THINKING AGAIN ABOUT
DETERRENCE-AND-INFLUENCE MEASURES

Having been through this notional exercise, let us now think again about the value of various deterrence-and-influence measures. Imperfect defenses may look useless to a conservative planner and yet be worrisome to the would-be attacker. Public-diplomacy efforts to encourage fierce rejection of WMD attacks by Muslim leaders, even revolutionary leaders, might be derided as unlikely to affect al Qaeda leaders, but perhaps such efforts would be just enough, on the margin, to make a difference. Is there not enough evidence about people in general, and even current al Qaeda leaders in particular, to imagine that they may disagree about evidence, disagree about risk taking, and differ about what "downsides" may be? Is this not even more obviously true when we recognize that individual people also perceive and reason differently as a function of their recent history and physical condition?

Next we might ask the same kinds of question about lower-level tiers of lieutenants and facilitators, and even supportive elements of the general population. Again, we should not fail to recognize the *potential* value of our efforts, even if they relate to deterrence or to forms of influence that some experts believe are implausible when dealing with religious extremists.

Finally, it can also be argued that deterrence is cumulative over the years and that viewing it as such can be very helpful. Doron Almog argues that case, drawing on the decades of struggle between Israel and Palestinian terrorists. He argues that over time terrorist organizations are forced by repeated defeats to reduce their objectives. Boaz Ganor, also drawing from the Israeli experience, provides a veritable text on the subject of counterterrorism, albeit one heavily laden with dilemmas as befits the subject.[42] And Shmuel Bar, in this volume, updates such reasoning and the evidence for it.

This chapter has sketched the case for using simple conceptual models to help guide thinking about how to deter or to otherwise influence potential, actual, or disengaging terrorists and the many people who support terrorist organizations directly or indirectly. Much more can and should be done. More analytic depth can be added to the models using decision-table methods, explicit characterization of uncertainty, and alternative models to reflect different mind-sets.

NOTES

1. Paul Davis and Brian Michael Jenkins, *The Deterring and Influencing Component of Counter Terrorism* (Santa Monica, CA: RAND, 2002).

2. Paul Davis and Kim Cragin, eds., *Social Science for Counterterrorism: Putting the Pieces Together* (Santa Monica, CA: RAND, 2009).

3. Paul Davis, *Using Simple Models to Analyze Opportunities for Deterrence and Influence in Counterterrorism* (Santa Monica, CA: RAND, 2010).

4. The White House (President George W. Bush), *National Strategy for Combating Terrorism* (Washington, DC: White House, 2006).

5. John Arquilla and David Ronfeldt, *The Advent of Netwar* (Santa Monica, CA: RAND, 1996); John Arquilla and David Ronfeldt, *Networks and Netwars: The Future of Terror, Crime, and Militancy* (Santa Monica, CA: RAND, 2001); Marc Sageman, *Understanding Terror Networks* (Philadelphia: University of Pennsylvania Press, 2004); Marc Sageman, *Leaderless Jihad: Terror Networks in the Twenty-first Century* (Philadelphia: University of Pennsylvania Press, 2008).

6. See also Alexander George and Richard Smoke, *Deterrence in American Foreign Policy: Theory and Practice* (New York: Columbia University Press, 1973); Alexander George, "The Need for Influence Theory and Actor-Specific Behavioral Models of Adversaries," in *Know Thy Enemy: Profiles of Adversary Leaders and Their Strategic Cultures*, ed. Barry Schneider and Jerrold Post (Maxwell Air Force Base, AL: Air War College, 2003), 271–310.

7. Paul Davis, *Synthetic Cognitive Models of Adversaries for Effects-Based Planning* (Santa Monica, CA: RAND, 2004).

8. Paul Davis, *Some Lessons Learned from Building Red Agents in the RAND Corporation Strategy Assessment System* (Santa Monica, CA: RAND, 1989); Paul Davis and James Winnefeld, *The RAND Corporation Strategy Assessment Center* (Santa Monica, CA: RAND, 1983).

9. Aleksandr Fursenko and Timothy Naftali, *One Hell of a Gamble: Khrushchev, Castro, and Kennedy, 1958–1964* (New York: W. W. Norton, 1997); Graham Allison and Philip Zelikow, *Essence of Decision: Explaining the Cuban Missile Crisis*, 2nd ed. (New York: Longman, 1999); Michael Dobbs, *One Minute to Midnight* (New York: Alfred A. Knopf, 2008).

10. Davis, *Lessons*.

11. This approach was demonstrated in work that focused on understanding Saddam Hussein and nuclear "proliferators." Paul Davis and John Arquilla, *Deterring or Coercing Opponents in Crisis: Lessons from the War with Saddam Hussein* (Santa Monica, CA: RAND, 1991); Paul Davis and John Arquilla, *Thinking About Opponent Behavior in Crisis and Conflict: A Generic Model for Analysis and Group Dis-*

cussion (Santa Monica, CA: RAND, 1991); National Academy of Sciences, *Post–Cold War Conflict Deterrence* (Washington, DC: National Academy Press, 1996).

12. Paul Davis, Jonathan Kulick, and Michael Egner, *Implications of Modern Decision Science for Military Decision Support Systems* (Santa Monica, CA: RAND, 2005).

13. Daniel Kahneman, "Maps of Bounded Rationality: A Perspective on Intuitive Judgment and Choice," Nobel Prize lecture given on December 8, 2002, at Stockholm University.

14. Paul Davis and James Kahan, *Theory and Methods for Supporting High-Level Decision Making* (Santa Monica, CA: RAND, 2007).

15. Paul Davis, "Representing Social Science Knowledge Analytically," in Davis and Cragin, *Social Science for Counterterrorism*, 401–52.

16. Ibid.

17. Darcy Noricks, "The Root Causes of Terrorism," in Davis and Cragin, *Social Science for Counterterrorism*, 11–70.

18. John Horgan, *Walking Away from Terrorism* (London: Routledge, 2009); Sageman, *Leaderless Jihad*; Bruce Hoffman, "The Myth of Grass-Roots Terrorism," *Foreign Affairs* 87:3 (2008): 133–38.

19. Todd Helmus, "Why and How Some People Become Terrorists," in Davis and Cragin, *Social Science for Counterterrorism*, 71–112.

20. Mark Stout, Jessica Huckabey, and John Schindler, *The Terrorist Perspectives Project: Strategic and Operational Views of Al Qaida and Associated Movements* (Annapolis, MD: U.S. Naval Institute Press, 2008), 39, 48.

21. Tore Bjorgo and John Horgan, *Leaving Terrorism Behind: Disengagement from Political Violence* (London: Routledge, 2009); Horgan, *Walking Away*; Darcy Noricks, "Disengagement and Deradicalization: Processes and Programs," in Davis and Cragin, *Social Science for Counterterrorism*, 299–322.

22. Martha Crenshaw, "Thoughts on Relating Terrorism to Historical Contexts," in *Terrorism in Context*, ed. Martha Crenshaw (University Park: Pennsylvania State University Press, 1995); Bjorgo and Horgan, *Leaving Terrorism Behind*; Horgan, *Walking Away*; Dipak Gupta, *Understanding Terrorism and Political Violence: The Life Cycle of Birth, Growth, Transformation, and Demise* (New York: Routledge, 2008); Gaga Gvineria, "How Does Terrorism End?" in Davis and Cragin, *Social Science for Counterterrorism*, 257–98 ; Audrey Cronin, "How al-Qaida Ends: The Decline and Demise of Terrorist Groups," *International Security* 31:1 (2006); Seth Jones and Martin Libicki, *How Terrorist Groups End: Implications for Countering Al Qa'ida* (Santa Monica, CA: RAND, 2008).

23. Christopher Paul, *How Do Terrorists Generate and Maintain Support?* (Santa Monica, CA: RAND, 2009).

24. David Petraeus and James Amos, *U.S. Army / Marine Counterinsurgency Field Manual* (Old Saybrook, CT: Konecky & Konecky, 2006).

25. Douglas Feith, *War and Decision: Inside the Pentagon at the Dawn of the War on Terrorism* (New York: Harper, 2008), 491–92. Other reasons existed, of course, such as general concern about Saddam's troublemaking in the region and long-standing support of terrorism (e.g., in Palestine).

26. Paul, *How Do Terrorists Generate and Maintain Support?*

27. Davis "Representing Social Science."

28. U.S. House of Representatives Committee on Homeland Security, Subcommittee on Intelligence, Information Sharing and Terrorism Risk Assessment, testimony of Kim Cragin, "Understanding Terrorist Motivations," December 15, 2009.

29. Lawrence Wright, *The Looming Tower: Al Qaeda and the Road to 9/11* (New York: Vintage, 2006), 35–45, 75–80.

30. Nick Tattersall, "Nigeria Bomber's Home Town Blames Foreign Schooling," Reuters, December 27, 2009.

31. Christine MacNulty, "Values as a Basis for Deterring Terrorists: Cultural-Cognitive Systems Analysis (Ccsa)," Proceedings of the Unrestricted Warfare Symposium 2008 Conference, Laurel, MD, Johns Hopkins University Applied Physics Laboratory, March 10–11, 2008; Christine MacNulty, "Perceptions, Values, and Motivations in Cyberspace," *IO Journal* 1:2 (2009), 32–38; Kim Cragin and Scott Gerwehr, *Dissuading Terror: Strategic Influence and the Struggle Against Terrorism* (Santa Monica, CA: RAND, 2005).

32. Robert Pape, *Dying to Win: The Strategic Logic of Suicide Terrorism* (New York: Random House, 2005).

33. Brian Jackson, "Organizational Decisionmaking by Terrorist Groups," in Davis and Cragin, *Social Science for Counterterrorism*, 209–56.

34. One issue that is not highlighted in Figure 3.8 is self-restraint, touched upon by referring to "acceptability of acts." As Brian Jenkins discusses, in this volume and elsewhere, we should expect quite a variation of self-restraint among individuals in the terrorist galaxy. Brian Michael Jenkins, *Will Terrorists Go Nuclear?* (New York: Prometheus Books, 2008).

35. Eli Berman and David Laitin, *Hard Targets: Theory and Evidence on Suicide Attacks*, National Bureau of Economic Research, Working Paper 11740 (2005); Claude Berrebi, *The Economics of Terrorism and Counterterrorism: What Matters, and Is Rational-Choice Theory Helpful?* (Santa Monica, CA: RAND, 2009).

36. Doron Almog, "Cumulative Deterrence and the War on Terrorism," *Parameters* 34:4 (2004–5): 4–19.

37. Office of the Director of National Intelligence, "Letter from al-Zawahiri to al-Zarqawi," ODNI News Release No. 2-05 (October 2005).

38. Andrew Morral and Brian Jackson, *Understanding the Role of Deterrence in Counterterrorism Security* (Santa Monica, CA: RAND, 2009).

39. Almog, "Cumulative Deterrence."

40. Robert Anthony, "A Calibrated Model of the Psychology of Deterrence," *Bulletin on Narcotics*, vol. 56, nos. 1 and 2 (2006), 49–64.

41. George Tenet, *At the Center of the Storm: My Years at the CIA* (New York: HarperCollins, 2007), 273–74.

42. Almog, "Cumulative Deterrence"; Boaz Ganor, *The Counter-Terrorism Puzzle: A Guide for Decision Makers* (New Brunswick, NJ: Transaction Publishers, 2005).

4 COUNTER-COERCION, THE POWER OF FAILURE, AND THE PRACTICAL LIMITS OF DETERRING TERRORISM

Frank Harvey and Alex Wilner

DETERRENCE AND COMPELLENCE are two strategies used to manipulate an adversary's behavior. Both are closely associated with coercion. "Coercion," explains Lawrence Freedman, is the threatened and "actual application of force to influence the action of a voluntary agent" by weighing on its "strategic choices."[1] Coercive strategies are effective when they produce a cost-benefit assessment within an adversary's calculus in which the expected utility of a given action is less than its expected cost, prompting changes in behavior. Coercion is, however, a dynamic process. It rarely ends with a defender simply applying a coercive strategy against a challenger. Challengers, too, can behave in ways that affect the defender's own utility calculus, its willingness to pursue potentially costly strategies, and its capability to act as it threatens. *Counter-coercion* is a challenger's ability to interfere with and diminish a defender's coercive strategy in ways that alter its preferences.

In thinking about deterring terrorism, counter-coercion figures prominently. Terrorist organizations retain enormous counter-coercion potential that can undermine a state's preferred deterrent/compellent strategy: they can turn a state's strengths into potential weaknesses and their own weaknesses into strengths; invalidate a state's deterrent message; and manipulate the manner in which states measure and weigh counterterrorism successes and failures. These counter-coercive advantages raise limitations concerning the applicability and utility of applying deterrence theory to counterterrorism.

The counter-coercion critique presented here offers a practical yet considerably understudied assessment of deterrence theory in the context of terrorism by reengaging important work on the prerequisites for deterrence/

compellence success. Theories of deterrence stipulate that threats must be clearly defined and communicated and that defenders retain the capability and resolve to punish noncompliance. While these prerequisites are well situated in studies of interstate deterrence, they are insufficiently addressed in the literature on deterring terrorism.

This chapter posits that counter-coercion complicates the manner in which deterrence can be properly applied in counterterrorism. The argument is structured as follows: The first section examines the traditional conception of counter-coercion, as it relates to interstate relations, and expands it to the context of terrorism. Two terrorist counter-coercion processes are then introduced: *active counter-coercion* (which involves terrorists taking concrete steps to impede a state's coercive effort) and *passive counter-coercion* (which is derived from the inherent characteristics of terrorism and counterterrorism). Sections two, three, and four examine these processes in greater detail, assessing how terrorists circumvent power asymmetries, invalidate coercive communications, and manipulate perceptions of counterterrorism success and failure. The chapter concludes by drawing out the implications of the analysis on deterring terrorism and suggests avenues for further research.

COERCION AND COUNTER-COERCION: THEORY AND PRACTICE

Coercion is about influencing adversary decision making. At its core, Karl Mueller writes, it is "an effort to *convince* the target to concede, not to force it to concede by physically precluding any alternative."[2] Its logic is that of deterrence and compellence: persuading an actor to willingly change its behavior rather than forcing it to do so because it has run out of other options. Crushing an opponent so that it can no longer retaliate is not coercion but rather "brute force" and overt military victory.[3] The goal of coercion is not the target's utter destruction but rather the manipulation of its behavior by the threat and use (and threat of future use) of destructive force. Coercion succeeds if and when an adversary "gives in while it still has the power to resist."[4]

At times, practicing coercion may involve going beyond the mere issuance of threats to the actual use of military force. Herein, the logic of coercion goes beyond that of deterrence in subtle but important ways: it relies on limited warfare for manipulative purposes.[5] It includes the demonstrative, restricted, and limited use of military force to both underscore threats and induce desired behavior. Deterrence and compellence, on the other hand, rely on threats and have, in fact, failed if one must be carried out in practice. While "coercive diplomacy" and "compellence" are used interchangeably, the difference rests with the fact that compellence is behavioral manipulation short of military use, while coercive diplomacy can include the use of force to emphasize compellent threats.[6]

Counter-coercion theory is derived from assumptions about the relationship between the application of coercive tactics and an adversary's motivation to find responses to counter those moves and/or exploit them in order to impose additional costs.[7] It is, elementally, about coercing the coercer (or deterring the deterrer). As Daniel Byman and Matthew Waxman suggest, "rather than simply [minimize] the effect of coercive threats, an adversary may try to impose costs on the coercing power."[8] That is, a challenger can respond to coercion in ways that manipulates a defender's cost-benefit calculus over whether or not to continue a given coercive strategy or develop and apply new, potentially less-preferred, approaches. The general idea is to defy, sidestep, and/or impose costs on a coercive strategy in order to compel a defender to alter its behavior in a way that better suits the challenger. For instance, an adversary may "escalate militarily," write Byman and Waxman, or attempt to "drive a diplomatic wedge between states aligned against it" in order to convince a defender to forgo a preferred coercive strategy. In either case, a challenger manipulates and amplifies the costs *associated* with imposing costs. "Viewing coercion dynamically," conclude Byman and Waxman, forces states to "incorporate the adversary's ability to neutralize," circumvent, or altogether eliminate the coercive costs it is willing and able to apply.[9] As a rule, the stronger the defender's motivation to pursue a specific military or political strategy, the more obvious the challenger's incentive to counter . . . and vice versa.

In relations between states and terrorist adversaries, counter-coercion is just as relevant and potentially more pronounced. For starters, terrorists develop and apply tactics that undermine state coercive strategies and impose costs on their preferred behavior in the same way as state adversaries do. *Active counter-coercion* is a terrorist group's attempt to undermine a state's coercive capability at the tactical level by undercutting the state's resolve and ability to pursue a favored coercive strategy. To a certain extent, terrorist groups do this already. They develop tactics and rely on violence that circumvents the discrepancies in absolute power upon which state coercion is often based and force states to use alternative, potentially more costly strategies. For example, the sensitivity Western states profess with regard to protecting civilians in counterterrorism and counterinsurgency operations invites obvious counter-moves by terrorist organizations: actively placing themselves in positions that invite civilian deaths.[10] The paradox, of course, is that in advertising a sensitivity to civilian casualties and advocating protective guidelines for theater operations, states inadvertently reward behavior that places civilians in harm's way.

Besides active counter-coercion, terrorists have other, altogether less obvious, counter-coercive strengths. The very organizational structure of terrorist groups and the nature of terrorism itself can diminish the utility and plausibility of a state's coercive threat. This phenomenon might be best described as *passive counter-coercion*, whereby terrorists, by virtue of their diffuse organization and the nature of the violence they employ, complicate and diminish the utility of a state's deterrent/compellent strategy. Passive counter-coercion weakens state coercion by invalidating deterrent processes and undermining practical prerequisites. For instance, consider that terrorist groups are said to lack a "return address."[11] While terrorists have other assets that can be held hostage in coercive bargains, statelessness complicates the process of constructing plausible threats. Statelessness might be thought of as a passive counter-coercive leverage that compels a defender to move away from its preferred coercive strategy (for example, threatening territorial assets) and forcing it to find other ways to produce desired outcomes. Other passive counter-coercive leverages associated with terrorism include the difficulty states have in properly communicating coercive threats with terrorists who are organized in confusing and nonhierarchical ways. One cannot deter an adversary one cannot reach. Likewise, the very manner in which states measure counterterrorism successes and failures inadvertently acts as passive counter-coercive leverage. Even small terrorist attacks represent disproportionately large losses that are usually perceived as significant deterrence and compellence failures.

ACTIVE COUNTER-COERCION: UNDERMINING STATE CAPABILITIES

In practice, coercion works when a defender properly communicates its intention and capability to an adversary, and a challenger accurately appreciates the threat, understands the consequences of its actions, and has a solid idea of what happens if and when a threat is ignored. When coercing terrorists, state capabilities are susceptible to active counter-coercion by non-state actors.

The crux of the problem stems from the difficulty states have in properly translating their offensive and defensive capabilities into credible deterrents and/or compellents and the subsequent ability of terrorists to actively exploit these difficulties. At issue is the very nature of asymmetric conflict: terrorism is the circumvention of disparities in absolute power capabilities. Weak adversaries use tactics that play to their advantages. Shmuel Bar's notion of the "power of weakness"—the relative power that the weaker side in a confrontation maintains vis-à-vis the stronger party—is crucial. Terrorists equalize power asymmetries by "neutralizing" features of a state's advantage.[12] They circumvent defenses, attack in novel and unexpected ways, escape detection, and render traditional forms of punishment ineffective. The flip side of the power of weakness is the "weakness of power."[13] Thomas Homer-Dixon describes it as a "cruel paradox": "by relying on intricate networks," he writes, "and concentrating vital assets in small geographic clusters . . . [states] amplify the destructive power of terrorists."[14] The cumulative result is that traditional conceptions of power that retain deterrent value in interstate relations are less relevant in asymmetric conflicts with terrorists. Traditional coercive capabilities become less credible and lose their deterrent/compellent edge. Terrorists can use these deficiencies to their advantage in order to limit, weaken, and altogether nullify a state's coercive strategy.

The attempted 2009 Christmas Day bombing of a commercial aircraft over the city of Detroit can be construed as a case of active counter-coercion at the tactical level. The attack was organized by al Qaeda in the Arabian Peninsula (AQAP), a regional franchise established in 2009 with the merger of al Qaeda's local Yemeni and Saudi Arabian chapters. AQAP has conducted numerous attacks, but it was its attempted assassination of Saudi Arabia's counterterrorism chief and deputy minister of the interior, Prince Muhammad bin Nayif, in August 2009 that resonates most with the Christmas Day plot. In that assassination attempt, the suicide bomber, Abdullah Asiri, reportedly hid a small amount of pentaerythritol tetranitrate (PETN) explosives in his body cavity in order to bypass the prince's robust security apparatus and gain personal access to him. The ensuing detonation, however, was of limited yield and barely harmed Nayif. Subsequent analysis suggests that the explosion was partially absorbed by Asiri's body, shielding the prince from the intended blast.[15]

It is likely that AQAP applied the lessons of its unsuccessful attack on Nayif when it equipped Umar Farouk Abdulmutallab with a near identical device to use over Detroit four months later. In the Christmas Day attack, Abdulmutallab used PETN sewn into and concealed in his underwear, the idea being that unlike in the assassination attempt, his body would not inadvertently degrade the device's blast, which would cause sufficient damage to destroy the aircraft. Gregory Johnson writes that "AQAP learned from its initial failure with PETN."[16] Consider further that PETN is the same explosive material that shoe bomber Richard Reid failed to detonate in his 2001 attack on American Airlines flight 63 and convicted shoe bomb plotter Saajid Badat planned to use in his own airline attack.

Seen as a cumulative process, AQAP's plot might be thought of as a creative attempt to circumvent U.S. denial capabilities and counter-coerce American efforts to protect airlines. To be sure, AQAP's primary goal was the destruction of the plane, but the counter-coercive effect of invalidating U.S. denial strategies was not lost on the organization. In its claim of responsibility, AQAP maintains that Abdulmutallab "waged a unique operation . . . by which he infiltrated all the advanced, new machines and technologies and the security boundaries in the world's airports. . . . He broke the American and international intelligence legend, and he showed their fragility and rubbed their noses in the mud, and he made all of what they spent on security development techniques a . . . heartbreak for them."[17] The various airport security measures enacted since 9/11 are meant to both protect passengers from terrorism and deny would-be terrorists the means to easily target planes. There is coercive meaning to these defenses. The coercive message is intended to be that aircraft are simply too difficult to attack successfully and that terrorist attempts to do so are likely to fail. AQAP's 2009 attack counter-coerced that denial message, signaling instead that airlines were in fact susceptible to novel attacks (like shoe bombs, liquid bombs, knicker bombs, and "ink cartridge" bombs) and that existing defensive measures were altogether ineffective. The attempted bombing had a counter-coercive quality to it and forced the United States to change its behavior, recalculate the effectiveness of its preferred coercive strategies, and establish new forms of airline defense and denial.

Other examples of active counter-coercion abound.[18] In each case, weak challengers relied on active counter-coercion to disrupt a defender's objectives, undermine its capabilities, impose costs on preferred strategies, and influence behavior. At root is that traditional military superiorities were not properly translated into counterterrorism coercive leverages. Whether in a symmetric or asymmetric deterrent relationship, coercion fails if a challenger perceives a threat as void, incredible, or impossible. Coercive credibility is based on a defender's ability to do as it threatens and communicate its intent and resolve to see threats through if and when compliance is lacking. In coercing terrorists, there is a credibility deficit. There are too many potential targets available for threats of denial to resonate effectively and too many sources of traditional military might that can be circumvented or nullified.

DELINEATING COERCIVE CAPABILITIES

A number of strategies exist that might help states better translate their traditional strengths into tactical counterterrorism coercion and reaffirm their coercive credibility. Succeeding at the margins is possible. One way to do so is to repeatedly illustrate certain strengths with the intent of specifically communicating capabilities. In its 2006 *Deterrence Operations Joint Operating Concept*, the U.S. Department of Defense suggests that key offensive and defensive capabilities "should be periodically demonstrated openly on the world stage—to ensure adversary decision makers fully comprehend the credible threats they face."[19] A capability to track, arrest, and indict terrorist financiers, for instance, might translate into a deterrent/compellent threat if successes are properly communicated and widely disseminated. The same can be said for defensive structures and plans that are meant to thwart attacks and offensive abilities that degrade terrorist strengths.

Military capabilities designed to impede terrorism by destroying terrorist infrastructure can be tailored, for instance, into specific deterrents that coerce state sponsors. Communicating deterrents with state facilitators can be achieved by shifting military planning to target specific states and by declaring policy publicly (through speeches and published declarations) and in private (through diplomatic channels and closed-door meetings).[20] Pursuing costly military signals might also be effective in coercing state facilitators. Elaine Bunn explains that "flexible deterrent options" including the deployment of forces can send a coercive message to adversaries that a state is serious about counterterrorism.[21] Doing so openly publicizes a state's capability and amplifies its resolve.

In the 1990s, for instance, the Kurdistan Workers' Party (PKK) based in Syria conducted cross-border attacks against Turkey. Though it did not sponsor PKK activity, Syria certainly facilitated it. When Turkey mobilized its forces on Syria's border and threatened invasion, it sent a clear coercive message to Damascus that it had the capability and intent to do as it threatened. Eventually, Syria acquiesced, clamped down on the PKK and expelled its leader, Abdullah Öcalan. From the 2006 Israel-Hezbollah case, post-conflict admissions from Iran confirmed that Tehran had supplied Hezbollah, before hostilities began, with Zelzal-2 missiles capable of striking Tel Aviv. According to Israeli assessments, Hezbollah's restraint in firing both its Fajr and Zelzal missiles during the conflict was due to Iranian opposition: without orders from Tehran, Hezbollah was "not allowed" to use these products.[22] It is conceivable that Israel, having proven its willingness to conduct a costly war in southern Lebanon, compelled Iran to rein in Hezbollah during the conflict lest the use of Iranian long-range weaponry give Israel the pretext to expand the war.

Other military capabilities can also be communicated as deterrents. Repeatedly illustrating a capacity to track, target, and capture or kill individuals, as near-daily drone attacks in Afghanistan and Pakistan do, can effectively signal a specific coercive capability. The assumption is that targeted eliminations represent a cost to participating in terrorism and have a psychological effect, cause despair, and lower moral among surviving cadres.[23] Each successful targeted killing communicates the state's technological, intelligence-gathering, and military ability to do as it threatens, all of which establishes credibility and signals resolve.

Turning counterterrorism defenses into denial mechanisms is a separate matter. Deterrence by denial manipulates an adversary's calculus by illustrating an ability to prevent the achievement and/or desired effect of a particular behavior. In counterterrorism, denial works by constraining the terrorism process (impeding access to targets), introducing operational uncertainty in planning (conducting random spot checks), mitigating terrorism's immediate sociopolitical and economic effect (strengthening first-response systems), and denying a group's long-term objectives (rejecting terrorist demands). Each of these processes frustrates terrorist objectives.[24] However, effectively converting defenses into coercive tools requires communicating these capabilities. Like punishment-based deterrents, denial mechanisms can be verbally communicated and visually illustrated, a point Wyn Bowen and Jasper Pandza take up in their contribution to this volume on denying radiological terrorism.

PASSIVE COUNTER-COERCION: INVALIDATING COMMUNICATION

Theories of coercion, when put into practice, are contingent on a number of prerequisites. As Frank Harvey submits, deterrence stipulates that an attack can be prevented if a defender (1) clearly "defines" the unacceptable behavior,

(2) "communicates" to the challenger a "commitment to punish violations," (3) retains the "capability" to either punish or deny as threatened, and (4) demonstrates "resolve" to carry out the punitive action if compliance is not met.[25] Each prerequisite relates to the underlying logic of deterrence by serving as a crucial element of communication and credibility. Coercion is never effective when done in secret. A defender must communicate to an adversary that it is the target of a deterrent policy and outline what action is unwanted. If and when threats are muddled, miscommunicated, weak, or altogether absent, deterrence and/or compellence will fail. In the case of coercing terrorists, satisfying all four preconditions proves difficult. Who is it states are trying to deter? What specific actions and general behavior are they trying to influence? How are they going to send the coercive message? Who is it states expect to communicate with, and what control do these actors have over the nature, scope, and ferocity of the terrorism challenge?

The communication dilemma is the basis for one of terrorism's passive counter-coercive strengths. By their very nature, terrorist groups are (usually) decentralized. Violence may be directed from above, but increasingly and especially in the case of al Qaeda, terrorists act with little central command. Organizational diffusion passively degrades a state's ability to properly communicate threats and apply coercion, thereby invalidating deterrent/compellent strategies. As Paul Pillar notes, "the less Islamist terrorism is instigated by a single figure, the harder it will be to uncover exploitable links."[26] But even when groups do have a degree of institutionalized hierarchy (like in Hezbollah, the Taliban, or FARC), states still lack reliable *access* to decision makers. There are no red phones connecting governments to terrorists, nearly no summit meetings between leaders, and very few diplomatic exchanges. All of this complicates the manner in which states can properly deliver coercive messages and degrades their ability to ascertain whether or not deterrents were properly received and accurately understood by the intended recipient.

In his study of Palestinian terrorism, Bar has found that some organizations augment these communicative difficulties by creating a situation within a target society that renders acquiescence to a deterrent "virtually impossible."[27] Groups may diffuse their centers of gravity in order to limit the amount of control leaders have over cadres, so that acquiescing to coercive threats and reining in those responsible for violence becomes impractical. The Taliban did so in 2007 after Mullah Dadullah Akhund, a top Afghan strategist, was killed in a Coalition raid. As a result of his death, Mullah Omar made major changes to the Taliban's command structure and set out new "guidelines" for his field commanders and shadow governors. Most importantly, control over military strategy was devolved and decentralized, passed down to lower-level commanders, so that the loss of key leaders would not jeopardize Taliban capabilities, as Dudullah's elimination had done.[28] Besides ensuring the continuation of Taliban operations, however, decentralization further complicated the manner in which Western and Afghan forces could communicate with and coerce Taliban leaders. Taliban devolution passively countered NATO and Afghan coercive strategies.

CLARIFYING COERCIVE COMMUNICATIONS

Thwarting and defusing the effects of this type of passive counter-coercion involves strengthening coercive communications. There are a number of strategies states might employ. First, strengthening communications with terrorists will involve limiting deterrent objectives and streamlining associated messages. In international relations, simplicity is often best; the more numerous the coercive threats and the broader their scope, the more complex the interactions between adversaries become, and the higher the odds that intentions and aims will be poorly communicated and improperly interpreted. Reconsidering the distinction between *broad* and *narrow* deterrence can assist states to zero in on their strategic objectives. Broad deterrence is all-encompassing in scope, aimed at deterring all acts of aggression between actors. The goal is to limit the occurrence of war and pacify relations. Narrow deterrence, on the other hand, targets a particular behavior within an ongoing conflict scenario. In "intrawar deterrence," defenders try to prevent challengers from conducting certain attacks all the while waging a war against them. Narrow deterrence, Freedman writes, assumes that "it is possible to deter a specific form of warfare even while other forms are progressing regardless."[29]

The global war on al Qaeda and its regional allies and franchises fits the broad-narrow dichotomy particularly well. Though the conflict endures, episodic violence does not negate the West's ability to influence the location, nature, and ferocity of al Qaeda attacks. The coercive objective is not the cessation of all violence but rather the achievement of some form of control *over* that violence. What this means in practice is to submit that qualitative differences matter; not all terrorist threats are equal. Accepting some form of terrorism as manageable while signaling that especially nefarious acts of terror (like mass-casualty attacks on civilians and CBRN terrorism) surpass a distinct threshold and will result in exceptionally costly retaliation, states might gain a degree of coercive control over terrorist adversaries.[30] The logic of deterrence in this case is to bind, restrict, and contain an ongoing conflict.[31]

That leads to the second component involved in strengthening coercive communications: streamlining associated messages. The imprecision with which states define their primary counterterrorism objectives and intentions dilutes the coerciveness of their actions. "Our enemy," President George W. Bush suggested in 2001, "is a radical network of terrorists, and every government that supports them. Our war on terror begins with al Qaeda, but . . . it will not end until every terrorist group of global reach has been found, stopped, and defeated."[32] These are the broadest of policy goals. While Bush's declaration might have had rhetorical value, it did little to provide the clarity of intent that deterrence theory and practice require. As Patrick Porter rightly notes, using "imprecise vocabulary" and "ignoring the discipline that strategy requires . . . fails to circumscribe the war within manageable boundaries and to direct resources towards the pursuit of precisely delineated interests."[33] If coercion is to work in counterterrorism, the actors and actions to be deterred will have to be precisely identified. Deterring all terrorism is not feasible, but deterring some terrorism might be. Likewise, coercing all terrorists is equally infeasible, though some groups and certain actors within those groups can be manipulated. Herein, coercion proves useful in delimiting the degree of violence inherent to a protracted conflict with terrorists.

PASSIVE COUNTER-COERCION: THE POWER OF FAILURE

In addition to the dilemmas associated with coercive credibility and communication, there is another structural impediment to successfully applying the logic of deterrence to counterterrorism: the inability of states to sustain balanced perceptions of their coercive successes and failures. Terrorists have significant counter-coercion leverage when it comes to passively shaping perceptions of victory and defeat in enduring asymmetric conflicts. That is not to suggest that terrorist groups do not perish over time. The recurring dilemma, however, is that even small terrorist attacks represent disproportionately large losses that are usually perceived as significant deterrence and compellence failures. Likewise, the costs of our failures are much greater than the costs of theirs—even foiled attacks carry weight. In deterring terrorism, these inherent limitations challenge the feasibility of constructing coercive relationships with terrorist adversaries, because perceptions of overall progress determine success and failure, not objective or balanced assessments of counterterrorist outcomes and achievements.

The capacity to manage real and perceived successes and failures is important to understanding the role of counter-coercion in counterterrorism and reveals the diminishing prospects for ending asymmetric conflicts with terrorists. There are several reasons why controlling perceptions of success and failure, victory and defeat, in Iraq, Afghanistan, Pakistan, and the larger battle against Islamist terrorists globally, is a losing proposition. The main coercive challenge for the United States is not its inability to win specific battles against terrorists, but rather its inability to sustain long-term impressions that the conflict is being won, that it has the stamina, intention, and resolve to see it through, and the right tools to credibly do as it threatens. As Amos Malka notes, the "10:1 principle" applies when combating terrorism: a state can "thwart ten armed operations, but if one succeeds in inflicting casualties and/or photographs well, then the effective result is a perceived victory for terrorism."[34] The intrinsic predisposition that states and their citizens have to overvalue the negative effects of security failures and undervalue and/or ignore the positive effects of successes is fundamental to understanding the passive counter-coercive advantage terrorists have. The net result is that the systemic manipulation of perceptions of success and failure influences a state's cost-benefit calculus concerning the efficacy of a given coercive strategy.

There are a number of reasons why terrorists have passive control over perceptions of success and failure. First, state losses (failures) loom larger than their gains (successes). Our sense of security following an attack is rarely, if ever, based on how many lives are saved but rather on how many were lost. Few individuals can recall the number of people evacuated from the World Trade Center on 9/11, but many can recite the number of deaths. The absence of a single post-9/11, mass-casualty attack on U.S. soil—essentially a perfect record—is almost completely excluded from the public's success-failure balance sheet, because we typically perceive a greater loss in security from a minor failure than a corresponding gain in security from news that major attacks were prevented.[35] These patterns are not likely to change; overall assessment of progress in the global war on terrorism will inevitably depend on the failures, never the larger and more numerous successes.

Second, security failures are ubiquitous, and their effects are consistently overestimated. Failures encompass an ever-expanding list of conceptually disparate images and facts that are readily identifiable and far easier to incorporate into assessments of overall security. As a result, "failures" are typically overvalued. The blurring of homeland security and the global war on terrorism means that almost any type of crisis becomes relevant to perceptions of security performance. Everything from mob violence following the publication of the Mohammad caricatures to videos of suicide bombings in Iraq combines to tip the balance in favor of systemic failure. Even non-terrorist events, like the collapse of relief efforts in New Orleans following Hurricane Katrina (2005), get inserted into our lists of potential security failures.[36] Whether the linkage to homeland security is real or derived through logical deduction is irrelevant. Evidence of failure is everywhere, not because states are actually failing but because the public will never assign the same relevance to successes.

Third, the costs of security failures add up, while successes are ignored. The price tag for launching a terrorist attack is significantly lower than the price for terrorism prevention and mitigation. For instance, according to estimates, the overall cost for the terrorists of the 2004 Madrid bombings (191 deaths) was $10,000.[37] And yet while terrorism is cheap, the costs to local and international business are in the billions. To the extent that terrorists experience failures at all, the negative impact on the organization does not resonate. By contrast, the enormous costs of failing to stop even a minor terrorist attack *do* multiply and produce combined economic, psychological, and political ripple effects that persist for years. Security successes, on the other hand, are often ignored. In contrast to the visceral image of counterterrorism failures, successes lack a reference point or image and are usually excluded from the security-insecurity balance sheet.

Fourth, security successes are inaccurately measured. Establishing balance in the public's assessment of success and failure is even more challenging because of the methodological hurdles that confound efforts to compile a list of counterterrorism successes.[38] With respect to selection bias, for instance, there is no generally accepted definition of "success." For example, the arrest of a terrorism suspect immediately *after* an attack would constitute a success when measured by the standards of law enforcement, but in counterterrorism, it is not the kind of success that counts. So while video surveillance allowed officials to identify the failed London July 21, 2005, bombers, images of the terrorists walking into the Underground also illustrated that the world's most expansive surveillance system was useless at deterring the attack. The result is that security failures are discoverable even in the absence of violence.

Fifth, counterterrorism successes are perceived as security failures. Deterrence in counterterrorism is difficult to prove because it is impossible to know whether a nonevent was the result of counterterrorist operations or the absence of any real threat in the first place. Moreover, legitimate counterterrorist successes are easily and logically reinterpreted by the public, media, and opposition groups as failures. Consider the rise in Canadian threat perceptions immediately following the June 2006 arrests in Toronto of seventeen terrorist suspects—Canadian threat perceptions escalated by over 70 percent following what was one of the most important counterterrorist *successes* in Canadian history.[39] Oddly enough, threat perceptions after this "success" were higher than those following a major counterterrorism "failure" in London the year earlier (July 2005). The discrepancy should concern security officials, who would obviously prefer a more balanced public assessment of the government's security performance.

Sixth, systemic media bias favors state failures over terrorist failures. The press usually contributes to reinforcing the sense of security failure by focusing almost exclusively on Western losses, errors, and mistakes while overlooking significant failures on the part of terrorists. Much less time is devoted to discussing the losses *caused* by Islamic extremists, their inability to recruit more than a minute fraction of Muslims, or their failure to transform Iraq and Afghanistan into states that espouse their views. The story is almost always about what the government is getting wrong and how much more needs to be done to fix the mistakes, omissions, and abuses. Post-9/11 counterterrorism successes—hundreds of multilateral agreements, changes in legislation, enhanced intelligence coordination, improvements in counter-financing, and so on—go unreported. The benefits emerging from all of this may be difficult to measure, but the obvious costs to terrorists receive almost no mention.

Finally, states and citizens alike overestimate the relevance of terrorist incompetence. Bruce Schneier illustrates the point with his description of the 2007 plot to destroy fuel tanks at JFK International Airport in New York City. A truly ridiculous plan, he argues, because "fuel tanks are thick-walled" and "separated from the pipelines by cutoff valves," so that even setting fire to the tanks would not have affected the pipelines. "If these are the terrorists we're fighting," he writes, "we've got a pretty incompetent enemy."[40] Perhaps, but officials never really know what kind of terrorist they are dealing with, or what proportion of competent to incompetent terrorists they are facing. Schneier never explains how easy it would be to distinguish wannabe terrorists (with an unrealistic plot) from the real thing, or how our policies should be guided by the risks of getting this wrong.

The cumulative result is that perceptions of counterterrorism success and failure are driven by terrorists and their actions, not by states and their security and coercive strategies. By virtue of the manner in which states interpret security threats and react to terrorism, their preferred coercive strategies are passively undermined. Every breach of security seemingly invalidates defensive structures, tactics, and strategies, forcing a state to reassess its current security policy and potentially compelling it to develop and utilize less-preferred tactics and strategies. Even if al Qaeda fails 99 percent of the time in its attacks on American interests, the remaining 1 percent defines the threat for the American public and determines perceptions of progress in counterterrorism. The problem with dismissing terrorists as incompetent is that their incompetence rarely matters; terrorist failures are successes. Terrorist failures succeed because they are just as likely to raise public anxieties as successes and force officials to implement measures to fill security gaps uncovered in each case.

Al Qaeda's repeated attempt to bomb commercial airplanes is a case in point. The potential economic loss of a successful attack, bombing, or shoulder-launched missile strike on an aircraft would measure in the trillions.[41] But the real problem surrounding these potential scenarios is even more disturbing—the impact on the airline industry and beyond of a single bombing or shoulder-fired missile aimed at any aircraft in North America or Europe would be enormous even if the attack failed. The "failure" would inevitably lead to huge investments in bettering security to address the threat, even if no damage occurred and not a single individual was killed. Following the failed plot in the skies over Detroit, hundreds of millions of dollars were invested to address the threat of PETN. The economic, political, and emotional effects of even minor security failures determine security policy, not the many successes. That terrorism drives the process complicates the manner in which states can apply coercion to counterterrorism.

CONCLUSION

Applications of deterrence theory to counterterrorism are bound by a number of constraints that are exacerbated by the very characteristics of terrorism. While the logic of coercion may, in some cases, inform counterterrorism policy, at the tactical level coercive applications are strained by considerations that are generally underplayed in interstate relations. Coercion is a dynamic process—challengers, like defenders, have the means to manipulate decision making in ways that compel their adversaries to behave in particular ways. Counter-coercion is the challenger's ability to influence the defender's coercive strategy to better suit its own goals. Terrorists have significant counter-coercive strengths over states in their ability to actively undermine state power, passively complicate the application of coercive strategies, and passively manipulate perceptions of coercive success and failure. To apply coercion to counterterrorism, these counter-coercive leverages will have to be better understood and circumvented. Doing so will require that states identify the specific terrorist actors and actions they aspire to deter, communicate coercive capabilities in a credible way, signal coercive intentions with decentralized adversaries, and deal with the structural impediments that shape perceptions of (in)security.

Further research is needed in two specific areas. First, the theoretical prerequisites of deterrence/compellence—defining and communicating unwanted behavior in a credible and resolute manner—will have to be reassessed in light of the characteristics of terrorism (substate/transnational, nonhierarchical, nonterritorial, unseen, asymmetric, et cetera). It may no longer be sufficient, for instance, for a state to merely possess the military and defensive means to punish or deny an adversary in order to coerce its behavior. What relevant capabilities do terrorists fear most? Constructing coercive credibility will require translating capabilities in a manner that resonates more effectively with non-state actors. Likewise, dilemmas in communication will have to be addressed. What relevant actions, statements, ultimatums, and other costly signals effectively communicate capabilities and resolve? Developing strategic communication with non-state actors in order to effectively communicate punishment and denial capabilities will have to take place.

Second, the dilemma over perceptions of systemic failure demands a much better understanding of how officials and the general public think about successes and failures in counterterrorism. This is an altogether neglected dimension of contemporary security policy. In the absence of systematic research on how these stories, images, and events interact to push perceptions in one or the other direction, leaders will continue to face an uphill battle in their efforts to establish some balance in public perceptions of coercive victory and defeat. And unless governments find innovative ways to clearly communicate credible signs of success, the only direction support will go is down.

Herein lies the policymaker's counter-coercion dilemma: if successes are too difficult to identify (or prove) and failures so easy to exploit, the only real policy option governments have left is to spend more to feed the illusion that something important is being accomplished. Paradoxically, the perception of action is precisely the strategy that continues to raise expectations the government is increasingly incapable of meeting.

NOTES

1. Lawrence Freedman, *Deterrence* (Cambridge, UK: Polity Press, 2004), 26.

2. Karl Mueller, "Strategies of Coercion: Denial, Punishment, and the Future of Air Power," *Security Studies* 7:3 (1998): 184.

3. Thomas Schelling, *Arms and Influence* (New Haven, CT: Yale University Press, 1996), 3.

4. Daniel Byman and Matthew Waxman, "Kosovo and the Great Air Power Debate," *International Security* 24:4 (2000): 9.

5. Coercive air power, for instance, attempts to manipulate behavior by strategically bombing targets, not by destroying the adversary. See Robert Pape, *Bombing to Win: Air Power and Coercion in War* (Ithaca, NY: Cornell University Press, 1996).

6. Janice Gross Stein, "Deterrence and Compellence in the Gulf, 1990–91: A Failed or Impossible Task?" *International Security* 17:2 (1992): 170–73; Martha Crenshaw, "Coercive Diplomacy and the Response to Terrorism," in *The United States and Coercive Diplomacy*, ed. Robert Art and Patrick Cronin (Washington, DC: United States Institute of Peace Press, 2003), 305–47.

7. Counter-coercion has received extensive treatment in theoretical and case study literature in international relations. See, for instance, Alexander George and William Simons, eds., *The Limits of Coercive Diplomacy* (Boulder, CO: Westview, 1994); Derek Smith, *Deterring America: Rogue States and the Proliferation of Weapons of Mass Destruction* (Cambridge: Cambridge University Press, 2006); Frank Harvey, "Getting NATO's Success in Kosovo Right: The Theory and Logic of Counter-Coercion," *Conflict Management and Peace Science* 23:2 (2006); Daniel Byman, Matthew Waxman, and Eric Larson, *Air Power as a Coercive Instrument* (Washington, DC: RAND, 1999).

8. Byman and Waxman, "Kosovo," 10.

9. Ibid., 10–11. See also Daniel Byman and Matthew Waxman, "Defeating US Coercion," *Survival* 41:2 (1999); Daniel Byman, Matthew Waxman, and Jeremy Shapiro, "The Future of U.S. Coercive Airpower," in *Strategic Appraisal: United States Air and Space Power in the 21st Century*, ed. Zalmay Khalilzad and Jeremy Shapiro (Santa Monica, CA: RAND, 2002).

10. Amos Malka suggests "Israel's sensitivity to [military] causalities" was actively "translated into power" by Hezbollah and exploited in order to influence Israeli

debates and compel the government to eventual withdraw from Lebanon in 2000. Amos Malka, "Israel and Asymmetrical Deterrence," *Comparative Strategy* 27:1 (2008): 6.

11. Richard Betts, "The Soft Underbelly of American Primacy: Tactical Advantages of Terror," *Political Science Quarterly* 117:1 (2002): 31–32.

12. Shmuel Bar, "Israeli Experience in Deterring Terrorist Organizations," presentation to the Herzliya Conference, Institute for Policy and Strategy, Herzliya, Israel, January 21–24, 2007.

13. Malka, "Israel," 2–5.

14. Thomas Homer-Dixon, "The Rise of Complex Terrorism," *Foreign Policy* 128 (January/February 2002).

15. Gregory Johnson, "AQAP in Yemen and the Christmas Day Terrorist Attack," *CTC Sentinel* special issue (January 2010): 1–3; United States Senate Committee on Foreign Relations, *Al Qaeda in Yemen and Somalia: A Ticking Time Bomb*, January 21, 2010; European Law Enforcement Agency (EUROPOL), "The Concealment of Improvised Explosive Devices (IEDs) in Rectal Cavities," SC5—Counter Terrorism Unit (The Hague, September 2008); Abdullah Al-Oreifij, "Bomber Had Half Kilo of Explosives Inside His Body," *Saudi Gazette*, September 5, 2009; Yossi Melman, "Inside Intel/He Had All the Signs," *Haaretz*, January 7, 2010. Other reports, however, suggest the bomber hid the PETN in his underwear. See Peter Bergen, "Similar Explosive on Plane Used in Saudi Attack," CNN, December 27, 2009; Jake Trapper, "The August Attempt on Saudi Prince Mohammed—and the Link to Flight 253," ABC News, January 3, 2010.

16. Johnson, "AQAP," 2.

17. The NEFA Foundation, "Al-Qaida in Yemen: AQIY Claims Responsibility for Christmas Airline Attack," December 28, 2009.

18. The Taliban adopted suicide bombings in 2005 to undermine NATO's superiority in Afghanistan. Al Shabaab did the same in Somalia. Hamas fires rockets from populated areas in order to impose costs on Israeli retaliatory policy in the form of civilian casualties and international condemnation. And Hezbollah, in 2006, neutralized Israel's coercive strengths by switching from long-range to short-range rockets once the former became vulnerable and protecting its leadership against targeted eliminations. It even compelled Israel to launch a costly ground incursion at the very end of the conflict.

19. U.S. Department of Defense, *Deterrence Operations Joint Operating Concepts*, December 2006, p. 41.

20. Daniel Whiteneck, "Deterring Terrorists: Thoughts on a Framework," *Washington Quarterly* 28:3 (2005): 196; Elbridge Colby, "Expanded Deterrence: Broadening the Threat of Retaliation," *Policy Review* 149 (2008); and Elbridge Colby, "The New Deterrence," *Weekly Standard*, April 9, 2008.

21. M. Elaine Bunn, "Can Deterrence Be Tailored?" *Strategic Forum* 225 (2007): 6.

22. *Jerusalem Post*, "Iran: We Supplied Zelzal-2 to Hizbullah," August 4, 2006. See also Anthony Cordesman, *Arab-Israel Military Forces in an Era of Asymmetric Wars* (Stanford, CA: Stanford University Press, 2008), 260–65.

23. Alex Wilner, "Targeted Killings in Afghanistan: Measuring Coercion and Deterrence in Counterterrorism and Counterinsurgency," *Studies in Conflict and Terrorism* 33:4 (2010).

24. Alex Wilner, "Deterring the Undeterrable: Coercion, Denial, and Delegitimization in Counterterrorism," *Journal of Strategic Studies* 34:1 (2011); James Smith and Brent Talbot, "Terrorism and Deterrence by Denial," in *Terrorism and Homeland Security: Thinking Strategically About Policy*, ed. Paul Viotti, Michael Opheim, and Nicholas Bowen (Boca Raton, FL: CRC Press, 2008).

25. Frank Harvey, "Practicing Coercion," *Journal of Conflict Resolution* 43:6 (1999): 840–43; Frank Harvey, "Rigor Mortis or Rigor, More Test: Necessity, Sufficiency, and Deterrence," *International Studies Quarterly* 42:4 (1998).

26. Paul Pillar, "Counterterrorism After Al-Qaeda," *Washington Quarterly* 27:3 (2004): 104.

27. Bar, "Israeli Experience," 7.

28. Syed Saleem Shahzad, "Dadullah's Death Hits Taliban Hard," *Asia Times*, May 15, 2007; Syed Saleem Shahzad, "Taliban a Step Ahead of US Assault," *Asia Times*, August 11, 2007.

29. Freedman, *Deterrence*, 33–34.

30. Robert Trager and Dessislava Zagorcheva, "Deterring Terrorism: It Can De Done," *International Security* 30:3 (2005–6): 102.

31. Patrick Porter, "Long Wars and Long Telegrams: Containing al-Qaeda," *International Affairs* 85:2 (2009): 296–305; Ian Shapiro, *Containment: Rebuilding a Strategy Against Global Terror* (Princeton, NJ: Princeton University Press, 2007); Jay Carafano and Paul Rosenzweig, *Winning the Long War: Lessons from the Cold War for Defeating Terrorism and Preserving Freedom* (Washington, DC: Heritage Books, 2005).

32. George W. Bush, Address to Joint Session of Congress, September 20, 2001; see also Department of Defense, *Deterrence Operations*, 18–19.

33. Porter, "Long Wars," 291.

34. Amos Malka, "The Power of Weakness vs. the Weakness of Power: Asymmetrical Deterrence," presentation to the Herzliya Conference, Institute for Policy and Strategy, Herzliya, Israel, January 21–24, 2007.

35. These tendencies explain why the negative effects of the July 7, 2005, bombings in London were more significant than the positive effects of the failed London bombings on July 21. There are parallels linking these tendencies to those compiled by "prospect theory," which explains why losses loom larger than gains. See Daniel

Kahneman and Amos Tversky, "Prospect Theory: An Analysis of Decision Under Risk," *Econometrica* 47:2 (1979); Amos Tversky and Daniel Kahneman, "Advances in Prospect Theory: Cumulative Representation of Uncertainty," *Journal of Risk and Uncertainty* 5:4 (1992).

36. Frank Harvey, *The Homeland Security Dilemma: Fear, Failure, and the Future of American Insecurity* (New York: Routledge, 2008).

37. Associated Press, "U.N.: Most Terror Attacks Cost Under $50,000," August 27, 2004.

38. Raphael Perl, "Combating Terrorism: The Challenge of Measuring Effectiveness," Congressional Research Service Report, November 23, 2005.

39. Harvey, *Homeland Security Dilemma*.

40. Bruce Schneier, "Portrait of the Modern Terrorist as an Idiot," June 14, 2007, post on blog *Schneier on Security*.

41. Tim McLaughlin, "Airlines Vulnerable to Shoulder-Fired Missile Attacks," *St. Louis Post-Dispatch*, August 20, 2006.

DETERRING WMD TERRORISM

5 THE TERRORIST PERCEPTION OF NUCLEAR WEAPONS AND ITS IMPLICATIONS FOR DETERRENCE

Brian Michael Jenkins

IN THE MONTHS following 9/11, a number of reports suggested that al Qaeda was planning even more cataclysmic terrorist attacks. In October 2001, a CIA source reported that al Qaeda had stolen a ten-kiloton nuclear bomb from Russia and had smuggled it into New York City.[1] In an interview with a Pakistani journalist the following month, Osama bin Laden claimed that al Qaeda had nuclear weapons.[2] With the invasion of Afghanistan, documents describing nuclear weapons were later found in various al Qaeda safe houses.[3] In 2002, a report deemed credible claimed that a Pakistani nuclear expert was working for bin Laden, with a larger group of Pakistani experts assisting him.[4] And at an October 2002 National Security Council meeting, President George W. Bush said bin Laden "may have a nuclear device" that could destroy half of Washington, DC.[5] Ordinarily, authorities would have treated such reports with great skepticism, but these were not ordinary times. The 9/11 attacks fundamentally altered perceptions of plausibility. Virtually no scenario could be summarily dismissed.

The reports turned out to be wrong. The source of the claim that al Qaeda had a bomb in New York proved unreliable. The Pakistani journalist embellished subsequent accounts of the same interview, adding previously unreported details, which diminished his credibility. After careful examination by scientists, the documents found in Afghanistan indicated that al Qaeda did not know how to build a nuclear bomb.[6] Two Pakistani nuclear scientists did meet with bin Laden a month before 9/11, but they testified that he had no fissile material and no active nuclear weapons program.[7] Nonetheless, reports of stolen or purchased Russian nuclear weapons, secret al Qaeda weapons labs staffed by Pakistani scientists, and nuclear weapons being smuggled into the United States—often recycled versions of the same stories—continue to circulate.

These reports have caused great alarm. In 2004, a highly respected authority estimated that the probability of a terrorist nuclear attack in the next ten years was greater than 50 percent.[8] According to a 2007 public opinion poll, more than 40 percent of Americans believed that terrorists were likely to detonate a nuclear bomb in an American city within five years.[9] In September 2008, the director of the U.S. Central Intelligence Agency stated publicly that al Qaeda was the agency's "number one nuclear concern."[10] Elevating al Qaeda to the number one spot, above North Korea, which we know has nuclear weapons, and Iran, which has a vast nuclear program, clearly resulted from an assessment of al Qaeda's intentions, rather than its capabilities. Terrorists are considered the greater threat because it is assumed that if they acquire a nuclear weapon, they will use it without hesitation. In 2003, a panel convened by the U.S. National Academy of Sciences concluded that American cities need to prepare for an attack that involves a homemade nuclear weapon.[11]

Putting aside estimates of probability, which have no predictive value anyway, a number of efforts are being made to prevent nuclear terrorism. First, these efforts aim at reducing both the number of nuclear weapons in current arsenals and the stockpiles of weapons-grade nuclear material, much of which is left over from decommissioning nuclear warheads. Second, security at weapons sites and anywhere fissile material is stored is being improved. And third, threat reduction has also involved preventing the emergence of new nuclear-weapons states. Some advocates go further and call for the "zero option"—the abolition of all nuclear weapons.

Can deterrence add a fourth component of efforts to prevent nuclear terrorism? Deterrence worked during the Cold War, but can terrorists be dissuaded from trying to acquire nuclear weapons? Or if they somehow acquired a nuclear device, could they be persuaded not to use it?

The idea of deterrence depends very much on how we view terrorists. Most people see them as wanton killers, constrained only by limits on their capabilities. Some analysts, however, view them as more complicated, not all willing to slaughter, constrained by concerns about alienating constituents or provoking backlashes that could harm their cause. Although terrorists are committed to violence in order to advance their beliefs, we do know that they often argue among themselves about when that violence may become counterproductive. This has been the focus of much of my own (admittedly controversial) research on the topic.

To better understand how terrorists might be deterred, we need to better understand how they may perceive the utility and risks of acquiring and using nuclear weapons. This, in turn, could reveal vulnerabilities that are not apparent when we view deterrence solely from our own perspective. This is clearly a speculative line of inquiry. Terrorists have not developed a nuclear doctrine. Evidence of how they might think about nuclear weapons must be inferred from their public statements and discussions of strategy. But additional insights can be gained from captured documents and interrogations and also may be drawn from what they do *not* say.

This chapter first explores possible terrorist motives for acquiring and using a nuclear weapon—how they think about nuclear weapons and how they could employ them to serve their cause. It then addresses the question of deterrence—specifically, what terrorists and their accomplices in any nuclear project might worry about and how we might build upon these worries to influence their calculations.

MY OWN BELIEFS

As we are in an area where evidence is sparse and presumptions are plentiful, let me first lay out my own views. I believe that nuclear terrorism—and by that I mean the detonation by terrorists of a nuclear bomb—is extremely unlikely. I doubt that terrorists themselves can make a nuclear bomb, and I do not believe that a government that has nuclear weapons will provide them with one. The most plausible mode of terrorist acquisition would be not the clandestine fabrication of a nuclear device, but the theft of a nuclear weapon, most likely with inside assistance, or the seizure of one during a period of political upheaval and chaos. This was the principal cause of concern immediately after the collapse of the Soviet Union, and it is what worries many about the situation in Pakistan today.

My skepticism is not limited to the possibility of acquisition, but also to terrorist intentions. I doubt that terrorists smart enough to think about how they could acquire a nuclear weapon will be dumb enough to try. I believe that terrorists see the possession, or the pretended possession, of nuclear weapons primarily as an instrument of terror. I believe that serious thinking by terrorists about how they might use a nuclear weapon—of which we have very little evidence—would cause all but a handful of nihilist fanatics to conclude that nuclear terrorism—actually detonating a device—would be counterproductive to their cause and their survival. Suicide bombings by terrorists do not alter this perception. The organization required to obtain and use a nuclear weapon would be far greater than that required to deploy a handful of fanatics eager to sacrifice their own lives.

Even if terrorists should somehow acquire a nuclear capability, in no foreseeable circumstances are they likely to acquire more than one or two weapons. And although terrorists with even one nuclear weapon could potentially cause catastrophic casualties, they could not hope to destroy an entire nation. Instead, they would only wound and enrage its people and their government. There would be retaliation. It is noteworthy that the countries considered to be the most likely targets of a terrorist nuclear attack—the United States, Israel, the Russian Federation, India, the United Kingdom, and France—themselves possess nuclear arsenals along with the sophisticated delivery systems necessary to retaliate with them if they choose to do so, while still maintaining sufficient weapons in reserve for other contingencies.

I am not persuaded that in the unlikely event that terrorists were to detonate a nuclear device, the absence of an exact terrorist address would necessarily preclude devastating retaliation. While massive retaliation might be welcomed by some terrorists, it would at the same time provide powerful incentives to others to assist in the prompt destruction of those groups as a matter of their own survival. As one wise observer noted, "Terrorists with a nuclear weapon will have no friends." After a terrorist nuclear explosion, they would have only enemies.

Obviously, there is great uncertainty here. We do not know enough about how terrorists might be deterred, in large measure because we have not analyzed their possible motives for going nuclear. Therefore, despite the low probability I would assign to nuclear terrorism, I believe it is nonetheless useful to explore how terrorists may think about the subject. Again, it should be emphasized that this is a speculative inquiry, and we can go only so far.

Deterrence, as a concept, did not arrive fully formed at the start of the Cold War. It developed over time, and in order for it to work, both sides had to be educated—their thinking had to be shaped. The theory continues to evolve. In a 2002 report coauthored by Paul Davis, we deliberately broadened the term "deterrence" to include "influence."[12] The question is: How might the thinking of terrorists be influenced? In talking about how terrorists might be deterred from going nuclear, we might influence the way terrorists themselves think about nuclear weapons. We begin with the questions, Why would terrorists want a nuclear weapon? What could it offer them that they cannot achieve with the weapons they currently possess?

NUCLEAR WEAPONS ARE ATTRACTIVE
TO FEW TERRORISTS

Despite the overall escalation in terrorist violence that clearly has occurred since the 1970s, nuclear terrorism may hold little attraction for many organizations otherwise willing to employ terrorist tactics. Those fighting for the independence or autonomy of a particular people or territory are constrained by the nature of their goal in the volume and quality of violence they may apply—they are not likely to destroy or contaminate what they hope someday to rule. They cannot expose a definable population to eternal revenge. A territorially defined constituency also provides a return address for retaliation. It is difficult to see, for example, how detonating a nuclear weapon would benefit separatist groups such as Spain's Basque *etarras* or Sri Lanka's Tamil Tigers. A nation founded upon nuclear destruction may never be allowed to live in peace.

Those employing terrorist tactics on behalf of specific causes like the protection of the environment or of animal rights are also unlikely to see nuclear weapons as beneficial to their campaign. A nuclear attack would constitute far too much violence—it would bring condemnation of their cause, the loss of their constituency. Criminal organizations and criminalized terrorist enterprises like Colombia's guerrillas, which draw continuing profits from trafficking in drugs, might see in nuclear weapons potential opportunities for extortion or sale, but probably not for actual use.

In fact, putting aside the aspirations of Palestinians for nuclear parity with Israel and the spontaneous boast of one German terrorist, which will be discussed later, only three groups appear to have thought about acquiring nuclear weapons: the Aum Shinrikyo cult in Japan, Chechen rebels in Russia, and al Qaeda. Aum Shinrikyo's leader, Shoko Asahara, was obsessed with visions of nuclear destruction. He warned his followers that a worldwide nuclear war was inevitable but that they could survive. While awaiting this apocalypse, the cult's scientists actively pursued the development of chemical and biological weapons. Aum also acquired a uranium mine in Australia and made inquiries regarding the purchase of a nuclear weapon from Russia, but beyond this there is no evidence of attempted acquisition. Aum's nerve-gas attack on Tokyo's subways in 1995 prompted a government crackdown that sentenced its leaders to death and ended the group's existence.[13]

Locked in a brutal war with Russia, the leaders of Chechnya's guerrillas contemplated elaborate nuclear scenarios, one involving the seizure of Russian nuclear-armed missiles, and they did plant a bomb to disperse radioactive material in Moscow. However, they chose not to detonate the device but instead notified the news media of its location. The purpose of this publicity stunt was to create terror in Russia, which the guerrillas thought would persuade the government to renew negotiations.[14] There is, however, no evidence that the Chechens actually attempted to acquire nuclear weapons. Russia's vast and supposedly inadequately guarded nuclear arsenal, the Chechens' advantageous geographic position, and their demonstrated operational capabilities put the Chechens in the best position of any group to acquire a nuclear weapon, and they certainly had ample motive. The fact that they did not attempt to do so seems significant. It would be useful to know more about their thinking, but there is little material to work with.

Al Qaeda's nuclear ambitions have been widely reported, but its lack of knowledge and amateurish acquisition attempts apparently have made it a victim of scams. Documents found at al Qaeda locations in Afghanistan provide evidence of interest, but no evidence of know-how or fissile material.

In sum, of the scores of terrorist groups in the world operating over a forty-year period, only one has come even close to attempting to acquire nuclear weapons. And that group did so without any apparent discussion about how it might use them. Either terrorists have a sound grasp of their own limitations, or they have dismissed nuclear terrorism as irrelevant to their cause. However, the fact that something has not happened thus far does not mean it may not happen in the future. Therefore, it is important to consider why terrorists might want a nuclear weapon.

WHY WOULD TERRORISTS WANT A NUCLEAR WEAPON?

Jihadist websites and chat rooms are filled with words and fabricated images of nuclear explosions—montages of mushroom clouds over the U.S. Capitol— but these are fantasies of the powerless. Although many believe that terrorists with a nuclear weapon would promptly use it, the terrorists' "first strike" policy may be a default position, easy to adopt because they do not have nuclear weapons and because such pretensions excite followers and alarm foes. If acquisition of a nuclear weapon became closer to becoming a reality, terrorists would have to think more seriously about how they would use it. I suspect that different terrorist actors would have different objectives. And not all of those within a single group would agree. Nevertheless, we can posit a spectrum of potential terrorist motives for acquiring a nuclear weapon.

Acquisition for Entrepreneurial Reasons

Terrorists could try to acquire a nuclear weapon first, then think later about how they might use it. It is reported that Osama bin Laden made attempts to acquire nuclear material while he was in Sudan in the early 1990s and that these ambitions continued during his residence in Afghanistan until late 2001, when al Qaeda was chased out of the country. But we have no evidence of any corresponding nuclear doctrine or discussions to indicate his thoughts about having or using such a weapon. It could be that in the 1990s, bin Laden was behaving like a typical entrepreneur of violence, building an organization, looking to acquire new capabilities, investing in various weapons acquisition efforts much as he invested in promising terrorist projects. It might be said that bin Laden dabbled in mass destruction.

Entrepreneurship, however, would seem to be only an early-stage motive. If nuclear weapons acquisition began to approach reality, terrorists would actually have to think hard about use. Acquire now, think later seems more likely to be the sequence for an opportunistic acquisition than an organizational commitment to a serious in-house development effort. If, for example, a trusted source were to offer a terrorist group a nuclear weapon, or if political chaos in a country with nuclear weapons suddenly provided an opportunity for terrorist operatives to get their hands on one, they might go for it without thinking what they would actually do with it.

Acquisition to Assert Status

In the 1970s, Palestinians asserted their right to develop nuclear weapons, since Israel by this time was widely believed to have developed them. The Palestinians appeared to be expressing the view that they would achieve equality with the state of Israel by matching its possession of nuclear weapons.[15] This seems to have been simply a claim of entitlement, as there is no evidence of any attempt by Palestinian groups to acquire a nuclear weapon. Outside the realm of terrorism, much of the impetus to develop nuclear weapons in the Arab countries and in the broader Muslim world did come from a desire to match the technological achievements of Israel and the West. Religious parity demanded nuclear parity. A Muslim nuclear bomb was needed to match the Christian, Jewish, and, after 1976, Hindu nuclear bombs.

Had Osama bin Laden been successful in his own acquisition efforts in 1992 or 1993, five years before Pakistan tested its first nuclear weapon, he would have acquired enormous prestige. With his status elevated among all Arabs, he would have become a leader to be reckoned with, not someone to be chased out of one country after another. Although Pakistan could claim strategic reasons for its development of nuclear weapons, simply being the first Muslim country to build the bomb provided a powerful incentive. (This is not intended to equate Pakistan with al Qaeda, but simply to illustrate status as a motive for nuclear weapons acquisition.) Nuclear weapons not only bring status—they are seen as scepters of statehood. Terrorist groups representing specific communities under threat might believe that a people defended by nuclear weapons will not disappear. They may see nuclear weapons as a guarantee against extinction.

Possession to Create Terror

The ability to create terror seems to be the most likely appeal of nuclear weapons for terrorists. In the past, terrorists have carried out attacks at nuclear venues—for example, nuclear power plants under construction—simply to provide a dramatic backdrop for their action. The mere proximity of the words "terrorism" and "nuclear" creates terror. Terrorists understand this. Al Qaeda's own operational planners reportedly dismissed as unrealistic the idea that the organization could develop its own nuclear weapon, but they decided to maintain the rhetoric of weapons of mass destruction for propaganda purposes, to excite followers and frighten foes.

Al Qaeda's online followers elaborated on the nuclear theme to fulfill their own aggressive fantasies and scare their enemies. The group's nuclear propaganda program does not appear to have been part of a centrally directed communication strategy, but more of a group project—an Internet phenomenon. It has, however, had an effect on already anxious governments and public audiences, making al Qaeda the world's first "virtual terrorist nuclear power."[16]

Possession as a Deterrent

One of bin Laden's few public statements on weapons of mass destruction suggests their use as a deterrent: if the infidels used weapons of mass destruction against the Muslims, he declared, al Qaeda would use such weapons against the infidels. But can we infer from this remark a deterrent posture?

That is, can we believe that if al Qaeda were to possess a nuclear weapon, it would hold it at the ready only to deter an enemy attack using nuclear or other weapons of mass destruction?

In al Qaeda's distorted worldview, Islam is already under assault from infidel Christian crusaders and Zionist Jews. Although the United States and Europe have made great efforts to correct this misperception, it continues to have resonance among many Muslims. Al Qaeda's leaders are correct, however, in interpreting the West's determination to wipe out al Qaeda.

Al Qaeda argues that its terrorist campaign has disrupted even greater aggression by the infidels. This is clever propaganda, allowing the organization to explain away its lack of visible progress by claiming credit for preventing something even worse. Al Qaeda does not need to actually possess a nuclear weapon in order to pretend to deter its enemies. A credible claim of possession might suffice, allowing it to claim credit for deterring actions that were never contemplated.

Possession to Coerce

Our views of how terrorists might use nuclear weapons (and the views of terrorists themselves) follow contemporary fashions in terrorist tactics. What we imagine as nuclear terrorism is usually a scaled-up version of what terrorists at the time are doing with conventional weapons. In an age of large-scale terrorist attacks, we therefore presume that terrorists would use nuclear weapons as weapons of mass destruction as they now use truck bombs (or used hijacked airliners on 9/11); but it was not always so.

Asked by a reporter in 1977 what terrorists might do if they had a nuclear weapon, Bommi Baumann, a member of Germany's Red Army Faction, responded that a nuclear weapon would give terrorists the ultimate power. With a nuclear weapon, he said, terrorists could make the chancellor of Germany dance atop his desk on national television.[17] It was a silly answer, but it followed the general line of thinking about nuclear terrorism in the 1970s. In that decade, roughly a fifth of all terrorist attacks involved taking hostages through kidnappings, hijackings, or building takeovers in order to make demands. It was therefore believed that terrorists would most likely use nuclear weapons as a means of coercion. Instead of holding a handful of captives, terrorists with nuclear weapons could hold entire cities hostage. Terrorists may have been thinking the same thing. "Nuclear blackmail," as it was then called, was the subject of numerous novels and screenplays, as well as of a number of simulations and strategic games in Washington. These simulations and games posited scenarios in which terrorists threatened to detonate a nuclear weapon in a heavily populated area unless their demands were met.

I participated in a number of these games—sometimes on the government side, but more frequently on the terrorist side—and found that nuclear blackmail turns out to be a difficult proposition. It was hard for the terrorists to establish their credibility. Then, unlike now, government officials tended to be very skeptical about terrorists' claims of possessing nuclear weapons. It was even more difficult to convince the government that if the terrorists' demands were met, they would surrender their nuclear weapon. After all, if they disarmed, the government might renege. But if terrorists could not convince the government that they would give up their weapon, terrorist blackmail became a contest of governance. If the government was convinced of more terrorist demands to come, it faced the question of who was going to run the country—its elected officials or the terrorists. The government's incentive to yield diminished. In fact, European terrorist groups active at the time of Baumann's response could think of nuclear weapons only in terms of coercion. The large-scale indiscriminate killing characteristic of the later religion-inspired terrorist groups had not yet begun. How would groups seeking local constituents, on whose behalf they claimed to be fighting, gain adherents by nuking them?

Possession to Achieve Mass Destruction

Possession of a nuclear weapon would enable terrorists to carry out an attack of true mass destruction. This is currently presumed to be terrorists' most likely course of action. It is feared that terrorists would detonate a nuclear weapon without offering any warning or making any demands, simply to punish and demoralize their foes for past misdeeds. Al Qaeda's commissioning and broadcast of religious fatwas, providing justification to kill millions of Americans, suggest nuclear destruction as the objective. The pronouncement of the fatwa, analysts argue, fulfills the Muslim requirement to give warning. However, one could also see the fatwas merely as a propaganda ploy aimed at drawing attention to America's culpability for the deaths of millions of Muslims, thereby justifying the continuation of al Qaeda's own bloody campaign.

Terrorists might also hope that a nuclear attack would provoke an overreaction by the targeted state. Many believe that al Qaeda hoped that its 9/11 attack would provoke an American war on all of Islam, which in turn would radicalize Muslims and bring them to al Qaeda's banner. This line of thinking appears often in the annals of terrorism. Terrorists have succeeded in provoking some massive crackdowns, but these often have been pyrrhic victories that resulted in the brutal destruction of the terrorists themselves. Indeed, strategists within the jihadist movement have criticized al Qaeda's 9/11 attacks on the grounds that they provoked a ferocious global campaign that imperiled the entire jihadist movement.

Instead of provoking the repression they hope would lead to a popular uprising, terrorists could use a nuclear weapon in an attempt to provoke a war. Lashkar-e-Taiba's terrorist attacks in India were intended to provoke retaliatory Hindu massacres of Muslims in India, thus dividing the two communities, but they were also intended to provoke hostilities between India and Pakistan. And they very nearly succeeded. A jihadist nuclear attack on India would significantly raise the risk of war between the two countries.

White supremacists and right-wing fanatics in the United States draw inspiration from a novel that describes white patriots detonating nuclear weapons in cities with large Jewish populations, thus fulfilling their visions of genocide and Armageddon-like battles.[18] Such Götterdämmerung scenarios are typical of neo-Nazis and other fascist fanatics who view power not as rising up from the masses but as descending from above in Wagnerian operatic fashion. In contrast to left-wing extremists, right-wing extremists are less constrained by the perceived need of support from the people; fascist ideologies also rule out pity for the masses.

ACQUISITION COULD INFLUENCE USE

The way terrorists acquire a nuclear weapon could influence the way they choose to use it. Secret accumulation of fissile material and clandestine fabrication of a device, although this seems the least likely and longest route for acquiring a nuclear weapon—far less complex terrorist attacks have taken years to plan—would give the terrorists the greatest autonomy in deciding how to use it. It would give them ample time to formulate a strategy, select a possible target, and develop a delivery plan. But it would also provide ample time for internal debate, which would involve not only terrorist leaders, but also the scientists and technicians working on the device. All participants may feel they have a voice in the matter. Almost certainly, there would be internal debate about a range of options. The need for consensus might argue against a strike without warning. Terrorists might instead want to announce possession and then use the device for prestige, coercion, and to cause terror.

In contrast, were a country with nuclear weapons to hand over one of its bombs to terrorists—an unlikely scenario—it would almost certainly be with the intention that the weapon be promptly used in a nuclear strike. Why else would a country do so? The only purpose of arming a protégé instead of itself using the weapon would be to avoid being connected with a nuclear attack. Also, the terrorists would probably not be allowed possession for any length of time lest the operation be exposed.

Overt theft of an intact weapon by terrorists would also put great pressure on them to act quickly. Fearful of losing the weapon before they could bypass the security measures built into it and rearm it for use, terrorists could try instead to exploit possession for the purposes of coercion, deterrence, and terror. Similarly, a fortuitous acquisition during a period of political chaos or civil war could provide terrorists with a weapon before they had figured out how to use it. There would be pressure to use it quickly and close by; or if they did not have an immediate target, they might try to hide the weapon and exploit its possession in order to make threats in the future.

CAN TERRORISTS BE DETERRED?

Reality is what people believe. During the Cold War, the Soviet Union and the United States warned each other that a nuclear attack by either side would lead to mutual destruction. Obviously, this could not be demonstrated. Nonetheless, the threat was credible because of the immense size of the two superpowers' nuclear arsenals; because the United States, during World War II, had not hesitated to use nuclear weapons; and because during much of the Cold War, many people still carried living memories of the massive destruction inflicted during World War II by both conventional and nuclear weapons. But deterrence ultimately rested upon the notion that if one side was crazy enough to start a nuclear war, the other side would be crazy enough to end the world. Mutual assured destruction was a mad idea. It worked because neither side was willing to test it.

Al Qaeda has succeeded in instilling the belief that it will someday acquire and use nuclear weapons. Indeed, al Qaeda has succeeded in becoming the world's first terrorist nuclear power without possessing any nuclear weapons. It is all illusion. But can terrorists be deterred? Many doubt it. Terrorists' use of suicide tactics and their presumption of God's approval are believed to obviate any notion of deterrence. We cannot retaliate against terrorists militarily—they have no territory or populations to protect, they offer no lucrative targets. Moreover, a terrorist nuclear attack might be anonymous—we would not know who did it, or we would lack convincing evidence. And as we are determined to wipe terrorists out anyway, we cannot threaten to escalate. Finally, terrorists themselves may not believe that target states will be ruthless enough to inflict death and destruction on any large scale, so our superior military arsenal is irrelevant. Therefore, terrorists are not deterrable.

There are, however, alternate views. Suicide tactics do not reflect the willingness of organizations to commit suicide. Terrorists seek guaranteed success, they typically abhor uncertainty, and they worry about unity. They have contemplated but have tended to avoid technologically complex operations where risks of failure are high. This inherent conservatism can be exploited as a deterrent.

Nuclear terrorism carries high risks of failure. Efforts to acquire nuclear weapons or fissile material may lead a group into stings, traps, and exposure. The weapon it builds or obtains cannot be tested and may not work. These doubts will fuel internal debate. Uncertainty about consequences may cause builders of a nuclear device to rethink what they are trying to do—the risks of disagreement and betrayal are high. Finally, the absence of forensic evidence may not prevent retaliation—a terrorist nuclear attack may instead be seen by some as an opportunity to attack enemies. This might not directly deter terrorists, but it could expose them to attack from unexpected quarters, which terrorists must anticipate if they go nuclear. The old rules may not apply in a post-nuclear-terrorist world; a terrorist nuclear attack that left tens or hundreds of thousands dead might make a ruthless response irresistible. Terrorist detonation of a nuclear weapon could lead to consequences that endanger the entire world—an additional incentive for all to prevent nuclear terrorism.

TERRORISTS' VULNERABILITIES WILL VARY

We have already discussed the lack of attraction nuclear weapons will have for most groups. We focus here on some of the groups that are more likely to attempt acquisition. Al Qaeda and its terrorist affiliates are already the targets of an intensive global campaign aimed at their total destruction. It is hard to get much leverage out of threats to annihilate those one is already trying to annihilate. But all terrorists depend on others for cover and ultimate survival.

On the other hand, some Pakistan-based groups may be primarily interested in "liberating" Kashmir from India. That introduces a territorial component—another inherent constraint. They could not expect to ever be allowed to govern Kashmir after detonating a nuclear weapon. Any military and political achievement brought about by nuclear destruction will provide the targets of the original attack with a lucrative target to go after. This is true of all separatist terrorist groups.

Al Qaeda's Afghan Taliban allies seek ultimately to rule Afghanistan under a caliphate. A nuclear attack would end the achievement of that goal forever. Pakistan's Taliban groups seek to overthrow the secular government and impose an Islamic republic on Pakistan, or at least autonomously rule a portion of the country. It is difficult to imagine them detonating a nuclear weapon in Pakistan unless they wanted to provoke perpetual civil war. Here again, any political gain would create a target for revenge.

Attempts to actually acquire a nuclear weapon, as opposed to boasts and threats aimed at exciting followers and alarming foes, involve actors beyond the terrorist leaders themselves, and those actors may be more vulnerable to various forms of retaliation. The people who supply the terrorists with nuclear weapons or fissile material—state sponsors, corrupt officials, criminal syndicates, weapons dealers, smugglers—may do so to avoid retaliation. Those motivated by profit would want to survive. Terrorists with a nuclear weapon have no reliable allies.

In early twentieth-century suspense novels, criminal masterminds like Fu Manchu could call upon a vast underworld army of operatives. Derived in part from accounts of the Assassins—an Islamic religious sect in twelfth-century Persia—the modern underworld servants were anonymous, obedient, ready to sacrifice their lives to carry out a murder or facilitate an escape. Ian Fleming updated the trope, providing his modern global syndicate of crime with an army of unthinking soldiers, human ants industriously serving their master. Fleming deprived even their criminal commanders of individual identities. They were addressed only by their numbers. The film versions of these stories elaborated upon this idea, depicting vast underground facilities filled with anonymous men wearing color-coded coveralls to further suppress individual identity, carrying out their assigned tasks without question or hesitation in response to a disembodied voice on a public address system.

This would not be an accurate description of any real-life terrorist group, since members often turn out to be more quarrelsome than obedient. Volunteers to violence, they are not easily controlled. Internal debates and schisms are common. Terrorist entry into the nuclear domain would exacerbate these existing tensions.

CAN THE UNITED STATES CREDIBLY BE
SEEN AS RUTHLESS?

Cold War deterrence depended upon a perception of utter ruthlessness, to the point of madness. For years, U.S. doctrine called for massive retaliation, and while U.S. administrations in the 1960s sought a more flexible response, there was no question that the United States would respond to any nuclear attack with large numbers of nuclear weapons. But how might terrorists assess the response to a terrorist nuclear attack?

In response to the attack on 9/11, the United States toppled the Taliban government in Afghanistan without hesitation. It launched a "global war on terrorism," which, although the label has been dropped, continues in its eleventh year, with the United States remaining fully committed to the death of al Qaeda's leaders and the complete destruction of their terrorist enterprise. Although this apparently has not dented the determination of those leaders to continue their struggle, there are few other terrorist groups that would envy al Qaeda's current circumstances. To hammer home this point, the pursuit of al Qaeda must be relentless. Al Qaeda must be destroyed, not simply because of 9/11, but because it even thought about nuclear weapons, thereby inviting its annihilation.

Because the U.S. administration chose not to run the risk of Iraq developing weapons of mass destruction, or perhaps because it cynically decided to exploit post-9/11 sentiments, American-led forces invaded Iraq, replaced its government, killed its leader's sons, and eventually captured and executed its leader himself. The issue here is not the quality of American intelligence or the legitimacy of the invasion, but the perception of what the United States might choose to do. Judging by these examples, the United States could be perceived as ruthless when aroused. Its actions were provoked by the deaths of fewer than three thousand Americans. Were the United States confronted with a terrorist nuclear attack involving ten or a hundred times as many deaths, the question is, What would it not be willing to do?

We ought not to presume that the terrorists' only target would be either Manhattan or Washington. It could just as easily be Moscow or Mumbai. Much would depend on exactly who acquires a nuclear device and the circumstances of acquisition, specifically where the device is acquired and the time pressures to use it. Chechens, who placed their "dirty bomb" in Moscow, contemplated seizing nuclear weapons to coerce the Russian government.

Moscow would be their target. Lashkar-e-Taiba, which attacked Mumbai in November 2008, focuses its violence on Pakistan and India. Indian cities would be in peril. Some terrorists talk about wiping Israel off the map. Al Qaeda in the Islamic Maghreb considers France to be a principal foe. In the aftermath of a devastating nuclear terrorist attack, what would these countries do?

A nuclear explosion in Russia probably would immediately be blamed on Muslim extremists in the Caucasus. The historical record implies that such an explosion would provoke a massive and brutal repression. A terrorist nuclear attack on India could lead to nuclear war in South Asia, with devastation on both sides and, quite possibly, the reduction of Pakistan's sovereignty. A terrorist nuclear attack on Israel would provoke immediate retaliation, possibly nuclear and not necessarily limited to terrorists or military targets. We are in uncharted territory here, the terra incognita of a post-nuclear-terrorist world.

A FINAL QUESTION

In one important respect, deterrence of terrorists is unlike the deterrence that existed during the Cold War. The United States (along with the United Kingdom and France) sought to deter attack by the Soviet Union, but Soviet possession of nuclear weapons was not challenged. There was no attempt to disarm the Soviet Union; instead, we chose to outbuild it.

With terrorists, the objective is to deter acquisition of nuclear weapons. But what would we do if an al Qaeda terrorist leader credibly claimed to have a nuclear weapon, providing convincing proof of possession—serial numbers, diagrams, photos, samples of fissile material? He might initially make no specific demands beyond vaguely warning his foes that the weapon would be used if the West persisted in its aggression against Islam, or more specifically, its military offensive in Afghanistan. Instead, he might tell us, we must retreat or negotiate. The announcement alone would serve terrorists' objectives. It would give them status. It would create terror, and it might provide some measure of deterrence. It would generate numerous alarming hoaxes. The threat alone might have serious economic effects.

Much would depend on the specific circumstances, but could we tolerate terrorist possession of a nuclear weapon? And if not, what could we do that we are not already trying to do? We probably would intensify our military efforts to destroy al Qaeda, but what further actions could we take? We would, of course, issue public warnings of the dire consequences that would follow any nuclear attack. Pakistan and Afghanistan could find themselves under virtual quarantine. Would we send more troops to Afghanistan? Could we increase pressure on Pakistan to find and deliver al Qaeda's leaders? Some might urge that we talk to the terrorists. Would we open a dialogue or threaten to seize any terrorist leader who showed up for negotiations? In the simulations I referred to earlier, terrorist blackmail did not work. Negotiations eventually fell apart, and the terrorists, if they possessed a nuclear weapon, had to decide whether to continue the standoff or use the weapon while the government prepared to be hit.

SOME PRELIMINARY CONCLUSIONS

Several tentative conclusions can be drawn from this preliminary inquiry. First, while nuclear weapons would theoretically provide terrorists with enormous destructive power and are the ultimate terrorist fantasy, in reality nuclear terrorism is simply not relevant to most terrorist campaigns; indeed, for most terrorists, nuclear terrorism would seem counterproductive. Only a few organizations have contemplated acquiring nuclear weapons, and only one, al Qaeda, has made any serious attempt to do so.

Second, a more serious effort by terrorists to acquire a nuclear weapon would require them to think more seriously about how they might use it. To the extent that they have thought about it at all, terrorists have considered nuclear weapons from a variety of perspectives; terrorists may seek nuclear weapons for status, terror, coercion, deterrence, or destruction. Or they may opportunistically try to acquire a nuclear capability with no clear purpose in mind. The current presumed terrorist nuclear "first-strike policy" seems to be a default position reflecting the lack of any nuclear capability.

Third, different terrorist groups would seek different objectives with nuclear weapons and would have different targets. Manhattan and Washington are not the only—or even the most likely—targets of nuclear terrorism. The target could just as easily be Moscow or Mumbai, Tel Aviv or Tokyo. And yet, not all terrorist objectives would require actual use of a weapon. Contrary to contemporary conventional wisdom, actual use of a nuclear weapon—that is, detonation without warning—while it remains the most worrisome scenario, may not be terrorists' automatic course of action. They could look for other ways to exploit possession or perceived possession of a nuclear capability. Possession alone, even a convincing pretense of possession, might suffice to achieve some terrorist objectives. Nuclear blackmail, however, remains a difficult proposition for terrorists, as compellence was for countries with nuclear weapons.

Fourth, the manner in which terrorists might acquire a nuclear weapon will influence how they might use it. Provision by a state patron would be aimed at swift use. Clandestine fabrication would give terrorists more autonomy and time and would require more actors, which means a wider range of options but more debate. Herein, attempts by terrorists to build or acquire a nuclear weapon are likely to foment internal discussion and debate about how it is to be used. Internal disagreement is a likely result.

Fifth, and finally, to work against terrorism, deterrence should be expanded to include supporting actors. Methods of applying deterrence in practice will also have to be expanded. Elementally, however, understanding how terrorists may think about nuclear weapons can inform deterrence strategies. Deterrence can build upon and exploit existing terrorist concerns and debates about counterproductive levels of violence. In counterterrorism, deterrence will depend on perceptions of the attack victims' ruthlessness. The message should be that an act of nuclear terrorism will fundamentally alter the rules of behavior and that pre-nuclear-terrorism constraints will not apply in a post-nuclear-terrorism world. As the only terrorist group to venture toward nuclear weapons, al Qaeda should be made an example of and destroyed.

NOTES

1. Graham Allison, *Nuclear Terrorism: The Ultimate Preventable Catastrophe* (New York: Henry Holt and Co., 2004), 1–4.

2. Hamid Mir, "Osama Claims He Has Nukes: If US Uses N-Arms It Will Get Same Response," *Dawn*, November 10, 2001.

3. David Albright, "Al Qaeda's Nuclear Program: Through the Window of Seized Documents," *Policy Forum Online*, Special Forum No. 47, Nautilus Institute, November 6, 2002.

4. For a description of bin Laden's contacts with Pakistani scientists, see Brian Michael Jenkins, *Will Terrorists Go Nuclear?* (Amherst, NY: Prometheus Books, 2008); 87–88.

5. The president's remark was quoted by former chairman of the Joint Chiefs of Staff General Richard Myers to the author and in his autobiography, *Eyes on the Horizon: Serving on the Frontlines of National Security* (New York: Simon & Schuster, 2010).

6. Albright, "Al Qaeda's Nuclear Program."

7. Jenkins, *Will Terrorists Go Nuclear?*

8. Allison, *Nuclear Terrorism*.

9. Harris Poll, "The War on Terror: What Is It? Who Are Our Enemies and How Likely Are Different Types of Terrorist Attacks in the United States?" Harris Interactive, June 22, 2007.

10. Pamela Hess, "CIA Chief: Al Qaida Is Top Nuclear Concern," *Huffington Post*, September 16, 2008.

11. Lewis Goldfrank et al., *Preparing for the Psychological Consequences of Terrorism: A Public Health Strategy* (Washington, DC: Institute of Medicine of the National Academies, 2003).

12. Paul Davis and Brian Michael Jenkins, *Deterrence and Influence in Counterterrorism: A Component in the War on al Qaeda* (Santa Monica, CA: RAND, 2002).

13. Jenkins, *Will Terrorists Go Nuclear?* 71–77.

14. Ibid., 77–84.

15. William Quandt, Fuad Jabber, and Ann Lesch, *The Politics of Palestinian Nationalism* (Berkeley: University of California Press, 1973).

16. Alex Spillius, "Nuclear Terrorism Is Gravest Threat to Global Security, Barack Obama Warns," *Telegraph*, April 12, 2010.

17. Baumann gave the interview in secret to a French reporter while still a fugitive. *Liberation*, October 7–8, 1978.

18. William Pierce, *The Turner Diaries* (Hillsboro, WV: National Vanguard Books, 1978).

6 WILL THREATS DETER NUCLEAR TERRORISM?

Martha Crenshaw

IN LATE 2008 the United States adopted a policy of deterring nuclear terrorism by non-state actors through threats of retaliation by overwhelming force.[1] The purpose of this chapter is to examine the implications of the threat and analyze the challenge of deterring terrorists from acquiring or using weapons of mass destruction, specifically nuclear materials. The barriers to effective retaliatory deterrence of non-state actors are high. There is disagreement over what al Qaeda's values and goals are. It is not clear that threats designed to inflict pain would be acceptable to the American public or world opinion even if they were not carried out. Deterrence of the intent to attack may not be compatible with "killing and capturing" and other uses of military force to reduce the adversary's capabilities. The "red line" that will trigger execution of the deterrent threat is not precisely defined. Threats may undermine efforts to convince non-state adversaries that the use of nuclear weapons is illegitimate. U.S. decision makers may not fully recognize the positive requirements of deterrence. Nor is it certain that there is an opponent's strategic calculus to be altered, if there is no central direction to a severely weakened al Qaeda beyond a common vision that links a diffuse and fragmented transnational movement. Nevertheless, the intent of the U.S. government is to deter this specific form of terrorism as part of a strategy of tailored deterrence. The issues of why and how do not appear to have been resolved, at least not in the public debate. The purpose of the declaratory policy remains ambiguous.

This chapter first outlines the evolution of the U.S. policy of "new deterrence," insofar as scrutiny of the public record allows, in order to specify exactly what the U.S. position is. It then evaluates policy in light of a theoretical interpretation of deterrence. The subsequent analysis is organized in terms of three questions about the requirements of effective deterrence. First, can the United States ascertain what the adversary values? Second, can a threat be designed that will harm those values and that the United States is willing and able to implement? Third, can the United States communicate and will al Qaeda understand the meaning and import of such a threat?

This chapter focuses on al Qaeda and affiliated groups because U.S. policy considers al Qaeda and its associates the preeminent non-state threat to U.S. interests, although it is possible that concentrating excessively on al Qaeda could lead to ignoring other threats. This chapter also stresses nuclear terrorism rather than acquisition or use of chemical or biological weapons because the official U.S. position is that nuclear terrorism is the most serious national security threat the United States faces.

My analysis does not explore the question of whether al Qaeda or any other non-state actor is likely to acquire or use nuclear materials, although what al Qaeda would want to achieve with their use and al Qaeda's level of determination to succeed are important to designing a deterrent threat. How the adversary might employ such weapons is also relevant: How provocative would an attack have to be in order to trigger retaliation? Would acquisition alone be sufficient? Have al Qaeda's nuclear strategies changed over time, especially with leadership shifts (particularly the death of Osama bin Laden and his replacement by Ayman al-Zawahiri) and shifting patterns of splits and mergers? Since there is little in the way of a historical record of the terrorist acquisition or use of nuclear weapons, opinions diverge with regard to both likelihood and consequences.[2]

DETERRENCE: POLICY AND THEORY

A review of the record reveals significant ambiguities and little consideration of how the policy would work in practice. Initially the adoption of a policy of deterrence by threat of retaliation seemed pronounced and definitive, but over time commitment to the policy has become hard to gauge.

In February 2008, President George W. Bush's national security advisor Stephen Hadley offered the following remark while speaking to the Center for International Security and Cooperation at Stanford: "[The United States] reserves the right to respond with overwhelming force to the use of weapons of mass destruction against the United States, our people, our forces and our friends and allies. *Additionally*, the United States will hold any state, terrorist group, or other non-state actor fully accountable for supporting or enabling terrorist efforts to obtain or use weapons of mass destruction."[3] Hadley's statement was apparently the first explicit indication of a change in American policy to include independent non-state actors as well as states and state-supported organizations in a policy of threatened retaliation for the use of weapons of mass destruction. The speech was initially off the record, but the text was released to the public by the White House three days later. Hadley continued to speak on the subject to various associations and groups, but as the *New York Times* noted later, the speech was "little-noticed."[4]

On October 28, 2008, Secretary of Defense Robert Gates, in a speech to the Carnegie Endowment for International Peace, made the policy official.[5] He explained that the United States already applied a deterrence strategy to "rogue regimes" and added:

> After September 11th, the president announced that we would make no distinction between terrorists and the states that sponsor or harbor them. Indeed, the United States has made it clear for many years that it reserves the right to respond with overwhelming force to the use of weapons of mass destruction against the United States, our people, our forces and our friends and allies.... Today we also make clear that the United States will hold any state, terrorist group or other non-state actor or individual fully accountable for supporting or enabling terrorist efforts to obtain or use weapons of mass destruction, whether by facilitating, financing, or providing expertise or safe haven for such efforts.

Deterrence was always a part of post-9/11 U.S. strategy, despite an early and emphatic emphasis on preemption and a continuing focus on prevention and homeland security.[6] Gates's 2008 announcement was foreshadowed by the September 2006 National Strategy for Combating Terrorism (NSCT), which contained a section specifically devoted to "denying" weapons of mass destruction to rogue states and their terrorist allies. It expressed the conviction that terrorists are determined to acquire such weapons and warned that the United States could not permit their efforts to succeed. The document referred to a "new deterrence calculus" that would deter terrorists from contemplating the use of WMD and dissuade them from conducting such attacks, through mitigating the effects of the attacks and guaranteeing accurate attribution of responsibility. It called for tailored deterrence—a strategy tailored to the situation and the adversary. The U.S. intention was to make clear that terrorists would face the prospect of an overwhelming response and to ensure that "our determination to respond overwhelmingly to any attack is never in doubt."[7]

In the spring of 2007, David E. Sanger and Thom Shanker of the *New York Times* reported a "vigorous but concealed" debate in the Bush administration about countering the terrorist threat.[8] According to their account, the president's top national security advisors, meeting in May 2006, decided that states should be held responsible for transferring weapons of mass destruction to terrorists but did not resolve the issue of how and when. On October 9, the North Korean nuclear test provoked the president to issue an explicit warning to North Korea. Administration officials believed that because North Korea was well aware that the United States knew the details of the North Korean program, the threat was credible because reliable attribution was near certain. For other potential state sponsors the threat would be less credible; without the requisite knowledge of where material originated, the threat would not be convincing to either terrorists or suppliers.

In March 2008, as Hadley was making the rounds with his speech, Eric Schmitt and Thom Shanker of the *New York Times* recalled the idea of "new deterrence" expressed in the 2006 NSCT, contrasted with the dismissive initial 2003 statement that traditional deterrence would not work against terrorism.[9] Administration officials were said to prefer defeating terrorists: "In some ways . . . the effort represents a second-best solution. Their preferred way to combat terrorism remained to capture or kill extremists, and the new emphasis on deterrence in some ways amounts to attaching a new label to old tools." The NSCT also recognized the familiar difficulties of crafting such a policy: the absence of physical targets, the difficulties of "decapitation," and the elusiveness of a transnational movement. But why would the U.S. government adopt a second-best solution?

In December 2006 the U.S. Strategic Command issued its "Deterrence Operations Joint Operating Concept" statement. Rather than embracing a concept of "new deterrence," the document is inconclusive, although it leans toward the negative. It briefly notes five rather daunting impediments: trying to identify terrorist decision makers, uncertainty about their decision calculus, their likely resistance to threats, our lack of understanding of their values, and absence of communication channels.[10]

Soon after Gates's speech, the Task Force on Department of Defense Nuclear Weapons Management, which Gates appointed, issued the second of two reports.[11] Although its primary focus was on renewing and strengthening the nuclear mission of the U.S. military, it also alluded to the issue of deterring non-state terrorist actors such as al Qaeda. Like the Joint Operating Concept statement, the task force report was pessimistic with regard to the likelihood of successful deterrence. The report concluded equivocally that deterrence by threat of retaliation is challenging and complicated.

In the spring of 2009, General Kevin Chilton, commander of the U.S. Strategic Command, and General Norton A. Schwartz, chief of staff of the Air Force, both published articles on the need to refashion deterrence for the modern world. Both advocated tailored deterrence and addressed the difficulties of deterring non-state actors in the context of an overall deterrence posture. Neither statement was definitive. General Chilton concluded by recommending that "we should work more aggressively on adding deterrence to our counterterrorism repertoire."[12]

At about the same time a Council on Foreign Relations task force on U.S. nuclear weapons policy concluded bluntly that traditional deterrence would not work against nuclear terrorism because stateless terrorists have no national territory that the United States can threaten to target—although the task force warned that the most likely nuclear detonation would be by a non-state actor rather than a state.[13] The solution, in the task force's view, was to increase security and to prevent weapons or materials from falling into the hands of terrorists. The question of what the government should do if prevention fails was not addressed.

The policy shift in the late Bush administration can be situated in two political contexts. One was the need to figure out what deterrent mission the U.S. nuclear arsenal was to serve in the post–Cold War era, especially in light of charges that the stockpile was badly in need of modernization, and calls for nuclear disarmament. Preventing nuclear proliferation to unfriendly states was a corollary area of acute concern. On a parallel track was the need to develop an effective post-9/11 counterterrorism policy, including countering the threat of terrorist acquisition and/or use of WMD, especially nuclear. The original 2003 counterterrorism strategy was reviewed and revised in 2006, as the preemptive or preventive war in Iraq that the original doctrine supported was foundering. By the time of the 2006 strategy review, the administration was facing extensive criticism of the global war on terror. Some influential critics had proposed substituting a strategy of containment.[14] The 2006 strategy statement explicitly compared the struggle against terrorism to the

Cold War and al Qaeda to adversaries such as the Soviet Union, a historical context in which deterrence seemed to have worked quite well. The discussion of deterrence at this time, however, still focused on states rather than non-states.

The Obama administration continued the policy announced by Gates in the fall of 2008. The 2010 Quadrennial Defense Review Report (QDR) can be seen as a step toward implementation. Recognizing a complex threat environment with multiple contingencies, the QDR identified successful counterterrorism, prevention of proliferation, and countering WMD as key missions. The QDR announced that new force planning guidance would ensure that the United States could prevent and deter attacks on U.S. territory and interests and the emergence of new transnational threats, as well as defeat al Qaeda. It noted the planned establishment of a "standing Joint Task Force Elimination Headquarters," which would develop "nuclear disablement, exploitation, intelligence, and coordination capabilities." It also called for enhanced nuclear forensic capabilities in order to enhance deterrence.[15]

The QDR merged prevention and deterrence into a single concept, "prevent-and-deter," the explication of which is confusing:

> The Department's prevent-and-deter activities will be focused on ensuring a defense in depth of the United States, preventing the emergence or reemergence of transnational terrorist threats, including Al Qaeda; and deterring other potential major adversaries.... The Department's efforts to deter threats to U.S. territory in-depth and prevent the growth or reemergence of transnational terrorist movements will continue and may grow in some areas. Our planning assumes even greater force availability for efforts to deter other would-be aggressors through forward presence and sustained operations to build partnership capacity.[16]

In April 2010, the Department of Defense Nuclear Posture Review Report named preventing nuclear proliferation and nuclear terrorism as the top priorities of the U.S. policy agenda and asserted that nuclear terrorism is the "most immediate and extreme threat today." It assumed that al Qaeda and its allies sought nuclear weapons and would use them if they obtained them. Although prevention was a key theme of the report, it also warned that if attacked, the United States would "take strong action" and, renewing the 2008 commitment, "hold fully accountable" any state, terrorist group, or other actor that had enabled the WMD attack.[17]

The first National Security Strategy of the United States of the Obama administration was issued in May 2010. It also defined nuclear terrorism as a preeminent threat to American national security and warned that a nuclear attack was more likely now than during the Cold War.[18] Otherwise the strategy statement downplayed terrorism and abandoned entirely the global war on terror in order to focus specifically on defeating al Qaeda and its affiliates, which are again said to be determined to buy, build, or steal a nuclear weapon. Yet the strategy appeared to admit that deterrence is challenging: "Instead of a single nuclear adversary, the United States is now threatened by the potential spread of nuclear weapons to extremists *who may not be deterred from using them*,"[19] while simultaneously repeating the commitment to tailored deterrence (although it explained that states that violate rules will be "isolated" rather than punished). The overall description of counterterrorism strategy said nothing about threats of force, instead referring to denying safe haven, strengthening allies, reinforcing homeland security, bringing terrorists to justice through law enforcement, and countering al Qaeda's extremist agenda.[20]

In June 2011, the administration issued a new National Strategy for Counterterrorism, focused on disrupting, dismantling, and defeating al Qaeda.[21] The strategy recognized nuclear terrorism as the gravest threat to global security and reiterated the assertion that acquisition of nuclear weapons or materials will lead to use. It referred to "deterring" theft, smuggling, or use but did not specify the means, and it considered deterrence as but one of several measures, not the centerpiece of the strategy. John O. Brennan, assistant to the president for homeland security and counterterrorism, in announcing the strategy, said only that "we are working to prevent al-Qa'ida from acquiring or developing weapons of mass destruction, which is why President Obama is leading the global effort to secure the world's vulnerable materials in four years."[22] There is no reference to threats of overwhelming force or what the United States would do if prevention fails.

THE APPLICABILITY OF DETERRENCE TO COUNTERTERRORISM

Since the 9/11 attacks, scholars and practitioners have extensively, indeed exhaustively, debated the question of applying deterrence to terrorism, and specifically to CBRN (chemical, biological, radiological, and nuclear) terrorism.[23] These discussions have raised or revealed a number of problems of "fit" of the theory of deterrence to counterterrorism.

One problem lies in the interpretation of the basic concept of deterrence. The theory of retaliatory deterrence rests on threatening the adversary with sufficient harm that he does not undertake an attack that he plans to make against you. It means preserving a status quo that the challenger wants to change.[24] However, what some experts are advocating or criticizing as deterrence seems to be general coercion, if that.[25] For example, Doron Almog calls for a policy of "cumulative deterrence" based on a gradual wearing down of the adversary through offensive and defensive measures as well as positive inducements, but it is not clear how continuous pressure and use of force can be defined as deterrence. Deterrence by retaliation involves a threat from the defender to do something new, not to continue a course of action. The defender does not say "we will keep hitting you over the head with this hammer so you don't even think of attacking us" but rather "we are not hitting you now but will hit you really hard later if you cross this line." In principle the "red line" is sharply demarcated in the eyes of both parties.[26] In addition, deterrence has a positive side, suggesting that the relationship between coercive diplomacy and pure deterrence is important, although it has not been studied.[27] In general, how are threats of retaliation related to positive incentives?

A state that decides to deter rather than destroy or defeat an enemy is sending a signal that it is prepared to live with that adversary because it assumes that the adversary can successfully be deterred from attack.[28] The elimination of the adversary is not necessary to the security of the defending state. This assumption provides a rationale for a policy of containment. Is this the signal that the United States wishes to send? It is not clear from the documentary evidence or from U.S. behavior that such is the intent, and the official statements do not consistently deal with the contradiction between *defeat* and *deter*. As noted, the first version of the NSCT in 2003 argued that traditional deterrence would not work against terrorism, while the second version in 2006 declared that there can be no peaceful coexistence with the enemy, while simultaneously advocating "new" deterrence.

American military operations in Iraq and Afghanistan, as well as the June 2011 official strategy statement, detract from the plausibility of the idea that the United States is prepared to live with al Qaeda, as distinguished from other non-state adversaries such as Hezbollah or Hamas. Drone attacks on the al Qaeda leadership in Pakistan, as well as their Taliban allies, conducted at high risk of causing civilian casualties, alienating the Pakistani public, and destabilizing an already weak Pakistani government, display a keen desire to destroy al Qaeda.[29] In October 2009 in a speech at the National Counter-terrorism Center President Obama declared firmly that the core mission of the United States was to disrupt, dismantle, and defeat al Qaeda and other extremist movements around the world.[30] The pursuit, the president said, would be unyielding. This intention was repeated in his justification for aug-menting troop levels in Afghanistan, while the 2010 QDR called for the de-ployment of additional drones. The use of drones and special forces to combat al Qaeda and its regional affiliates such as AQAP is the essence of the 2011 counterterrorism strategy. The risks taken in sending in a SEAL team to ap-prehend or kill bin Laden in the center of Pakistan demonstrate full well the importance to the United States of destroying al Qaeda. American decision makers must have anticipated that the raid would result in the most strained relationship with Pakistan in the history of the alliance. Moreover, Pakistan is one of the potential sources of the nuclear materials that terrorists might ac-quire, so its destabilization portends consequences that far exceed those of the non-nuclear failed state.

As noted earlier, a major theoretical question is whether deterrence is com-patible with killing, capturing, and defeating. Wyn Bowen concludes that, at best, deterrence is a short-term delaying option, a way of buying time so that physical disruption and destruction can work.[31] Other analysts think that deterrent threats are reinforced by carrying them out.[32] However, offensive actions may also undermine the logic of deterrence. The 2006 Joint Operating Concept recognized this contradiction: "Credibly threatening to impose additional cost on a non-state actor against whom the US is already waging a global war . . . can be difficult. Such an actor may well perceive that the US is already doing everything under its power to impose costs on them, whether they take the additional action we seek to deter, or not."[33] In addition, under threat such an actor might cross the red line out of desperation.

This statement also implicitly recognizes another positive dimension to deterrence. The threat of retaliation conveys a promise that the defender will refrain if the challenger does not undertake the proscribed action. That is, the threat will be implemented if and only if the challenger crosses the red line. The logical implication is that if al Qaeda does not acquire or use nuclear weapons, the United States will not carry out the deterrent threat of over-whelming force, whatever that may be. The defender's restraint is the reward for the challenger's compliance. Yet, as in all cases of deterrence, the defender typically cannot know whether the adversary is refraining from fear or for myriad other reasons, such as patiently waiting and planning for the opportune moment to mount a challenge.

THE REQUIREMENTS OF EFFECTIVE DETERRENCE

In principle, effective deterrence has three minimum requirements. The defender needs to know the challenger's values, how to credibly threaten those values, and how the threat will be received and acted on.

The Adversary's Values

What does al Qaeda value?[34] What assets does al Qaeda possess that it would not wish to see harmed, especially after the death of bin Laden as well as many other secondary leaders? Numerous compilations and translations of al Qaeda statements as well as analyses of those documents are available, including many posted on the website of the Combating Terrorism Center at West Point.[35] Al Qaeda values some present assets, but other attainments al Qaeda values are what it aspires to in the future. So in theory the defender might threaten harm to something the challenger currently has or to block the path to achieving important goals in the future.

How does the U.S. government view al Qaeda's objectives? In 2006 it was assumed that the goals of al Qaeda were to expel the West from Muslim lands, promote the establishment of regimes governed according to its version of Islamic law, and continue to attack the United States and its allies, including Israel. Some elements of al Qaeda were presumed to seek a caliphate extending from Spain to Southeast Asia. There was recognition of divisions within al Qaeda, but a common goal was said to be totalitarian rule.[36] By June 2011, the Obama administration was disparaging such conceptions:

> Our strategy is . . . shaped by a deeper understanding of al-Qa'ida's goals, strategy, and tactics. I'm not talking about al-Qa'ida's grandiose vision of global domination through a violent Islamic caliphate. That vision is absurd, and we are not going to organize our counterterrorism policies against a feckless delusion that is never going to happen. We are not going to elevate these thugs and their murderous aspirations into something larger than they are.[37]

Relying on leaks from analysts studying the documents found in bin Laden's Abbottabad house, the *Washington Post* reported that, oddly enough, bin Laden appeared to agree.[38] He apparently cautioned leaders of al Qaeda in the Arabian Peninsula (AQAP) that now was not the time to try to establish an Islamic state and that they should remain focused on attacking the United States.

Within al Qaeda, whether the far enemy or the near enemy should take priority has long been a matter of debate, but in practice the two aims are related. In order to accomplish domestic revolution and construct a regional caliphate, al Qaeda would have to both defeat and expel the foreign allies of local regimes, who provide essential military, economic, and political support and also offend true believers by their presence on Muslim land. Thus, attacks on the U.S. homeland would be an integral part of a strategy to seize back what al Qaeda leaders regard as rightfully theirs.[39] Focusing on the United States does not mean abandoning the aspiration of the caliphate.

All the same, in the short or long term, al Qaeda must value territorial control. Al Qaeda's infrastructure is not substantial (for example, current training camps are apparently minimalist and easily rebuilt if destroyed, in comparison to the camps that were operated before the U.S. invasion of Afghanistan). The purpose of safe havens is to provide space for leaders to organize and plan.

Interpretations differ as to whether or not al Qaeda values the support of a constituency. In a tangible sense, popular support can be the source of funds and recruits as well as protection and security. The famous letter from Ayman al-Zawahiri to Abu Musab al-Zarqawi in Iraq in 2005 is often cited as evidence of sensitivity to local public opinion in terms of taking power. There are fierce debates within Islamist circles over the morality of killing Muslim civilians and, occasionally, killing civilians at all. On the other hand, a view of al Qaeda as apocalyptic (which the Obama administration appears to avoid but which influenced the Bush administration and might influence a successor to the Obama administration) implies that the organization cares nothing for an earthly constituency. Groups motivated by religion are said to be indifferent as to whether people are killed or not, since the good will enjoy life after death and the bad deserve their punishment. "Suicide" terrorism is a proud hallmark and symbol of willingness to die.[40]

Another possible al Qaeda resource or value is electronic communications capabilities. Internet presence and the capacity to distribute audio and videotapes are key assets for al Qaeda, perhaps the virtual equivalent of territory. Although al Qaeda may not recruit directly from Internet connections, the phenomenon of radicalization or homegrown terrorism that currently preoccupies Western governments is encouraged and stimulated by al Qaeda propaganda. It could be thought of as preparing the ground for recruitment. The ability to broadcast intentions makes it possible for self-generated groups to act on the message. This capability is likely to matter to the Obama administration, whose 2011 strategy stresses defense of the homeland and the danger of recruitment within the country.

There is also the familiar argument that al Qaeda values most intensely the Muslim holy sites, which goes beyond territorial possession to highly symbolic and affective values. Al Qaeda's objections to an American presence in Muslim lands are predicated on a defensive theory of protecting holy sites, chiefly Mecca, from the infidel. This can be seen as a religious duty as much as a way of garnering popular support.

Bush administration officials also believed that al Qaeda valued its reputation and credibility with Muslims, intangible values based on perceptions. Consequently the organization was thought to wish to avoid operations that would be shameful or embarrassing; its leaders feared failure.[41] Thus image, reputation, and status might be key values. Similarly, a white paper prepared for the Secretary of Defense Task Force on DoD Nuclear Weapons Management suggested that the central value for al Qaeda was its ideological narrative.[42] It could be that through this justifying narrative or story al Qaeda gains support, sanctuary, and resources.

A corollary worth noting is that some analysts have proposed that deterrence not aim at al Qaeda as a collective entity but at selected individual members, who might value their lives, families, and fortunes, and fear personal retribution.[43] Such an approach to disaggregated deterrence resembles a criminal justice approach more than international relations theory.

Designing and Implementing Threats

For the purpose of this analysis I will assume that al Qaeda values first survival as an organization and continuing to fight, and second the actual and potential assets mentioned above: preserving a territorial foothold or sanctuary; the protection of holy sites from the contamination of the infidel; the support of the *ummah*, or community of Muslim believers; and the reputation established by its ideological narrative and its ability to transform that narrative into action, especially via its communication capabilities. How can a threat be formulated that would threaten these interrelated values? Are multiple threats required for multiple values? How credible would such a threat or threats be? Beyond designing a threat that would inflict unacceptable pain on al Qaeda, a critical question is whether the United States would be willing and able to execute it.

Issuing a credible deterrent threat requires that the defender demonstrate the capability to both know and be able to prove convincingly who attacked. The defender must be able to identify who was responsible and convince the challenger that he cannot escape detection (possibly the latter could occur without the former, but this seems unlikely). In deterring nuclear terrorism, absence of reliable attribution in a timely way will make it hard to hold accountable or punish, as the 2010 QDR recognized.[44] There are a number of facets to this issue. One is the distinction between *acquisition* of materials and *use* of materials. The second is the distinction between knowing who committed the attack or acquired the material and where and how they gained possession and expertise that translated acquisition into use.

In the case of acquisition of nuclear material, as opposed to use, it will be difficult for American policymakers to know whether al Qaeda has crossed the barrier or not. Does acquisition refer to materials or knowledge and plans for use? Would recruiting nuclear scientists constitute acquisition? How certain of acquisition would the United States have to be in order to carry out a threat? Furthermore, even if the U.S. government could reliably identify the physical source of nuclear materials, it could not necessarily conclude anything about direct responsibility. Materials or even weapons could be stolen from a careless state (although the fact that as far as we know such a theft has not happened suggests that it is not at all easy). A state that willingly gave or sold materials or weapons to a terrorist organization could still claim that they were lost or stolen, or that independent agents in the bureaucracy were responsible, not the nation's leaders.

Another issue is whether acquisition necessarily means use. As Brian Jenkins notes in his contribution to this book, employment might not automatically follow acquisition, despite the U.S. assumption that it would.[45] Nuclear weapons or materials might be most useful for blackmail or deterrence, not use, even though the U.S. government believes that al Qaeda would not stop with mere possession. Acquisition without use would be risky for al Qaeda, but the intention might be to bide one's time and wait for the appropriate moment for use or revelation of possession.

Attribution is an unresolved problem. After noting that nuclear terrorism had been one of the gravest threats to American security for the past ten years, a 2010 report from a committee of the National Research Council cautioned that much remained to be done to ensure reliable attribution. The committee explained that the recently established National Technical Nuclear Forensics Center, under the direction of the secretary of homeland security, was intended to coordinate a national effort but that a number of challenges remained, such as dispersion of authority, inadequate adaptation of forensics capabilities to real-world emergencies, and absence of a clear implementation plan. The time necessary for post-detonation evaluation and analysis is too long. In fact, U.S. capabilities, while robust, were still "fragile, under re-sourced, and, in some respects, deteriorating."[46] The entire forensics pro-gram is a holdover from the Cold War nuclear weapons program, which sug-gests that extensive modernization is in order if capabilities are to be adapted to a terrorist threat.

Assuming resolution of the attribution dilemma, how can the United States design an appropriate threat? One possibility would be to revive the classic deterrence stratagem from the Cold War: the threat of harming the adversary's civilian population. But in operational terms which target would that be? Where is the *ummah* located? Countries with the largest numbers of the world's 1.5 billion Muslims are Indonesia, next Pakistan, then India. Tur-key and Egypt are the largest Sunni Muslim majority states in the Middle East, and both are long-standing American allies. It is not conceivable that the United States would threaten overwhelming force against Muslim popu-lations, even if they supported al Qaeda (which they do not). Of course during the Cold War the United States did not necessarily assume that the Soviet Union's population supported the Communist regime. The original Gates speech also suggested the issue of whether or not "overwhelming force" meant the use of nuclear weapons, since the original context of the extension of de-terrence to non-state actors was a justification of the need to maintain a nu-clear arsenal. It seems unlikely that nuclear weapons would be employed as counterterrorism, considering the toll in civilian casualties, but it would be worth asking what considerations would either encourage or prohibit a re-sponse in kind.

Alternatively the threat could be designed not to harm a population or constituency directly but to deprive al Qaeda of its legitimacy and popular support. However, methods directed at this end would hardly be called deter-rence, whether by retaliation or denial. Depriving al Qaeda of its popular sup-port and undermining its image as defender of the faith are efforts at persua-sion, endeavors that so far have not been particularly successful, despite major steps by the Obama administration such as the Cairo speech. Initiatives to promote moderate counterparts to al Qaeda or to discredit its message may be undermined by threats of force.[47]

Another possibility for deterrence is threatening the holy places al Qaeda wishes to safeguard. The United States could threaten their destruction or their occupation.[48] Force could easily be applied, but, as the CTC report observed, threats of bombing or other military strikes are more likely to produce rage than fear. As for occupation or regime change, it is highly unlikely that the United States would threaten to occupy another majority Muslim country, its military capacity in this regard already being severely overextended, especially with the addition of Libya to the list of involvements (and remote military intervention in Yemen and Somalia). Moreover, holy sites are located on the sovereign territory of American allies: not just Saudi Arabia but Israel. In fact, from al Qaeda's perspective, Jerusalem is already occupied by the enemy.

A more limited conception of threat would apply to al Qaeda's relatively constrained desire to gain a territorial foothold. For example, the United States could threaten al Qaeda with increased military support for the domestic counterterrorism efforts of vulnerable regimes, which include weak states such as Yemen, Somalia, and Pakistan, or not-so-weak states such as Algeria. Such a threat does not necessarily involve "overwhelming force," but it does imply a "kinetic" or military approach. Yet the prospect of this threat also raises serious problems, since it would run counter to the American aim of spreading democracy. Although this goal is no longer the centerpiece of American foreign policy, it is still a guiding principle. In addition, military assistance has proved troublesome in practical terms. Indigenous armies and police forces are not easily or quickly trained and equipped. The historical record as well as contemporary experience in Iraq and Afghanistan shows how hard it is for outside powers to establish stable local governments capable of prosecuting successful counterterrorism offensives. The United States currently faces dilemmas of central control in both Yemen and Pakistan, making the idea of relying on proxies for counterterrorism even less practical in policy terms. In Libya and in Egypt, Islamist groups have allied or tried to ally themselves with the opponents of authoritarian regimes that the United States wishes to promote. The Obama administration's message is that the "Arab spring" undermines al Qaeda's narrative, but slow democratization and/or disorder could create opportunities for jihadist movements. If the popular push for democracy falters and authoritarianism is reinstituted, especially in Egypt, al Qaeda could benefit.

In sum, most conceptions of a threat of overwhelming force involve potential value conflicts or practical difficulties of implementation that are extremely consequential. In some cases merely issuing a threat would be inflammatory. Thus the credibility of many of the possible deterrent threats is questionable. Looking at the historical record, retaliation for provocative terrorist attacks is extremely rare. States are more likely to exercise restraint than to retaliate even after attacks on their homelands. India after the Mumbai attacks in 2008 is a case in point. The reason for India's restraint goes beyond fear of escalating a conflict with nuclear-armed Pakistan. The question is whether terrorist acquisition or use of some sort of nuclear device would erode the constraints that have operated consistently in other contexts.

Thus one consideration, and a possible solution to the credibility dilemma, is that should al Qaeda use nuclear devices against the United States, the immediate emotional reaction would support an extraordinarily harsh response. As Jenkins notes, normative restraints might vanish in the horror of the moment, and democratic publics might favor measures that they would otherwise find abhorrent. Likewise, U.S. threats might be more plausible because al Qaeda would probably lack a second-strike capacity. Paul Kapur argues that U.S. threats against al Qaeda would be more believable than those issued during the Cold War because, first, a nuclear weapon would have been detonated in the American homeland, as opposed to a Soviet conventional attack on Europe, and, second, al Qaeda could not inflict the devastating response on the United States that the Soviet Union could have.[49] However, it is not out of the question that al Qaeda could possess some capacity for a second strike.[50] Its first use of a nuclear device might be a shot across the bow aimed at establishing credibility, with capabilities held in reserve. American decision makers could not be confident that no second strike was forthcoming, and even if they were, they might not be able to convince a frightened public. In addition, American policy is extended deterrence, and many allies are vulnerable. What if al Qaeda's second-strike threat were an attack on an American ally, such as Turkey, Israel, or India? What if the prospective second strike did not involve nuclear devices but conventional explosives that would nevertheless cause large numbers of deaths?

Communicating and Understanding Threats

Once a threat is defined, how can it be communicated so as to be understood? Does the adversary have the ability to comprehend and act on the deterrent threat or threats? How would the United States send its message, and would al Qaeda receive it as the United States intends? What made American threats before 9/11 unconvincing?

There is extensive disagreement as to what type of actor al Qaeda is. Is it an organization with leaders in control of plans and actions, or is it a decentralized network of local subsidiaries and imitative freelancers who act on impulse and inspiration, on the spur of the moment? Is it something much more complex and in between, as Jeffrey Bale argued?[51] What we have learned about bin Laden after his death suggests that there was an operational central leadership. There is also the question of the decision-making capacity of subsidiaries or affiliates in Pakistan, the Maghreb, Somalia, or Yemen, who are capable of directing attacks against the U.S. homeland.

Alternative futures are possible. Going forward, if extreme decentralization and fragmentation characterize the al Qaeda movement, then it is difficult to think of a common adversarial "strategic calculus" that would permit a reasoned response to a threat. Unconnected small conspiracies, composed of personnel with minimal training, formed to conduct one attack and possibly die in the attempt, would not seem to pose a WMD threat that would warrant a retaliatory deterrence posture. Ultimately it seems unlikely that such a pluralistic and shifting set of adversaries could be deterred, even if they were capable of understanding the threat. Crafting a set of threats to fit each component of a complex transnational organization (such as financiers, bomb makers, planners, couriers, media specialists, and ideologues, across different contexts including different languages and cultures), as Paul Davis contends in this volume, seems inordinately complicated and time-consuming for decision makers. Even with the best of efforts, the impact of any threat will be uncertain.

However, if there is the continuation or reconstitution of a unified transnational organization under the authority of al-Zawahiri, then there might be a common strategy and a motivation that could be influenced. If the expectation is a weak central al Qaeda and stronger local organizations such as AQAP, then it will be imperative to understand the calculus of regional actors.

Whatever the organizational future, in light of the determination expressed in the Obama administration's June 2011 counterterrorism strategy, it is reasonable to assume that communication and control will be extremely difficult for al Qaeda. This means that its response to threat will be erratic and unpredictable even if there is a consolidated organization.

If for the sake of argument we leave this problem aside, logic says that decision makers in al Qaeda must believe that the United States will execute the threat, or that the likelihood of execution is high even if uncertain. Al Qaeda leaders must also be convinced that the executed threat will be painful, which leads back to the question of what al Qaeda values. The threat could be perceived as credible, but acceptable or even perversely helpful to the long-term cause. Possibly al Qaeda welcomed the wars in Afghanistan and Iraq precisely because they fulfilled their predictions of a hostile West pressing to invade Muslim nations and kill Muslims. Presumably another attack on a Muslim country would only confirm al Qaeda's expectations. In general, the issue of adversary perception of threat has received scant attention, and there is little evidence of how al Qaeda responds to threats from the West.

It is not a good sign that in the lead-up to the American invasion of Afghanistan in 2001, neither al Qaeda nor the Taliban acquiesced to American threats. Pakistan appeared to, as General Musharraf went on state television to announce a change of allegiance, but its sincerity is still in doubt (in fact, now more than ever). The Taliban leadership was divided. Some Taliban leaders believed that the United States would attack, but others did not. Some miscalculated that Pakistan would stand with them, while others thought that the United States would invade no matter what they did, so why abandon honor? Another lesson from this experience is that the more the United States exerted military pressure on the Taliban, the less able the Taliban was to comply with the demand to turn over bin Laden. Similarly, in the present conflict, al Qaeda's decision-making ability and control over the organization and its response to threat erode as the United States escalates its drone attacks. If some subset of al Qaeda acquired nuclear materials, the central leadership might not be able to ensure compliance even if it were inclined to do so.

CONCLUSIONS

This chapter analyzed the challenge of deterring terrorist acquisition and use of nuclear weapons or materials, which is a main focus of U.S. attention in the national security realm. Effective deterrence of non-state actors is not easy and may not be possible. Al Qaeda's values are not entirely transparent. It is hard to craft credible and painful threats. Deterrence comes into conflict with other high-priority U.S. policies, particularly the twin aims of destroying al Qaeda while dissuading those populations whose support it seeks.[52] We do not know enough about al Qaeda's decision making to understand how threats are received, but the past record of noncompliance by similar entities such as the Taliban is not promising.

The idea of retaliatory deterrence is not well integrated into an overall strategic conception that is logically coherent in relating ends to means and practical in the sense of the prospects of its implementation. It is difficult to see how threats of retaliation could be effective or to predict how the United States would actually respond should the danger of nuclear terrorism materialize. We are left questioning the purpose of the rhetorical threats that both the Bush and Obama administrations have endorsed. Why should the Cold War doctrine of deterrence have proved so compelling? If the interest of the United States is actually the defeat of al Qaeda, then it would seem more logical to deny the contemporary relevance of deterrence for counterterrorism. This is a puzzle that this chapter has not solved.

NOTES

1. This research is supported by the Science and Technology directorate of the U.S. Department of Homeland Security under Grant Award Number 2008-ST-061-ST0004, made to the National Consortium for the Study of Terrorism and Responses to Terrorism. The views and conclusions contained in this chapter are those of the author and should not be interpreted as representing the official policies of the U.S. Department of Homeland Security or START. I am grateful first to the editors and then to Scott Sagan and Nil Santana for their comments. I also benefited from discussions at the International Relations Colloquium, University of California, Berkeley, the International Society for Research on Aggression annual meeting at the University of Connecticut, and the International Society of Political Psychology annual meeting in Istanbul, July 2011.

2. Anne Stenersen and Brynjar Lia, *Al-Qaida's Online CBRN Manuals: A Real Threat?* (Kjeller: Norwegian Defence Research Establishment [FFI], 2007), and Rolf Mowatt-Larssen, *Al Qaeda Weapons of Mass Destruction Threat: Hype or Reality?* (Cambridge, MA: Harvard-Belfer Center for Science and International Affairs, 2010).

3. Stephen Hadley, "Remarks by the National Security Advisor to the Center for International Security and Cooperation," Stanford University, February 8, 2008. Emphasis added.

4. Thom Shanker, "Gates Gives Rationale for Expanded Deterrence," *New York Times*, October 29, 2008.

5. Robert Gates, "Nuclear Weapons and Deterrence in the 21st Century," speech at Carnegie Endowment for International Peace, October 28, 2008.

6. Jeffrey W. Knopf, "Wrestling with Deterrence: Bush Administration Strategy After 9/11," *Contemporary Security Policy* 29:2 (2008): 229–65.

7. Government of the United States of America, *National Strategy for Combating Terrorism*, September 2006, 14.

8. David Sanger and Thom Shanker, "U.S. Debates Deterrence for Nuclear Terrorism," *New York Times*, May 8, 2007.

9. Eric Schmitt and Thom Shanker, "U.S. Adapts Cold-War Idea to Fight Terrorists," *New York Times*, March 18, 2008. See also Eric Schmitt and Thom Shanker, *Counterstrike: The Untold Story of America's Secret Campaign Against Al Qaeda* (New York: Times Books, 2011). Shortly after 9/11, the Defense Advanced Research Projects Agency (DARPA) asked the National Academy of Sciences, RAND, and the Institute for Defense Analysis to consider the question of whether terrorism could be deterred. See the report, *Discouraging Terrorism: Some Implications of 9/11* (Washington, DC: National Academy Press, 2002). I served on this committee.

10. U.S. Department of Defense, *Deterrence Operations Joint Operating Concept Version 2.0*, December 2006, 18–19, 65–67. See also Brad Roberts, *Deterrence and WMD Terrorism: Calibrating Its Potential Contributions to Risk Reduction* (Washington, DC: Institute for Defense Analyses, 2007).

11. Report of the Secretary of Defense Task Force on DoD Nuclear Weapons Management, *Phase II: Review of the DoD Nuclear Mission* (Arlington, VA, December 2008).

12. Kevin Chilton and Greg Weaver, "Waging Deterrence in the Twenty-First Century," *Strategic Studies Quarterly* 3:1 (2009): 38; Norman Schwartz and Timothy Kirk, "Policy and Purpose: The Economy of Deterrence," *Strategic Studies Quarterly* 3:1 (2009): 11–30.

13. Council on Foreign Relations Independent Task Force Report No. 62, "U.S. Nuclear Weapons Policy," April 2009. For a perspective agreeing that it is almost impossible to deter WMD terrorism by "religious fundamentalists," see David Auerswald, "Deterring Nonstate WMD Attacks," *Political Science Quarterly* 121:4 (2006): 543–68.

14. Stephen Biddle, *American Grand Strategy After 9/11: An Assessment* (Strategic Studies Institute of the U.S. Army War College, 2005). Biddle was advisor to General David Petraeus during the "surge" in Iraq.

15. Government of the United States of America, *Quadrennial Defense Review Report*, September 2010; United States Department of Defense, "DoD News Briefing with Secretary Gates and Adm. Mullen from the Pentagon," February 1, 2010.

16. *Quadrennial Defense Review*, 37.

17. Government of the United States of America, *Nuclear Posture Review Report*, April 2010, 3, 12.

18. Government of the United States of America, *National Security Strategy*, May 2010, 23.

19. Ibid., 17, italics added.

20. Ibid., 4, 19–22.

21. Available at http://www.whitehouse.gov/sites/default/files/counterterrorism _strategy.pdf.

22. John O. Brennan speech, June 29, 2011. Text at http://www.whitehouse.gov /the-press-office/2011/06/29/remarks-john-o-brennan-assistant-president-homeland -security-and-counterterrorism.

23. Analysis of the applicability of deterrence was not uncommon before 9/11: see my article, Martha Crenshaw, "Transnational Terrorism and World Politics," *Jerusalem Journal of International Relations* 1:2 (1975): 120–24.

24. Thomas Schelling, *The Strategy of Conflict* (Cambridge, MA: Harvard University Press, 1960); Thomas Schelling, *Arms and Influence* (New Haven, CT: Yale University Press, 1966); Alexander George and Richard Smoke, *Deterrence in American Foreign Policy* (New York: Columbia University Press, 1974).

25. In an account of the arrests of bomb makers in Queens, New York, the *New York Times* reported that "[Najibullah] Zazi and his confederates were deterred before any plot had a chance to take shape." David Johnston and William Rashbaum, "Terror Suspect Had Bomb Guide, Authorities Say," *New York Times*, September 21, 2009. It would be more accurate to say that the conspirators were preempted.

26. Doron Almog, "Cumulative Deterrence and the War on Terrorism," *Parameters* 34:4 (2004/5): 4–19. The relationship between the use of force and threats of force is not straightforward. Does the use of force enhance the credibility of threats, or does it reveal that deterrence has failed? The difference may lie in the timing of threats. For example, a government might employ limited force and then threaten significant escalation later if the adversary attacks.

27. Martha Crenshaw, "Coercive Diplomacy and the Response to Terrorism," in *The United States and Coercive Diplomacy*, ed. Robert Art and Patrick Cronin (Washington, DC: United States Institute of Peace, 2003).

28. I am indebted to David Holloway for this observation.

29. The debate over whether to pursue a "counterterrorist" or a "counterinsurgency" strategy vis-à-vis Afghanistan had implications for this aspect of deterrence. The counterterrorist posture advocated by Vice President Biden presumably ruled out coexistence with al Qaeda. I did not see references to deterrence in that debate, nor in the June 2011 strategy reevaluation.

30. Barack Obama, "Remarks by President Obama at the National Counterterrorism Center," McLean, VA, October 6, 2009.

31. Wyn Q. Bowen, "Deterrence and Asymmetry: Non-State Actors and Mass Casualty Terrorism," *Contemporary Security Policy* 25:1 (2004): 54–70.

32. For example, Shmuel Bar, "Deterring Terrorists: What Israel Has Learned," *Policy Review* 149 (2008): 29–42. See also Alex S. Wilner, "Targeting Killings in Afghanistan: Measuring Coercion and Deterrence in Counterterrorism and Counterinsurgency," *Studies in Conflict and Terrorism* 33: 4 (2010): 307–29.

33. Department of Defense, *Deterrence Operations Joint Operating Concept Version 2.0*, 18.

34. For present purposes, assume that there is an al Qaeda with a set of common values. It is likely, however, that subunits within al Qaeda and other nationally based affiliates or subordinates have values that differ from those of al Qaeda central.

35. The Harmony Program database, Combating Terrorism Center (http://www.ctc.usma.edu/programs-resources/harmony-program). In print, consult, among others, Devin Springer, James Regens, and David Edger, *Islamic Radicalism and Global Jihad* (Washington, DC: Georgetown University Press, 2009); Raymond Ibrahim, ed. and trans., *The Al Qaeda Reader* (New York: Broadway Books, 2007); Gilles Kepel et al., *Al-Qaida dans le texte* (Paris: Presses Universitaires de France, 2005); Brynjar Lia, *Architect of Global Jihad: The Life of Al-Qaida Strategist Abu Mus'ab al-Suri* (New York: Columbia University Press, 2008).

36. The 2010 NSS is largely silent on al Qaeda's intentions other than to say that they are killers who slaughter innocents and should not be regarded as motivated by religious belief.

37. Brennan, June 29, 2011.

38. Greg Miller, "Bin Laden Document Trove Reveals Strain on al-Qaeda," *Washington Post*, July 1, 2011.

39. Here prospect theory might be relevant. Al Qaeda believes that it is recovering lost territory, not expanding.

40. See my arguments against the "new terrorism" idea in *Explaining Terrorism* (London: Routledge, 2011).

41. Schmitt and Shanker, "U.S. Adapts."

42. Combating Terrorism Center, *Terrorism, Deterrence, and Nuclear Weapons* (2008), 31.

43. Lewis Dunn, *Can Al Qaeda Be Deterred from Using Nuclear Weapons?* (Washington, DC: National Defense University Press, Center for the Study of Weapons of Mass Destruction, 2005); Paul Davis and Brian Jenkins, "A Systems Approach to Deterring and Influencing Terrorists," *Conflict Management and Peace Science* 2:1 (2004): 3–15.

44. Over half of anti-American attacks included in the Global Terrorism Database at START (1970–2004) cannot be attributed to any identifiable actor.

45. See Dunn, *Can Al Qaeda Be Deterred?*

46. Committee on Nuclear Forensics, Nuclear and Radiation Studies Board, Division on Earth and Life Studies, National Research Council, National Academies, *Nuclear Forensics: A Capability at Risk (Abbreviated Version)* (National Academies Press, 2010), 5.

47. This observation reinforces my earlier contention that we need to reexamine theories of coercive diplomacy (a combination of carrots and sticks).

48. In Paul Kapur's view, occupation is preferable to destruction because such a strategy would be a form of holding hostages, which would give the occupier leverage as well as avoid the moral condemnation of destroying significant symbolic targets. Paul Kapur, "Deterring Nuclear Terrorists," in *Complex Deterrence: Strategy in the Global Age*, ed. T. V. Paul, Patrick Morgan, and James Wirtz (Chicago: University of Chicago Press, 2009), 120, 129 (n. 55).

49. Ibid., 124.

50. Al Qaeda also has a strategy of deterring its adversaries, though it is based on actions rather than threats. Theoretician Abu Mus'ab al-Suri explained that al Qaeda uses terrorism in order to deter the enemy with fear. American allies "will be deterred," he writes, "if one sets an example by striking or severely punishing a few of them." He applauds the 2004 Madrid bombings as a successful example, which compelled the Spaniards to retract their support for the United States in Iraq. Al-Suri was captured in Pakistan in 2005. Lia, *Architect of Global Jihad*, 414–15.

51. Jeffrey Bale, "Jihadist Cells and 'I.E.D.' Capabilities in Europe: Assessing the Present and Future Threat to the West," unpublished paper, May 2009.

52. For a review of the Obama administration's counterterrorism strategy, see Marc Lynch, *Rhetoric and Reality: Countering Terrorism in the Age of Obama*, Center for a New American Security, June 2010. See also Martha Crenshaw, "The Obama Administration and Counterterrorism," in *Obama in Office: The First Two Years*, ed. James Thurber (Boulder, CO: Paradigm Publishers, 2011).

7 STRATEGIC ANALYSIS, WMD TERRORISM, AND DETERRENCE BY DENIAL

James M. Smith

THOMAS SCHELLING, in his foreword to this volume, reminds us of the slow progress that marked developments and applications of deterrence theory during the Cold War. Today, a decade after the 9/11 attacks forced global terrorism to the top of the United States' security agenda, Schelling's assertions could be made again regarding the pace of progress and state of thinking about deterrence and its application to terrorism. Operational and policy responses to terrorism have dominated time and attention, and thinking on adapting and refining deterrence for application to terrorism has taken a back seat to action. The lack of focus was heightened not only by the operational imperatives of responding to 9/11, but also by the initial assertions, widely accepted and little challenged, that terrorists could not be deterred.

The departure point for this chapter is that the target of deterrence thinking here should be terror*ism* and not terror*ists*, and at the leadership level of terrorism, not the tactical trigger-puller; that terrorism is a deliberate tool applied in pursuit of objectives derived from an ideological/political strategy; that this strategy is in fact rational, although in terms of its proponents' rationality and not necessarily ours; and that while traditional practice of nuclear deterrence may not adapt readily to this fight, foundational concepts of deterrence do in fact have utility in crafting a strategy to at least seek to deter the acquisition and employment of weapons of mass destruction (WMD) within

The views expressed in this chapter are those of the author and do not necessarily reflect the official policy or position of the United States Department of the Air Force, Department of Defense, or the U.S. government.

current and future strategies of terrorism. This chapter touches on these as-sertions in its development of that final point: it directly addresses adaptation and application of deterrence concepts to affect decisions and actions on the acquisition and use of WMD within strategies of terrorism.[1] It addresses the hardest and most dangerous WMD cases: biological and especially nuclear weapons. Most of the concepts and applications developed here also apply in general to radiological and chemical weapons, but the unique aspects of those categories of weapons are not specifically and completely addressed herein.

This chapter, then, addresses adaptation and application of deterrence concepts to affect decisions and actions on the acquisition and use of the most dangerous and potentially destructive WMD within strategies of terrorism. It begins by reviewing foundational concepts of deterrence and identifying a framework for applying denial strategies toward deterrence effects on the WMD decisions and actions of terrorism. It then applies a system's perspec-tive and systematic analysis to describe basic terrorism and specific WMD terrorism processes and actors against which the denial framework can be applied. The application of that framework and its deterrence concepts then identifies promising denial effects toward formulation of an overall strategy of denial with cumulative deterrence effects. Finally, conclusions are drawn on the relevance of concepts of traditional deterrence and their applicability to strategic responses to terrorism today.

DETERRENCE FOUNDATIONS

Classical Cold War deterrence focused on the use of one's nuclear capability to apply psychological reinforcement to an adversary's existing behavior—on his *not* using his nuclear weapons to change that status quo. Deterrence was thus seen as "the power to dissuade."[2] This basic statement points to several key characteristics of Cold War military doctrine. It had at its core the nonuse of nuclear weapons. As Bernard Brodie put it, in the nuclear age the purpose of military force had shifted from war winning to a new imperative on war avoidance.[3] The emphasis was now on the psychological effect conveyed by possessing weapons and destructive capability rather than their actual physi-cal employment. These capabilities were deployed to reinforce the status quo rather than win ground or force changes in behavior. And there was a distinct divide between nuclear deterrence forces and conventional defense forces. So deterrence was seen as nuclear forces withheld for discrete psychological reinforcement of nuclear nonuse by the adversary.

In implementation the operative levers were force posture (signaling capability), declaratory intent (conveying credibility), and a strategy of punishment-based targeting (holding at risk the core assets of the targeted government and society). Terms such as "massive retaliation" and "assured destruction" ruled the day as shorthand for threatened punishment in terms of nuclear annihilation. In theory, denial capabilities and strategies were also possible, but these posed technological and policy problems, and they did not come into realistic play in deterrence strategy until the latter days of the Cold War.

Deterrence effects were always theoretically possible by creating the psychological impression that the adversary could not attain his desired objectives; nonuse of nuclear force on his part could be reinforced by posing the inevitability of an outcome where he could not fulfill his strategy through nuclear weapons use. Denying success to the adversary, however, would require unquestioned defense capabilities in concert with the ability to disarm that adversary's strike capabilities; it would require on our part a disarming first strike of assured accuracy and the ability to reach all adversary nuclear force targets with little or no warning backed up by an impenetrable defense to catch any adversary delivery vehicles that the disarming strike missed. The required technical capabilities and accuracy did not exist at least until late in the Cold War, and both the ability to achieve surprise and an umbrella defense still elude realistic capability and/or affordability. So denial was sent to the "back burner" early in the era, and it never fully emerged as a mainstream concept at that time.

Like denial, another secondary deterrence concept that resided behind the mainstream emphasis on nuclear retaliation was intrawar deterrence. In this case, deterrence of nuclear use was seen as applicable even in the midst of limited—here meaning non-nuclear—conflict. As Schelling noted, even in active conflict, "bargaining" takes place; bargaining via demands, proposals, positive and negative assurances, signaling, and "communicating the limits of one's tolerance."[4] And in addition to the ultimate outcome of the conflict, the other central object of this deterrent signaling would be "the mode of conducting the war itself."[5] So deterring the use of nuclear weapons does not require an absence of conflict. Denial actions and deterrence effects toward the nonuse of WMD are possible within active, non-WMD conflict.

Today, as we look toward applicability of these traditional concepts and practices to WMD terrorism, nuclear deterrence and deterrence by punishment have only limited roles for all of the reasons generally cited as applying to the overall concept of deterring terrorism. However, the more applicable concepts are those underlying denial of WMD terrorism even within an active campaign of terrorism and counterterrorism. Deterrence by denial targets the adversary strategy; it operates via a counterstrategy aimed at denying the adversary strategic success. As Glenn Snyder put it, denial capabilities "deter chiefly by their effect on . . . his estimate of the probability of gaining his objective."[6] Or for Schuyler Foerster, denial is simply stated as "deterrence by the threat of denying victory."[7] For WMD terrorism, denial focuses on reducing one's own vulnerability while formulating and implementing a coherent strategy targeting both adversary capabilities and policy; it entails both active and passive defense; it applies even within an otherwise active fight against all of the non-WMD dimensions of terrorism. A strategic analysis of modern terrorism and the critical components of WMD terrorism will provide the framework for such a denial strategy with deterrence effects.

STRATEGIC ANALYSIS: DECISION-TO-ACTION DYNAMICS

A strategy to counter and deter WMD terrorism must begin with an analysis of the target of that strategy: whom we are trying to deter, what behaviors we are trying to affect, what objectives and strategy we are trying to deny, and what critical processes and people we must deny and influence. The brief analysis used here begins with attention to what stages of terrorism generate significant WMD threats. It then addresses the central decision-to-action dynamics, processes, and players that characterize a terrorist organization at the most dangerous level of development. Finally, it revisits that decision-to-action chain with specific attention to the dynamics, processes, and players critical to terrorist acquisition and use of WMD.

Terrorism Life Cycle and WMD Terrorism

Terrorist organizations experience a life cycle just like other organizations, and that life cycle can tell us important information about the potential for and danger of WMD acquisition and use. For this analysis we describe and analyze a representative four-stage development cycle: gestation, growth, maturity, and transformation.[8] Across the initial, or *gestation* phase, the group has yet to take form or differentiate its functions. It is here that the root identity cleavage is defined, the failure of government to address those roots is recognized, and the process of transforming the identity cleavage toward collective violence begins. The key concept here is identity: a perceived grievance of substantial consequence is defined in terms of an "us-them" divide with the "us" the deprived party, and the "them" defined around the causes of that deprivation. If this condition is widely perceived and defined in terms of an identity divide, and particularly if that identity cleavage is mobilized by charismatic leadership, a nascent organization and an accelerated pathway toward collective violence will result. But that violence would seldom, if ever, take the form of WMD terrorism at this phase of development.[9] The organization is not yet sufficiently sophisticated to be able to plan such an act, or to acquire, maintain, deploy, and employ complex weapons such as biological and nuclear weapons.

As the organization takes root, its goals are articulated and initial functions defined; the organization enters a *growth* phase. The focus here is on recruitment and socialization, basic resource development, and organizational development. Violence is most likely designed to "establish legitimacy, enhance recruiting, collect intelligence, and test tactics."[10] A relatively simple chemical action may be possible at this point, particularly as the organization transitions to maturity, but the nuclear or biological action of focus here would not yet generally be supported.

The *mature* phase of the organizational life cycle should be the primary focus of attention for interest in WMD terrorism. Organizational development is complete, the chosen form and functions are in place along with established internal and external relationships and linkages, a clear ideology and strategy have been formulated and articulated, and action output toward operational and strategic objectives has been generated. It is here that the organization has established the infrastructure to allow it to accept more-complex technologies and undertake more-complex operations; it is in the mature phase that WMD terrorism might be possible and plausible for a small number of advanced terrorist groups.

The final phase of the life cycle is the *transformation* phase. Terrorist organizations, like all other organizations, will inevitably experience a loss of congruence and vitality unless they can successfully regenerate, reinvigorate, learn, and adapt.[11] Some groups remake themselves in another form, perhaps joining the political process in a nonviolent form. Others divide into factions, perhaps with at least one faction even more violent than its parent organization. Others regenerate at an earlier phase in an altered form. Still others may die a natural or a violent death. Adaptive mature organizations, newly broken off super-violent organizations, or dying organizations all might be prone to and capable of WMD terrorism if the resources and weapons are in place at the end of the mature phase, so this phase warrants some attention as an extension of mature-phase WMD potential.

WMD weapons are complex, and even well-developed and otherwise technically competent groups have experienced prohibitive barriers to effective acquisition and use of WMD. Unformed, ill-formed, and unsophisticated organizations are not likely to be able to pose a significant WMD threat, nor are they likely to be successful targets of complex psychological coercion. It is acknowledged that a growth-phase group that came into possession of a fully operational weapon could pose a threat of WMD use on a local or limited scale. As noted, a transformation-phase group might pose a similar threat. However, this analysis focuses on terrorist organizations that have developed to maturity and that exhibit a fairly advanced level of technical, organizational, and operational infrastructure behind their decisions and actions. The denial strategies and deterrence effects developed here are tailored to that mature phase with advantageous spillover to limit or even prevent the catastrophic effects of limited WMD use by a group at a different stage of development.

Terrorism Processes and Players

In addition to indicating organizational life-cycle stages of concern, strategic analysis and a systems perspective can be used to identify critical dynamics, processes, and players in the organizational decisions and actions of terrorism. Identification of these key components allows the specification of targets for effective denial strategies. We begin by describing a dynamic chain of linked decisions and actions characteristic of mature terrorist groups.

As indicated at Figure 7.1,[12] the group decision-making process is founded in its identity. As discussed in addressing the gestation stage of the organizational life cycle above, identity is the foundation for the group's ideology and organization. Identity cleavages underlying collective violence can be based in ethno-political divides, economic or environmental conditions, or social and societal fractures, but perhaps most significant for catastrophic WMD terrorism are religion-based identity cleavages. Terrorism based in religious identity is characterized by uncompromising divides—the deepest division between the strategic "us" and the strategic "them," with no room for bridging that divide—and willingness to undertake mass-casualty attacks as sacramental acts.

Figure 7.1. Terrorism decision-to-action dynamics

The defined identity is mobilized via the group's ideology—its narrative that wraps strategic goals and purpose with traditional texts, myths, legends, values, beliefs, and norms. Identity provides the base and organizational vector, and ideology provides the vehicle for identity mobilization and the heart of organizational dynamics. Any strategic analysis of terrorism must proceed from a deep understanding of the critical foundation of identity and ideology.

From this expression of identity with its designation of goals, audiences and targets, and ideology, with its bounding context and justification, the guiding strategy provides a "theory of victory," an action plan that specifies and guides the range and interaction of efforts—political, social, psychological, and "military"—that proceed to fulfilling strategic objectives. Again, the strategy flows directly from identity and ideology, forming an objectives-driven chain of ideas, motivations, and actions. This chain then flows directly on to the organizational structure that accepts transformed recruits and other inputs, shapes that transformation and organizational sustainment, frames operational preparation and capability, and converts energy and resources into applied action as directed by the strategy and its objectives.

Finally, the flow proceeds to the specification of an operational doctrine—the operational code that translates strategic guidance, objectives, and organizational resources into instrumental, orchestrated acts that provide ever-advancing steps within the framing strategy and toward the ultimate goals. Tactics and targets at the operational point of attack are thus linked to and flow from this chain, from initial roots to ultimate objectives, with messages and audiences, weapons and targets, training and planning, all derived from identity and ideology through strategy and structure in an unbroken flow. This chain describes a deliberate and at least internally rational process that guides decisions and action for a mature terrorist organization.

Mature terrorist organizations depend on organizational processes, each with a cast of critical players, to sustain their organization and carry out actions. One characterization of the processes and players is at Figure 7.2, with the processes and players associated with the components of the dynamic decision-to-action chain. Decisions and actions begin with identity, and the associated foundational sub-process is leadership.

Leadership is a critical and core requirement for success for any activity, and it is certainly the critical core for any effective employment of terrorism. Richard Shultz discusses leadership as the most critical component of success for violent non-state actors. Since Clausewitz's "remarkable trinity" of state conflict (the military, the government, the people) does not apply for non-state actors and in characterizing al Qaeda by 2008 as pursuing a global insurgency strategy, Shultz states "the remarkable trinity for revolutionary insurgency movements, the *sine qua non* for success is an effective interrelationship between *leadership*, *ideology*, and *organization*."[13] And the role of leadership is to articulate and continuously revitalize the ideology and to build, maintain, and sustain the organization. Charismatic appeal and the ability to mobilize identity are often seen as central to success in ideological leadership. Several groups of the past and today differentiate these tasks, with a team leadership structure—separate ideological leadership and organizational/operational leadership—but in any case, and especially for decisions of consequence such

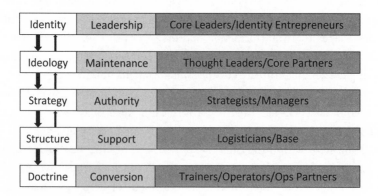

Figure 7.2. Terrorism key processes and players

as those revolving around WMD terrorism, a small core representing both the ideological and organizational elements will be involved. It is this small, central leadership core that will ultimately be the target of deterrence effects.

Successful terrorist organizations, those that progress to maturity and become capable of complex actions, must maintain ideological relevance and organizational vitality. The process that focuses on these internal organizational dynamics is *maintenance*.[14] Even as the ideological component of leadership works to socialize, energize, and guide a renewing and possibly growing human resource base, it also identifies the external audience that most closely identifies with that ideology. It is here that the organization looks for recruits and for its most critical partners.

The *authority* (or cognitive) process is focused on observation and learning, on formulating and adapting strategy toward achieving instrumental objectives en route to strategic goals, and on designing communications and specialized functional structures that the organization will rely on to enact that strategy. This is the operational and organizational brains of the group, as well as its command and control infrastructure.[15] These tasks require the blend of operational experience and expertise with clear strategic perspective, and the ability to structure and manage the implementation of strategy through other processes and players.

Support is the process that focuses on resources acquisition.[16] Terrorist organizations require human, financial, material, and operational resources, many of these specialized to the unique nature of terrorist activities. To list a few, terrorists require documents and travel assistance, operational weapons and expert knowledge of weapons types, safe havens from which to organize and operate, and financial assets sufficient to sustain the enterprise and its operations. The logisticians are important members of the group, and the linkages they forge with suppliers and supporters—their outreach to the broader base of ideologically aligned support as well as to profit-motivated suppliers of specialized goods and services—are indeed critical to organizational success.

Conversion is the output-oriented process that converts resources into action.[17] This process includes the provision of both basic and specialized training, and the tactical planning and direction as well as the actual conduct of tactical action. This action can be political, it can be focused on propaganda, it can involve economic and social operations designed to weaken an adversary, and it often does entail acts of applied collective violence. This is where the "rubber meets the road," and where expert and specialized operational knowledge must be imparted and applied, where specific teams, weapons, delivery mechanisms, and targets must be matched to ensure the generation of specific messages to specific audiences. Trainers and operators, sometimes including partner operators who can add specific expertise, are essential to success.

So mature terrorist organizations develop around specialized processes, each undertaken by its own specialized cast of players, and with each generally aligned with a link in the dynamic chain from decisions to actions for the group. A representative set of processes and players were presented here as relevant to mature terrorism in general, and examining these processes and players as tailored to WMD terrorism allows the designation of the levers and targets that can constitute denial strategies in that particular case.

Terrorism and WMD

The general terrorism analytical framework developed above can be refined to focus directly on WMD terrorism decisions and actions, processes and players. This refinement of dynamics for WMD terrorism is outlined at Figure 7.3.[18] The five factors identified here lead us to questions that must be asked and answered to determine whether and how a particular terrorist group might seek to acquire and plan to use WMD. Our position, one shared by others in this volume, is that terrorist groups do not universally covet WMD; that as with states, acquisition does not automatically equal use; and that any planned use would be the result of a most deliberate and strategically driven process.

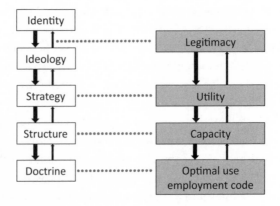

Figure 7.3. WMD terrorism decision-to-action dynamics

The identity and ideology that flow as the lifeblood of the terrorist organization directly determine the legitimacy, and thus the desirability, of acquisition of WMD weapons or materials. Identity plays a central role here. For states, "leaders' *conceptions of their national identity* . . . drive their choices for or against the [nuclear] bomb."[19] Jacques Hymans goes on to cite the *"self-other comparison"* when it is starkly dichotomized and when the state leadership interprets the relationship as one in which their group is rightfully equal to (or superior to) the other as central to decisions to acquire nuclear weapons.[20] And if leadership identity is the central component of state WMD decisions, collective and coherent identity across the terrorist core leadership, and out into its core partner base, would be central for terrorism as well. WMD must be seen as legitimate in terms of that defined and shared identity and its associated identity divide.

That identity is the foundational input to ideology for the group, so shared vision of the relationship between ideology and WMD is also crucial. The group leadership will undertake a careful analysis of how acquisition of those weapons, and particularly their use, would be perceived and reacted to by multiple audiences. The perceptions of the inner group members, particularly the core partners and direct support base as well as the primary recruitment base, and also of the broader and more general audience of desired influence, are central here. No group will willingly alienate its base, and the compatibility between the defined identity, guiding ideology, perceptions of legitimate use, and the consequences of WMD use must be carefully studied. Identity entrepreneurs and ideological thought leaders may make statements of justification to ease anticipated issues here, but the group will monitor reaction and test these waters continuously before the acquisition or use of WMD weapons. The WMD decision and direction cadre within the group will be small and will be close and trusted associates of the core leader(s). WMD possibilities and realities will not be shared outside the core until the weapons are actually acquired and postured, or possibly employed.

Strategy defines the group's "theory of victory," its strategic and operational objectives and broad action plan to achieve them. Good strategy integrates the objectives (ends) with avenues toward attaining those objectives (ways) and capabilities required to pursue those avenues of action (means). The operational component of group leadership must determine that in fact mass destruction "means" are both a compatible and superior "means" toward the near- and long-term "ends." It may well be that WMD are incompatible with the ends and/or the ways, offering operational and strategic effects that send the wrong messages to or generate the wrong reactions from the target audiences. Too much destruction and too many casualties may be counterproductive, alienating parts of the base and generating severe reactions from the target adversary. Further, for terrorist groups with territorial linkages and national bases, the externalities, lingering effects, and degree of destruction on their own territory might argue strongly against WMD as a viable option. In other cases, for apocalyptic groups for example, WMD might be a perfect fit with their identity, ideology, and strategy. However, in all cases these questions must be addressed before denial targets and strategies can be determined.

We began by asserting that only mature terrorist organizations would generally have the organizational capacity to acquire, maintain, deploy, and employ WMD. These weapons are complex and extremely difficult and expensive to acquire and use. The basic materials required for biological or nuclear weapons are difficult to process and bring to a level where weapons use is possible. Terrorist organizations, even those with sanctuary and advanced financial/technical capabilities, are not going to build cascades to enrich uranium to weapons grade, or to successfully and fully weaponize biological agents. Only states or state-based entities (state-linked agents operating covertly or as rogue actors) would realistically be able to provide either finished weapons or already weapons-grade materials. And even then, a significant level of sanctuary or safe haven, plus very significant expertise and resources, would be required to finish assembling and maintaining these weapons.

To examine only one aspect of capacity—expert knowledge—we borrow again from the state-based proliferation literature. Dennis Gormley in examining missile proliferation finds that "true technical knowledge is rarely just the product of explicit phenomena, such as easily acquired materials, drawings or blueprints, formulas, or even engineering notes, all of which can be purchased or transmitted via the internet. . . . Tacit knowledge cannot be written down: rather it is acquired through an often lengthy process of apprenticeship."[21] One often hears that you can get everything that you need to know to build nuclear or produce biological weapons from the Internet. However, Gormley's observation that "book knowledge" also requires "tacit knowledge," or actual experience, we assert applies equally here as it does to missiles, and the history of attempts to produce and employ biological weapons by terrorists certainly testifies to that requirement. Even in cases where rudimentary weaponization has taken place, the inability to deliver/employ has led to failure except in the case of a state-based player with access to state capacity.

So, expertise and experience, or human capacity, must be added to physical capacity, financial capacity, and other aspects of organizational capacity to support WMD terrorism. Acquisition and use of WMD requires the clear ability to absorb, assemble or otherwise prepare, maintain, deploy, and employ WMD, and those requirements exceed the capacity of all but a very few terrorist organizations.

Assuming all of the above hurdles are successfully overcome, at the operational level doctrine translates into questions of optimal use and tactics according to the group's employment code. We approach WMD terrorism as deliberate and as ideology and strategy driven. Just as ends and ways decisions from strategy determine the strategic utility of WMD means, types of WMD weapons, audiences and desired messages/effects, timing, and other strategic considerations will dictate the selection of tactical targets and attack details. Not every city or population, not every time and place, is optimal to enhance WMD terrorism in furthering the group's ideology and objectives. Even if the group arrives at this point of employment planning, it can still dilute or even counter the desired effects of WMD by selecting the wrong target and tactical details. Mature and sophisticated terrorist organizations will undertake a very deliberate and detailed study, planning, surveillance, and training process to optimize the use of this unique WMD asset.

These planning and operational details will also be consistent with the doctrinal and tactical practices that constitute the employment code, the modus operandi, of the group. Tactical team composition—for some groups and weapons this includes a member with tacit knowledge of the weapon and delivery or a charismatic "cheerleader" to ensure group motivation and commitment—will likely be tailored only slightly for the unique aspects of the weapon. Planning and preparation will be if anything more deliberate and intense for WMD. Movement to the target(s), particularly movement of WMD weapons, will be characterized by extreme care and stealth, but must also be undertaken within the group's capacity and may be consistent with past successful practices. Other aspects of operational security, limiting knowledge of or access to the weapon and operation, will be a core practice. If multiple targets are part of the code, then every effort to procure and deploy more than one weapon to more than one target should also be a characteristic of the operation. In short, the means may be uniquely WMD in this case, but the traditional known practices of the group will be present to at least a significant degree.

Thus, the identity-ideology-strategy-structure-doctrine chain defines the internal dynamics and external outreach of a mature terrorist organization. There are distinct processes—from leadership though maintenance, authority, support, and conversion—each with specialized players and roles, that can be identified and studied to determine a more complete picture of the specific dynamics of any given terrorist group. And finally, one can identify a parallel set of components that define the WMD dynamics, specializations of the processes, and designation of a smaller set of specialized players required for WMD terrorism. It is this set of dynamics, processes, and players that offers targets and strategies of denial to combat and ultimately deter WMD terrorism.

STRATEGIES OF DENIAL

Denial strategies should target adversary WMD capabilities as well as defend any targets that might, by denying those targets, render the adversary unable to achieve his strategic success.[22] The systematic, strategic analysis of a mature terrorist organization seeking to undertake WMD terrorism provides a map to appropriate denial targets. We return to the analysis above, and proceed to suggest representative denial targets and strategies from the tactical level on the WMD decision-to-action chain and work up.

Anticipating and disrupting the employment code, especially as it would be adapted for WMD employment, presents the first targets for denial. General antiterrorism actions applied at this level, such as national entry controls and documentation scrutiny for both humans and materials, can be enhanced and tailored toward specific WMD-relevant targets. Nuclear materials screening at ports and other entry points, for example, can be expanded and supplemented in cases where there is an indication of increased WMD threat. Specific personnel with tacit expertise can be added to watch lists at entry points, and patterns of "team" constitution and movement can be added to monitoring procedures. Physical requirements for WMD support and movement can be identified and monitored as well. Any indicators consistent with likely WMD movement and employment patterns for identified terrorist organizations or following identified training patterns can be highlighted for specific attention and interdiction.

Denial targeted at a group's employment code may seem too broad to implement with any hope of success. However, most actions there entail adjusting existing systems and practices to bring more focus to routine practices. These adjustments are narrowed by adding denial actions derived from targeting the terrorists' optimal-use calculations. Key here is that specific group identities, ideologies, and strategies will indicate optimal targets for WMD attack. For example, not every city constitutes an optimal target for such an attack. Given the likelihood that a group would only be able to acquire and deploy one, or at best a very small number of mass destruction weapons, it would not want to dilute the weapon's optimal effects by wasting it on a secondary or tertiary target. A nation can conduct a serious "red team" analysis of terrorist group optimal target criteria combined with an equally serious "blue team" assessment of a group's assets and come up with a short list of probable WMD target sites. The employment-code denial analysis can then be tailored for enhanced implementation with these sites as the base. The optimal-use denial analysis can then construct a short list of probable physical targets for hardening.

The point of denial at this tactical level is to deny access and opportunity to the targets and to deny or disrupt use of employment tactics that the terrorist group finds enhance its objectives and further its ideological goals. Which groups are targeting us with WMD? What do they stand for, and what are their ultimate and immediate objectives? What kind(s) of WMD are they capable of acquiring and using? How would they deploy, maintain, and employ such weapons? What targets in or related to my country are optimal within that context? How do I deny them access to those targets and their desired effects? Denial here seeks to delink terrorism from strategy-enhancing targets and effects. Denial actions of hardening, protection, blocking entry, and disrupting movement focused on the highest-value targets can at least delay or deflect WMD terrorism on their own, and they can contribute to wider effects when combined with denial actions at the operational and strategic levels.

Denial strategies aimed at capacity targets are a major focus of the overall effort to deny and deter. As developed above, capacity is the central determinate of WMD potential for the terrorists, and it also presents a range of targets for denial action. The full set of national and international policies aimed at countering WMD proliferation are relevant here, and these policies should be tailored to address proliferation networks as well as state proliferation to non-state actors. All "supply-side" WMD policy elements, from countering smuggling to weapons and materials accountability and controls, and from precursor and enrichment monitoring to law enforcement enhancements, can play a role in limiting capacity. Important efforts include countering terrorist finance, monitoring tacit expertise as well as special materials transfers, and denying sanctuary or safe haven within which to assemble or finalize weapons from prepared materials already acquired.

One set of targets and actions aimed at limiting terrorist capacity involves sponsors and enablers, and for WMD that implies state or state-based sponsors and enablers. Again, WMD final weapons and ready-to-finish materials are beyond the capacity of almost all terrorist groups. Only states and non-state providers possessing state WMD programs can provide these "finished" WMD resources. The United States under the Bush administration, Martha Crenshaw illustrates in her contribution to this volume, applied traditional deterrence-by-punishment threats in this case. While this strategy implies a traditional deterrence warning to both terrorists and sponsors, in effect the traditional deterrence is aimed at the state sponsors/enablers, which amounts to a denial effect on the terrorists themselves.

Note that as denial at the tactical level—denial of employment code and optimal use—was generally focused on one's own national territory and policy, much of the denial at the operational level aimed at denying capacity involves international cooperation and the use of multinational levers like treaties and laws. Denial strategies cannot be fully effective from a unilateral base, and national coordination—even integration—as well as international cooperation are essential for success.

Just as denial at the operational level built on and provided synergies with tactical denial efforts, denial at the strategic level builds on operational denial of capacity. Strategic denial targets, first, the terrorist strategy. Strategy specifies the goals and actions that will lead to attainment of the ideological end state. WMD must be seen as consistent with, as adding utility to, the execution of the strategy. Denying optimal-use targets or organizational capacity blocks the effective implementation of strategy. Psychological hardening of one's own population to terrorist intimidation, advancing international condemnation and cooperation against terrorism and its support infrastructure, and building barriers between terrorists and their key supporters act to deny strategic success.

The central element at the strategic level is the determination of legitimacy of WMD use by the terrorist leadership. It is difficult to act to deny that perceived legitimacy because it is founded deep within ideology, often with religious justification. If you are an outsider to that religion and its cultural traditions, active efforts to delegitimize WMD on that basis or attack the religious justification can easily backfire, and can actually harden the terrorist argument by generating the perception that you are interfering in or attacking their religion. Denial based on shared values and traditions emphasized through strategic communications efforts can perhaps weaken the "us-them" divide, thus weakening the argument for ultimate action on the terrorists' part, and other counterstrategy efforts can also contribute to raising questions in the terrorists' minds of utility and legitimacy. There also may be divided positions within the terrorist leadership on WMD legitimacy that can be accentuated. However, we must tread carefully, working quietly within their systems and communities but not creating any impressions of external manipulation or control that would actually fuel the terrorist cause.

WMD TERRORISM AND DETERRENCE BY DENIAL

So the strategic, systematic analysis of WMD terrorism presented a range of denial targets, as well as several levels of complementary denial strategies that together provide a framework for the design and implementation of a comprehensive effort to deny the terrorist organization successful use of WMD. This framework is summarized at Figure 7.4.

At the tactical base, the framework's focus is *denial of opportunity*, or access to the targets and tactics that would contribute best to the attainment of the terrorists' strategic goals. Blocking or muting a terrorist group's messages

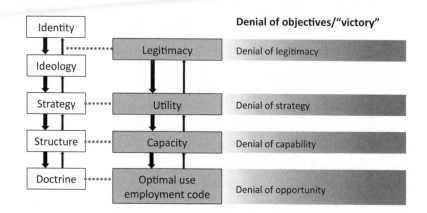

Figure 7.4. WMD terrorism and strategies of denial

to its intended audiences, forcing it away from the primary targets and forcing it to abandon its trained and trusted tactics that would ensure the generation of those messages and also lead to its other, shorter-term objectives, can contribute doubt and lead to delays, diversion to other targets, or decisions to abandon targets and WMD use. Adding the operational level, the focus here is on *denial of capability*, or blocking the resources needed to support WMD terrorism and ideally the weapons themselves. WMD are complex, expensive, technology intensive, and difficult to acquire and use even for states, and these barriers are even higher for terrorist organizations. Denying access to weapons or weapons-ready materials is a central goal. However, deterrent effects can also be achieved by denying organizational capability and support resources. Finances, technical (especially tacit) expertise, sanctuary or safe haven in which to finish and/or maintain the weapon—these are all targets that can lead to denial effects. Building on and adding to the overall effort, at the strategic level, focus is placed on *denial of strategy and legitimacy*. The goal is to create the perception in the mind of the terrorist leadership that it cannot achieve its objectives or fulfill its ideological goals through the use of WMD terrorism. Targeting terrorist strategy, blocking objectives and countering messages, building barriers between the terrorist and his support base add to these efforts. And ultimately the goal is to create doubt as to the legitimacy of WMD use within the context of the terrorist's ideology and collective identity.

CONCLUSION

This chapter has suggested an application of denial strategies designed to negate the objectives and rationale for WMD terrorism. The question remains, however, as to whether denial strategies constitute deterrence, or are simply considered tools in defending oneself against WMD terrorism. We argue that as you build from the tactical through the operational and to the strategic level, as you begin to attack and deny terrorist strategy and the foundation of legitimacy upon which it is based, that elements of deterrence are achieved. The terrorist leadership becomes convinced that WMD terrorism cannot fulfill its strategy and ideological goals; this amounts to denial of its theory of victory. This constitutes *net effect deterrence by denial* as envisioned but never fully enacted by the forefathers of deterrence. Further, if you reject that argument and insist that this can only be called denial actions in defense against WMD terrorism, the practical effects are nonetheless the same: muting and altering the threat, with net positive outcomes likely in the form of avoided or mitigated WMD attacks.

Our conclusions, then, are first that deterrence applied to WMD terrorism may not be *the* answer, but it certainly is an answer and is worth further consideration and analysis. Second, we conclude that terrorist organizations at the mature phase of development and at a level of sophistication that might enable systematic WMD terrorism are deliberate, internally rational entities, and that their core leadership and support elements are likely vulnerable to coercive influence. Third, we note that there may be at least limited roles for traditional, punishment-based deterrence strategies—particularly against state sponsors and enablers—but that these levers amount to denial of support to the terrorists. Fourth, we assert that there are critical dynamics, processes, and players within the terrorist organization, that these elements can be mapped as relevant to WMD terrorism, and that denial targets and layered strategies can be identified and designed toward the creation of a net effect of deterrence by denial of "victory" in the mind of the terrorist leadership. Fifth, these strategies are applicable and their WMD denial effects attainable even when applied within active campaigns of non-WMD terrorism and counterterrorism. Sixth, we argue that these denial efforts, even absent the posited net deterrence effect, constitute sound elements of combating WMD terrorism. Seventh, we see deterrence—and particularly deterrence by denial—as a fertile area of continuing inquiry as applied to terrorism beyond just that applied here to address the WMD threat. Finally, we conclude that piecemeal efforts at the national and international levels may be individually positive steps against WMD terrorism, but orchestrated synergies within a deliberate denial framework can magnify the individual effects of these efforts toward net effects that can indeed act to deter terrorism in at least some forms and directions.

NOTES

1. The most widely accepted definition of "WMD" is probably that adopted by the United Nations in 1948: "Atomic explosive weapons, radio-active material weapons, lethal chemical and biological weapons, and any weapons . . . which have characteristics comparable in destructive effect to those of the atomic bomb or other weapons mentioned above." This definition cites, in today's terms, nuclear, radiological, chemical, and biological weapons. Commission for Conventional Armaments, UN document S/C.3/32/Rev.1, August 1948, as quoted in United Nations, Office of Public Information, *The United Nations and Disarmament, 1945–1965*, UN Publication 67.I.8, p. 28. Cited

in W. Seth Carus, *Defining "Weapons of Mass Destruction,"* Center for the Study of Weapons of Mass Destruction Occasional Paper 4 (Washington, DC: National Defense University Press, February 2006), p. 3.

2. Glenn H. Snyder, *Deterrence and Defense: Toward a Theory of National Security* (Princeton, NJ: Princeton University Press, 1961), 9.

3. Bernard Brodie et al., eds. *The Absolute Weapon* (New York: Harcourt, Brace, 1946), 76.

4. Thomas C. Schelling, *Arms and Influence* (New Haven, CT: Yale University Press, 1966), 135.

5. Ibid.

6. Snyder, *Deterrence and Defense*, 15.

7. Schuyler Foerster, "Theoretical Foundations: Deterrence in the Nuclear Age," in *American Defense Policy*, 6th edition, ed. Schuyler Foerster and Edward N. Wright (Baltimore: Johns Hopkins University Press, 1990), 49.

8. Troy S. Thomas, Stephen D. Kiser, and William D. Casebeer, *Warlords Rising: Confronting Violent Non-State Actors* (Lanham, MD: Lexington Books, 2005), 96–98.

9. Ibid., 96.

10. Ibid., 97.

11. Ibid., 98.

12. Derived from James M. Smith, "Strategic Culture and Violent Non-State Actors: Concepts and Templates for Analysis," in James M. Smith, J. Mark Long, and Thomas H. Johnson, *Strategic Culture and Violent Non-State Actors: Weapons of Mass Destruction and Asymmetrical Operations Concepts and Cases*, USAF Institute for National Security Studies Occasional Paper No. 64, February 2008, p. 4.

13. Richard H. Shultz, *Global Insurgency Strategy and the Salafi Jihad Movement*, USAF Institute for National Security Studies Occasional Paper No. 66, April 2008, p. 26. Italics in original.

14. Ibid., 104–7.

15. Ibid., 107–12.

16. Ibid., 100–104.

17. Ibid., 112–14.

18. Derived from Smith, "Strategic Culture," 5.

19. Jacques C. Hymans, *The Psychology of Nuclear Proliferation: Identity, Emotions, and Foreign Policy* (Cambridge: Cambridge University Press, 2006), 16. Italics in original.

20. Ibid., 20–25. Italics in original.

21. Dennis M. Gormley, *Missile Contagion: Cruise Missile Proliferation and the Threat to International Security* (Westport, CT: Praeger International Security, 2008), 87.

22. This section builds on earlier ideas presented in less mature form in James M. Smith, "A Strategic Response to Terrorism," in *After 9/11: Terrorism and Crime in a Globalized World*, ed. David A. Charters and Graham F. Walker (Halifax, Nova Scotia: University of New Brunswick Centre for Conflict Studies and Dalhousie University Centre for Foreign Policy Studies, 2005); James M. Smith and William C. Thomas, "Deterring WMD Terrorism," US-Russian Federation Workshop on Strategic Crisis Management, Moscow, May 23, 2006; and James M. Smith and Brent J. Talbot, "Terrorism and Deterrence by Denial," in Paul Viotti, Nicholas Bowen, and Michael Opheim, eds., *Terrorism and Homeland Security: Thinking Strategically About Policy* (New York: Taylor and Francis, 2008).

8 PREVENTING RADIOLOGICAL TERRORISM
Is There a Role for Deterrence?

Wyn Q. Bowen and Jasper Pandza

IN THE CONTEXT of preventing radiological terrorism, most emphasis in the literature to date has been placed on making it increasingly difficult for terrorists to acquire and transit the necessary radioactive materials. Emphasis has also been placed on limiting the adverse effects should the worst happen, including the development of decontamination capabilities and educating the public about the health effects of radiation. Such defense and mitigation measures are important for obvious reasons. However, very little, if any, attention has been placed on strategies that could deter radiological terrorism, a gap this chapter starts to address by examining the potential for a deterrence approach that denies terrorists the success of a radiological attack.[1]

In thinking about deterrence theory, one can distinguish between deterrence by punishment and deterrence by denial.[2] In publications that focus on deterring terrorist use of an improvised nuclear device, most attention has been given to deterrence by punishment, which involves threatening terrorists and their sponsors with retaliation should they attempt to carry out a nuclear attack.[3] This would rely in part on nuclear forensic capabilities to swiftly and accurately attribute an attack to a particular state or non-state group. Yet the success of nuclear attribution—and consequently what deterrence by punishment could potentially achieve—remains unclear given the challenges associated with creating comprehensive data sets of fissile material signatures from around the world. It is even more problematic to use deterrence by punishment to counter radiological terrorism in particular, because the widespread availability of many different kinds of relevant radioactive materials and their higher susceptibility to theft combine to make attribution extremely difficult.[4]

The emphasis in this chapter will thus be on deterrence by denial. A denial strategy would seek to convince terrorists that they would not be able to achieve their objectives by carrying out a radiological attack. In other words, the aim would be to make non-state actors perceive the possible and probable gains to be lower than the possible and probable costs they would likely incur by preparing for and carrying out such an attack. Seeking to influence the outcome of their cost-benefit analysis would require effectively communicating the existence of capabilities to defend against and/or mitigate the consequences of an attack, so a deterrence approach will have to build on existing defense and mitigation capabilities rather than replace them.

The aim of this chapter is to identify and sketch out the potential for applying deterrence to counter radiological terrorism. The first section provides some background on what radiological terrorism entails, including the basic mechanisms of how radioactive materials cause harm, the materials of greatest concern, and relevant radiological "incidents" that have helped to shape understanding of the possible consequences of a radiological attack. This section also summarizes the general consensus view about the likely nature and impact of a radiological event, which, while unlikely to have massive catastrophic effects on the nuclear scale, would still have significant local and global security, political, and socioeconomic implications.

The second section then discusses deterrence by denial, making a distinction between "pre-event denial" and "post-event denial." The final section examines some of the thorny issues raised by thinking about a "post-event denial" approach to deterrence in this field. The lack of a historical record in the context of the terrorist use of radiological materials makes research related to how such use might be deterred in the future a challenging exercise. Nevertheless, by drawing on various scientific, technical, medical, and social science literatures, including both primary and secondary documentation, the chapter reaches some academically important and policy-relevant conclusions.[5]

RADIOLOGICAL TERRORISM

One of the most worrying aspects of radiological terrorism is that the range of attack scenarios is very wide, including some that could be classed as mass-casualty terrorism. While most scenarios would hardly cause any casualties, they would still likely cause widespread panic and have significant economic implications. This chapter considers all radiological attack scenarios with the exception of sabotage attacks on nuclear facilities, which require terrorists to overcome much larger physical protection measures compared with obtaining certain radioactive sources that are widely used in commercial, medical, and research applications and applicable to a variety of attack scenarios.[6]

Radiological dispersion devices (RDDs) have received most attention from security analysts thus far. They are devices that disperse radioactive material, either by the use of conventional explosives ("dirty bomb") or by technologically more challenging means involving sprayers.[7] As discussed below, the overall consensus in the literature is that an RDD would be very unlikely to cause many casualties, but it could cause significant public fear and anxiety and result in significant and long-term decontamination costs.

A more disquieting set of attack scenarios was identified by James Acton and colleagues, who considered the potential malign uses of radioactive materials through ingestion, inhalation, and immersion (termed "I³" attacks).[8] Getting victims to ingest or inhale radioactive materials is more challenging, but it has a greater potential to cause radiation casualties compared with a "dirty bomb" attack. The authors' discussion also raises awareness of the fact that radiological terrorism does not require a device that weaponizes radioactive material—the sheer use of radioactive materials for terrorist purposes is the defining feature of radiological terrorism.

Lastly, a radiological exposure device (RED) fully retains its material and relies only on ionizing radiation to pose an external health threat.[9] To suffer significant damage, however, a person would have to remain in close proximity to the source for an extended period of time, unless a very strong gamma emitter is used that could cause damage even with short exposure times. Figure 8.1 places these attack scenarios into the broad picture of radiological terrorism, though the figure is not necessarily complete, and certain scenarios might fit into more than one category.

Materials and Availability[10]

All radioactive materials cause physical damage to human health because of their ionizing radiation. This radiation ionizes atoms and molecules in a victim's body, leading to the breaking or alteration of DNA and the creation of free radicals that cause cellular damage (for example, radiation burns). At

Radiological terrorism					
Have terrorists obtained their own radioactive material?					
No	Yes				
Sabotage attack, e.g. on civilian nuclear infrastructure	Is the radioactive material to be dispersed?				
	No	Yes			
	Radiation emission device (RED); only gamma emitters would be useful	Is a device used to facilitate the wide dispersal of the material?			
		No		Yes	
		Simple scattering of radioactive materials	Inhalation, ingestion, immersion attack (I^3), i.e., an attack directly aimed to utilize the internal health effects of radiation	Radiological dispersal device	
				Is the dispersal facilitated with conventional explosives?	
				No	Yes
				Non-explosive options include sprayers, etc.	"Dirty bomb"

Figure 8.1. Major scenarios of radiological terrorism

radiation doses larger than roughly 0.7 gray, a very wide range of health effects can occur that are grouped as acute radiation syndrome (ARS). Symptoms of ARS will only become apparent days or weeks after exposure. Much further delayed is the development of cancer, which can occur two to ten years after radiation exposure and which follows a random or "stochastic" model.[11]

A wide range of radioisotopes are used in industrial and medical applications. In the context of radiological terrorism, about nine radioisotopes are considered to be of high security risk should they lose their physical protection or should they become abandoned ("orphaned").[12] Factors that determine the security risk include "energy and type of radiation; half-life of the radioisotope; amount of material; shape, size, shielding, and portability of the source; prevalence of use; and how dispersible is the source material."[13] The material's half-life is the time it takes for half of the radioactive nuclei in a sample to undergo radioactive decay. A half-life shorter than a few days will mean a source loses most of its radioactivity before it can be used in an attack. A half-life longer than a few thousand years means that the source's level of radioactivity is too low to cause much harm to human health. The dispersibility of a radioisotope depends on its physical and chemical properties. Powdered forms, for example, will be much easier to disperse than metallic forms. Gram quantities of some radioisotopes are sufficient to see them as a security concern.[14]

Ionizing radiation is a by-product of the nuclear decay of radioisotopes and can be roughly divided into alpha, beta, and gamma radiation.[15] The kind of radiation determines whether a certain radioactive source, which contains many atoms of a particular radioisotope, poses an internal or external health hazard and what kind of shielding is required to protect the human body from damage and to hide the source from detection. Radioactive sources often emit a number of different kinds of radiation, but one usually dominates. For example, a cobalt-60 source predominantly emits gamma radiation and some smaller amounts of beta radiation; cobalt-60 is therefore classed as a gamma emitter.[16]

Radioisotopes emitting gamma rays are the only ones that pose an internal *and* significant external hazard to health, meaning they are dangerous even when they are not ingested or inhaled by the victim. In contrast to alpha or beta radiation, gamma radiation does not consist of small particles, but of electromagnetic waves that can penetrate significant amounts of matter without being weakened.[17] One can think of them as very strong X-rays known for their medical uses. Gamma radiation can only be confidently shielded with sheets of lead or thick layers of other dense materials. While a wide dispersion of gamma ray emitters would make the work of first responders and decontamination teams very difficult (full body protection and a respirator mask can only reduce the radiation dose to some extent), terrorists would likewise find it difficult to hide these materials from detectors. Gamma radiation is readily and easily detectable. Furthermore, terrorists handling a strong gamma source are likely to receive a very large and potentially lethal radiation dose themselves, as adequate shielding is difficult to achieve with limited technical capabilities. This is a point that might be exploited in constructing a pre-event denial approach to prevent radiological terrorism, as some terrorists may not be willing to put themselves in such danger. Three of the nine high-risk radioisotopes are strong gamma ray emitters: cesium-137, cobalt-60, and iridium-192. They are used in commercial and medical applications (for example, to sterilize food or to irradiate cancer tumors). The effects of removing physical protection from powdered cesium-137 are evident from the 1987 Goiânia incident, discussed in detail below.

As mentioned, sources emitting alpha and beta radiation pose a significant risk to health only when they are inhaled or ingested. Alpha radiation, made up of relatively large helium nuclei, cannot penetrate the outer layer of skin or even a few centimeters of air.[18] Yet alpha particles carry a large electric charge and, should they be emitted from inside the body, can cause substantial internal damage. Beta particles, essentially highly energetic electrons, carry less electric charge than alpha particles, but they are much lighter.[19] Consequently, thin sheets of metal or thick layers of fabric can be used to shield against beta radiation, so it predominantly poses an internal health hazard.

Alpha and beta emitters are mostly used for industrial purposes, and they come in various physical and chemical forms. The 2006 assassination of Alexander Litvinenko in the United Kingdom demonstrated the lethality of ingesting the alpha ray emitter polonium-210. Because polonium-210 almost exclusively emits alpha radiation, which does not escape the body, it was only identified as the poison after Litvinenko's death.[20] Alpha sources are particularly easy to transport, and in contrast to gamma emitters they will appeal to terrorists who want to minimize the radiation dose they themselves receive. A notable radioisotope emitting beta rays is strontium-90. Within the former Soviet Union, it was used as a power source for small generators placed in isolated locations.[21] Each of these generators contains a very large amount of this radioisotope and therefore continues to pose a security risk.

Terrorist Appeal

In a summary of cases where terrorists' interests in radiological weapons have surfaced, it has been noted that "there have been relatively few examples of terrorists in general showing unambiguous interest in radiological weapons."[22] Yet at the same time, it must be emphasized that both security experts and intelligence services have been in agreement for several years that it is well within terrorists' ability to acquire radiological weapons.[23] The closest terrorists appear to have gotten in using a radiological weapon involved the 1995 placement of an undetonated dirty bomb in Moscow's Izmailovsky Park by Chechen rebels.[24]

The lack of historical cases of terrorist use of radiological weapons evidently complicates how we think about preventing and responding to large-scale radiological events. The closest and most relevant case in this area was a nonterrorist-related radiation accident in Goiânia, Brazil, in 1987.[25] This event involved the discovery of an abandoned radiotherapy unit by scrap metal workers at an old hospital site in Goiânia. The therapy unit had used a cesium-137 radiation source. Cesium-137 is a strong emitter of gamma and beta radiation and, when used for medical purposes, comes in the form of soluble and readily dispersible cesium chloride salt. The workers were fascinated by the blue glow of the cesium chloride, and fragments of the substance were consequently distributed among family and friends. It took fifteen days from the time the source was discovered until staff in the local hospital realized that a major radiological incident was unfolding. By then, several people had become very ill due to radiation sickness, and many more had received significant radiation doses. Table 8.1 illustrates the scale of the challenges that confronted the authorities in Goiânia.[26]

In the context of deterring radiological terrorism, three important points can be highlighted when considering Goiânia. First, just a handful of cesium-137 chloride can evidently produce significant human suffering and enormous economic and psychological effects. Second, the economic and psychological effects were predominantly the result of individuals who were worried about the health effects of radiation and consequently overwhelmed the health-care system. The 112,000 people who sought medical attention were disproportionate to the number of people who actually needed it—the latter figure being only 0.22 percent of the 112,000. Third, the dispersal of the cesium chloride was not facilitated by any kind of relatively sophisticated mechanism, such as a sprayer or the detonation of conventional explosives. When discussing the terrorist use of radiological materials, a limited focus on RDDs and dirty bombs may therefore be misguided, because potentially greater harm can be generated without terrorists having to overcome significant technological hurdles. The delay in detecting the Goiânia event by the local authorities obviously holds relevant lessons for terrorist events that use more surreptitious methods of dispersal than a detectable explosion.

The public perception following the more recent radiological poisoning of Litvinenko appears to confirm the above conclusions. To understand the public perception of risk to health, a telephone survey was carried out by researchers at the King's College London Institute of Psychiatry. About 12 percent of the survey respondents perceived their health to be at risk, despite the UK Health Protection Agency communicating that risk existed only if people had visited one of two potentially contaminated locations within a specific time frame. Interestingly, most of the 12 percent wrongly believed that Litvinenko's poisoning was linked to terrorism rather than being an assassination and therefore a criminal act targeting one person. The study concluded that both successful risk communication by the Health Protection Agency,

Table 8.1. Consequences of the Goiânia accident

Health effects	• 249 people were found to be radioactively contaminated, and 49 of these were admitted to hospital.
	• 4 people died within one month from conditions associated with the ARS (having received doses of 5.5–6 gray). All of them had extremely close contact with the cesium powder.
Decontamination	• 85 houses were significantly contaminated, and seven had to be demolished.
Waste issues	• 3,000m³ of radioactive waste remains to be stored close to the city and must stay there for another 300 years.
Public response and resulting effects on health care and the economy	• 112,000 people went to be monitored for radiation sickness. The majority did so at an improvised screening station set up in a stadium.
	• Nearly 75 percent of these people went spontaneously. The vast majority were not contaminated or otherwise directly affected by the incident.
	• The accident had "great psychological impact" on the population due to fears of "contamination, irradiation . . . and fatal diseases."
	• Due to those widespread psychological effects, the sale of the produce of Goiás State (in which Goiânia is located) fell by 25 percent.

and the predominant perception that the incident was related to crime or es-
pionage, contributed to limiting the public's concern about their health. These
findings suggest that public health concern would be much larger if a similar
incident of the same scale had in fact been terrorist in nature.[27]

Both cases provide valuable empirical insights into the public's reaction to
a major radiological attack. Should terrorists carry out a radiological attack,
they are likely to create large-scale social and psychological disruption, although not necessarily on the scale of the Goiânia event. Moreover, understanding the likely public reaction allows governments to work toward
minimizing the potential negative aftereffects of an attack before it takes
place. Thus, efforts to build resilience and to manage public risk perception
can be important parts of a post-event deterrence-by-denial approach.

Casualties Due to Radiation

The impact of a dirty bomb in an urban setting has received by far the greatest attention in publications that study the effects of radiological terrorism.
The magnitude of the health effects that could be inflicted on the public
would depend, among other things, on the radioisotope used, the degree to
which the material is dispersed, atmospheric conditions such as wind speed

and direction, and whether victims are subject to internalizing radioactive material or just external exposure.[28] The general consensus is that a dirty bomb scenario would cause very few, if any, casualties due to radiation effects. Indeed, one study has estimated that being directly involved in a dirty bomb attack carries a lifetime health risk of smoking five packs of cigarettes.[29] Yet, it is worthwhile to consider two further empirical studies that suggest that the number of casualties in such events is likely to be very low.

First, the Sandia Aerosolization Program at the U.S. Sandia National Laboratories has been running for twenty years, and over six hundred RDD-related explosions have been carried out to study how radioisotopes disperse following an explosion. The amount of material aerosolized influences how many people would be likely to inhale it and subjected to more severe internal health effects. The program has found that both the properties of the radioactive material and the RDD device design have a significant influence on the amount of material aerosolized.[30] So, the amount of radioactive material aerosolized is highly variable and depends on the amount used and design issues; it appears therefore that terrorists would be unlikely to build an efficient RDD without advanced knowledge of material properties and bomb design.[31]

Second, researchers at the Institute for Transuranium Elements, a European Commission nuclear research institute located in Germany, applied a simple mathematical model to understand the long-term health effects related to cancer after the dispersion of radioactive materials. The excess number of cancer deaths over a period of fifty years (short-term ARS effects were not included in the study) after a detonation of a cobalt-60 dirty bomb in a large city was calculated to be just one. If two kilograms of highly radioactive mixed oxide (MOX) nuclear reactor fuel were dispersed, the excess number of cancer deaths was calculated to be 335. Yet even this number is too small to have a statistical significance in cancer deaths.[32]

It would appear, then, that the lack of radiological terror attacks to date could well be due, in part at least, to terrorists wanting to inflict large-scale casualties and their related perception that the possible gains from using radiological materials (in terms of casualties) are insufficient to warrant this unconventional approach. This may be especially relevant given that more-conventional terrorist methods have a proven track record in this respect. While Acton and colleagues have done some preliminary investigation on I^3 attack scenarios—events that may well cause more radiation casualties than dirty bombs—further in-depth studies on the feasibility and consequences of such attacks would be valuable.

Psychological and Economic Impact and Mitigation Measures

It is useful to define the phrase "psychological effects" used throughout this chapter in more precise terms. Psychological effects can broadly be divided into short-term distress and long-term psychological disorders.[33] All disasters can cause such effects and terrorist events even more so because they are initiated deliberately and are usually perceived to be unpredictable and uncontrollable. Distress is a normal reaction to a terrifying event and dissipates over time. Psychological disorders occur more rarely but require long-term specialized treatment. They include post-traumatic stress disorder, anxiety disorders, and depression. One aspect that remains consistent across different scenarios of radiological terrorism is that both the psychological and economic effects are likely to be very high. Indeed, these effects offer greater traction for terrorists contemplating the use of radioactive materials in hopes of generating fear and confusion. As Daniel Barnett and colleagues submit: "Radiation is an especially powerful terrorism weapon because it instills considerable fear. . . . It is physically imperceptible, requiring sophisticated monitoring equipment for detection; its carcinogenic potential includes a long latent period; exposure—especially from a terrorist act—is involuntary; and such exposure is potentially fatal."[34] Radiological terrorism is therefore likely to have a significant impact on the mental health—in terms of causing distress and psychological disorders—of people directly affected by an attack, but is also likely to have a similarly strong psychological impact on those who are not directly affected. It has been suggested that in a worst-case scenario, the use of radiological weapons could potentially "disrupt social order and overwhelm emergency response and medical systems."[35]

The Goiânia incident illustrates the discrepancy between actual public health risks and public perception of these risks. In order to manage public risk perception and minimize the adverse psychological impact that a radiological attack could have on society, preparing the public for a radiological event in order to create a degree of resilience, as well as ensuring effective government communication once an event has occurred, would appear to be essential if the consequences of an attack are to be effectively mitigated. When a government communicates the risk of CBRN terrorism after an event,

Brooke Rogers and colleagues write, "it is critical that truthful, consistent information is provided and regularly updated by trusted sources." The authors continue: "Effective public communication has been shown to encourage appropriate protective actions from at risk populations, reassure individuals who are not directly at risk by reducing rumours and fears, facilitate relief efforts, and maintain public trust and confidence in the agencies responsible for ensuring the welfare of the public."[36]

In addition to these psychological effects, radiological terrorism is likely to have an economic impact by making affected commercial areas temporarily unusable and by necessitating potentially very costly decontamination activities.[37] Decontamination is understood as the removal of radioactive material from buildings and structures. In this regard it must be noted that technologies and expertise for decontaminating large urban areas appear to be wanting. In 2004, it was concluded that "there are no well-established technologies for wide area decontamination of modern built-up areas."[38] A later study based on interviews with officials in relevant U.S. government agencies found that "existing decontamination techniques and procedures cannot facilitate quick, efficient recovery in a large urban environment" and that, in worst-case scenarios, effective decontamination would take "billions of dollars and years or even decades to complete."[39] Moreover, as of 2009 in the United States, there was no official guidance for identifying cost-effective decontamination methods in the event of a radiological attack, according to the U.S. Government Accountability Office.[40]

In summary, a radiological attack is unlikely to cause mass casualties. However, there is significant scope for such an attack to cause major economic and societal disruption. On this basis alone, some non-state actors may view the use of radiological materials as worthy of exploration because of the potential to cause mass effects. If there is to be a role for deterrence, then, one option might involve seeking to manipulate terrorist perceptions of the potential economic and societal disruption associated with a radiological event.

DETERRENCE AND RADIOLOGICAL TERRORISM

This section focuses on working through a denial-based concept for deterring radiological terrorism, likely the most realistic way of applying deterrence theory in this context. Indeed, there is a case for building on the consensus view already established—that few people will be killed in a radiological attack—by focusing on post-event denial capabilities that aim to make terrorists believe that states can effectively minimize the economic and societal disruption of radiological events. A denial approach would involve seeking to convince non-state actors actively pursuing (or contemplating) the acquisition and/or use of radiological weapons that capabilities exist to prevent them from realizing their objectives. In short, deterrence would focus on the fear, concern, and anxiety on the part of the actors to be deterred that they would not easily realize their objectives. Importantly, there are pre-event and post-event dimensions to this "deterrence-by-denial puzzle."

Pre-event Deterrence by Denial

The pre-event dimension involves deterring terrorists by convincing them that their operations will be thwarted prior to any planned dispersal of radiological materials because capabilities exist to prevent them from first acquiring the necessary materials and, if that fails, to then detect and disrupt subsequent operations before any release occurs. Some aspects of the "capability" in this area are directly related to counterterrorism as a whole, including intelligence collection and analysis on the intentions and operations of non-state actors, while others are specifically targeted at the radiological and nuclear dimensions. Key examples of the latter type include the development and deployment of radiation-detection capabilities designed to detect the presence and movement of radioactive materials. Operation Cyclamen in the United Kingdom is one example of a specific project to develop a national radiation-detection capability targeting radiological terrorism.[41] Detection involves large portal-monitoring systems, on road access points at ports and land borders, for example, but also the use of smaller, hand-held radiation detectors.

Another approach specific to radiological and nuclear terrorism includes threat-reduction activities in Russia and other former Soviet states to secure potential source materials. In the years ahead, risks will need to be addressed as part of the potential "nuclear renaissance" where relevant infrastructure and knowledge may spread to regions prone to inter- and intra-state conflict, like the Middle East and Southeast Asia.

Binding all this together, of course, is the challenge of how to communicate denial capabilities to specific or generic individuals and groups with the aim of deterring a radiological terrorist attack. Pre-event denial communication would need to raise the perceived effectiveness of capabilities to secure materials and protect borders. This could involve publicizing the implementation of new physical security measures or of instances where radiological material has been interdicted at borders. Additionally, most terrorists are not suicidal, so communications should also emphasize the likelihood of receiving a dangerous or lethal dose when handling and transporting strong gamma emitters, even when materials are not ingested.

Post-event Deterrence by Denial

By demonstrating an advanced capability for rapidly responding to a radiological attack, minimizing its physical, psychological, and economic impact, and quickly recovering (or at least generating the perception that such a capability exists), it may be possible to create sufficient uncertainty in the minds of non-state actors about their ability to achieve their strategic objectives. The end result might be to convince terrorists that radiological attacks are not worth the time and effort. This post-event dimension also involves a perceived resolve on the part of the deterring party—including government officials and decision makers, emergency responders, and perhaps most important, the general public—to deal with the consequences of a radiological event in a robust and comprehensive fashion if and when pre-event deterrence should fail. How consequences are managed and mitigated is of central importance. As Barnett and colleagues write, "The response to a radiologic terrorist event will involve multiple disciplines from all levels of government, including emergency medical systems, fire, law enforcement, radiation experts, hazardous material (HazMat) teams, public health officials and health care providers."[42] A radiological event may also require "the ability to manage large populations in contaminated urban areas for long periods of time, potentially years."[43] There are three key areas in terms of post-event response: decontamination, the medical response, and risk communication to the general public. Each of these capabilities and activities would need to be built into a post-event denial approach for deterring radiological terrorism.

ISSUES AND PROBLEMS ASSOCIATED WITH POST-EVENT DENIAL

Now that the general appearance of a deterrence-by-denial approach has been outlined, the next section identifies some of the issues, dilemmas, and problems that are raised when thinking about building deterrence on post-event capabilities and activities.

Decontamination and Medical Countermeasures

Decontamination (that is, cleanup) is central to the recovery process, yet as illustrated in the first section, it is likely to be an expensive and time-consuming process measured in weeks, months, and potentially years, depending on the quantity and type of radiological material dispersed. However, deterrence by denial requires convincing terrorists that a relatively quick and politically acceptable level of recovery from a radiological attack is feasible. Issues related to standards and levels of decontamination are central to thinking about mitigating the effects of a radiological event. An example here might be the technical capability to accurately measure the extent of radioactive contamination following an attack, as a U.S. Government Accountability Office report outlines. If baseline radiation levels are already on record for a city or region as a result of previous background radiation surveys, it would be possible, following an attack, to focus on decontaminating areas "up to pre-existing levels of radiation rather than fully removing all traces of radiation."[44] This will reduce the time required for and the overall costs of cleanup and more quickly allow for a rapid return to normal life.[45]

Is there room to incorporate such thinking into a deterrence-by-denial strategy? As already noted, there are two important audiences: the non-state actors that might contemplate carrying out a radiological attack, and the general public. With the former, the focus is on putting terrorists off from carrying out their plans by undermining their confidence that sufficient disruption would be caused by such events. With the latter, there is the question of whether lowering decontamination standards, and communicating this ahead of any event as part of a public strategy, would have unintended and detrimental effects—notably reducing public confidence rather than reassuring them about the potential for recovery.

Investment in pre- and post-event medical countermeasures could also ameliorate the negative psychological effects likely to be associated with a radiological event and contribute to deterrence by denial. After an event, medical treatment always starts with the external decontamination of patients, unless immediate life-threatening problems exist that have to be dealt with first.[46] Radioactive materials sitting on the skin or on the clothes of the patient pose an immediate health risk because they can easily be inhaled or enter the body through open wounds and cause internal damage. External decontamination involves the removal of clothes, followed by washing hair and skin. Should the patient be internally contaminated, more-complex toxicological challenges and procedures apply. This may involve attempts to facilitate the excretion of the radioactive material and, depending on the internalized radioisotope, the administration of relevant treatment, such as Prussian blue (ferric ferrocyanate) for cesium-137 or diethylenetriaminepentaacetate (DTPA) for americium-241.[47]

In the case of a radiological attack that involves the dispersal of a large amount of radioactive material, many victims will have to be treated at the same time. Treatment would likely take place close to the scene of the incident with triage of casualties that includes the external decontamination of all victims and the provision of first aid.[48] Whether patients are internally or externally contaminated, or whether they were only irradiated but not contaminated, ARS symptoms will only occur at a later stage. Treatment will then depend on the actual dose received. Patients can be managed as outpatients if they have received up to 2 gray, while others require hospitalization.[49]

For an effective post-event response, medical staff treating victims need to be trained and prepared prior to any event, and the capability must exist to decontaminate many people, as quickly as possible and at short notice. However, multiple studies have found that "most general practitioners are uncertain about the health consequences of exposure to ionizing radiation and the medical management of exposed patients."[50] Besides establishing appropriate decontamination capabilities to respond to radiological incidents, this deficit in training will need to be tackled to maximize the likelihood of an efficient response to a worst-case scenario. Communicating such preparedness and capabilities ahead of time should help the public realize that mortality rates can be reduced significantly, even after a severe radiological attack. If the same message is simultaneously transmitted either directly or indirectly, overtly or covertly, to terrorist groups, then this may influence their decision calculus against pursuing radiological attacks.

Communicating with the Public

Public resilience in the face of terrorism is one of the most important factors in denying terrorists the fruits of their labor. Utilizing resilience to inform denial-based approaches to deterrence is essential. One of the key issues here is public communication and the ability to maximize the scope for reassuring people about the risks associated with radiation—which are usually exaggerated in the public psyche—and to sell the prospects for cleanup and effective medical countermeasures. Doing so should help build public confidence that something can and will be done if an event occurs. However, communicating to the public in this area is fraught with difficulties. How much information should be given to the public, and how should it be communicated? Moreover, as the U.S. National Academies have noted, this "type of attack would likely involve localized loss of life and no immediate danger to surrounding populations or property, but the potential for misinformation and public panic would be high."[51] In the radiological field, the public education aspect is absolutely essential if the aim is to bolster the prospects for deterrence. A measured approach will obviously be needed, one that develops over time to incrementally educate the public.

However, it is difficult not to view the public communication dimension in the radiological field as a potentially double-edged sword. For example, are not politicians, in particular, likely to be wary about overselling mitigation capabilities, given the risk of political backlash should a radiological event prove disastrous?

Communicating with Terrorists

On the issue of communicating with terrorists, an initial question that arises is whether this should be done overtly or covertly. The latter approach suggests the targeting of specific groups or individuals, while the former approach appears better suited to a more generic target audience. There are some risks to communicating deterrent messages to non-state actors in this area. For instance, does communicating radiological response capabilities risk unintentionally identifying capability gaps and vulnerabilities for terrorists to target? Relatedly, there is a risk that preparing for and communicating an ability to mitigate the impact of a radiological event might inadvertently send a contradictory message to adversaries that measures to prevent an attack are weak and/or likely to fail. Does post-event deterrence by denial, then, interfere with and potentially negate communication on pre-event denial capabilities?

Likewise, some terrorists might even interpret denial communications as a challenge to *pursue* radiological attacks. What are the risks, for instance, that groups not currently contemplating the use of radiological terrorism might be motivated to do so given government communications that demonstrate a real worry about these types of attacks? If the motivation to use radiological materials is in fact low, then the best denial strategy might be to focus on post-event denial but with limited pre-event communication. This is obviously a question of finding a balance, but providing an answer in the absence of previous events against which to measure policy options is difficult. Consider further the potential for negative displacement effect. By effectively eliminating a particular activity, do we inadvertently force terrorists to identify alternative approaches that are worse in terms of their effect (for example, abandoning explosive RDD dispersal for passive RDD dispersal)? Finally, given the inevitably limited resources available to most governments, are there post-event trade-offs in terms of the types of capabilities that governments should focus their investment and energy on in the context of deterring radiological attacks? Is there an optimal balance that can be struck between specific post-event capabilities in the pursuit of effective deterrence?

No Comparable or Previous Event

As suggested, assessing the prospects for deterring radiological terrorism is difficult in the absence of previous events. This leads to the important question of whether it will take a failure of prevention and/or deterrence in the field of radiological terrorism to actually strengthen future deterrence prospects. The answer to this, of course, will be dependent on how such an event (the first of its kind) is dealt with, how the worst aspects of radiological terrorism are mitigated, and how resilient the targeted society turns out to be. If, following the first radiological attack, a society and state successfully deal with the crisis in a relatively effective manner, then future deterrence prospects might get a boost. On the other hand, if the first radiological attack is perceived as a major terrorist success, then other groups may be motivated and encouraged to pursue similar attacks. Deterrence will be weakened as a result. It has been argued, for example, that "the degree of social disruption" following a radiological event "will influence whether RDDs might continue to be used as a terrorism modality."[52] The lack of previous events obviously complicates the issue of communicating to both terrorists and the public because of the absence of what might be called a "baseline experience." There is no way to compare crisis events, reconstruction efforts, defensive capabilities, and so on. Public exercises in dealing with radiological scenarios, though limiting, offer one way through which to communicate preparedness in the absence of such a baseline.

CONCLUSION

This chapter was designed as a "straw man" to stimulate a debate over the desirability and feasibility of applying a denial-based approach to deterrence in the context of preventing radiological terrorism. Particular emphasis was placed on the post-event aspect of denial. This was done by providing some technical background on radiological terrorism, including the materials of greatest concern, their widespread availability in the industrial and medical sectors, and relevant radiological "incidents" that have helped to shape understanding of the potential for terrorist use of radioactive materials. The application of deterrence to prevent these types of incidents was then discussed, with a main focus on the role of deterrence by denial rather than deterrence through the threat of punishment. A distinction was also made between deterrence based on "pre-event denial" capabilities and deterrence based on "post-event denial" capabilities.

The latter part of the chapter then examined some of the issues raised by thinking about a "post-event denial" approach to deterring radiological terrorism. It is evident that the thorniest issues relate to communicating deterrence. At one level it involves communication to the general public about the risks associated with radiological terrorism and the capabilities that exist to mitigate the effects of a radiological event. Importantly, for deterrence to work, public resilience is a key aspect of the "capability" to deter through a denial-based approach. Striking the right balance in terms of how much and what type of information to publicly communicate prior to any future radiological event is a delicate matter and fraught with challenges, notably avoiding unnecessary public anxiety. Moreover, the lack of a radiological event to date, and therefore the lack of real experiences in dealing with the aftermath—the Litvinenko affair notwithstanding—complicates the process of communicating to both the public and to hostile non-state actors. A related problem is communicating preparedness to non-state actors, either openly or more covertly. Doing so might unintentionally identify capability gaps and vulnerabilities and provide terrorists with insights into what they need to do to get around those post-event denial capabilities that exist.

NOTES

1. This research was carried out at the Centre for Science and Security Studies at King's College London as part of a MacArthur funded grant. Deterrence in the context of conventional and WMD terrorism has been addressed by, for example, Michael Levi, *Deterring State Sponsorship of Nuclear Terrorism*, Council Special Report No. 39 (New York: Council on Foreign Relations, 2008); Lewis Dunn, "Can al Qaeda Be Deterred from Using Nuclear Weapons?" Occasional Paper 3, Center for the Study of

Weapons of Mass Destruction (Washington, DC: National Defense University Press, 2005); Michael Powers, "Deterring Terrorism with CBRN Weapons: Developing a Conceptual Framework," Occasional Paper 2, Chemical and Biological Weapons Arms Control Institute (2001); Wyn Q. Bowen, "Deterrence and Asymmetry: Non-State Actors and Mass Casualty Terrorism," *Contemporary Security Policy* 25:1 (2004); Wyn Q. Bowen, "Deterring Mass-Casualty Terrorism," *Joint Force Quarterly* 31 (2002); Robert Trager and Dessislava Zagorcheva, "Deterring Terrorism: It Can Be Done," *International Security* 30:3 (2005/6).

2. Lawrence Freedman, *Deterrence* (Cambridge, UK: Polity Press, 2004), 36–40; Glenn Snyder, *Deterrence and Defense: Toward a Theory of National Security* (Princeton, NJ: Princeton University Press, 1961), 14–15.

3. See, for example, Michael Miller, "Nuclear Attribution as Deterrence," *Nonproliferation Review* 14:1 (2007); Michael May et al., eds., *Nuclear Forensics: Role, State of the Art, Program Needs* (Joint Working Group of the American Physical Society and the American Association for the Advancement of Science, 2008).

4. However, the basic technical capabilities to apply forensic analysis on radiological sources exist: Klaus Mayer, Maria Wallenius, and Ian Ray, "Nuclear Forensics—a Methodology Providing Clues on the Origin of Illicitly Trafficked Nuclear Materials," *Analyst* 130:4 (2005).

5. We are indebted to Andreas Wenger, Alex Wilner, and G. James Rubin for their feedback on this chapter.

6. National Research Council Committee on Science and Technology for Countering Terrorism, *Making the Nation Safer: The Role of Science and Technology in Countering Terrorism* (Washington, DC: National Academies Press, 2002), 41–48.

7. Charles Ferguson and William Potter, *The Four Faces of Nuclear Terrorism* (Routledge: New York, 2005), 259; Daniel Barnett et al., "Understanding Radiologic and Nuclear Terrorism as Public Health Threats: Preparedness and Response Perspectives," *Journal of Nuclear Medicine* 47:10 (2006): 1645.

8. James Acton, M. Brooke Rogers, and Peter Zimmerman, "Beyond the Dirty Bomb: Re-Thinking Radiological Terror," *Survival* 49:3 (2007); Peter Zimmerman and James Acton, "Radiological Lessons—Radiation Weapons Beyond 'Dirty Bombs,'" *Jane's Intelligence Review* (2007).

9. Ferguson and Potter, *Four Faces*, 271.

10. For an elaborate technical introduction see Charles Ferguson, Tahseen Kazi, and Judith Perera, "Commercial Radioactive Sources: Surveying the Security Risks," Center for Nonproliferation Studies, Monterey Institute of International Studies, 2003, 2–7.

11. Barnett et al., "Understanding Radiologic and Nuclear Terrorism," 1656–57; Doran Christensen et al., "A Practical Basis for Early Management of Radiological Injured or Ill Patients: Ionizing Radiation Physics and Instrumentation, Radiation

Protection, Contamination Control, Dosimetry, and Radiological/Nuclear (R/N) Terrorism," in *Toxico-Terrorism: Emergency Response and Clinical Approach to Chemical, Biological, and Radiological Agents*, ed. Robin McFee and Jerrold Leikin (New York: McGraw-Hill Medical, 2007), 447.

12. The nine are americium-241, californium-252, cesium-137, cobalt-60, iridium-192, plutonium-238, polonium-210, radium-226, and strontium-90. See Ferguson, Kazi, and Perera, "Commercial Radioactive Sources," 16; and Argonne National Laboratory "Radiological Disperal Device" (2005).

13. Ferguson, Kazi, and Perera, "Commercial Radioactive Sources," 13–14.

14. Ibid., 15.

15. James Turner, *Atoms, Radiation, and Radiation Protection*, 3rd ed. (Weinheim, Germany: Wiley-VCH, 2007), 55–61.

16. Argonne National Laboratory, "Radiological Disperal Device," 3.

17. Turner, *Atoms*, 68–71.

18. Ibid., 62–65.

19. Ibid., 65–68.

20. BBC News, "Timeline: Litvinenko Death Case," July 27, 2007.

21. Ferguson, Kazi, and Perera, "Commercial Radioactive Sources," 12; Argonne National Laboratory, "Radiological Disperal Device," 3.

22. Charles Ferguson, "Radiological Weapons and Jihadist Terrorism," in *Jihadists and Weapons of Mass Destruction*, ed. Gary Ackerman and Jeremy Tamsett (Boca Raton, FL: CRC Press, 2009), 185.

23. Central Intelligence Agency, "Terrorist CBRN: Materials and Effects," 2003, 2.

24. Ferguson, "Radiological Weapons," 186.

25. This paragraph draws from International Atomic Energy Agency, "The Radiological Accident in Goiânia," 1988, 1–2 and 22–26.

26. Ibid., 2–4; International Atomic Energy Agency, "Goiânia's Legacy Two Decades On," March 7, 2008.

27. G. James Rubin et al., "Public Information Needs After the Poisoning of Alexander Litvinenko with Polonium-210 in London: Cross Sectional Telephone Survey and Qualitative Analysis," *British Medical Journal* 335:7630 (2007): 1143–45.

28. Barnett et al., "Understanding Radiologic and Nuclear Terrorism," 1645.

29. Joseph Ring, "Radiation Risks and Dirty Bombs," *Health Physics* 86:2 (2004): S42.

30. Frederick Harper, Stephen Musolino, and William Wente, "Realistic Radiological Dispersal Device Hazard Boundaries and Ramifications for Early Consequence Management Decisions," *Health Physics* 93:1 (2007): 1–4.

31. Ferguson interprets the results as showing that "most dirty bombs would not produce significant amounts of aerosolized radioactive material and thus would not pose significant health risks for inhalation." Ferguson, "Radiological Weapons," 184.

32. Joseph Magill et al., "Consequences of a Radiological Dispersal Event with Nuclear and Radioactive Sources," *Science and Global Security: The Technical Basis for Arms Control, Disarmament, and Nonproliferation Initiatives* 15:2 (2007): 113–17.

33. M. Brooke Rogers et al., "Mediating the Social and Psychological Impacts of Terrorist Attacks: The Role of Risk Perception and Risk Communication," *International Review of Psychiatry* 19:3 (2007): 280–85.

34. Barnett et al., "Understanding Radiologic and Nuclear Terrorism," 1658.

35. Ibid., 1655.

36. Rogers et al., "Mediating," 283, 279.

37. Peter Zimmerman and Cheryl Loeb, "Dirty Bombs: The Threat Revisited," *Defense Horizons* 38 (2004): 9–10; Barnett et al., "Understanding Radiologic and Nuclear Terrorism," 1655.

38. Zimmerman and Loeb, "Dirty Bombs," 9.

39. Jennifer Bulkeley, "Decontamination and Remediation After a Dirty Bomb Attack—Technical and Political Challenges," *Nonproliferation Review* 14:1 (2007): 132–33.

40. United States Government Accountability Office, "Combating Nuclear Terrorism: Preliminary Observations on Preparedness to Recover from Possible Attacks Using Raiological or Nuclear Materials," 2009, 10.

41. UK Home Office, "Pursue Prevent Protect Prepare: The United Kingdom's Strategy for Countering International Terrorism," 2009, 126.

42. Barnett et al., "Understanding Radiologic and Nuclear Terrorism," 1657.

43. Committee on Science and Technology for Countering Terrorism, *Making the Nation Safer*, 58.

44. United States Government Accountability Office, "Combating Nuclear Terrorism: Federal Efforts to Respond to Nuclear and Radiological Threats and to Protect Key Emergency Response Facilities Could Be Strengthened," 2007, 3.

45. The extent to which pre-event radiation surveys really decrease the cost of urban decontamination efforts is probably small, however, because it is the aim of decontamination efforts to reduce radiation levels so that they do not pose a significant health threat, and it is unlikely that pre-event radiation levels were at such high levels already. Nonetheless, knowledge about pre-existing radiation levels alone, and the capability to determine them, demonstrate some advanced decontamination capability to both the public and potential terrorist adversaries.

46. Doran Christensen et al., "Diagnosis and Medical Management of Radiation Injuries and Illnesses," in McFee and Leikin, *Toxico-Terrorism*, 452.

47. Barnett et al., "Understanding Radiologic and Nuclear Terrorism," 1658; Christensen et al., "Diagnosis," 460.

48. Barnett et al., "Understanding Radiologic and Nuclear Terrorism," 1658.

49. Ibid.

50. István Turai et al., "Medical Response to Radiation Incidents and Radionuclear Threats," *British Medical Journal* 328:7439 (2004): 568; M. Carol McCurley et al., "Educating Medical Staff About Responding to a Radiological or Nuclear Emergency," *Health Physics* 96:5 (2009): S50.

51. Committee on Science and Technology for Countering Terrorism, *Making the Nation Safer*, 58.

52. Barnett et al., "Understanding Radiologic and Nuclear Terrorism," 1655.

EMPIRICAL EVALUATIONS

9 DETERRENCE OF PALESTINIAN TERRORISM
The Israeli Experience

Shmuel Bar

THE OBJECTIVE of this chapter is to analyze Israeli successes and failures in deterring and/or compelling non-state Palestinian terrorist groups since the beginning of the Second Intifada (2000).[1] During this period, Palestinian terrorist organizations posed the greatest threat to day-to-day Israeli security. While not a primary objective, deterrence played a role in shaping Israeli counterterrorism responses.

The threat to Israel posed by Palestinian terrorist organizations is an expansive one. A number of diverging subgroups with disparate allegiances, motivations, goals, and capabilities threaten Israeli security. First, highly institutionalized terrorist organizations, like Fatah Tanzim, the Al-Aqsa Martyrs' Brigades, and the Popular Resistance Committees, originate from the ruling political party, Fatah, of the Palestinian Authority (PA) and continue to enjoy political, organizational, and financial links with PA security apparatuses. Second, opposition organizations within the PA, like Hamas, retain both a terrorist and a social-political infrastructure within the Palestinian territories, have strong roots to the populace, and offer various levels of spiritual, political, and military leadership. Third, pure terrorist organizations with little social or political infrastructure, like the Palestinian Islamic Jihad and Ahmad Jibril's Popular Front for the Liberation of Palestine / General Command (PFLP/GC) act as proxies of Iran, have no real political leadership within the Palestinian territories, and are effectively run from Syria and Iran. And fourth, residual Marxist organizations, like the Popular Front for the Liberation of Palestine (PFLP) and the Democratic Front for the Liberation of Palestine (DFLP), continue to organize violence, if only sporadically, but have increasingly transitioned into political actors and have achieved a certain degree of legitimacy as a result. The complexity of Palestinian terrorism complicates the manner in which Israel can develop and apply deterrence to counterterrorism. The primary focus here is to assess Israel's deterrent relationship with Fatah and Hamas in particular.

In evaluating Israeli deterrence in combating terrorism, the chapter asks three interrelated questions. First, how do Fatah and Hamas threaten Israel, and what factors motivate these organizations? Second, did Israel have a clear policy of deterrence in its relations with these terrorist organizations, and if so, how did it signal and communicate its deterrent (direct/indirect, military/diplomatic), and was its policy consistently upheld by different governments? And third, how did Fatah, Hamas, and the Palestinian Authority interpret Israel's deterrent capability and willingness to respond to provocations, and were these perceptions situation dependent or linked to specific Israeli leaders?

These questions are addressed with reference to events that repeatedly tested and shaped Israel's deterrence vis-à-vis these organizations. Three recent milestones are of particular importance: (1) Israel's withdrawal from Lebanon in May 2000; (2) the outbreak of the Intifada in October of that year; and (3) Hamas's takeover of Gaza, the abduction of Israeli soldier Gilead Shalit in 2006, the shelling of neighboring Israeli towns, and Israel's eventual military response in January 2009 (Operation Cast Lead).

General findings suggest that Israel was able to achieve a degree of intermittent deterrence against Palestinian terrorists. That success, however, was limited to the very few occasions where terrorist leaders were in firm control over the violence orchestrated by their followers and in cases where Israel properly and credibly communicated deterrent threats. More often than not, neither factor was particularly prevalent, to the overall detriment of Israeli deterrence/compellence.

The argument is structured as follows: Section one introduces the core concepts of deterrence/compellence and applies them to counterterrorism. Section two outlines Israel's deterrent doctrine with respect to counterterrorism. Section three evaluates how Israeli deterrence functioned in practice against Fatah and Hamas. Section four assesses the coercive effects and unintended consequences of Israeli targeted killings in particular. The chapter concludes by expanding on the lessons derived from the Israeli case study on the subject of deterring terrorism more generally.

DETERRING TERRORISM: RELEVANT CONCEPTS

The concepts used in this study are borrowed from modern theories of deterrence. However, these concepts tend to focus on the relationship between states and on the high end of potential conflict: confrontation between regular armies and/or nuclear conflict between states. The result is that these theories naturally overshadow traditional descriptions of coercion that have existed since time immemorial both in the relations between states and between states and non-state actors (insurgents, guerrillas, terrorists). Today's asymmetric relationship between states and non-state terrorist organizations renders state-to-state doctrines of deterrence unsuitable to many cases. Importantly, however, the asymmetry differs from case to case. The degree of statelike attributes of the organization, for instance, or the functional links between an organization and a state can have a significant influence on the type of strategies that can be implemented to coerce the organization in question.[2] Hence, two "entities" that are usually overlooked in accounts of classical interstate deterrence must be addressed when applying deterrence to terrorism: the "host state" and the "patron state." The relationship between the terrorist organization to be deterred and the host/patron state can help determine where deterrence is best applied (whether against terrorist leaders, supporting populations, and/or external facilitating entities). In the case of Fatah and Hamas, their relations with various host and patron states created both avenues and shortfalls for Israeli deterrence.

This study also makes a distinction between *strategic* and *tactical* deterrence. Israel succeeded in maintaining strategic deterrence vis-à-vis neighboring states with both high-end conventional capabilities on the ground and in the air and with its perceived possession of nonconventional (that is, nuclear) capabilities. These capacities, however, had little relevance to Israeli attempts to deter terrorist organizations. Furthermore, strategic interstate deterrence has been based on the *perception* of Israel's capabilities rather than on the use of these capabilities. State adversaries trust that Israel has the capability to act as it threatens. Deterrence of terrorist organizations, on the other hand, has been based—when it existed—on tactical deterrence through day-to-day actions, which accumulate and shift perceptions of Israeli deterrent objectives and resolve. Perceptions of Israeli counterterrorism resolve and willingness to act are far less objectively constructed than perceptions of its military capability. These perceptions are also laden with cultural and psychological overtones that pass through overlapping prisms of history, culture, language, ideological axioms, modes of transmission, and reception of information by non-state adversaries. Transmitting signals of resolve to combat terrorism requires that Israel identify the decision makers (and their interests) to be threatened, adapt its signals to resonate with the individual psyche of the adversarial leadership in question, and uncover the dynamics underpinning the leadership's threat assessment. In discussing and evaluating tactical deterrence, all of these processes must be assessed.

Finally, any discussion of deterring terrorism must also address individual characteristics related to adversarial leadership, societal factors, and ideology. In the first case, the type of leadership against which deterrence is directed, along with attitudes toward risk, the nature of the assets leaders value, the kind and quality of relations between leaders and other elites, the particular mechanisms of decision making, and, most important, the degree of personalization of the political cause with the leadership itself, all leave a mark on how deterrence is applied to counterterrorism in practice. In terms of societal factors, the influence social and economic elites have on the decision-making process and fault lines that exist between different sectors within society may render deterrent threats against one group irrelevant when applied to another. Finally, ideology, whether secular or religious, can complicate deterrence by manipulating a target's Weltanschauung (or worldview) in ways that diminish the efficacy of deterrent messages. This is not to propose that the "rational actor model" does not apply to religiously motivated terrorist groups, but rather suggests that the information on which these groups make their decisions may include elements that are considered irrelevant or even nonexistent by the deterrer. Without taking into account the possibility that the target leadership may be factoring in divine intervention, for instance, it may be difficult to understand its actions. While one might correctly argue that all of these same factors are relevant to decision-making processes within states (and influence strategic deterrence as a result), most governments and regimes are less "polycratic" and tend to operate within organized decision-making mechanisms. For the most part, these critical issues remain relevant to the theory and practice of deterring terrorism rather than deterring states. In light of these factors, the following section explores Israeli policy and doctrine of deterring terrorism.

ISRAELI POLICY AND DETERRENCE DOCTRINE

Did Israel have an actual doctrine or policy of deterrence vis-à-vis Palestinian terrorist organizations, or was Israeli policy exclusively directed at prevention, disruption, and preemption of terrorist attacks? A preliminary conclusion of this study is that Israel never formulated a comprehensive doctrine for deterring terrorism. The conventional wisdom in Israel holds that terrorist organizations cannot be effectively deterred and must be fought until extirpated.[3] Consequently, the political sensitivity associated with counterterrorism in Israel precluded any official doctrine of deterrence, as doing so would necessarily have implied an acceptance that terrorists could not be eradicated.

Nevertheless, there was a consensus among Israeli security leaders that the preventive and preemptive steps that were implemented had a temporary and tactical deterrent effect on terrorist organizations. In light of Israeli pressure, Palestinian leaders did seem to weigh the launching of terrorist attacks according to a cost-benefit calculus that factored in whether or not Israel's reaction would neutralize the anticipated benefits of the attacks. Israeli security experts tended to characterize this phenomenon as "operational discretion" on the part of the terrorist leadership, rather than deterrence. Importantly, the calculus was not due to the mere threat of Israeli force but rather to the actual application of force and the fear that it would be reapplied in the future.

These preventive and preemptive policies became the backbone of Israel's de facto deterrence doctrine for the Palestinian theater. They can be divided into two main categories: *preventive* and *proactive* strategies. Preventive security measures included a variety of strategies meant to impede terrorist movement and communication. They included bolstering defensive security at potential target sites, imposing travel restrictions on Palestinians, closing passages to Gaza, and erecting other roadblocks. These steps were taken as disruptive tactics intended to compel terrorists to postpone attacks or to change their plans in a manner that would facilitate further disruption, but they were also used as a means to bring popular pressure to bear on terrorist leaders. Other preventive tactics included punitive measures, like the demolition of a terrorist's home and the expulsion of suspected terrorists from Gaza to the West Bank (and vice versa), and economic and political pressure applied directly against the populace, like curfews and territorial closures. It was assumed that these pressure tactics would result in a groundswell of petitions from the local leaders to the "warlords" within the Palestinian territories and from there to the terrorist operators living abroad to rein in the level of violence—if only temporarily—and facilitate an easing of Israeli sanctions.

Proactive security measures included both offensive and defensive tactics. They included targeted killings (known in Hebrew as "focused disruption") of key terrorist planners and leaders both in the Palestinian territories and, according to unverifiable reports, abroad; arrests inside Palestinian population centers; wide-scale military actions, like Operation Defensive Wall (or Defensive Shield, March–May 2002); the "siege" of Yasser Arafat's compound in Ramallah; and threatening Arafat with expulsion from the West Bank/Gaza (WBG). Israeli counterterrorism policy in WBG has been one of constant disruption to arrest and eliminate wanted terrorists and confiscate arms. While the primary motivation of these proactive measures was operational in the context of disrupting terrorism, the corollary of deterrence, when it emerged, was added value.

Of all preventive and proactive counterterrorism tactics, the targeted killing of top- and medium-level terrorist leaders has been a central (and controversial) feature of Israel's struggle with Palestinian terrorism and a key element of deterring future terrorism.[4] A number of historic examples are widely perceived as showcasing the tactic's efficacy. First, the elimination of the Fatah/Black September terrorists involved in the Munich Olympics massacre (1972) in Operation Spring of Youth was viewed by Israel not only as retribution but as projecting a message of deterrence by demonstrating the "long arm" of Israel's operational capability, intelligence dominance, and resolve.[5] As a result of these operations, Fatah effectively ceased orchestrating international terrorism for a period of years, and Black September—the pseudonym of the "Unified Security" apparatus of Salah Khalaf (Abu Iyyad)—ceased to exist altogether. The decision to refrain from international terrorism was formalized by the Palestine Liberation Organization (PLO) in 1974.

By 1985, however, Fatah, the PLO's largest faction, renewed its involvement in international terrorism by killing three Israeli tourists in Larnaka, Cyprus, torturing two Israeli sailors to death in Barcelona, Spain, and hijacking the cruise liner *Achille Lauro* and murdering Jewish American passenger Leon Klinghoffer. Israel responded by bombing PLO headquarters in Tunis, Tunisia, in October 1985. After this episode, Arafat concluded that the price of orchestrating international terrorism was too high and committed Fatah to the "Cairo Declaration" and a cessation of such acts. The Israeli bombing in Tunis served two deterrent purposes. Not only was it direct deterrence by punishment against the PLO and its leadership, but it also functioned as indirect deterrence against the PLO's host country—Tunisia. Unlike Lebanon, which did not have the capability to impose its will on terrorist organizations active within its territory, the Tunisian government did, and effectively put pressure on Arafat following the bombing.

Targeted killings do have their detractors, though. The debate within Israel, and between Israel and other countries, concerns the possible counter-productivity of targeted killings insofar as they potentially increased the mo-tivation of the targeted organization. The fact that many terrorist attacks in Israel were attributed by their perpetrators as acts of revenge for the elimina-tion of certain figures by Israel contributed to the belief that targeted killings not only failed to deter terrorism but actually fed a cycle of violence. This logic, however, was never accepted within Israel's security community, which continued to assert that a leadership with a sense of impunity contributed to the scope of terrorist planning, whereas a leadership dedicating operational resources to evasion and survival was less capably involved in terrorism. This assumption was borne out at the beginning of the Second Intifada. The Pales-tinian organizations and Fatah in particular acted on the premise that their political leadership would enjoy immunity and that Israel would only target field operatives. This assumption was based on a number of factors, including the outcome of the Khaled Masha'l affair,[6] Israel's de facto policy of refraining from targeting political leaders, domestic considerations in light of links be-tween Palestinian leaders and influential Israelis, and the general assumption that international pressure would constrain Israel from targeting political figures.

As the Intifada intensified, however, Israeli policy changed. Israel began targeting high-echelon Palestinian leaders as well as low-echelon "ticking bombs." From 2001 onward, Israel implemented a comprehensive policy of targeting leaders and individuals involved in terrorism from a range of Pales-tinian organizations, from the Palestinian Islamic Jihad (PIJ) and Hamas to Fatah and the PFLP. It was believed that such actions, though primarily meant to disrupt terrorism, had a cumulative deterrent effect because the cost of planning attacks (in the loss of terrorist infrastructure and know-how and in the death of a large number of terrorist leaders and operatives) was greater than the expected benefit the attacks were meant to achieve.[7] Following al Qaeda's 2001 attack on the United States, the international political climate also shifted dramatically in Israel's favor, and there was greater international understanding for its predicament in combating suicide terrorism and greater leeway for carrying out targeted killings.

As the level of Palestinian violence increased, Israel continuously raised the price of involvement in terrorism. From the outbreak of the Intifada, Israel gradually added more prominent leaders and erstwhile "immune" figures to its list of targeted individuals. Notable watersheds included the killing of the PFLP's secretary general in August 2001 and the siege of Arafat's Ramallah headquarters in April 2002, which indicated that even heads of organizations with political wings were not immune; the arrest of Fatah leader and member of the PA legislative council Marwan Barghouti, in April 2002, which signaled that members of the Palestinian legislature who had close connections with Israelis could also be targeted; and the killings of Hamas leaders Salah Shehadeh in July 2002, Sheikh Ahmad Yassin in March 2004, and Abd al-Aziz Rantisi in April 2004, which indicated that all levels of the Hamas leadership were "fair game." Israel's targeted killing policy was both preventive and deterrent. It was believed that the elimination of leaders and operatives served not only a disruptive goal but also induced an atmosphere of fear and caution within leadership circles that translated into less terrorist activity. This belief rang true. Israeli statements following the killing of Yassin and Rantisi that the targeted killings of Hamas leaders would continue virtually paralyzed the group's leadership in Gaza. The top echelon of the organization went underground, and it was rarely seen in public. Furthermore, though the organization announced that it had selected a new leader to replace Rantisi, it chose not to name him publicly.

Notwithstanding these reputed successes, there have been unintended consequences of eliminating Hamas's Gazan leadership, with deleterious effect on Israeli deterrence. Israeli targeted killings gradually marginalized the decision-making power of Hamas's local leaders, shifting the organization's power base to Hamas's "external" leadership living outside the WBG. Thus, while Israel may have weakened Hamas locally by targeting its leadership, it also inadvertently complicated (and weakened) its subsequent ability to deter/ compel Hamas activity by shifting the organization's balance of power outside its immediate field of operations. In the following section, this and other paradoxes of Israeli deterrence of terrorism are explored in greater detail.

ISRAELI DETERRENCE: ARAFAT, ABBAS, AND HAMAS

In the years prior to the Oslo Accords (1993), Israel's deterrent image was at its acme: it had demonstrated its military prowess by killing Arafat's deputy and head of the "Western Sector" of Fatah, Khalil al-Wazir (Abu Jihad), in Tunis in 1988, the First Intifada had all but fizzled out, and Israel had come out of the first Gulf War (1990–91) with tangible gains (like the Madrid peace conference and American assurance that the PLO would not take part in it). At the same time, the PLO leadership was at an all-time nadir: Saudi Arabia and the Gulf states had boycotted Arafat, the PLO was suffering serious cash-flow problems, and its international leadership (exiled to Tunisia) had lost its influence in the West Bank and Gaza to a burgeoning local leadership. The PLO's much-diminished status played a role in enhancing Israel's own perception of its deterrent image.

In the beginning of the Oslo Accord era (1993–96), Israel had no strategy of deterrence toward Arafat. Its strategy was to entice him to renounce terrorism and to dismantle his terrorist apparatuses by offering future benefits derived from the success of the Oslo process. It is widely accepted by Israeli decision makers that Arafat's refusal to accept these incentives was both ideological and strategic; he could neither forgo the "armed struggle" nor list those involved in it as "enemies of the state" and, at the same time, believed that by keeping Fatah as a "strategic reserve" for future terrorism (all the while Hamas continued to perpetrate terrorist attacks), Israel would be forced to make future concessions. By the mid-1990s, however, Israel shifted its policies and put pressure on Arafat and the PA, which it considered responsible not only for terrorism perpetrated by Fatah and the PA's security apparatuses but for being complacent in Hamas attacks as well. Ostensibly, then, Israeli efforts to deter/compel Fatah by pressuring and/or threatening the PA (and Arafat personally) were also intended to have an indirect deterrent effect on Hamas.

The period of the Second Intifada (2000 onward) was fraught with Israeli attempts to dissuade Arafat from encouraging terrorism. Early Israeli threats of retaliation during the first few months of the Intifada lacked credibility in Palestinian eyes. However, this changed after the 9/11 attacks and following the February 2001 election of Ariel Sharon as Israel's prime minister. Arafat's appeal of December 16, 2001, to refrain from terrorism was motivated by his ultimate understanding that 9/11 had tipped the scales in Israel's favor: al Qaeda's attack had caused a fundamental change in the Western world's (in) tolerance toward terrorism; Israeli reactions to Palestinian attacks would be viewed more sympathetically; and U.S. military engagement in Afghanistan would overshadow Israeli action against the PA. In addition, from mid-November 2001, public opinion polls in Israel indicated that Ehud Barak's

Labor government would fall and that Arafat's historical nemesis, Sharon, would be elected prime minister with a mandate to more firmly deal with Palestinian violence. Arafat's assessments enhanced Israel's deterrent positions and compelled him to attempt to diminish the level of terrorism. In fact, following Arafat's call of December 16, the number of weekly terrorist attacks diminished from one hundred to seventy-nine, and then from forty to twenty.

The Israeli "siege" of Arafat's Ramallah headquarters in May 2002 effectively imprisoned him until his illness and death in November 2004. Israel's ostensible goal was to induce Arafat, who still had broad control over Fatah's various factions and apparatuses, to rein them all in. In effect, the Israeli policy was based on the assumption that direct personal pressure on the group's top leadership would bring about a change concerning the sponsorship and facilitation of terrorism. Ultimately, in the case of Arafat, this did not materialize. He withstood Israeli pressure until his death, rejecting pleas by Fatah colleagues and leaders to acquiesce to Israeli demands.[8] While the Israeli siege strategy did result in protracted negotiations over the terms for freeing Arafat, it did not produce the deterrent or coercive effect that was intended. Inasmuch as personal pressure did result in commitments on the part of Arafat to restrain Fatah terrorist activities, these commitments were given in order to satisfy international (U.S. and British) and Arab pressure and were not the result of public Israeli pressure.

At the same time, the Israeli military and security leadership debated whether or not Palestinian terrorism was a "bottomless pit" or one with a floor, and if the latter, how close Israeli counterterrorist efforts were to reaching that floor. The former view was espoused by Military Intelligence, while the director of the Israel Security Agency (Shin Bet), Avi Dichter, adopted the latter. The "bottomless pit" view led to the conclusion, as it was formulated by the chief of staff, Moshe (Bugi) Ya'alon, that Israel had to "burn into the Palestinian and Arab consciousness" that terrorism simply did not pay.[9] This goal called for building a "blocking wall" that would demonstrate to the terrorist organizations that their efforts to cause significant damage to Israel were in vain while simultaneously directing measures against the Palestinian population (as detailed above) to induce it to put pressure on the Palestinian organizations to end terrorism against Israel.[10] None of these steps achieved the desired goal of deterrence or compellence either.

The reasons for Israel's failures during the Arafat era are many. First, Arafat's personalized authoritarian rule and focus on personal interests reduced his willingness to acquiesce to Israeli pressure. When petitioned by Fatah leaders to restrict Fatah's terrorist activity and to crack down on Hamas in order to lower Israeli pressure, Arafat refused, on the grounds that any concession he would give would only be used to increase the pressure upon him. Israeli pressure was employed against the "Palestinian Authority" as an entity, on the assumption that Arafat would perceive threats against PA interests as detrimental to himself. However, this classic deterrence cost-benefit calculus did not apply; Arafat's frame of reference was personal, not collective. His main interest was his own personal survival as head of the PA, and he perceived any concession to Israeli demands as a contribution to a greater Israeli scheme to depose him.

Second, Arafat governed with a strategy of "controlled chaos," the intention of which was that he, and only he, would be able to rein in and control the anarchy that he encouraged. The strategy preserved his indispensability. And yet, eventually the policy diminished Arafat's own ability to control the chaos he himself had generated. Since deterrence is predicated on the existence of a command structure that can translate a leadership's deterrent acquiescence to the ground, the chaotic decentralization that took place in the PA and Fatah made such translation difficult. This problem was compounded by the fragmentation of the Palestinian society, which made it virtually impossible for Israel to find a deterrent or incentive that could operate equally on all—or even most—political factions and terrorist groups. Any Israeli act that created a deterrent on one group only encouraged another to inherit its place and initiate further acts of terrorism.

Finally, the level of violence inherent to Palestinian society since the First Intifada (and increasingly so since the Second Intifada) precludes the "public's" influence over violent organizations. Palestinians who eschew the culture of violence or those that do not want to pay the price for terrorism simply do not have the confidence in their personal security to protest or act against terrorist groups. This characteristic of the "host society" neutralized Israel's ability to apply indirect deterrence through Palestinian society with threats against its collective interests.

Some of these deterrent limitations disappeared with the demise of Arafat. Others, however, remained permanent factors of the Palestinian theater. Arafat's policy of controlled chaos eventually created a multipolar terrorist space in the West Bank and especially in Gaza. No one "address" existed for Israeli deterrence. While Arafat was at the helm, he could conceivably have used his personal influence and financial clout to rein in the various groups and factions. With his death, no individual within the PA had enough power to influence the plethora of warlords who had taken over the Palestinian territories.[11] The result was that subsequent leaders, like Mahmoud Abbas (Abu Mazen), lacked the control over Fatah operatives that Arafat had. Even if Israel were to compel him to rein in the violence, Abbas had no way of doing so in practice; he had no leverage for transferring Israeli deterrence to the "warlords" of Fatah, and even less with regard to Hamas. Even with Abbas's 2005 presidential election, the PLO and the PA denied Israel its deterrent levers that had existed under Arafat. Not only did Abbas lack the power to respond to Israeli pressures, but the very fact that he, and not Arafat (whose international credibility had been tarnished), had became the target of Israeli deterrence restricted the scope and breadth of coercive pressure Israel was willing to wield. Israeli restraint was not due to international pressure but rather based on an interest to perpetuate and enhance Abbas's leadership. Israeli leaders understood that Abbas's position on the peace process offered the most likely avenue to foster reengagement and future negotiation, so they self-imposed restrictions on their deterrent/compellent tactics.

The election of the Hamas government in the 2006 legislative elections was interpreted by some in Israel and in the international community as a potential blessing in disguise. According to one theory, gaining legislative power provided Hamas with "something to lose," its electoral victory giving Israel a deterrent/compellent leverage to wean it away from its policies of terror. It was assumed that the Palestinian public, in dire need of a respite from violence and of a pragmatic relationship with Israel, would pressure Hamas from below, leading to a gradual moderation of its ideology and a diminution in its propensity to rely on terrorism.[12]

Neither came to pass. The Hamas leadership would have preferred wielding influence over a Fatah-run PA, free of public accountability and the related risks of a potential loss in public support due to Israeli responses to acts of terrorism emanating from the PA's territory. Hamas knew, however, that even if it wanted to, it would fare as poorly as Fatah in reining in the multitude of warlords active in Gaza. It simply could not impose a central authority over PA territory and all groups active within it. Furthermore, Hamas's leadership, divided as it was between individuals living within GWB and those living abroad, complicated the nature of the organization's decision making and Israel's ability to influence that process. External leaders still called the shots.

The abduction of the Israeli soldier Gilead Shalit in 2006 illustrated that it was not the political figureheads of Hamas within the PA government who controlled the terrorist infrastructure in Gaza but rather the organization's external leadership. Living abroad insulated this latter group from Israel's indirect deterrent strategies, and it was much less susceptible to coercive pressures emanating from Palestinian society than was Hamas's local leadership.

ISRAELI DETERRENCE: TARGETED KILLINGS

An internal and unpublished study conducted by the Israeli government reviewing the deterrent value of targeted killings found a steep decline in the number of Israeli casualties from suicide attacks immediately after the "Defensive Wall" operation of 2002.[13] This finding, of course, can be attributed to the disruptive value of Israel's military operation: Israeli forces reentered Palestinian cities for the first time since the Oslo Accords and were performing wide-scale arrests and uncovering weapons caches. However, during this period, the number of attempted suicide attacks continued to rise. These figures suggest that the efficacy of Israeli disruption and not deterrence (that is, a decline in the motivation to perpetrate suicide attacks) was the reason for the decline in successful attacks. For instance, the percentage of attempted suicide bombings that were disrupted rose following "Defensive Wall" to 80 percent, from 20–40 percent previously. The corresponding decrease in the odds of success of a planned suicide attack did not seem to have a measurable effect on the motivation of the planners.

However, starting in the summer of 2003, this changed. Not only did the number of successful suicide attacks continue to drop, but there was also a steep decline in the number of overall suicide bombing attempts. This can be partially attributed to the construction of Israel's security barrier, of which 130 kilometers were in place and operational by July 2003. There is ample evidence from interviews with terrorist planners and would-be suicide bombers that the barrier reduced the ease of planning terrorist attacks and forced organizers to shift their energy toward circumventing it.[14]

However, the barrier was not the only factor that reduced the number of attempts to send suicide bombers into Israel. Targeted killings became instrumental in reducing the motivation for preparing attacks.[15] From the beginning of 2003, Israel's targeted killing strategy had changed. Whereas until Operation Defensive Wall targeted killings had been used as a purely defensive tactic—in extremis—when the target was clearly defined as a "ticking bomb," from 2003 onward Israel adopted a strategy of targeting individuals from the "production line" of the suicide bomber industry.

This policy shift was based on the assumption that without command-level recruiters, handlers, and "engineers" (those who were critical in preparing and facilitating attacks) the motivation of potential suicide bombers would not come into play. It was believed that suicide bombers could not be deterred, but that their recruiters and handlers could be.[16] This assumption was derived from Israel's experience at the beginning of the Intifada, in which the IDF succeeded in surrounding safe houses of senior operatives, who preferred to surrender themselves rather than fight to the death.[17] When asked why they chose not to blow themselves up alongside enclosing Israeli soldiers, the captured operatives explained that there was a difference between those destined to become martyrs and those who had the expertise to prepare the martyrs. Whether their lack of enthusiasm to become martyrs themselves was due to a natural aversion toward death or because of a professed commitment to their larger cause, Israeli targeted killings compelled them to take precautionary measures that ultimately reduced the scope of their operations.

Over time, the targeted killings also demonstrated Israel's "intelligence dominance" in the field. A Hamas directive to operatives, for instance, warned that "the Zionist enemy has succeeded in assassinating many of the brother fighters . . . the electronic spy planes do not leave the sky of Gaza, the many [Israeli] eyes on which the task has been placed do not slumber and the Apache helicopters are ready with missiles and waiting for an opportunity. You are under close surveillance 24 hours a day. You are a target for assassination every day and every hour."[18] The result in this case was an augmentation of Israeli coercion. On the other hand, unsuccessful targeted killings, particularly politically damaging events following a large number of Palestinian civilian casualties or episodes that elicited international condemnation, frequently had an adverse effect on deterrence. This was most evident in the failed 1997 attempt to kill Masha'l and in the various botched attempts to kill Mohammad Dif, the commander of Hamas's Izadin Qassam group. In the first case, Hamas knew that Israel's failure had purchased Masha'l an "insurance policy" against future Israeli attempts to kill him; in the second case, Hamas understood that Israel would continue to attempt to kill Dif—who was responsible for the deaths of hundreds of Israelis—whether or not he refrained from terrorism.

When Israel's 2003 targeted killing strategy started producing results, the Palestinians first regarded the shifting momentum as a failure of Palestinian defensive measures rather than an Israeli military success, and they called for the adoption of a list of further defensive steps.[19] Over time, however, the targeted killings were interpreted as a clear expression of Israeli military and intelligence dominance, and Palestinian leaders began to take Israeli strengths into strategic account. There was also a belief that the targeted killing strategy was an Israeli attempt to provoke the Palestinians to retaliate with more terrorism, thus justifying what was perceived as Sharon's attempt to reduce the Israeli-Palestinian conflict to an equation of "security and terror." One conclusion, then, called for Palestinians to formulate a single, coordinated strategy based on a cessation of suicide attacks.[20] This line of thought suggested that even very successful terrorist attacks would not deter Israeli retaliation since Israel would continue to dominate all military affairs. The remaining option was to adopt a paradigm of nonviolent resistance that would have a better chance of promoting Palestinian national goals while restraining Israel's traditional military strengths.[21]

On examination of the historical record, the targeted killings eventually served a deterrent role. This is evident in reviewing the debates within the Palestinian leadership, both in the PA and abroad, over establishing a *hudnah* (cease-fire) or *tahdiyah* (temporary cease-fire) with Israel.[22] The debates began in June 2003, and Israel interpreted them as a direct result of the deterrent effects of its concerted campaign of targeted killings.[23]

The Palestinian debate went through a number of stages. First, in January 2004, under Israeli fire, Rantisi, then Hamas's Gazan leader, offered Israel a ten-year *hudnah* in return for Israel's complete withdrawal from all territories captured in the 1967 Six Day War and the establishment of a Palestinian state in the West Bank and Gaza. Rantisi justified the offer on the basis that liberating all of Palestine at that stage was too difficult. Second, in June 2004, after Sheikh Yassin and Rantisi were killed, Hamas switched tactics and declared a unilateral *hudnah*. Israel agreed informally to restrict its military action to individuals on their way to conducting attacks. The *hudnah* lasted for a period of between one month (with the Palestinian Islamic Jihad and al-Aqsa Brigades) and two months (with Hamas). The unilateral cease-fire was a clear indication that proactive Israeli counterterrorism activity had had an effect on the Palestinians, which compelled them to seek a period of calm. In this case, almost all channels of deterrence were involved: direct military action against the organizations, targeted killings of their leaders, pressure on the host state (the PA) and of surrounding states (Egypt), and indirect pressure achieved through the Palestinian public. Third, after the election of the Hamas government, the concept of the *hudnah* morphed into a more limited *tahdiyah*, which called for a moratorium on terrorist attacks inside Israel but allowed for the continued launching of rockets. In light of the declining rate of success of suicide attacks, the proposed *tahdiyah* was in fact a formalization of the limitations on Hamas's terrorist activities. Finally, in the wake of Israeli military operations (including a resumption of targeted killings) that began after the 2006 kidnapping of Shalit and the shelling of the border town of Sederot, Hamas again called for a unilateral *tahdiyah*, which it succeeded in preserving despite violations on the part of Fatah forces.

CONCLUSION

Israel has achieved intermittent success in deterring terrorism in the Palestinian theater. Ultimately, its deterrent record is linked to three factors: the existence of a terrorist leadership against which a deterrent could be directed and communicated; that leadership's command and control over elements responsible for terrorism; and the credibility of Israeli threats. An important conclusion from this case study is the relevance of the characteristics of Palestinian society and of the organizations themselves on shaping coercive outcomes. Leadership qualities and ruling style, societal factors, relations with host and patron states, ideological factors, and Palestinian interpretations and assessment of Israeli deterrence all inform and shape Israeli deterrent efforts and outcomes. Each of these factors is further discussed below.

First, since 1993, Fatah's leadership was concentrated in the WBG, reducing the political divisions that traditionally marked Palestinian politics and bridging the "interior" and "exterior" halves of Fatah's leadership. For most of the period studied here, Yasser Arafat was the sole source of authority in Fatah, the PLO, and the PA, and arguably the ultimate decision maker against which all Israeli attempts at persuasion and deterrence were directed. The total identification of the "Palestinian national interest" with his own personal interests made deterrence of Fatah and the PA dependent on Arafat's believing that any intensification or reprieve of Israeli pressure would apply to him as well.

Arafat's death created a vacuum of authority that Palestinian society was unable to fill and led to a subsequent decentralization of authority. His successor, Abbas, could not benefit from Arafat's personal status, nor could he re-create Arafat's control over Palestinian financial or military levers. Out of necessity, decision making under Abbas was collective, consensual, and decentralized, in sharp contrast to the centralist and individualist mode of Arafat's rule. This shift in leadership style had a detrimental effect on Israel's ability to deter Fatah/PA terrorism. Whereas in the past Israel could focus on an individual leader, it now had to find a way to influence complex interactive processes between a large number of individuals and coalitions. As Abbas's regime weakened, the number of relevant individuals and groups grew in number, and the complexity of Israel's task increased with it. Hamas, on the other hand, has remained split between an "interior" and "exterior" leadership, with clear predominance of the latter. When Israel killed Yassin and Rantisi, no authoritative local leader emerged in Gaza. The result was to amplify the dominance of Hamas's "exterior" leadership and diminish Israeli deterrence capabilities. Hamas's "exterior" leadership, living in relative comfort aboard, was less susceptible to both Israeli pressures and internal pressures directed from the Palestinian population living in the West Bank and Gaza. This development reduced the responsiveness of Hamas's terrorist organs to Israeli deterrence, even in the event where Israel successfully pressured Hamas's "interior" leadership.

Second, concerning societal factors, two characteristics of Palestinian society and politics are pivotal for understanding how Israeli deterrent signals were received. In the first case, there is dissonance in terms of the interests, vulnerable assets, and levers of influence between Palestinians living outside the West Bank and Gaza and those living inside these territories. The former include the refugee populations in Jordan, Lebanon, and Syria, who share a common goal in an eventual return to pre-1948 Palestine. They experience Israeli pressure against Gaza and the West Bank differently and with less intensity, and their leaders are less susceptible to Israeli coercion. However, this external Palestinian leadership—in the case of both pre-1993 Fatah/PLO and present-day Hamas—has dominated the "inside-outside" relationship by dint of its control over the financial assets of Palestinian organizations and its political links with the Arab world. Thus, not only are "outside" groups less susceptible to Israeli coercion, but they also have greater control over the affairs and behavior of "inside" Palestinian factions. The second societal characteristic that inhibits the reception of Israeli deterrence is the inherent weakness of Palestinian democracy, embodied as it is in the legislative, secular civil society, and indigenous Palestinian economic oligarchy. For instance, while Israeli economic pressure imposed as a response to the Second Intifada took a toll on the economic welfare of regular Palestinians, it did not have a critical influence on the existential interests of the ruling oligarchy. Neither did economic pressure on the populace translate into indigenous pressure on Palestinian elites. Consequently, Israeli attempts to deter terrorist leaders from acts of terrorism though economic pressures on the "host" populace were doomed to failure.

Third, the complex interaction between various political and terrorist groups and the Palestinian "host state" (embodied in the PA) complicated Israeli deterrence strategy. Since the Oslo Accords, Fatah's leaders were the PA's leaders. Consequently, the "state" interests of the PA, particularly the main economic sectors that were dominated by the "exterior" Fatah oligarchy, were inherently linked to that oligarchy. The February 2006 elections that brought Hamas to power in the governmental branch of the PA (the presidential branch remained in the hands of Fatah and Abbas) changed the nature of the relationship between Hamas and the PA, in a manner somewhat analogous to the relationship that existed between Fatah and the PA beforehand. Hamas's landslide victory came as an unpleasant surprise to its leadership, however, which much preferred wielding influence over the PA rather than actually having to operate the PA. Hamas was well aware that with political power came responsibility and accountability for terrorism perpetrated from within the PA's territory. It also became responsible for the consequences of terrorism in the form of Israeli reprisals, economic sanctions, and subsequent hardships for Palestinians. Nevertheless, damage to Hamas's constituency did not deter the organization from perpetrating further acts of terrorism; that decision-making process took place far from Gaza's borders and beyond the reach of Hamas's local political branch. While the local Hamas leadership in charge of the PA might have been concerned over the ramifications of terrorism and over its popularity and standing with the Palestinian populace, it was impotent to actually influence Hamas's terrorist policy, over which it had little control.

Fourth, a similarly complex set of interactions mark Palestinian relations with other Arab "patron" states. The weakness of the Palestinian Authority and its dependence on the charity and goodwill of Arab states provide these donor states with potential leverage over Palestinian affairs. The integration of the different Palestinian organizations within the PA makes them all a party to that dependence. There is, however, no single "patron" of the Palestinians that Israel might target in order to achieve indirect deterrence over Palestinian terrorism. Before the Oslo Accords, the PLO was heavily dependent on the Arab Gulf states for its financing. These countries could theoretically have served as conduits for indirect pressure on the PLO. However, during the Oslo era, the PA's financial reliance on the Gulf states diminished due to Western support, so that economic pressure on Arab "host" states became less relevant as a lever over the PA. As for Hamas, Israeli calculations regarding coercive pressure on Syria and Iran (Hamas's "patron" states) has had to take into account broader geopolitical interests and the possibility of igniting a broader confrontation with these countries.

Fifth, ideology plays a role in determining the susceptibility of the various Palestinian groups to Israeli deterrence. Fatah was founded as a secular nationalist organization and remained relatively pragmatic in its political maneuvering. As a political movement, it raised the banner of an "independent Palestine" and claimed the title of the "sole legitimate representative of the Palestinian people." Its ideology was largely autonomously developed. Over the years, Fatah acquired a pragmatic approach toward its "armed struggle" with Israel, shifting the use of political violence from its original status as "the only means to liberate Palestine" to "the main means" and finally as "one of the means along with other forms of struggle."[24] This shift provided the Fatah leadership with the ideological justification it needed to reach political agreement with Israel, including formally renouncing terrorism. It also allowed Fatah to justify taking steps against its own terrorist elements in light of "Palestinian national interests." All these ideological characteristics made Fatah more amenable to Israeli deterrence. Hamas, on the other hand, is tied with an ideological umbilical cord to the dominant Islamic source of authority accepted by its "mother movement," the Muslim Brotherhood (MB). The Hamas-MB ideological bond is exceptionally pronounced. Unlike other regional MB movements that have their own national spiritual leaders, Hamas has never had an indigenous authoritative spiritual leadership that could rule on matters of Islamic principle. Strategic issues, therefore, have to be referred to various spiritual guides living abroad. These individuals are neither necessarily synchronized with life in the WBG, nor are they as astutely aware of Israeli pressure as local Palestinians are. Hamas's ideology is much less flexible as a result, and the organization is altogether less amenable to Israeli deterrence.

Sixth and finally, Palestinians in general have a better collective acquaintance with Israel than does any other Arab society and tend to have a more realistic assessment of Israel's capabilities and constraints. Local Palestinian leaders are generally more adept at interpreting and assessing Israeli deterrent signals and tend to hold a more realistic view of Israel's interests and possible policies than their "external" colleagues do in Tunis or Damascus. Unfortunately, the strategic assessment that informs decisions on terrorism is not in the hands of the more pragmatic "interior" leadership but the "external" leadership. Israeli deterrence often deteriorates as a result. During the Arafat era, the "intelligence assessment" process was almost exclusively in the hands of Arafat. Much of his decision making when confronted with Israeli coercion was derived from his tendency to exaggerate Israeli constraints and ignore the power of Israeli public opinion in the face of increasing terrorism. Hamas's assessment of Israel, on the other hand, differs greatly between the "interior" and "exterior" components of the organization. The former has, as noted above, a clear and sober view of Israel's strength and willingness to use its power. The "exterior" leadership, however, draws much of its assessment from various patron actors like Iran, Syria, and Hezbollah. The absence of high-level Hamas leaders in the West Bank and Gaza who could command the respect of the exterior leadership renders much of the perceptions of the "interior" irrelevant to contemplating Israeli deterrent strategies.

An examination of trends in Palestinian terrorism and of intelligence on the planning of attacks since 2000 shows that at times Israeli attempts to deter terrorism were successful. During this period, Israel engaged in wide-scale proactive actions (particularly involving targeted killings) that resulted in a decline in terrorism alerts and a diminishment in the number of overall attacks. While part of this decline is attributable to Israeli efforts at disruption, the conclusion of this study is that proactive Israeli actions also reduced the motivation of terrorist leaders to plan attacks out of fear of even more painful Israeli reactions. On the other hand, preventive security measures directed against the Palestinian population with the intention of deterring terrorism indirectly were much less successful. A widely debated strategy in public and professional circles in Israel, the assumption holds that putting pressure on the Palestinian populace could act as a leverage against the leadership orchestrating and facilitating terrorism. However, Israeli counterterrorism has always been curtailed by Israel's obligations as the occupying power in the West Bank and Gaza and as a result of Israeli public opinion and political debates.

The fact that Israeli public opinion is readily available for interpretation by various terrorist organizations has reduced the efficacy of preventive operations in terms of deterring terrorism.

NOTES

1. The author would like to thank Shmuel Bachar and Rachel Machtiger for their assistance in researching and writing this chapter.

2. The most salient of these attributes include leaders who have command and control over the affairs of a territory, the existence of a vertical hierarchy, the existence of a social agenda and responsibility toward a given population, methods of financing political affairs, and national or transnational/religious agendas.

3. Such a position was evident in interviews with a number of members of the Knesset Defense and Foreign Affairs Committee. The immediate response of one former chairman of the committee, for example, to the question of the study was: "Deterrence is relevant to states. Terrorist organizations have to be eradicated." The interviews with Israeli officials cited in this chapter include virtually all surviving heads of Mossad, Shin Bet, and Military Intelligence, and many of their staff. All interviews were contingent on the nonattribution of participants, a necessary and unavoidable precondition. Formal governmental authorization would have had to been granted otherwise.

4. Shabtai Shavit and Danny Yatom, interviews with author, June–July 2006.

5. Shavit interview; Avi Dichter, "Lessons from the Fight Against Terrorism," Washington Institute for Near East Policy, *Peace Watch* no. 533 (2005).

6. In 1997 the Israelis botched an assassination attempt on Masha'l in Amman, Jordan, in which Israeli agents were captured and Israel was compelled to provide the antidote that saved Masha'l's life and to release Sheikh Ahmad Yassin from prison.

7. This is the conclusion—in retrospect—of a number of interviews with senior officials. It is doubtful, however, that in the heat of the action such "strategic" considerations were thought out systematically. At the time, the Israeli political and military leaders were faced with the need to prove to Israeli citizens that they were doing all that could be done to prevent and preempt terrorism. The slogan "Let the IDF win" (i.e., remove political constraints from IDF command), which was popularized by the political Right, also put pressure on Israeli leaders to demonstrate a willingness to employ military action and to show that Israel had not forgone its traditional defensive strategy of preemption.

8. A senior Fatah leader narrated a meeting with Arafat a month before his hospitalization. He had begged Arafat to at least tactically accept some of the Israeli and American demands. Arafat's reply was that "as long as I am under siege, you will all be under siege and all of Palestine will be under siege." Personal interview with a senior Palestinian official, who spoke on the condition of anonymity.

9. Moshe Ya'alon, interviewed by Ari Shavit, "The Enemy Within," *Haaretz*, August 30, 2002.

10. Personal communication with General Amos Malka (retired), former director of Military Intelligence.

11. The situation was likened by one senior Israeli intelligence officer to deterring organized crime versus deterring a multitude of small nonorganized criminals. The former is much easier to do once the "godfather's" interests are known. With the latter case, there is no way to develop a comprehensive policy of deterrence that would apply to hundreds of autonomous warlords.

12. This attitude was raised in Israeli security circles after the elections, though it did not gain much currency afterward.

13. The government study is not publicly available. The author received a copy of it with permission to cite its findings but not the source itself.

14. Moussa Abu Marzouq, deputy chairman of the Hamas Political Bureau, and Ramadan Shalah, Palestinian Islamic Jihad leader, both publicly admitted that Israel's security fence in the West Bank was an obstacle to carrying out suicide bombing attacks in Israel. See Intelligence and Terrorism Information Center, "Moussa Abu Marzouq Confirms Security Fence Makes Attacks More Difficult," June 7, 2007; Intelligence and Terrorism Information Center, "Ramadan Shalah Admits Security Fence an Obstacle," November 15, 2006.

15. Brigadier General (reserve) Dr. Itshak Ben-Israel, "Dealing with Suicide Terrorism—the Israeli Case" (Hebrew), unpublished.

16. This was the explicit position of the Israel Security Agency (the Shin Bet).

17. Cases included Abdallah Barghouti, Ibrahim Hamed, and Muhanmad Abu Ouda (Hamas engineers responsible for the death of tens of Israelis), Amjad Ubeidi (PIJ), and Marwan Barghouti (Fatah), who had dispatched suicide bombers for the Tanzim.

18. The document was retrieved in Gaza by the IDF during Operation Cast Lead (2008–9). A copy was provided to the author by the Center for Special Studies in Glilot, Israel.

19. See Hani Habib, Ahmad al-Majdalani, and Abdallah Awwad writing in *al-Ayyam*, August 27–30, 2001.

20. See Muhannad abd al-Hamid, *al-Ayyam*, April 23, 2004.

21. See Hani al-Masri, *al-Ayyam*, March 27, 2004.

22. The idea of a *hudnah* was first raised by Yassin, spiritual leader of Hamas, in 1993, when he distinguished between "peace" or "reconciliation" (*sulh*) with Israel, which he rejected, and a cease-fire or truce (*hudnah*). *Sulh* is an Arabic term used in the context of reconciliation between tribes or families and includes a cessation of the pretexts for vengeance. It is usually perceived as having a stronger legal and obligatory meaning than the alternative word—*salam*. The concept of *hudnah* is derived from

Islamic sources and is a classic outcome of deterrence. *Hudnah* is a temporary cease-fire, which warring Muslims may accept if they are constrained by weakness. A *hudnah* must be restricted in time, and while it is maintained the two sides do not engage in military hostilities, though they continue to prepare for the next engagement. In Islamic history, the concept is associated with the Hudaybiya Treaty that the Prophet Muhammad signed with the Meccan tribe of Quraysh in 628. The treaty was to last ten years and stipulated the conditions under which Muslims could enter Mecca, unarmed, for their annual pilgrimage. The treaty dissolved, however, two years later. In the Palestinian context, the concept of *hudnah* was revived by Arafat in a private speech to a Muslim audience, when he compared the Oslo Accords to the Hudaybiya Treaty, implying that this *hudnah*, like Hudaybiya, could be rendered null and void if the circumstances permitted. While this comparison did not augur well for the peace process, it did shed light on the effects of Israeli deterrence on Arafat: he had expressed his acceptance of Israeli predominance and deterrence at this stage.

23. This was the interpretation of almost all the Israeli officials interviewed.

24. Aryeh Yodfat and Yuval Arnon-Oḥanah, *PLO Strategy and Politics* (Hebrew version) (London: Croom-Helm, 1981), 112–21; Anat Kurz, *Fatah and the Politics of Violence: The Institutionalization of a Popular Struggle* (Sussex, UK: Sussex Academic Press, 2007).

10 TURKISH AND IRANIAN EFFORTS
TO DETER KURDISH INSURGENT ATTACKS

David Romano

DETERRENCE AND INFLUENCE

Traditional deterrence refers to a foreign policy strategy deployed by one state against another. By either raising the perceived costs (deterrence by punishment) or lowering the anticipated benefits (deterrence by denial) of an adversary's potential and unwanted actions, a state tries to dissuade certain behavior. Compellence strategies seek to make an actor reverse actions already taken or initiate new actions. Positive inducements, on the other hand, offer rewards in return for desired behavior. Rational states should respond in predictable ways when these clearly communicated exercises in power—deterrence, compellence, and positive inducements—alter their cost-benefit calculations.[1]

Deterring non-state actors also has a long history, and takes different forms, depending on the context. Within states, government authorities, police forces, and complex systems of legal sanctions serve to deter individuals from engaging in behavior deemed illegal. State responses to terrorism typically rely exclusively on coercive mechanisms, since offering positive inducements to terrorists invokes high political costs with domestic constituencies. Often confused with antiterrorism policies (or purposely labeled together), counterinsurgency strategies attempt to contain, deter, and defeat significant domestic groups in full revolt against a state's political and legal system.[2] Such counterinsurgency programs typically include coercive military tactics, including threats aimed at whole communities. Because uncertainty exists regarding state authorities' ability to identify and apprehend domestic insurgents, the more clearly identifiable and vulnerable communities from which insurgents come, the more they are credible targets of deterrent threats and punishment. Such direct or indirect threats of harm to the larger community, as well as coercive punishments, are meant to (1) deter insurgents from further violence; (2) deter the larger community from cooperating with insurgents; and (3) compel community members into cooperating with the government rather than the insurgents. Counterinsurgency strategies do not always rely exclusively on military and covert coercion, however, and can also include positive inducements such as liberalization and reform intended to address the grievances that sparked revolt in the first place. States typically add positive inducements to their repertoire after more coercive tactics fail to put an end to an insurgency.

Influencing non-state actors (NSAs) based outside one's state boundaries, however, presents a more complicated challenge. While modern states as disparate as Israel, India, Britain, and the Democratic Republic of the Congo have faced NSA attackers from outside their borders for many years, the urgency of deterring violent attacks from such groups achieved center stage in the West after the September 11 attacks, the African embassy bombings, and other attacks carried out by local radicals assisted, directed, or inspired by foreign militants (such as the London and Madrid train bombings). A foreign policy aimed at influencing non-state actors differs from counterinsurgency strategies in important ways. Justifiably, in such circumstances states appear much less willing to entertain positive inducements—reforming or changing their policies to address NSAs' grievances—when those NSAs are foreign or based outside the state in question. Coercive state responses—whether military strikes or covert operations—must also, by definition, be conducted on the sovereign territory of another state, often without acquiescence. Typically, indirect exercises of power toward NSAs thus form a more readily pursued course of action: deterring, compelling, or inducing the authorities of states in which attacking NSAs reside to take action against them, or at least contain them. Such pressure can take the form of coercive diplomacy—warnings of reprisals against host states of NSAs should attacks occur (deterrence); threatening host states with military action or economic sanctions should they fail to act against NSAs in their territory (compellence); promises of financial and military aid in return for host state cooperation (positive inducements); or even "soft power" appeals for cooperation based on commonly accepted international norms. Interstate governmental organizations can also be appealed to, putting NSAs on terrorist lists, Interpol watch lists, and financial blacklists.

An examination and comparison of two lesser known cases can help illuminate several of the difficult and complex issues at play when addressing foreign policies aimed at deterring or containing non-state actors. Mountainous northern Iraq, also known as South Kurdistan and Iraqi Kurdistan, serves as a base of operations for a number of non-Iraqi Kurdish dissident organizations. Since the 1980s, Turkey largely failed to stop attacks from Iraqi Kurdistan–based fighters of the PKK (Kurdistan Workers' Party), or terrorist bombings from likely PKK front organizations, such as the TAK (Kurdistan Freedom Hawks). In contrast to Turkey, Iran until very recently successfully deterred and contained a number of Iranian Kurdish dissident groups based in Iraqi Kurdistan. Fighters of the Kurdistan Democratic Party of Iran (KDPI), Komalah (also referred to as "Marxist Komalah"), and a splinter Komala group (referred to as "nationalist Komala"), all have headquarters and bases in Iraqi Kurdistan yet refrain from launching attacks into Iran. Only recently has a new Iranian Kurdish opposition group emerged to launch a series of significant attacks in Iranian territory: PJAK (the "Kurdistan Free Life Party") is closely linked to the PKK and is thought to share PKK bases, supplies, and even manpower.

What explains the different levels of success experienced by Turkey and Iran in their efforts to stop Kurdish insurgent attacks emanating from northern Iraq? Why did the PKK end a five-year unilateral cease-fire (1999–2004) with Turkey and resume attacks, including a number of bombings in western Turkey? Why did PJAK emerge to launch scores of guerrilla attacks on Iranian forces, at a time when other Iranian Kurdish opposition groups appeared deterred and quiescent? The fact that all these dissident groups operate out of Iraqi Kurdistan allows us to apply an interesting control, since all of them exist within roughly the same geostrategic conditions and a territory controlled by the same political authority—the Kurdistan Regional Government of Iraq (KRG).

Important insights may come from the fact that Turkish and Iranian policy toward the KRG, in both substance and style, has differed. Can we contrast an Iranian foreign policy approach to gaining KRG cooperation in containing Kurdish dissidents to a less successful Turkish approach? Does PJAK indicate a limit to Iranian deterrence strategies? If so, why? Finally, what can the Turkish and Iranian approaches to deterrence tell us about deterring non-state actors in general? Can lessons from cases involving ethnic nationalist (a.k.a. national liberation) movements offer valid insights to other kinds of non-state actors willing to resort to terrorism?

Finally, it seems prudent to add something more about conceptual terminology before proceeding further. While "deterring terrorism" forms the overall theme of this collection of essays, I feel it is sometimes more useful to examine the issue of preventing attacks from non-state actors in a more general sense. Just as states sometimes commit war crimes, NSAs occasionally use terrorism to pursue their objectives. The PKK certainly employed terrorism since it began armed attacks in the early 1980s, directly and probably indirectly as well, via front organizations. In contrast, the KDPI, the Komalas, and PJAK appear to have largely eschewed the targeting of civilians, and limit their attacks to Iranian security forces. Defining any of these groups as "terrorist organizations" would either categorize them inaccurately or lead us to ignore other important aspects of the nature of these groups. In addition to deterrence, consideration of compellence strategies and positive inducements aimed at NSAs, the populations they depend upon for support, and the authorities of territories from which they operate offers a more complete picture of the ways states try to exercise power against such opponents.

THE POLITICAL CONTEXT

Since the creation of the Turkish Republic, the state of Iraq, and the modern Iranian state, dissidents from each country's Kurdish minority periodically broke out into armed revolts.[3] The post–World War I redrawing of political boundaries left Kurdistan divided where the borders of Turkey, Iraq, Iran, and Syria converge. The very rugged Zagros mountain range lies at the heart of what the Kurds refer to as Kurdistan ("land of the Kurds"), with the headwaters of the Tigris and Euphrates rivers and the Anti-Taurus mountain range, as well as Mount Ararat and Mount Cudi, as prominent landmarks of the region. The terrain is ideal for guerrilla warfare and remained under only tenuous control of not only modern states, but the Ottoman and Persian empires as well.

Iraq, Iran, Syria, the USSR, the United States, and Israel all used various Kurdish dissident groups at different times as pawns to weaken their rivals: Syria supported the PKK from the early 1980s until 1998 in order to pressure Turkey on water issues; Iraq's Saddam Hussein supported Kurdish rebels in Iran; the Shah of Iran, the United States, and Israel supported Iraqi Kurdish revolts; and the USSR supported Kurdish rebels in Iran (the 1945–46 Republic of Kurdistan) and secretly in Iraq during the 1960s (in order to pressure

Baghdad to request more Soviet assistance).[4] Today, Kurds number roughly fifteen million of Turkey's population of seventy-seven million (about 20 percent of the population), seven million of Iran's sixty-six million citizens (roughly 10 percent), and five and a half million of Iraq's total twenty-nine million people (just under 20 percent).

After 1991, the PKK, the KDPI, and both Komala and Komalah found more secure sanctuaries in a de facto autonomous Iraqi Kurdistan, from which they could continue to oppose Ankara (the PKK) and Tehran (the others). PJAK emerged into public view in Iraqi Kurdistan as well, around 2004, and claimed to have larger numbers of fighters and sympathizers in Iranian Kurdistan. What follows is a comparison of how Turkey and Iran dealt separately with various Kurdish NSAs and how the logic and practice of deterrence informed both states' policies.

TURKEY AND THE PKK

The PKK began armed attacks against Turkish military and police targets in the rural, mostly Kurdish southeast of Turkey in 1984. The organization had already begun targeting rival Kurdish groups shortly after its founding in the late 1970s. The group's leader, Abdullah Öcalan, and much of its top leadership enjoyed safe haven in Syria and Lebanon, while most of the lower-ranking militants operated within Turkey itself. PKK recruits who completed training elsewhere, such as at the Mahsum Korkmaz academy in Lebanon's Bekaa Valley, then moved on to forward staging bases in northern Iraq before reentering Turkey. Since Saddam's government in Baghdad faced a worsening war with Iran and Iraqi Kurdish insurgents by the mid-1980s, it lacked sufficient control of its own territory to deny the PKK operating bases in northern Iraq. During the 1980s the Kurdistan Democratic Party of Iraq (KDP) also assisted PKK militants in its area of operations. Some PKK training and recruitment activities also occurred within Iran in the 1980s and 1990s.

By the late 1980s, the PKK's insurgency reached the stage of a full-blown guerrilla war. In addition to Turkish military and police, civil servants and teachers (accused of providing intelligence to the state and furthering Ankara's assimilation program toward the Kurds) also became targets. Ankara's response soon degenerated into a dirty counterinsurgency campaign, complete with thousands of unsolved murders and disappearances. The Turkish state by the late 1980s also began pursuing a common counterinsurgency strategy of arming Kurdish tribes and villages in "village guards" to help fight the PKK, and forcibly evacuating and destroying villages that refused to join the village guard system or were suspected of sympathizing with the insurgents. Some three thousand Turkish Kurdish villages were destroyed in this way. The PKK in turn attacked village guards, frequently killing not just the guards themselves, but their families as well.

Besides pursuing a military-based counterinsurgency strategy and economic development plans for southeastern Turkey (none of which ever bore much fruit), Ankara, beginning in November 1992, convened regular tripartite meetings with Syrian and Iranian leaders to coordinate strategy against Kurdish dissident groups[5] (after 2003, Ankara also held such meetings with central Iraqi government officials).[6] Given Syrian support for the PKK at the time, and Iranian support for Islamist movements in Turkey, the meetings produced little beyond a consensus that no one wanted the emergence of a Kurdish state in the region. The timing of the commencement of tripartite meetings between Turkey, Syria, and Iran was not random: the establishment of a de facto Iraqi Kurdish autonomous region in early 1992 had raised regional fears of Kurdish secession from Iraq and nascent Kurdish statehood.

More important for the discussion here, the Kurdish Autonomous Zone (hereafter the KAZ) provided Kurdish dissident groups from Turkey and Iran a more natural and secure sanctuary from which to operate. Turkey's 1984 "Protocol of Security" agreement with Baghdad[7] led to a number of significant Turkish military incursions into northern Iraq, in an attempt to deny PKK militants sanctuary there. More than two dozen Turkish military incursions occurred from 1984 to 1999. The operations in the 1980s—in 1984, 1986, and 1987—were fairly minor in scope. The four most significant invasions of the 1990s, however, involved much larger numbers of troops for extended periods of time. They included Operation Northern Iraq (1992), Operation Steel (1995), Operation Hammer (1997), and Operation Dawn (also in 1997). Each of the operations saw the involvement of tens of thousands of troops. The largest, Operation Steel, sent thirty-five thousand Turkish troops into the KAZ for two months in 1995 to hunt for PKK militants. Sixty-four Turkish soldiers were killed in the operation, but with 555 militants supposedly killed on the other side, the Turkish general staff claimed another victory against the PKK.[8] According to the Kurdistan Democratic Party representative in Turkey at the time, however, cooperating Iraqi KDP *peshmerga* (fighters) neutralized more PKK militants than the Turkish military did during these operations. He explained that "You can't use a wagon to chase mice," meaning that tanks and aircraft were ill-suited to chasing down guerrillas hiding in mountain caves and ravines, and the KDP *peshmerga* knew the terrain while Turkey's soldiers did not.[9]

Turkey secured the cooperation of Iraqi Kurds of the KDP through a combination of compellence and positive inducements. When the KAZ emerged in 1992, the main Iraqi Kurdish groups there faced an exceedingly difficult situation. They were completely free of Saddam for the first time, but landlocked and surround by Saddam's forces to the south, Turkey to the north, Syria to the west, and Iran to the east—the perpetual Kurdish problem with difficult neighbors. They faced a double embargo (the international sanctions on Iraq as well as sanctions placed by Saddam on the KAZ) and no ready sources of income apart from smuggling. Iraqi Kurdish society was also exhausted and devastated in 1992—from the 1980–88 Iran-Iraq War, the genocidal Anfal campaign of 1987–88 (in which somewhere between 70,000 and 180,000 Iraqi Kurds were exterminated by Baghdad), and the Gulf War and crushed uprisings of 1991. It was only the Turkish, U.S., British, and French creation of a safe haven in Iraqi Kurdistan (aimed in part at encouraging Iraqi Kurdish refugees who fled Saddam's onslaught in 1991 to return home before they exacerbated Turkey's problems) and resulting autonomy that offered any hope. Still, the continuation of Allied protection of the KAZ depended on Turkish acquiescence to the use of its Incirlik airbase. Also, what little travel and trade entered the KAZ mostly did so from Turkey, ironically providing the only lifeline for fairly desperate Iraqi Kurds attempting to make their autonomy work. Dependent to such an extent on Ankara, Iraqi Kurds could scarcely refuse when Turkey demanded assistance against the PKK. The promise of more open borders for Iraqi Kurdistan combined with the threat of ending the KAZ's very existence proved a potent combination of compellence and inducement. That the PKK had begun to compete with the KDP and the Patriotic Union of Kurdistan (PUK—the other leading Iraqi Kurdish party) for support among the Iraqi Kurdish population only encouraged cooperation with Turkey even more. In terms of intelligence and joint operations, the Iraqi Kurdish cooperation proved crucial. However, when civil war broke out between the main Iraqi Kurdish parties in 1994 (they were mainly fighting over the scraps of revenue entering Iraqi Kurdistan through smuggling), the PKK benefitted as both the KDP and PUK weakened each other. The PUK often cooperated with the PKK, given that they shared an enemy in the KDP, while occasionally Turkey assisted the KDP against the others. Once the Iraqi Kurdish civil war ended in 1998, competition between the PKK and PUK also picked up, however, leading to some armed clashes between them (with the encouragement of Turkey) in 1999 and 2000. The combined opposition of the KDP and PUK by 1999, together with the significant problems the PKK faced in Turkey itself, thus eventually pushed the PKK onto the defensive. The group kept a very low profile from 1999 to 2004.

Turkey's policy toward Syria also forms a crucial part of any explanation for the PKK's decline in 1998–99, however, and must not be overlooked. Ankara achieved a significant victory when it successfully compelled Syria to evict Abdullah Öcalan and other PKK leaders from Damascus and Lebanon. Turkey had repeatedly demanded that Syria cease its support for the PKK, but to no avail. By 1998, however, a number of factors combined in Turkey's favor: a burgeoning military and economic cooperation between Turkey and Israel seemed aimed squarely at Damascus; Syria's Soviet Union patron was no longer available; the Oslo Peace Accords between Israel and the Palestinians threatened to leave Syria facing Israel alone; and Ankara assured Damascus that it need not fear the Ataturk Dam project threatening Syria's water supply. The final push to persuade Syria to stop supporting the PKK came in the form of military brinkmanship—in the autumn of 1998 Turkey mobilized and moved tens of thousands of troops to the Syrian border and made ominous statements about the "repercussions of continuing to shelter Ocalan" (a clearer compellent threat of the use of force could not exist). Syria found the Turkish threat sufficiently credible, promptly expelled Öcalan, and ceased sheltering or aiding the PKK in any significant way. After an odyssey across several continents, Öcalan was captured by U.S. and Turkish agents in Kenya the next year.

All in all, the combination of a brutal Turkish counterinsurgency strategy in southeastern Turkey, cooperation from the Iraqi Kurdish KDP, and successful coercive diplomacy toward Syria severely damaged the PKK's ability to continue its guerrilla war. Facing a losing battle and with its leader in enemy hands, the PKK announced a unilateral cease-fire from 1999 to 2004, which kept the Turkish-Iraqi border quiet for a time. When the Turkish Grand National Assembly voted against allowing U.S. and Coalition troops to transit through Turkey in order to open a northern front in the invasion of Saddam's Iraq, however, Turkey lost a great deal of say in the new, post-Saddam Iraq. An officially recognized Kurdistan Autonomous Region emerged in Iraq, and the

Iraqi Kurds became the United States' replacement for the Turkish assistance denied to them. Iraqi Kurds of the KDP and PUK put aside the divisions that plagued them during most of the 1990s and quickly placed themselves in a position to take full advantage of the momentous changes occurring in Iraq. Jalal Talabani, leader of the PUK, became president of Iraq, and a number of Kurds took up other important posts in Baghdad, including foreign minister (Hosyar Zebari of the KDP) and deputy prime minister (Barham Salih of the PUK). A greatly strengthened KRG (by 2005 an increasingly amalgamated government of the KDP and PUK), although still relatively weak and fearful of Turkish, Iranian, and Syrian intervention in its affairs, appeared more difficult to coerce into cooperation with Turkey against the PKK. Whereas the Iraqi Kurdish parties were too weak to deal the PKK too much damage in the 1990s, Ankara could still successfully demand their cooperation in its military forays against the group. After 2003, however, the much stronger Iraqi Kurdish parties in close cooperation with the United States became better placed to resist Turkish compellence.

Relations between the KRG and Turkey neared a crisis after the PKK resumed attacks in Turkey in 2004. In the PKK's view, Turkey never reciprocated with a cease-fire of its own from 1999 to 2004, and the resumption of the PKK's fight actually amounted to self-defense. It seemed as though all the incursions and counterinsurgency operations of the 1990s had come to naught, as PKK militant activity picked up once again. Attacks included ambushes that killed scores of Turkish soldiers and even overran an isolated Turkish military base; roadside improvised explosive devices (IEDs—a tactic copied from the Lebanese and Iraqi theaters of conflict and not previously used by the PKK); and bombings in Turkish cities such as Diyarbakir, Ankara, and Istanbul. A July 2005 bus bombing in an Aegean resort town also killed a number of foreign tourists and Turks, and was blamed on the PKK and the Kurdistan Freedom Hawks, a possible front organization of the PKK.[10] Turkey reacted to the renewed attacks from the PKK with a series of aerial and artillery bombardments of PKK bases and rural Iraqi Kurdish communities living near the bases, culminating in the February 2007 Operation Sun, in which some ten thousand troops and commandos entered the KAZ for close to a week. Although Ankara claimed a resounding victory from Operation Sun, no PKK camps were captured or destroyed, and even Turkish claims to have killed some 250 militants seemed suspect.[11] Crucially, and contrary to its incursions of the 1990s, Turkey lacked any direct Iraqi Kurdish cooperation for the offensive of 2007. At the time of this writing, the PKK also remains ensconced in its usual Qandil Mountain bases of Iraqi Kurdistan, its leaders still give interviews to journalists, and its militants still cross into Turkey and conduct operations from bases within Iraq. Although Turkey was able to secure some intelligence-sharing on the PKK from KRG officials and the United States, and following Operation Sun the KRG leadership agreed to work harder at limiting the PKK's freedom of movement, publicity, and resupply in Iraqi Kurdistan, it seems clear that Turkish deterrence of the group has failed. What explains the resumption of PKK attacks after the 1999–2004 five-year cease-fire, and the organization's continuing ability to operate out of northern Iraq?

The most basic explanation revolves around two concurrent factors: (1) Turkey squandered a five-year opportunity to resolve Kurdish disaffection in the country and bring the militarily chastised PKK leadership down from the mountains, offering the group virtually no positive inducements to lay down arms; and (2) since 1997, Turkey failed to persuade, compel, or induce Iraqi Kurds to make any significant moves against the PKK presence in Iraqi Kurdistan. In the first case, amnesties offered to PKK militants never extended to any of the leadership or militants who had "blood on their hands," and included a requirement that surrendering cadres provide "useful" intelligence concerning their comrades still in the mountains.[12] PKK leaders meanwhile insist that they long ago gave up any secessionist ambitions and that they are eager for reconciliation. At the same time, the overall pace of social, political, and economic initiatives addressing Kurdish grievances in Turkey also proceeded much slower than anticipated, and at times seemed insincere. When politicians in Ankara granted minority-rights concessions (although they still refuse to recognize the Kurds in Turkey as a minority), such as the right to teach the Kurdish language, the new rights came with so many caveats— lessons could only happen in special private schools, teachers had to be native Turkish speakers, schools must charge a certain amount of money, building codes must be more scrupulously adhered to in potential classroom sites than anywhere else, and all teaching material must pass a rigorous state approval process—that the concessions seemed to be insincere and aimed more at European Union accession than at Kurdish citizens of Turkey. While the new, moderately Islamist AKP government in Ankara undoubtedly made more democratic reform progress after 2002, and garnered many Kurdish votes in return, the pace of reforms and innumerable continuing humiliations dealt out to Kurds and their identity by the military and civilian state bureaucracy left enough Kurds sufficiently disappointed to sympathize with a resumption of PKK armed operations.[13]

In addition to thus failing to address its own domestic problems quickly enough, Ankara simultaneously pursued a somewhat blunt and ineffective foreign policy toward Iraqi Kurds, at least until 2010. Turkey refused to recognize Kurdish autonomy in Iraq, or even pronounce the official name of the "Kurdistan Autonomous Region." Almost all of Ankara's high-level official diplomatic initiatives were thus aimed at the government in Baghdad, which today wields no power in Iraqi Kurdistan. In February 2010 Turkey had yet to open a consulate in the Kurdistan Region, and Turkish officials until May 2008 refused even to officially meet with KRG leaders.[14] KRG president Massoud Barzani (of the KDP) described the situation accordingly: "You [Turkey] do not talk to me in an official capacity. You do not accept me as a partner for talks. You do not maintain a dialogue with me. Then suddenly you want me to take action for you against the PKK? Is this a way to do things?"[15] Only in October 2009 did Turkey send its foreign minister to the Kurdish region— Foreign Minister Ahmet Davutoğlu arrived in Erbil shortly after opening a Turkish consulate in Basra, near Iraq's border with Kuwait.[16]

The lack of recognition from Turkey, combined with the fear that Ankara intends to subvert any experiment in Kurdish self-rule in Iraq (or anywhere else), provides Iraqi Kurds with little inducement to squander precious resources in an attempt to dislodge the PKK from its remote mountain bases. Iraqi Kurdish leaders also have enough worries from other neighbors and brewing conflicts with Arab Iraqis, potential confrontations for which they must conserve their military assets. They may even need the PKK's help against other opponents one day. Cooperating with Turkey to fight fellow Kurds in the PKK would also cost KRG leaders a good deal of sympathy from their own constituents. Turkish threats to invade their region, or close off their mutual border, have thus failed to elicit much cooperation from the KRG.[17] As a result, the most that Iraqi Kurdish leaders seem willing to do for Turkey involves helping to mediate between Ankara and the PKK (an option Ankara has expressed, until recently, little interest in pursuing) and, since February 2007, working a little harder to circumscribe and limit the PKK's political activities in Iraqi Kurdistan. Turkey nonetheless maintains its demand that PKK militants in Iraq be apprehended and turned over to them, and interprets a refusal to do so as collaboration with the PKK.[18]

Ankara enjoyed much greater success in its diplomacy toward Syria, in fact, than it has with the KRG. More recently, Turkish diplomacy toward Iran also bore more fruit after 2002, when the AKP was elected in Turkey. Iranian policy now seems to focus on pursuing good relations with the AKP government rather than supporting more-radical Islamist subversive groups in Turkey, and this permits greater Turkish-Iranian cooperation against the PKK and PJAK.

IRAN AND ITS OPPOSITION GROUPS

In contrast to Turkey, Tehran displayed a good deal more finesse in its attempts to neutralize Iranian Kurdish opposition groups. Although it is not possible to provide many details of a very complex historical relationship between Kurds and the Iranian state here, or the numerous splits that occurred within the Iranian Kurdish movements, for our purposes the 1960s may serve as a relevant starting point. In the early 1960s, the Kurdistan Democratic Party of Iran (KDPI) was providing support to Iraqi Kurdish groups rebelling against Baghdad, sending supplies such as food, clothing, and ammunition over the border.[19] The KDPI also established secure bases in Iraqi Kurdistan, from which it could send militants back into Iran almost at will. Mohammad Reza Shah, appraising the situation, pursued a strategy designed to weaken two of his enemies at once: First, Tehran began providing very significant quantities of supplies and weapons to the Iraqi Kurdish KDP. In short order the Iraqi Kurds became dependent on the shah's aid, which greatly surpassed what the KDPI could offer. Tehran then demanded that its Iraqi Kurdish clients move against the KDPI as the price for continued aid. In a low moment for pan-Kurdish nationalists, the Iraqi KDP eventually complied, evicting the KDPI from its territory, killing some of its leaders and handing over others to the shah's forces, who executed them. After the signing of the 1970 Autonomy Accord in Iraq, KDPI cadres asked Mustafa Barzani (leader of the Iraqi KDP) for permission to return to Iraqi Kurdistan and operate from there once again, but he refused and told them to ask the government in Baghdad for territory south of Iraqi Kurdistan to operate from. The government in Baghdad offered to help the KDPI if the group would help it against Barzani's KDP, which, despite the betrayal of a few years past, they refused to do.[20] Until the revolution in 1979, the KDPI was thus reduced to a few hounded militants in Iran, with its remaining leadership attempting to reorganize in Europe.

The overthrow of Mohammad Reza Shah in February 1979 immediately saw the KDPI and its leadership reemerge in Iranian Kurdistan, along with a more leftist Kurdish movement, the Komala. They quickly organized themselves publicly and joined the political debate and jockeying in Tehran to create a new political order. The Kurds soon came into conflict with Ayatollah Khomeini's emerging theocratic government, and by the summer of 1979 Khomeini rejected Kurdish demands for autonomy. Two hundred thousand troops, including the new Pasdaran Revolutionary Guards, were deployed to retake control of Iranian Kurdistan, killing thousands in the process.[21] The 1980 Iraqi invasion of Iran saw the KDPI, Komala, and other Kurdish groups take advantage of the situation to again declare autonomy and push Iranian troops out of Kurdistan. By 1984, however, Iranian troops recovered the territory, KDPI and Komala militants turned on each other due to a number of ideological differences and personal quarrels, and both groups were pushed into the mountains of Iraq.[22] In Iraq, the PUK helped the KDPI and Komala find sanctuary and evade Iranian troops.

In 1989, Iran arranged a meeting with Dr. Abdul Rahman Ghasemlou, the leader of the KDPI, to discuss reconciliation, but assassinated him and two of his associates at the meeting place in Vienna, Austria. A few weeks after that, a senior Komala leader was assassinated in Cyprus. Ghasemlou's successor, Dr. Sadegh Sharafkindi, was assassinated in Berlin, Germany, in 1992.[23] Although Tehran assassinated many more opposition figures before and after these particular incidents, Ghasemlou and Sharafkindi stood out as particularly important coups for the Iranian intelligence services. The KDPI experienced difficulties recovering from the loss of two successive and well-regarded leaders.

With the creation of the Kurdish Autonomous Region in 1992, the KDPI and Komala gained more secure tenure over their sanctuaries in Iraq, however. They were allowed to establish bases in Khoy Sinjak (hills between the cities of Suleimaniya and Erbil) and near Suleimaniya. Iran initially demanded the expulsion of both groups, and sealed its border with Iraqi Kurdistan to add pressure to its demand. Under protection of U.S.-led Operation Provide Comfort, Iraqi Kurds this time refused to hand them over. The KDPI and Komala launched occasional armed activities in Iran in the early 1990s, but mostly focused on propaganda activities and building a stronger political base. They played a cat-and-mouse game with Iranian agents in the area (who by all accounts still have a pervasive presence there), losing many of their cadres to assassination. KDPI cadres claimed that because of these Iranian agents, "if a *peshmarga* [who] belonged to the KDPI or Komala went to the city of Suleimaniya alone, the chances of him returning back alive was only five per cent [sic]."[24] Iranian air raids on the KDPI and Komala bases occurred a number of times in the 1990s, as did a ground attack in 1996 involving Iranian troops that the PUK had allowed to transit through the area (though the PUK also called and warned the Iranian Kurds in advance that the troops were coming).

By the late 1990s, the parties had reached an understanding of sorts. The Iraqi Kurds allowed the KDPI and the two factions of the Komala(h) to become comfortable in their Iraqi Kurdish bases as long as they limited their activities to political propaganda and did not launch armed attacks against Iran. The Iranians were unhappy about this but tolerated it, and allowed the KDP and PUK to open representation offices in Tehran (similar to those in Ankara). Iran in turn supported a growing Kurdish Islamist movement in Iraqi Kurdistan, including some groups like Ansar al-Islam (which had links to al Qaeda) that occasionally clashed militarily with the Iraqi Kurds, conducted terrorist bombings, and occasionally served as agents of Iran targeting KDPI and Komala cadres.[25] Iran effectively used the Islamist Kurdish movement as both a deterrent and coercive asset vis-à-vis the Iraqi Kurds, forcing them to continue containing Iranian Kurdish groups in their territory. The Iraqi Kurds (especially the PUK) were unhappy about this, but were forced to accept it. The Iranian price for keeping their border with Iraqi Kurdistan open and supporting the PUK against the KDP (between 1994 and 1998) also included closing down a KDPI radio station broadcasting into Iran (the broadcasting station was promptly moved to Kirkuk, in the part of Iraq controlled by Saddam).[26] Tehran thus effectively neutralized the threat from the KDPI and Komala(h), which no longer pursue armed resistance in Iran.[27] According to KDPI leader Mustafa Hijri, "Yes, we have guerrillas but now we have no military action. We are organizing politically within Iranian Kurdistan. We are not allowed by the Iraqi Kurdish organizations to establish an army here and have them act. We believe that in time that organizing people inside Iranian Kurdistan is more effective than military action."[28] None of these Iranian Kurdish opposition groups chose to resort to terrorism either, unlike the non-Kurdish Iranian opposition group Mojahedin-e Khalq (MEK), which from its bases in Saddam's Iraq has launched a number of spectacular terrorist bombings in Iranian territory since 1979.

The 2003 invasion of Iraq initially put Iran on the defensive, as it feared becoming the next U.S. target for regime change. One of Iran's Kurdish Islamist client groups, Ansar al-Islam, was also ejected from its mountainous bases in Iraqi Kurdistan by a combined U.S. Special Forces and PUK offensive in March 2003. The Iranians acted quickly to take advantage of the monumental changes in Iraq, however, establishing two consulates in Iraqi Kurdistan (in Erbil and Suleimaniya)[29] and enjoying a great deal of influence through Shiite parties in Baghdad as well. Approximately nineteen foreign consulates have since been opened in Iraqi Kurdistan, with Turkey (despite its shared border and deep interests in the region) one of the last to follow suit in 2010. Unlike their Turkish counterparts, Iranian diplomats from the beginning expressed no hesitation in holding official meetings with officials of the Kurdistan Regional Government in Erbil and Suleimaniya. KRG officials regularly travel to Tehran for high-level meetings as well. Although Iran very much opposes the creation of a Kurdish state, it seems to have less problem than Turkey initially did with a Kurdish autonomous region that it can wield a great deal of influence on.

The KDPI and Komala(h) dissidents are thus still prevented from engaging in armed operations from Iraq, despite widespread Kurdish unhappiness with the regime in Tehran[30] and the increased security that U.S.-supported Iraqi Kurds enjoy vis-à-vis Iranian pressure and the threat of invasion. When the United States occasionally arrested Iranian diplomats in the KRG and in Baghdad (a total of twenty such arrests occurred),[31] Iraqi Kurdish officials quickly demanded their release—despite the fact that these individuals were almost certainly involved in Iranian intelligence activities detrimental to Iraqi Kurdish interests. This stands in stark contrast to the July 2003 American arrest of a dozen Turkish Special Forces soldiers, which KRG officials remained mum about.[32]

In 2004 a new Iranian opposition group emerged, however, which proved quite willing to pursue armed struggle against the regime in Tehran. PJAK, the Free Life Party of Kurdistan, declared itself from bases in the Iraqi Kurdish Qandil Mountains, not far from the bases of the PKK. Although the group insists that it is separate from the PKK, links between the two appear extensive, and both pay a great deal of homage to incarcerated PKK leader Öcalan. Many former members of the PKK, which included Iranian, Iraqi, and Syrian Kurds since the 1980s, now lead and fight for PJAK. Taking advantage of increased disaffection among Iranian Kurds since Mahmoud Ahmedinejad's election in 2005, PJAK has, since its founding, launched scores of operations targeting Iranian military and police forces. PJAK appears to field a couple of thousand armed fighters in Iraq, with many more supporters inside Iran itself. The group's English-language website (pjak.org) provides a good idea of its platform and typical activities.[33] As the history of its activities indicates, PJAK completely eschews terrorism and seems intent on projecting a progressive image designed to elicit international support.[34]

An Iranian failure to liberalize and reform also contributed to the resurgence of the conditions that foster Kurdish unrest in the first place. Rather than offering positive inducements, Iranian efforts to combat PJAK include (1) increased coordination with Turkey, which views PJAK and the PKK as one and the same organization; (2) artillery barrages against PJAK's Qandil bases and nearby Iraqi Kurdish villages; (3) an increased military (around 200,000 troops) and police presence in Iranian Kurdistan; (4) demands to the KRG and Baghdad that the group be contained or evicted from Iraqi territory; and (5) improved border posts, surveillance, and in some cases barriers. Iran's inability to secure sufficient KRG or Iraqi cooperation in this matter seems to place it in a situation similar to Turkey's vis-à-vis the PKK, although PJAK does seem to enjoy less freedom to move around the KRG region than the PKK does. The principal explanation for the failure to deter PJAK, as opposed to the KDPI and Komala(h), also appears similar: PJAK based itself in the most rugged mountains of Iraq, which the KRG cannot control. According to KRG official Safeen Dizayee, "5,000, even 50,000 troops" could not control Qandil, just as Saddam never managed to control the area either.[35] Dizayee added that "the United States does not want another Tora Bora," meaning that U.S. forces would also find dislodging the PKK and PJAK next to impossible. PJAK's presence in Qandil may also serve the interests of the United States and the KRG as a card to play against Iran. PJAK also denies radical Islamists like Ansar al-Islam or al Qaeda in Iraq use of the Qandil Mountains, or free passage in that area from Iran into Iraq. PJAK leader Rahman Haji Ahmadi described the situation in this way: "Turkey wants to control the Qandil mountains with Iran. When they do, they will open the border and allow al Qaeda and Ansar al Islam fighters to come in. And this will make Erbil [the capital of Iraqi Kurdistan] like Fallujah used to be."[36]

CONCLUSION

Both Tehran and Ankara possess a great deal of familiarity with their respective Kurdish dissident groups as well as with the neighboring Iraqi Kurds. This has allowed both states to deter, coerce, and occasionally offer positive inducements in a fairly effective fashion. Nonetheless, the Iranian approach appears to have been somewhat more successful than that of Turkey, at least vis-à-vis the KDPI and Komala(h). The indirect strategy of having the Iraqi Kurdish Regional Government contain these groups, but not insisting that they be expelled, proved especially effective. Iranian diplomacy and recognition of the Kurdistan Regional Government appears to have secured Iraqi Kurdish cooperation, even after 2003 and despite the close relationship the KRG now enjoys with the United States. While Turkish efforts to recruit Iraqi Kurdish allies against the PKK also bore occasional fruit in the 1990s, Turkey witnessed a return of PKK attacks in 2004 and not much cooperation from the KRG.

For Turkey and Iran, the limits of both coercive strategies and inducements against the KRG appeared in the rugged terrain of Iraqi Kurdistan's Qandil Mountains. The fact that PKK (and now PJAK) militants seem to have nowhere else left to turn also exacerbates the problem, together with, of course, Kurdish disaffection with both states. From where the Kurdistan Regional Government securely controls its territory, however, no dissident group attacks neighboring states. While stronger than in the 1990s, the KRG remains too weak and threatened to move against PKK and PJAK forces in their mountain bases, even assuming that the Iraqi Kurds had enough of an interest to do so. An apt parallel may be found in Israel's dealings with its neighbors: armed attacks against Israelis today come not from Egypt, Jordan, or Syria, but from the territory of a much weaker Lebanese state and weakly consolidated Palestinian Authorities. The lesson appears to be as follows: unconsolidated, weak neighbors provide non-state actors with territory to operate in and attack from. More-consolidated, stronger states (such as Syria and Jordan after 1970) or pseudo-states such as the KRG can be expected to act rationally when coerced or threatened, and cooperation from such authorities is essential when trying to contain non-state actors outside one's own territorial boundaries. Hence it would appear to be in Turkey and Iran's interest to have a stronger and more secure KRG that can eventually control all its territory, including the Qandil Mountains, but which will undoubtedly remain weaker, and hence easier to influence, than its neighbors.

In the cases examined here, Turkish and Iranian strategies for ending terrorist attacks also appear identical to strategies aimed at stopping attacks on uniformed soldiers and security forces. Dissuading groups such as the PKK from resorting to terrorism in the course of their armed struggle probably depends more on the international community's policies than those of the Turkish or Iranian states. Successful Turkish or Iranian deterrence of guerrilla attacks by these groups may lead to an insurgent calculus wherein terrorist attacks (on "softer" targets, by definition) remain the only available means of armed struggle. If the international community clearly communicates and acts on its revulsion for terrorist tactics, irrespective of the legitimacy of the goals sought by Kurds, Palestinians, Tamils, Sikhs, Punjabis, Irish, or Islamists, militarily contained groups will more likely limit themselves to non-violent tactics, as the KDPI and Komala(h) have done. Terrorism is not just the tactic of the weak—it is the tactic of weak and ruthless utilitarians. If the price in public sympathy and international support for resorting to such tactics, as opposed to guerrilla warfare or peaceful protest, appears too high, even the ruthless will eschew it, as PJAK seems to be doing today. Even the PKK has tried to shed its terrorist image and designation.[37] Although the PKK targeted many civilians in the 1980s and 1990s, mostly "village guards" and their families—armed by Ankara to fight the PKK—as well as Turkish civil servants, PKK officials insist that they have eschewed such a policy in recent years.[38] In contrast to groups such as Hamas, which glorify suicide bombings against civilian targets, the PKK today denies targeting civilians. In January 2008, PKK military commander Bahoz Erdal (a.k.a. Fehman Hussein) unequivocally stated: "We are not fighting without cause, but are defending our national values, and we show sensitivity—especially when it comes to civilians. We have never harmed civilians intentionally, and we will not do so in the future."[39] The PKK thus claims that its attacks are limited to the armed forces of the Turkish state and national infrastructure such as power plants.

Their denials notwithstanding, possible PKK front groups may now conduct the occasional terrorist strike on behalf of the organization. Commander Erdal, for instance, recently warned tourists to avoid Turkey: "Turkey is not safe for tourists, and we advise them to stay away from it. Extremist Kurdish organizations like the Kurdistan Freedom Hawks (TAK) have targeted tourists in the past, and continue to threaten them in Turkey [today]. We cannot predict what will happen in the future."[40] A very logical PKK strategy would include harming Turkey's tourism industry and the income it generates. Other bombings such as the January 3, 2008, bomb blast in Diyarbakir—in which five people, including three children, were killed—lacked any claim of responsibility, but Ankara blamed the PKK. In any case, the PKK remains on not only Turkey's list of terrorist organizations, but that of the United States, Canada, Australia, the UK, and the European Union as well.

PKK leaders seem to be trying to find a way to come down from the mountains, however, and the best deterrent strategy probably involves giving them a way to do so. PKK leaders insist that their goals no longer involve carving a separate Kurdish state from eastern Turkey and that they are open to a negotiated peace to achieve "Kurdish rights and democracy." Although it would prove exceedingly difficult for a Turkish politician or Iranian leader to make visible concessions to groups such as the PKK and PJAK, robust minority-rights reforms paired with some kind of amnesty that includes the leadership of such groups could serve as a much more effective long-term strategy for dealing with them.

Given that all the Kurdish dissident groups examined here wish to avoid the terrorist label, the international community could also play a role in reducing terrorism—by not labeling groups such as PJAK, the KDPI, and the Komalas as "terrorists,"[41] and offering to take the PKK off the terrorist lists should it stop targeting civilians for a sustained period of time. While Turkey and Iran probably lack the political will or ability to offer such a positive inducement to groups willing to eschew the targeting of civilians, the international community's view does matter to these groups. If no amount of internal reform and sincere changes in tactics can get a group off international terrorist lists, however, it will obviously have less incentive to eschew terrorism. Casualties, especially innocent lives, will then remain higher than they need be.

NOTES

1. For some of the classic theoretical texts on power, influence, deterrence, and compellence, see Robert Dahl, "The Concept of Power," *Behavioral Science* 2:3 (1957): 201–15; Kal Holsti, "The Concept of Power in the Study of International Relations," *Background* 7:4 (1964): 179–94; and Thomas Schelling, *Arms and Influence* (New Haven, CT: Yale University Press, 1966).

2. The distinction between a "terrorist" and an "insurgent" is a difficult one to make. For the purposes of this discussion, a terrorist intentionally targets civilians in the pursuit of political goals. An insurgent enjoys the sympathy and support of a proportion of a state's population. Of course, an insurgent may employ terrorist means (a "terrorist insurgent," if you will), and whether or not insurgents target civilians, they are typically labeled "terrorists" by the states they oppose. The distinction between "counterterrorism" and "counterinsurgency" thus also poses difficulties that are not completely resolved here. It appears, however, that while "hearts and minds" campaigns

and negotiated settlements can form part of counterinsurgency policies, this does not usually hold true for counterterrorism strategies.

3. Well known revolts include the Sheikh Said Uprising (1925), the Mount Ararat Rebellion (1927–30), the Dersim Revolt (1937–38), and the Kurdistan Workers' Party (PKK) guerrilla war (early 1980s to present day) in Turkey; the Barzinji Rebellions (1920s and 1932) and various revolts led by Mullah Mustafa Barzani (1940s through the 1970s) and his son and other associates (1970s, 1980s, and 1991) in Iraq; and the Simko Revolt (1920s), the secession of the Republic of Kurdistan in Mahabad (1945–46), and the attempt of various Kurdish groups to get autonomy within the Islamic Republic (early 1980s) in Iran.

4. Galia Golan, *Soviet Policies in the Middle East: From World War Two to Gorbachev* (Cambridge: Cambridge University Press, 1990), 157–75.

5. Mahmut Bali Aykan, "Turkish Perspectives on Turkish-US Relations Concerning Persian Gulf Security in the Post–Cold War Era: 1989–1995," *Middle East Journal* 50:3 (1996): 354.

6. Joshua Itzkowitz Shifrinson, "The Kurds and Regional Security: An Evaluation of Developments Since the Iraq War," *Middle East Brief* No. 14 (2006).

7. Funda Keskin, "Turkey's Trans-Border Operations in Northern Iraq: Before and After the Invasion of Iraq," *Research Journal of International Studies* No. 8 (2008).

8. *Hurriyet* (Turkish mass-circulation daily), http://fotoanaliz.hurriyet.com.tr/GaleriDetay.aspx?cid=6755&p=1&rid=4369 (accessed November 2010).

9. KDP official Safeen Dizayee, interview with author, June 11, 1999, Ankara. *Peshmerga* is a Kurdish term for Kurdish fighters that literally means "those who face death."

10. BBC News, "PKK 'Behind' Turkey Resort Bomb," July 17, 2005.

11. See David Romano, "PKK Triumphant as Turkey Retreats from Northern Iraq," *Eurasia Daily Monitor* 5:40 (2008).

12. Militants in the Qandil Mountains that I spoke to in 2004 found the demand that they inform on their comrades the most objectionable, and dishonorable, of the amnesty's myriad conditions.

13. It remains impossible to conduct a credible survey on the opinions of Kurds in Turkey regarding this issue, of course. The assessment presented here of popular Turkish Kurdish sentiment is thus the author's own subjective opinion, based on discussions held on numerous trips to both western and eastern Turkey since 1999. Examples of humiliations include refusing to recognize Kurdish as a language, belittling Iraqi Kurdish leaders as "tribal chieftains," finding various excuses to forbid parents from giving their children some Kurdish names, and referring to "a Kurdish problem" while simultaneously denying the existence of a Kurdish minority in Turkey (or rejecting the existence of a "Kurdish problem" and insisting that there exists only "a terrorism problem").

14. Turkish businessmen have, in contrast to their government, moved quickly to deal with Iraqi Kurdistan and invest heavily in the region; Turkish companies built the region's two airports, much of its new road system, and a new university in Suleimaniya. In 2009, Turkey's foreign minister did announce a change in Turkish policy, however, stating that Turkey would open a consulate in the Kurdish region.

15. Massoud Barzani, interview with Turkish mass daily *Milliyet*, October 30, 2007. Turkish columnist Mehmet Ali Birand adds: "Massoud Barzani eats at the White House with President [George W.] Bush. Then he goes to the European Parliament and has lunch with the representatives. He even tours Europe and makes friends with leaders. What does he find when he goes back home? Turkey calls him a tribal chieftain. He is refused admittance. He's treated as a nobody. This is the attitude that upsets Massoud Barzani most and goads him into protecting the PKK." Mehmet Ali Birand, "Should We Start to Take Barzani Seriously?" *Turkish Daily News*, November 10, 2007.

16. Foreign Minister Davutoglu's trip to Erbil was a successful one, however, and may well signify a new era of improved relations between the KRG and Turkey. KRG authorities surprised Davutoglu at the airport with a group of Kurdish children waving the Kurdish and Turkish flags. In the past, displaying the Kurdish flag along with Turkey's flag would have led a Turkish official to cancel his visit, but Davutoglu instead took the Kurdish children into his arms and kissed them (author's discussion with KRG representative to the United States, Qubad Talabani, November 15, 2009, Memphis, Tennessee). In early 2011, Turkish prime minister Recep Tayyip Erdoğan made his first visit to Iraqi Kurdistan, signaling that relations had indeed taken a new turn. The results of the new improved relationship will take a bit more time to evaluate, however.

17. Tözün Bahçeli and Peter Fragiskatos write that "Ankara has accused the KRG, and Barzani in particular, of not merely tolerating the PKK but providing the organization with logistical support." At a press conference in Istanbul on June 1, 2007, Yaşar Büyükanit, Turkey's chief of the general staff, darkly threatened that a military operation might involve wider aims than attacking the PKK. He asked: "Are we going to fight only the PKK once we enter northern Iraq or will something happen with Barzani?" Tözün Bahçeli and Peter Fragiskatos, "Iraqi Kurdistan: Fending Off Uneasy Neighbours," *International Journal of Contemporary Iraqi Studies* 2:1 (2008): 67–82.

18. Sources in the KRG confided in the author their suspicion that Iran provides false intelligence reports to Turkey, implicating the KRG, the United States, and Israel in supporting the PKK. The Turks in turn appear eager to believe the reports, which quickly circulate through Turkish mainstream media. Such a strategy could certainly serve Iran's interests, should it manage to alienate Turkey from the KRG and its U.S. and Israeli allies.

19. David McDowall, *A Modern History of the Kurds* (New York: I. B. Tauris, 1997), 253.

20. Hussein Tahiri, *The Structure of Kurdish Society and the Struggle for a Kurdish State* (Costa Mesa, CA: Mazda, 2007), 134–41.

21. For more details on the 1979–80 "pacification" of Iranian Kurdistan, including mass executions, destruction of villages, and the creation of "village guard" movements, see Tahiri, *Structure of Kurdish Society*, 141–58.

22. McDowall, *History of the Kurds*, 275–76.

23. Ibid., 277.

24. Quoted in Tahiri, *Structure of Kurdish Society*, 303.

25. See David Romano, "An Outline of Kurdish Islamist Groups in Iraq," *Jamestown Occasional Papers Series*, September 17, 2007, 1–20.

26. Tahiri, *Structure of Kurdish Society*, 303–4.

27. Author's interview with Central Committee members of Komalah, Komala, and the KDPI, April 21, 25, and 29, 2004, Khoy Sinjak and Suleimaniya camps, Iraqi Kurdistan.

28. Author's interview, April 29, 2004, Khoy Sinjak, Iraqi Kurdistan.

29. Kenneth Katzman, "Iran's Activities and Influence in Iraq," Congressional Research Services Report for Congress, June 4, 2009, 7.

30. For more on Tehran's poorly publicized discrimination against Iranian Kurds, see Kerim Yildiz and Tanyel Taysi, *The Kurds in Iran: The Past, Present and Future* (London: Pluto Press and Kurdish Human Rights Project, 2007).

31. Katzman, "Iran's Activities," 5–6.

32. The Turkish Special Forces were probably in Iraqi Kurdistan to foment instability, thereby giving Turkey an excuse to intervene. The intelligence leading to their arrest and detention by the United States probably came from the KRG as well. They were quickly released after Turkey threatened to deny the United States access to the Incirlik airbase.

33. For instance, an "activities report" for PJAK's military activities in July 2008, reads: "Media and Publication Center of the Free Life Party of Kurdistan—PJAK 05 July 2008, Military dispatch for the month of July: Eastern Defense Forces of Kurdistan-HRK: Iranian's military large scale operations: 5; HRK fighters military operations: 8; Total of Iranian forces Killed: 51; Commandos: 13; Revolutionary Guards: 30; Colonel of the Revolutionary Guards killed: 1; Contra-guerillas: 7; Iranian military vehicles destroyed: 10; Iranian armored vehicles destroyed: 1 . . . HRK fighters destroyed two local important revolutionary guards headquarters. HRK forces attacked a group building a military quarters, they captured an engineer and released him. Our fighter Mr. Jalil Karimi was martyred during clashes against the Iranian army in Kirmanshah city area. . . . The Iranian army and Revolutionary Guards shelled the areas under PJAK control for 7 different times including Kandil mountain

and the borders villages in Iraq-Kurdistan Regional Government (KRG) inflicting damages on the Kurdish civilian and their properties. During this heavy arterially bombardment our military forces did not sustain any loss or damage. American spy airplanes were seen 7 times before and during the Iranian army shelling. . . . These military operations are in response to the Iranian coordinated attacks and atrocities against PJAK, the Kurdish and Iranian people. PJAK is for democratic values, freedom and peace. It is against any suicide or terrorist attacks and killing of civilians, it adheres to the United Nations Human rights declaration and international laws. It is a freedom fighters movement for the Kurdish and Iranian people. . . . Free Life Party of Kurdistan (PJAK), Media and Publication Center."

34. PJAK's refusal to ever target civilians differentiates it from the PKK.

35. Interview with Turkish mass circulation daily *Hurriyet*, February 28, 2008.

36. Kenneth Timmerman, "Obama Blacklists Kurdish Group in Gesture to Tehran," *Newsmax*, February 9, 2009.

37. Portions of this paragraph and the next are adapted from my article "Turkey and Iraqi Kurds Agree to Disagree on PKK's Terrorist Status," *Eurasia Daily Monitor* 5:25 (July 1, 2008).

38. Author's interview, PKK Qandil Mountain base, Iraq, April 2004.

39. Elaph Publishing, "PKK Military Wing Commander: Turkey May Become Exact Replica of Iraq," January 31, 2008, http://www.kurdishaspect.com/doc030408MEM .html#anchor_62 (accessed January 2012).

40. Ibid.

41. At the time of this writing, the U.S. Treasury Department (but not other branches of the U.S. government) designates PJAK as a terrorist organization (see Timmerman, "Obama Blacklists Kurdish Group").

11 MISSION IMPOSSIBLE?
Influencing Iranian and Libyan Sponsorship of Terrorism

Michael D. Cohen

CAN STATES DETER or influence the sponsorship of terrorism by other states?[1] A large body of research has addressed the deterrence of the use of conventional and nuclear force in interstate relations. In the "fourth wave" of deterrence literature, theorists have also assessed whether terrorists and state sponsors of nuclear, chemical, biological, and radiological terrorism might be deterred. But very little research has addressed the state sponsorship of terrorism. More specifically, we do not know what causes cross-national variation in the state sponsorship of conventional terrorism. We do not know what is required to successfully influence such sponsorship.

This is a serious shortcoming. While many of the most threatening terrorist groups, like Hezbollah, Hamas, and al Qaeda, for instance, no longer require the state support that they once received, state sponsorship helped these groups develop their core competencies and organizational and technical expertise. Furthermore, not only have various terrorist groups required different types of state sponsorship to achieve their goals, but some states continue to sponsor terrorists to achieve their security objectives. State-sponsored terrorism in South Asia, the Middle East, and elsewhere is today considered a critical national security threat. If we are to retard the growth of existing terrorist groups and impede the birth of new ones, understanding what aspects of state sponsorship of conventional terrorism can be influenced and deterred is a critical question.

The chapter is structured as follows. The first section addresses the literatures on coercive diplomacy and state sponsorship of terrorism. The second section outlines four variables that might explain variation in state sponsorship.

The third section offers comparative case studies of Iranian and Libyan sponsorship and shows how these variables varied. The chapter concludes that successfully influencing state sponsorship of terrorism is likely to be exceptionally difficult because other variables, like the state of the international economy and domestic responses to economic uncertainties, caused Libyan cessation. Successfully coercing state sponsorship may be impossible without the right economic weaknesses in the sponsor.

INFLUENCING STATE SPONSORSHIP

Many scholars assume that most terrorist groups require different types of state sponsorship. However, which types of groups tend to rely on what types of state sponsorship is unclear. Ian Shapiro has argued that it is implausible to think that any terrorist group able to present a serious and ongoing challenge to American security would be able to do so without some form of state sponsorship.[2] Bruce Hoffman has also suggested that over 90 percent of terrorist groups do not survive their first year. Of those that do, nearly all obtained state resources for military training, financial support, territorial sanctuary, logistical and organizational aid, and/or diplomatic and ideological support.[3] Other studies suggest a strong link between domestic terrorist groups in the West and other actors.[4] Daniel Byman showed that of the thirty-six terrorist groups designated as foreign terrorist organizations by the U.S. secretary of state in 2002, twenty (55 percent) had enjoyed "significant" state support at some point in their history.[5] But it is difficult to ascertain the degree to which terrorist groups depend on different types of state sponsorship throughout their development and what to do about it.

There is often little evidence connecting terrorists to their sponsors.[6] While Joseph Lepgold asserted that terrorists may be easier to influence and manipulate as their dependence on states increases, accurately predicting that relationship is difficult.[7] It is often hard to detect when terrorist groups have weaned themselves off their sponsor and become self-reliant. It is thus problematic for an influence strategy to stipulate which type of support will be met with which type of punishment. Moreover, any threats by the coercer may increase the legitimacy of the terrorist group among certain audiences. This could then place additional pressure on the state to continue sponsoring it. Efforts to influence or deter state sponsorship of terrorism could thus cause what they were designed to prevent. The specific properties of terrorism, as Martha Crenshaw concludes, complicate the case for coercive diplomacy.[8]

Byman has contributed the most to address the causes of state sponsorship and the means to influence it. He offered a rich empirical study of the main state sponsors of terrorism. He noted that state sponsors value the benefits of sponsorship, believe that the costs are tolerable, have few strategic alternatives but to facilitate terrorism, and are often motivated by ideological rationales. State sponsors also usually show more resolve to continue facilitating terrorism than the coercer does to stop such activity. Moreover, Byman found that the United States and other major powers often misunderstand the logic behind the state sponsorship of terrorism.[9]

However, Byman's study does not explain variation in state sponsorship. Why did Libya stop sponsoring terrorists in the early 1990s while Iran continues to do so twenty years later? He notes that coercive pressure can induce concessions from the target state, but does not specify which types of pressure cause which type of concessions. Furthermore, while Byman notes that a decline in revolutionary fervor correlates with a decrease in sponsorship, it is hard to know whether revolutionary fervor masks other strategic imperatives. Declining revolutionary zeal may neither be necessary nor sufficient to cause a cessation of state sponsorship if changing economic conditions, for instance, help diminish enthusiasm for particular ideologies. Whereas Byman notes that threats and the use of military force might be necessary to stop state sponsorship, he does not address which of these strategies explain variation in state sponsorship.

Bruce Jentleson and Christopher Whytock assessed why Libya relinquished its nuclear weapons program and renounced the sponsorship of terrorism.[10] However, they do not address which coercive variables explain what behavior in this case, so it is hard to know what lessons to infer for this and other cases of terrorism sponsorship. American strategy during the Bill Clinton administration and early George W. Bush administration combined threats of force and deft diplomacy. Likewise, other states contributed to a U.S.-led multilateral sanctions regime, opposition to cooperation within the Libyan elite was minimal, and the weak Libyan economy was unable to sustain the costs of defying U.S. and international pressure. However, Jentleson and Whytock do not address which of these variables might explain variation in state sponsorship in other cases. What successes from the Libyan case offer insights that apply elsewhere?

WHAT IS TO BE INFLUENCED?

What is state sponsorship of terrorism? One can start with the distinction between active and passive sponsorship. Active sponsorship involves the intentional transfer of resources such as money, arms, and logistics, or the provision of territorial sanctuary to the terrorist group by the regime or state. It can also involve assistance with organization, training and operations, ideological direction, and diplomatic support or recognition.[11] Shmuel Bar refers to this category of sponsorship as proxies and partnerships.[12] On the other hand, passive sponsorship involves a state not intervening to stop a terrorist group from raising funds, from enjoying sanctuary within a given territory, and/or from recruiting or being supported by other individuals or groups within the state's territorial jurisdiction. Passive sponsors have the capacity to hinder terrorist development within their borders but choose not to.[13] A third category involves states that have tried and failed to hinder terrorist development within their borders, governments that were genuinely unaware of terrorist activity on their territory, and states that lack the ability to counter terrorism effectively though they may want to.

The type of active sponsorship most crucial to the survival and long-term success of terrorist groups includes the provision of territorial sanctuary, money, arms, and logistics. Obstructing, influencing, and deterring this type of sponsorship is a central goal for coercive diplomacy directed at state sponsorship.[14] The provision of money, arms, and logistics to terrorist groups should be easier to influence than the providing of sanctuary. There will always be weakly governed regions that terrorists can relocate to and regimes unable or willing to convincingly feign an inability to challenge terrorist groups located within their sovereign jurisdiction. Alternatively, a terrorist group may have widespread, local legitimacy such that threatening removal of territorial sanctuary is to threaten the survival of the regime or government itself. Claims by representatives of such states that they have no ability to influence terrorist groups are thus partially true because the legitimacy of the state partly depends on the survival (and at times even the success) of the terrorist group. State sponsorship of money, arms, and logistics could involve either state control, coordination, or contact.[15] Full control is rare (and by definition not state-sponsored terrorism but state terrorism). Contact is more common but generally difficult to influence effectively. Coordination is more than contact but not control and entails a state influencing some aspect of an autonomous terrorist group's agenda. State sponsors of terrorism can include ruling elites, a non-state group supported by the state, and competing elites or bureaucracies within the state. The latter is perhaps best thought of as fragmented sponsorship, because the sponsor(s) and the relationships between them and other non-state and substate groups are often hard to detect. Ruling elites, for instance, could delegate the sponsorship of terrorism to elements within the bureaucracy in order to escape detection or to increase leverage over other leaders and rivals. The bureaucracy could betray the trust of its principal backer and encourage the terrorist group to engage in activities that increase its power vis-à-vis the ruling elites. Alternatively, powerful individuals or interest groups within a state could also sponsor terrorism. A final distinction to be made is between deterring state sponsorship (before it occurs) and compelling the cessation of state sponsorship (after it has occurred). The latter is harder to accomplish, although in practice the distinction between the two processes is difficult to recognize. Moreover, successful coercive diplomacy aimed at recovering what a state has already gained through terrorist sponsorship should be harder still to accomplish.

A comparative assessment of the causes of sponsorship cessation by two similar sponsors will explain the causes of variation in these cases. Both Iranian and Libyan sponsorship was authorized by elites, involved extensive forms of coordination and contact, and was expressed in the deliberate transfer of money, arms, and logistics. Yet Libya stopped sponsorship in 1993, while Iran continued through the 1990s and continued to do so more recently in Iraq, Afghanistan, Lebanon, and elsewhere.[16] What explains this variation, and what do the answers offer other efforts to deter similar types of state sponsorship elsewhere?

WHAT INFLUENCES STATE SPONSORSHIP?

To understand how state sponsorship can be influenced, we need to know why states sponsor terrorists. The coercer will seldom be more motivated than the state sponsor because sponsorship of terrorism may be necessary for political survival, whereas an inability to deter or even influence the state sponsorship of terrorism will rarely lead to political suicide for the coercer.[17] There are multiple strategic incentives for states to sponsor terrorism. Sponsorship can challenge efforts by major powers to contain undesirable behavior and increase the sponsor's bargaining leverage, enable power projection in both local and more distant regions where conventional superiority is impossible, and influence neighbors and regional adversaries.

Coercive diplomacy in interstate relations does not have an impressive re-cord.[18] There is no reason to believe that influencing state sponsorship of ter-rorism will fare any better. Yet if terrorists are hard to deter, influencing states from sponsoring them should be easier (but not easy). Most governments not only want to survive, but also seek sustainable economic growth, a substantial military potential, or some combination of these and other goals. What they desire can be threatened. Accordingly, state sponsorship of terrorism should be easier to influence than the terrorists themselves.

Key here is the asymmetry of resolve. Robert Jervis argued that conflict and crisis initiation is explained better by the balance of resolve than by the balance of power.[19] Alexander George noted that the three variables explain-ing most of the variation in cases of successful and failed coercive diplomacy are closely related to the opponent's perceptions of the balance of resolve. Coercive diplomacy is facilitated if the challenger believes that an asymmetry of motivation operates in favor of the coercing power, that it is time urgent to respond to the coercing power's demands, and that the coercing power will engage in escalation that would impose unacceptable costs.[20] Influencing state sponsors of terrorism will be difficult because the target states must be-lieve that the coercer is more motivated to successfully influence sponsorship than the target is to resist. Yet, the targets of coercion will usually find state sponsorship so attractive that the coercer will find it difficult to threaten and/ or punish them sufficiently to cause cessation.[21]

The coercive diplomacy literature suggests that there are at least four variables that may influence state sponsorship: (1) a strategy that contains the right configuration of proportionality, reciprocity, and coercive credibility; (2) international support for the coercing state's strategy; (3) opposition groups within the target state who believe that the benefits derived from stop-ping sponsorship are greater than those that come from defiance of the inter-national coercive effort; and (4) an inability of the state sponsor's domestic economy to recover some of the potential costs incurred by defying coercive demands. Each is individually addressed below.

First, devising a successful influence strategy will depend on achieving the proper balance between threats of force and diplomacy that is consistent with the criteria of proportionality, reciprocity, and coercive credibility.[22] Propor-tionality refers to the relationship between the scope of the objectives being pursued and the instruments being used to achieve them. If the demand to stop sponsoring terrorism carries a high cost of cooperation, the strategy must increase the costs of noncompliance and/or increase the benefits of compliance. If the means to influence the cessation of terrorism sponsorship are limited, the objectives of the strategy should be similarly limited such that there is proportionality between means and ends. Limited means require limited goals; the main source of disproportionality is an objective that goes beyond mere policy change to regime change.[23] Moreover, forcible regime change is indicative of a failure of influence strategies. Reciprocity involves an explicit understanding of the linkages—perhaps incremental—between the coercer's carrots and the target's concessions. The balance lies in neither offering too little too late or demanding too much in return nor offering too much too soon or for too little in return. Credibility requires that the coercer convincingly convey to the target state that noncooperation has consequences and that it has the means to carry out the threatened punitive action.

Second, if third-party states—especially those that can reduce the costs of state-sponsor defiance—cooperate with the coercer, the more likely state sponsorship of terrorism will be successfully influenced. Costs typically involve a combination of economic sanctions and embargoes of varying severity, the withholding of aid and other economic and military assistance, and perhaps limited uses of force. The more other countries compensate for these losses, the more likely it is that coercive efforts will fail.

Third, influencing state sponsorship is more likely to be successful if opposition to cooperation within the sponsoring state and society is limited. Even when costs are to be borne from defiance, an external threat can often enhance the domestic legitimacy of the target regime, increasing its tolerance to pay costs and run risks. Coercive threats can also increase the audience costs a particular regime faces, making it more difficult for the regime to offer concessions. Is regime security augmented by defiance, or are there domestic political gains to be made from acquiescing to and genuinely improving relations with the coercing state? Much depends on the power of the ruling elites and other substate actors. To the extent that these other groups' interests are threatened by the ruling elite's compliance with the coercer's demands, they will help block external pressure imposed on the regime. To the extent that their interests are better served by accepting the concessions being demanded of the regime, they will intensify the pressure to comply.

Fourth, influencing state sponsorship will depend on the costs that military force, sanctions, and other coercive instruments can impose on the sponsoring state's economy and the benefits that trade and other economic incentives offer. This is partly a function of the strength, flexibility, and resilience of the target state's domestic economy and its capacity to absorb, alleviate, or counter the costs being imposed through ample budget resources, import substitution, or trade diversification.

IRAN: CONTINUING SPONSORSHIP

Mutual antagonism between Iran and the United States has endured since Iran's 1979 Islamic Revolution. Different U.S. administrations have expressed their concern over Iranian terrorism sponsorship, disruption of Middle Eastern peace initiatives, and efforts to acquire nuclear and other weapons of mass destruction. U.S. concern is based on Tehran's postrevolutionary hostility toward the United States and the regime's sponsorship of terrorism. Iran has objected to Washington's support for Israel and to U.S. interference in Iranian and regional politics (for example, its roles in the 1953 Iranian coup and the 1980s Iran-Iraq War). Iranian anger was reinforced following the 1988 U.S. missile attack on an Iranian airliner and, more recently, by the U.S. failure to recognize Iran's conciliatory behavior during the 1990–91 Persian Gulf War and the 2001 Afghanistan War. American objectives have varied over time, but economic sanctions have been the central feature of U.S. coercive strategies since 1979.

Proportionality, Reciprocity, and Credibility

Several shortfalls undermined the efficacy of U.S. efforts to influence Iranian sponsorship of terrorism. First, the Iranian behavior to be influenced was never clearly articulated. The United States sought to influence not only multiple behaviors simultaneously but also did not specify the degrees of action and inaction it sought. For instance, the Antiterrorism and Effective Death Penalty Act of 1996 stipulated that U.S. sanctions would be waived and Iran removed from the U.S. list of state sponsors of terrorism if Tehran ceased its efforts to acquire weapons of mass destruction. President Clinton stated that the goal of his executive order banning virtually all economic transactions with Iran was to curb Iran's pursuit of WMD along with its support for international terrorism.[24] In 2006 President George W. Bush stated bluntly that Iranian sponsorship of terrorism "in the Palestinian territories and Lebanon . . . must come to an end."[25]

Influencing such state sponsorship is difficult if the benefits of cooperation require concomitant change on two unrelated fronts. Cooperation on either front alone is still regarded as defiance, and simultaneous cooperation on both may be politically untenable for the target state in question. With only a tenuous diplomatic relationship with Iran, it is difficult for the United States to establish precisely what aspects of nuclear proliferation and/or terror sponsorship are to be stopped. Because the unacceptable Iranian behavior was never specified, the consequences of defiance could never be established, and the benefits of cooperation were unclear. Coercive credibility might have been established by the American display of force against Libya in the 1980s, in the Persian Gulf in the 1990s, against Afghanistan and Sudan in 1998, and more recently in Afghanistan and Iraq. But without stipulating what Iranian action or inaction would lead to the use of force, coercive credibility was hard to achieve, because the desired behavior was unclear. Moreover, the general hostility that marks Iranian-American relations suggests that U.S. assurances against forcible regime change may be necessary for generating Iranian concessions.[26] Without clear guarantees regarding American concessions, Iranian elites may have worried that forcible regime change was inevitable.

Multilateral Cooperation and Economic Sanctions

American unilateral sanctions forced Iran to diversify its economic partnerships. But lack of cooperation from Russia, China, and various European countries ensured that U.S. economic sanctions would have at best a weak effect on influencing Iran's sponsorship of terrorism and its nuclear development program. U.S. efforts to isolate Iran proved most successful in the military arena, where some multilateral cooperation was eventually established.[27] Yet even these measures encompassed only selected countries and failed to fully choke the flow of military hardware to Tehran. A more effective military containment of Iran might have been achieved had the United States been able to secure a United Nations arms embargo. Such efforts were never seriously pursued because of persistent doubts regarding Russian and Chinese support for such a resolution.

A 1995 executive order issued by President Clinton closed a loophole that had allowed American companies—who had become the largest consumers of Iranian oil—to resell four billion dollars' worth of Iranian crude annually to third markets. Iran initially experienced short-term costs as it struggled to find companies to take control of the oil that American firms had been responsible for marketing (which, at the time, represented nearly 25 percent of Iranian production).[28] Iran sold its oil at discounted prices and incurred a loss of several million dollars over three months.[29] It was also forced to salvage for spare parts for sophisticated oil extraction and treatment machinery, equipment that had been supplied by the United States. However, shortly after this discomfort, foreign companies took up the slack created by the departure of American firms.[30] Although Iranian oil exports—which still generated about 80 percent of Tehran's foreign exchange—dropped slightly in 1995 when broader U.S. sanctions against Iran were imposed, they had fully recovered by 1996.[31]

The United States also pressed for a moratorium on the extension or rescheduling of new export credits and new lending by international institutions. In 1991, for instance, shortly after the World Bank decided to resume its program in Iran by approving $847 million for six development projects, the United States pressured the institution into again suspending its lending. However, several states were dissatisfied with the World Bank's policy, eventually leading to the resumption of lending in 2000 and 2001 with loans totaling $232 million and $700 million respectively. Thus, although the United States received some support for its sanctions from other states and global institutions, Iran was ultimately able to diversify its trade and finance partners to deflect economic pressure over the long run.

Likewise, extensive economic ties between European states and Tehran—along with diplomatic positions that put much of Europe at odds with American initiatives—impeded broader U.S.-European cooperation. The 1996 Iran and Libya Sanctions Act (ILSA) mandated that the U.S. president impose sanctions on any foreign entity investing more than twenty million dollars a year in the Iranian or Libyan energy industry. The European Union quickly responded by issuing a regulation forbidding its companies to comply with ILSA. The EU further threatened to bring the matter before the World Trade Organization on the grounds that ILSA violated extant trade agreements against the extraterritorial application of national laws.[32] The deterrent value of ILSA virtually collapsed after May 1998 when the Clinton administration, prodded by Congress, issued the first waiver to a company violating the terms of American law and promised additional waivers for similar investments by foreign companies. American unilateral sanctions against a country not considered a threat by much of Europe and Asia failed to significantly influence Iranian sponsorship of terrorism. And as Iranian trade with American and to a lesser extent European companies declined over the past two decades, ties to Asia and other developing economies grew.

Domestic Opposition

Gauging the role that domestic opposition groups, including sociopolitical and religious elites, have had on either supporting or opposing Iran's sponsorship of terrorism is difficult. The 1997 election of moderate president Mohammad Khatami and Iran's young, Western-leaning population suggest that elements of the Iranian ruling elite and society might prefer not to sponsor terrorism. Some scholars argue that the costs of U.S.-led sanctions have taught Iran's ruling elite that the spread of the Islamic Revolution and the sponsorship of Palestinian terrorism are less important than sustained economic development, domestic stability, and integration into the global economy.[33] Iran also stopped sponsoring attacks by Shia militant groups on American forces in the Persian Gulf after the 1996 Khobar towers bombing in Saudi Arabia because of the fear of multilateral diplomatic, economic, and military pressure.[34] However, much of this speculation has neglected the role intra-elite dynamics might have on influencing policy change. Of particular importance is whether both the ruling elites and other influential opposition groups advocate less sponsorship of terror because of the possibility of multilateral sanctions or because they have learned that sponsoring terrorism is not in their interests. The forces for sponsorship seem to currently prevail over those for cessation of it.

The Costs of Defiance

Although Iran was able to circumvent most of the potential losses that resulted from unilateral sanctions, Washington's temporarily successful efforts to block World Bank and IMF funding partially undermined Iran's response to its 1990s debt crisis. The debt crisis was caused by high inflation, unemployment, and economic underdevelopment, plunges in world oil prices, Iran's long war with Iraq, and general economic mismanagement. All these factors impeded Iran's economic development, which had long been dependent on large volumes of foreign and domestic investment to help sustain key sectors and spur growth in new ones. U.S. sanctions had their greatest effect precisely during the debt crisis.[35]

Only at the turn of the century did rising oil prices allow sustainable economic development.[36] Moreover, Iran's ambitious debt repayment schedule gave Tehran strong incentives to attract foreign direct investment just before the cost of the U.S. sanctions peaked in the mid-1990s. In 1997 and 1998, when the effects of ILSA were being felt, low oil prices nearly forced Iran to default on its debt once again. While the sanctions had a limited effect on Iran's economy until other trade and financial partners could be found, the variability of world oil prices and other aspects of Iranian economic misman-agement may have influenced sponsorship of terrorism independently of U.S. influence strategies. Indeed, much of the moderation of the Khatami admin-istration may have been a result of internal dissatisfaction with the evolution of the Iranian Revolution and a growing desire for modernization rather than as a result of the sanctions.

LIBYA: CESSATION OF SPONSORSHIP

The United States and Libya enjoyed a warm relationship in the decade fol-lowing Libya's independence in 1951. After the discovery of oil in 1959, Ameri-can companies assumed a leading role in developing the Libyan oil industry, and by 1967 Tripoli was the fifth-largest producer of oil among members of the Organization of the Petroleum Exporting Countries (OPEC). Strong, mutu-ally beneficial ties gave the United States reason to hold off passing immediate judgment when a young Muammar Qaddafi took control of the country in a coup in 1969. Although Qaddafi banned the United States from using Libyan soil for military bases and even nationalized some American and other for-eign oil interests in 1973, U.S. officials still hoped that the new regime would continue to shun the Soviet influence that many of Libya's neighbors had welcomed.

However, Libya's behavior throughout the 1970s—its alleged sponsorship of the 1972 massacre of Israeli athletes at the Munich Olympic Games and the 1973 assassination of the U.S. ambassador to Sudan—gave rise to increased hostility. American alarm grew further in response to Qaddafi's open support of radical Palestinian groups, the Irish Republican Army, and his opposition to the Camp David Peace Accords between Israel and Egypt (1978). Qaddafi's radicalism and warming relationship with Moscow made Tripoli an imme-diate target of the Ronald Reagan administration when it took office in Janu-ary 1981.

Proportionality, Reciprocity, and Credibility

Eager to project an image of American resolve in response to the 1979 Soviet invasion of Afghanistan and the Islamic Revolution in Iran, Reagan commit-ted his administration to a more confrontational approach with Libya. Sever-ance of official ties was followed by the curtailment of unofficial contacts, and ended with covert action and limited military confrontations. Throughout the 1980s, the United States repeatedly voiced its opposition to Libya's sponsorship of terrorism, its weapons of mass destruction program, its opposition to the Middle East peace process, and its general regional adventurism. Qaddafi objected to U.S. support for Israel and what he perceived to be U.S. imperialism in the Middle East and Africa. A bitter relationship became poisoned following U.S. military action against Libya at the Gulf of Sidra in 1986 and after Libya took responsibility for the 1988 bombing of Pan American Flight 103 over Lockerbie, Scotland.

Following the Reagan administration's unsuccessful attempt through demonstrations of force to deter Qaddafi from sponsoring terrorism, Presidents George H. W. Bush and Clinton rejected regime change as a U.S. policy objective for Libya. However, U.S. preferences for Libyan behavior given these concessions were never specified. Coercive credibility, on the other hand, was established by Reagan's earlier uses of force against Libya and George H. W. Bush's threats and uses of force against Saddam Hussein in Iraq in 19901. The absence of reciprocity, however, undermined the proportionality and coercive credibility of the U.S. influence strategy and limited its potential to influence Libyan sponsorship, which persisted until the mid-1990s. Libyan back-channel overtures around this time appeared to show flexibility on sponsorship and WMD development.[37] But the United States showed little immediate desire to actively pursue these overtures, not least because a powerful domestic coalition—which included the families of those killed in the Lockerbie bombing—demanded that the United States not deal with Libya until all U.S. stipulations had been unconditionally satisfied.

Qaddafi, apparently frustrated by American lack of interest in his offers, turned to Britain. Secret talks laid the foundations for what became in May 1999—a month after the Lockerbie suspects had been handed over for trial— U.S.-British-Libyan secret talks. U.S. demands, however, were no different from earlier stipulations. The Americans wanted to accept Qaddafi's offer to hand over the Lockerbie suspects for trial to a third, neutral country, but feared such a development would have brought pressure on the United States to end multilateral UN sanctions. Furthermore, the Americans wanted several other concessions before lifting sanctions and began the negotiations on the condition that Qaddafi stop lobbying for an end to the sanctions.

At the first meeting in Geneva, U.S. delegate Martyn Indyk established reciprocity. He told his Libyan counterpart that multilateral sanctions would be lifted if Libya compensated the Pan Am victims and got out of terrorism.[38] Other American carrots then came in stages. In February 2004, U.S. officials reopened their diplomatic mission in Tripoli and lifted the travel ban preventing Americans from visiting Libya.[39] In 2005, the United States lifted its unilateral sanctions against Libya, and full diplomatic relations were restored, while in 2007 the United States did not block Libya's entry to the UN Security Council as a nonpermanent member. Coercive credibility was also maintained by the 2003 Iraq War and the capture of Saddam Hussein. In restricting its goals to Libyan policy change and not regime change, the United States also maintained proportionality between ends and means. The U.S. strategy to influence Libya to cease sponsorship thus contained reciprocity, proportionality, and coercive credibility.

Multilateral Cooperation and Sanctions

The United States was able to increase the pressure it already applied on Libya with its 1982 unilateral sanctions by devising and applying multilateral UN sanctions in 1992. The unilateral sanctions banned American imports of Libyan crude. However, the sanctions were mitigated by the continued import of Libyan oil into the American market through purchases on the spot oil market or as a refined product. Moreover, the appeal of Libyan oil—a high-quality crude on Europe's doorstep—led countries like Germany and Italy to assume the Libyan exports that the United States forfeited. The UK, too, increased its imports from Libya by 350 percent over the first year following the U.S. ban.[40] A similar outcome resulted when U.S. sanctions were extended to cover all U.S.-Libyan bilateral trade in 1986; Libya's ability to find substitutes greatly diminished the costs of U.S. unilateral sanctions.

Only with Libya's refusal to comply with UN Security Council Resolution 748—which demanded the surrender of the Lockerbie bombing suspects— were UN multilateral sanctions applied in April 1992. In November 1993, UNSC Resolution 883 was also passed, strengthening extant restrictions targeting Libya's airline industry, banning exports critical to its oil and gas sectors, and freezing all of Libya's international assets. Libya's inability to replace many of the banned items hurt its aviation industry, which had already been hobbled by the U.S. sanctions. Libya's tourism industry was also critically affected. More seriously, however, the UN ban on the equipment needed for the maintenance of oil refineries and other related operations forced Libya into a costly scramble for spare parts. The restrictions also prevented Libya from upgrading refineries in order to produce more gasoline for domestic consumption.[41]

There was also global uncertainty regarding the continued application of the multilateral sanctions; nobody knew whether they would be intensified or weakened at each mandated 120-day review. The result was a weakened Libyan currency and soaring inflation. Qaddafi, as a precaution, devoted substantial resources to a reserve asset bank that could be relied on if the sanctions were toughened. But the stockpiling limited the availability of funds that the government could devote to satisfying daily needs and/or investment in capital-intensive projects.[42] This forced the government to curtail most development projects. Uncertainty also further reduced incentives for foreign investors to compensate for this loss. Only with the suspension of multilateral sanctions in April 1999, along with the upswing in oil prices shortly thereafter, did Libya witness an economic revival. Growth became robust, inflation subsided, and foreign reserves swelled.

Domestic Opposition

While conservatives in Iran seem to have been able to circumvent domestic pressure to comply with U.S. demands, Libya's economic malaise translated into domestic pressure on Qaddafi to comply with U.S. and global interests. Economic discontent in the 1990s fueled political unrest, while small initiatives toward political liberalization failed to appease Qaddafi's political opponents. Qaddafi's regime faced growing political challenges from competing elites, Islamic tribal groups, militant Islamic groups, and opposition groups living in exile.[43] Military discontent also became a problem. Several coup attempts occurred, including one that warranted the arrest of an estimated two thousand dissidents and the execution of six senior army officers.[44] All these developments made Qaddafi more amenable to U.S. efforts to influence Libya's sponsorship of terrorism. While it is unclear whether such domestic resistance to the regime would have occurred in the absence of the costs inflicted by multilateral sanctions, much of it seems to have been generated by frustration with the costs of Qaddafi's political leadership and poor economic planning.

An extraordinary dispute apparently broke out in the higher echelons of Qaddafi's regime in the mid-1990s between those underscoring the need for structural economic reform and international investment and those wanting to continue to defy U.S. and other Western pressure.[45] Qaddafi was initially indecisive, but in 1998, after having ordered his military to annihilate the rural Islamic dissidents, he sided with the pragmatists. This increased the influence of officials in the regime who had become frustrated with Libya's diplomatic and economic isolation.

The Costs of Defiance

The Libyan economy had begun to weaken at about the same time that U.S. unilateral sanctions were imposed in the early 1980s. Export revenue decreased, growth rates leveled out and dropped, imports dried up, and several critical development projects geared toward the diversification of the economy were retrenched.[46] Much of Libya's energy infrastructure, unlike Iran's, was based on U.S. technology, and modernization was therefore dependent upon the assistance of American oil firms. U.S. unilateral sanctions caused the steady downturn in oil production at fields and projects once operated by American companies. Yet Libyan developmental plans and the success of U.S. coercive efforts were also closely linked to the uncertainties of global oil markets; oil revenues generated more than 95 percent of Libya's foreign exchange. From 1992 and 1999, the price of oil continued to drop. Fluctuating prices caused Libya's export earnings to vary tremendously during these years, which had serious repercussions on the whole economy. Multilateral sanctions only exacerbated the inability of Libya's already weak economy to recover.[47] Libya, unlike Iran, had little means to absorb the costs of U.S. multilateral sanctions.

CONCLUSION

A summary of efforts to coerce Iran and Libya to stop sponsoring terrorism is presented in Table 11.1. Any of the variables addressed in this chapter—other than coercive credibility—could have been necessary to influence Libya's sponsorship of terrorism. But attention to the sequencing of their effects suggests that multilateral sanctions—strong support for the coercive effort by other major powers—were probably necessary to influence Libyan sponsorship. Multilateral economic sanctions preceded and exacerbated the domestic challenges to Qaddafi's regime and partially generated the costs that severely constrained Libyan economic development. The multilateral UN sanctions went into effect in 1992 and 1993, and the domestic unrest and significant costs to Libya's economy occurred only in subsequent years. In the absence of the multilateral sanctions, Qaddafi may have been less susceptible to U.S. and British demands in the 1990s.

Table 11.1. Coercive efforts against Iran and Libya

	Iran	Libya
Proportionality	No	Yes
Reciprocity	No	Yes
Coercive credibility	Yes	Yes
Multilateral support for sanctions	No	Yes
Domestic opposition to regime	No	Yes
Insufficient economic resilience	No	Yes

In the Libyan case, proportionality and reciprocity were both established only after sponsorship stopped. This suggests that neither was necessary to cause cessation of sponsorship. Yet both were influential in persuading Libya to end its international isolation and comply with other U.S. demands. On the other hand, neither was evident in the U.S. strategy toward Iran. Indeed, proportionality and reciprocity ensured that the Qaddafi regime would survive to enjoy the benefits of acquiescing to further coercive demands. Major powers may have to credibly commit to *not* engage in forcible regime change against their weaker adversaries in order to influence their behavior. Some have argued that U.S. coercive credibility derived from the 2003 Iraq War and toppling of Saddam Hussein's regime was also necessary to compel Libya to cease terrorism sponsorship.[48] But U.S. uses of force in the first Gulf War and elsewhere did not cause Iran to cease sponsorship of terrorism, while Libya was prepared to negotiate an end to such sponsorship a decade before 2003.[49]

Severely constraining economic conditions forced Qaddafi into a desperate bargaining position. Multilateral economic sanctions may be necessary to influence the sort of state sponsorship of terrorism practiced by Iran and Libya, but they are not sufficient. They are probably less important than the right configuration of economic weaknesses that these can exploit. The fact that Qaddafi was willing to cooperate long before Washington was emphasizes that even successful influencing strategies will have limited results if the state sponsor faces moderately promising economic contexts that can foster a steadfast unwillingness to cooperate. Most cases of state sponsorship will exhibit the less-than-total dependence on the coercer that drove Gaddafi to desperation and made him willing to stop sponsorship. This sort of dependence is unfortunately rare.

A number of factors suggest that even if state sponsorship can be influenced under some limited conditions, there are good reasons to be modest about the impact of deterrence strategies in stopping state sponsorship. Thomas Schelling explained long ago that deterrence strategies can be easily overcome by a series of small developments that are each individually hard to detect and contain.[50] State sponsorship of terrorism is hard to detect and can easily be secretly reinitiated by incremental steps. Moreover, the sponsorship of terrorism will often not be the only—or even most desirable—state behavior to be influenced. State sponsors of terrorism tend to show resolve to engage in a variety of other, undesired behaviors. Iraq's nuclear ambitions, its use of chemical agents in 1988, and its treatment of minority communities, for instance, worried Western decision makers more than its sponsorship and facilitation of Palestinian suicide bombers. All this suggests that influencing the sponsorship of terrorism may be one aspect of a long list of behaviors to be challenged, and not even the most pressing one.

But public opinion in the coercing state may push for unilateral concessions on several fronts that will make devising practical influencing strategies politically untenable. Both the Libyan and Iranian cases produced strong American public pressure not to offer concessions to either state until they had acquiesced to demands to stop terrorism sponsorship and WMD development. Demanding such unilateral concessions up front may not only make the target state less likely to change its behavior, but might even spur the behavior that the threats are designed to influence. British intermediaries were highly influential in allowing secret three-way negotiations—which were themselves necessary for Qaddafi to cease sponsorship—to begin.

Finally, while reciprocity will be hard to achieve domestically, multilateral sanctions will be hard to achieve internationally. The Pan Am bombing over Lockerbie killed not only American but British, German, and French nationals, and was a catalyst for Western European cooperation in the multilateral sanctions regime. If this much has to be done to elicit multilateral sanctions, state sponsors may pressure their terrorist groups to avoid behavior that will turn international opinion against them. If other states do not perceive the state sponsor as a sufficient threat and/or greatly value the gains they acquire from continuing trade and diplomatic relations, multilateral sanctions will be very difficult to achieve.

Libya, but not Iran, exhibited an extremely high dependence not only on oil revenues but also on American machinery to generate its wealth. Libya also had a weakened economy a decade before the sanctions took effect, which were followed by requests by senior Libyan officials to engage in negotiations over terrorism sponsorship, WMD acquisition, and Libya's general isolation. Multilateral sanctions may have been necessary to induce Libya to stop sponsoring terrorism, but they were not sufficient. The economic weaknesses that compelled Qaddafi to cease sponsorship and seek reconciliation with the West will not exist in most other cases of state sponsorship. At best, the right combination of several other variables will be required for influence strategies to have limited effects. At worst, state sponsors will be able to mitigate the costs imposed on them such that influencing state sponsorship of terrorism will be almost impossible. The state sponsorship of terrorism, like terrorism itself, may be another weapon of the weak that the strong can rarely overcome.

NOTES

1. This chapter is concerned with the sponsorship of terrorism by "rogue states." Some crucial dimensions of these state sponsors of terrorism are expressed hostility to major-power interests, domestic oppression, violation of international law and norms, and unpredictability. I do not address influencing sponsorship of terrorism by the United States or its allies. Influence refers to a more diverse set of tools than punishment or denial—as in standard deterrence theory—to impede state sponsorship. Lewis Dunn, "Deterrence Today: Roles, Challenges, and Responses," *IFRI Proliferation Papers* (2007); Janice Gross Stein, "Deterrence and Reassurance," in *Behaviour, Society and Nuclear War*, vol. 2, ed. Philip Tetlock et al. (New York: Oxford University Press, 1991), 8–72.

2. Ian Shapiro, *Containment: Rebuilding a Strategy Against Global Terror* (Princeton, NJ: Princeton University Press, 2007) .

3. Bruce Hoffman, *Inside Terrorism* (New York: Columbia University Press, 1998), 84.

4. Ignacio Sánchez-Cuenca and Luis de la Calle, "Domestic Terrorism: The Hidden Side of Political Violence," *Annual Review of Political Science* 12 (2009): 31–49.

5. Daniel Byman, *Deadly Connections: States that Sponsor Terrorism* (New York: Cambridge University Press, 2005), 2–3.

6. Daniel Whiteneck recommends that states communicate that punishment will be based on reasonable evidence of state linkages. Daniel Whiteneck, "Deterring Terrorists: Thoughts on a Framework," *Washington Quarterly* 28:3 (2005): 187–99.

7. Joseph Lepgold, "Hypotheses on Vulnerability: Are Terrorists and Drug Traffickers Coerceable?" in *Strategic Coercion: Concepts and Cases*, ed. Lawrence Freedman (New York: Oxford University Press, 1998), 131–50.

8. Martha Crenshaw, "Coercive Diplomacy and the Response to Terrorism," in *The United States and Coercive Diplomacy*, ed. Robert Art and Patrick Cronin (Washington, DC: United States Institute of Peace Press, 2003).

9. Byman, *Deadly Connections*, 259–72. See also Daniel Byman, "The Changing Nature of State Sponsorship of Terrorism," Saban Center for Middle East Policy Analysis Paper No. 16 (2008).

10. Bruce Jentleson and Christopher Whytock, "Who 'Won' Libya? The Force-Diplomacy Debate and Its Implications for Theory and Policy," *International Security* 30:3 (2005/6): 47–86.

11. Byman, *Deadly Connections*, 53–78.

12. Shmuel Bar, "Deterring Terrorists: What Israel Has Learned," *Policy Review* 149 (2008): 6.

13. Daniel Byman, "Passive Sponsors of Terrorism," *Survival* 47:4 (2005/6): 118.

14. Of Byman's sixteen cases of state sponsorship, four involved the provision of sanctuary, two included the provision of money, arms, and logistics, and seven were considered to have had a "high impact" on the target government's counterterrorism efforts. Byman, *Deadly Connections*, 74.

15. Byman, "Changing Nature," 16–7.

16. See, for example, "Mullen Accuses Iran of Arming Anti-U.S. Forces in Iraq," McClatchy Newspapers, http://www.mcclatchydc.com/2011/07/07/117227/mullen-accuses-iran-of-arming.html (accessed July 9, 2011).

17. Crenshaw notes that state sponsors have more to lose than non-state terrorist groups in resisting compliance, but that their isolation may also limit their interests beyond terrorism. Crenshaw, "Coercive Diplomacy," 312.

18. Robert Art, "Coercive Diplomacy: What Do We Know?" in *The United States and Coercive Diplomacy*, ed. Robert Art and Patrick Cronin (Washington, DC: United States Institute of Peace Press, 2003), 359–420.

19. Robert Jervis, *The Illogic of American Nuclear Strategy* (Ithaca, NY: Cornell University Press, 1984), 135.

20. Alexander George notes that successful coercive diplomacy is closely related to the opponent's perceptions of the balance of resolve. Alexander George, *Forceful Persuasion: Coercive Diplomacy as an Alternative to War* (Washington, DC: United States Institute of Peace Press, 1991), 14. See also Alexander George and William Simons, eds., *The Limits of Coercive Diplomacy* (Boulder, CO: Westview Press, 1994), 267–94.

21. Lepgold, "Hypotheses on Vulnerability," 148.

22. Jentleson and Whytock, "Who 'Won' Libya?" 47–86.

23. George and Simons, *Limits of Coercive Diplomacy*.

24. William Clinton, "Remarks at the World Jewish Congress Dinner in New York City," April 30, 1995.

25. George W. Bush, Address Before a Joint Session of the Congress on the State of the Union, January 31, 2006.

26. Quoted in *Washington Post*, "Iranian Abandons Push to Improve U.S. Ties," May 30, 2002.

27. Meghan O'Sullivan, *Shrewd Sanctions: Statecraft and State Sponsors of Terrorism* (Washington, DC: Brookings Institution Press, 2003), 89.

28. Ibid., 66.

29. Patrick Clawson, "Iran," in *Economic Sanctions and American Diplomacy*, ed. Richard Haass (New York: Council on Foreign Relations, 1998), 93.

30. The loss of American investment in the Iranian energy industry was compensated by foreign interests. In 1995, the French firm Total invested $600 million in two Sirri oil fields. In 1997, $2 billion in investments were made in the South Pars gas field. Two years later, the French firm Elf Aquitaine and the Italian firm Eni signed a deal worth nearly $1 billion to develop the Doroud oil field.

31. O'Sullivan, *Shrewd Sanctions*, 67.

32. Hossain Alikhani, *Sanctioning Iran: Anatomy of a Failed Policy* (New York: Tauris, 2000), 288–360.

33. Gawdat Bahgat, *American Oil Diplomacy in the Persian Gulf and the Caspian Sea* (Gainesville: University Press of Florida, 2003), 175; Byman, *Changing Nature.*

34. Anoushiravan Ehteshami, *After Khomeini: The Iranian Second Republic* (New York: Routledge, 1995), 152; Gary Sick, "Iran: Confronting Terrorism," *Washington Quarterly* 26:4 (2003): 93; Mark Gasiorowski, "Iran: Can the Islamic Republic Survive?" in *The Middle East in 2015: The Impact of Regional Trends on US Strategic Planning*, ed. Judith Yahphe (Washington, DC: National Defense University Press, 2002), 136.

35. By 1993, Iran had already fallen $3 billion in arrears of its repayment commitments. Vahe Petrossian, "Iran: Hard Times Persist as the Isolation Eases," *Middle East Economic Digest*, December 23, 1994.

36. Jahangir Amuzegar, "Iran's Post-Revolution Planning: The Second Try," *Middle East Policy* 8:1 (2001): 25–42.

37. Gary Hart, "My Secret Talks with Libya and Why They Went Nowhere," *Washington Post*, January 18, 2004.

38. Martin Indyk, "The Iraq War Did Not Force Gadaffi's Hand," *Financial Times*, March 9, 2004.

39. Jentleson and Whytock, "Who 'Won' Libya?" 77; Eben Kaplan, "How Libya Got Off the List," *Council on Foreign Relations Backgrounder*, October 16, 2007.

40. O'Sullivan, *Shrewd Sanctions*, 190.

41. Judith Gurney, *Libya: The Political Economy of Oil* (New York: Oxford University Press, 1996), 221–22.

42. Tim Niblock, *Pariah States and Sanctions in the Middle East: Iraq, Libya, Sudan* (Boulder, CO: Lynne Reinner, 2001), 66–67.

43. Mary Jane Deeb, "Qadhafi's Changed Policy: Causes and Consequences," *Middle East Policy* 7:2 (2000): 147.

44. Lisa Anderson, "Qadhafi's Legacy: An Evaluation of a Political Experiment," in *Qaddafi's Libya, 1969–1994*, ed. Dirk Vandewalle (New York: St. Martin's Press, 1995), 233–34.

45. Ray Takeyh, "The Rogue Who Came in from the Cold," *Foreign Affairs* 80:3 (2001): 65–66.

46. O'Sullivan, *Shrewd Sanctions*, 186.

47. Milton Viorst, "The Colonel in His Labyrinth," *Foreign Affairs* 78:2 (1999): 61.

48. John Hannah, "Stopping an Iranian Bomb," *Washington Post*, May 19, 2009.

49. See Indyk, "Iraq War"; Hart, "My Secret Talks."

50. Thomas Schelling, *Arms and Influence* (New Haven, CT: Yale University Press, 1966).

12 A TOXIC CLOUD OF MYSTERY
Lessons from Iraq for Deterring CBRN Terrorism

Fred Wehling

> *To people of distinguished skills and high levels of expertise in the*
> *sciences . . . we call on you to tell you that we are in need of you.*
> *The battlefield will accommodate your scientific aspirations. The*
> *vast areas in the American camps will be the best test site for your*
> *unconventional so-called germ or dirty bombs.*
>
> **—Abu Hamza al-Muhajir, September 28, 2006**

IN OCTOBER 2006, Iraqi insurgents began a campaign of terrorist bombings using chlorine gas to enhance the effect of improvised explosive devices (IEDs). In July 2007, these attacks abruptly stopped. Can the cessation of the chlorine attacks be attributed to a successful application of deterrence? This question, while easily stated in theoretical terms, is deceptively complex to answer in practice. This case study will attempt to do so by examining the intensive efforts undertaken by Coalition military and security forces in Iraq to halt insurgent use of chlorine and other chemical agents and relating these efforts to the logic of deterrence. The chapter asks and investigates a set of related questions: Who carried out the chlorine attacks and why? What attacks were attempted, and what effect did they have? Could the perpetrators have been deterred? Did Coalition forces attempt to deter the use of chlorine in IEDs, and if so, how? And did these efforts succeed in deterring the perpetrators from using this mode of attack?

Investigating these questions is crucial for determining what lessons the Iraqi case study offers for deterring chemical, biological, radiological, and nuclear (CBRN) terrorism more generally. However, as previous studies illustrate, answering these questions with certainty or even a high degree of confidence is difficult.[1] Findings from this study, for instance, suggest that while a concerted counterterrorism effort to stop the chlorine attacks was eventually successful, success was not a result of deterrence but rather of neutralizing key proponents of the CBRN attacks within the organization of al Qaeda in Iraq.

Nevertheless and despite the cloud of mystery that continues to surround the case, the Iraqi chlorine campaign still offers lessons for deterring terrorists from using CBRN. These lessons include a better appreciation for the difficulty of applying deterrence by punishment in counterterrorism, the need to focus efforts at deterrence by denial on critical points within the CBRN "kill chain" (from acquisition to use), and the crucial role champions of CBRN have within terrorist organizations. The case also offers a rare opportunity to study deterrence theory when terrorists demonstrate both a clear motivation and capability to use CBRN. While the study exemplifies the difficulty of assessing the efficacy of deterrence in specific instances, it also indicates that our limited ability to demystify the black box of terrorist decision making does not prevent contemporary deterrence theory from offering sound strategic guidance for combating terrorism.

WHO WERE THE PERPETRATORS, AND WHAT WERE THEIR MOTIVATIONS?

The precise identity of the group responsible for the Iraqi chlorine campaign remains uncertain. No organization claimed responsibility for any of the attacks, and although a number of suspected perpetrators were apprehended, no evidence from interrogations or court proceedings is available to definitively establish the culpability of a specific insurgent group. Nevertheless, it is possible to identify the perpetrators with a sufficient level of confidence to analyze the effectiveness of deterrence.

Iraqi insurgent groups first threatened to use chemical weapons in September 2005, when an individual calling himself Abu Usama, claiming to speak for Jaysh al-Ta'ifa al-Mansoura (Army of the Victorious Community), warned that his group would use chemical weapons in Baghdad's Green Zone.[2] Subsequently, a U.S. Army spokesman reported on September 13 that unknown insurgents wired barrels of unspecified chemicals with conventional explosives in the northern city of Tal Afar, speculating that the intended attack would have been blamed on Coalition forces.[3] However, no attacks using chemical agents are known to have followed this first attempt, and no connection between Jaysh and the subsequent chemical campaign has been suggested.

When the wave of chlorine attacks began in October 2006, Coalition forces quickly assumed that the most likely perpetrator was Tanzim Qaidat al-Jihad fi Bilad al-Rafidayn ("Organization of the Base of Jihad in the Land of the Two Rivers"), commonly known as al Qaeda in Iraq (hereafter AQI).[4] This assumption was eminently reasonable, since in the previous month the suspected leader of the organization, Abu Hamza al-Muhajir (alias Abu Ayyub al-Masri) had called upon Muslim scientists to assist AQI in producing unconventional weapons.[5] Subsequent captures of chlorine containers in weapons caches believed to be held by AQI provided further evidence to confirm the group's role. One of the largest of these caches, located in Al Garma east of Fallujah in Anbar Province, was described as a "chlorine bomb factory" after it was seized on February 21, 2007.[6]

The present author considers it highly probable that the Coalition's assumption that AQI was in fact behind the chlorine attacks was correct and will base the following analysis on that assumption. Some analysts, citing gaps in Coalition intelligence, have nonetheless argued that allied forces tended to exaggerate AQI's capabilities and were sometimes too quick to attribute attacks to AQI, given its relatively small size and the large number of other militant groups operating in Iraq.[7] While this study regards AQI as the most likely perpetrator of the chlorine campaign, the criticism and uncertainty are important, because deterrence has little value if deterrent and compellent threats are misdirected. If Jerrold Post's argument that "one cannot deter an adversary one does not understand"[8] is valid, the task of deterrence becomes exceptionally more difficult when an adversary cannot be properly identified. This is just the first of several problems encountered when attempts are made to assess the potential efficacy of deterring terrorists.

Proceeding from the conclusion that AQI was responsible for the chlorine attacks, a second problem is encountered: properly gauging the organization's motivation for using chlorine as a weapon of terror. Chlorine is one of the most widely produced and used chemicals in the world. The active component in chlorine bleach, it can be found in almost any household, has a wide variety of commercial and industrial uses, and is used extensively to purify drinking water. Chlorine has a distinctive yellow-green color and a pungent, irritating odor that is easily detected in very low concentrations, usually providing ample warning of exposure. Although chlorine gas, classified as a choking agent, was one of the earliest chemical agents used in warfare, its lethality is much lower than that of vesicants, nerve agents, and other agents specifically developed for military applications.[9] As a potential agent for terrorist use, chlorine can be obtained very easily, acts rapidly, and does not require special expertise or training to use in crude dispersal devices with or without explosives, but it has very low lethality in concentrations likely to be caused by such devices.

Chlorine's irritant qualities and easily detected and identified smell can cause people to believe they have been exposed to dangerous concentrations when the level of actual exposure is barely sufficient to cause few (if any) symptoms of irritation. Chlorine is therefore an ideal agent to cause psychological casualties while causing few serious injuries or deaths.[10] Did AQI, which had access to and expertise in using a plethora of lethal conventional weapons, choose to use chlorine to enhance the psychological effect of terror attacks while limiting the casualties they would cause? The possibility cannot be ruled out. However, considering that the leaders and operatives of the organization repeatedly demonstrated that they had no qualms about causing massive levels of civilian casualties, it seems unlikely that AQI would choose a chemical agent specifically because of its low lethality. It is more likely that the group's leaders, or specific individuals within its leadership, saw chlorine as the most readily available means of carrying out al-Muhajir's call to use chemical and biological agents in attacks on Coalition troops, Iraqi security forces, and other political and operational targets. But this motivation must remain speculative, and the dearth of better evidence on the reasons why chlorine was used complicates the task of assessing the effectiveness of deterrence.

WHAT ATTACKS WERE ATTEMPTED?

The first attack of the chlorine campaign in 2006 caused few casualties, none of which resulted from exposure to toxic chemicals, and attracted little media attention. By contrast, the spectacular chlorine attacks in March 2007 were widely reported in international media, denounced as a "heinous crime" by the Iraqi government,[11] and condemned by the Organization for the Prohibition of Chemical Weapons[12] and UN Secretary-General Ban Ki-moon.[13] The targets, methods, and effects of the attacks carried out and attempted as part of the campaign attributed to AQI are summarized in Table 12.1. The source of all information in the table is the Center for Nonproliferation Studies WMD Terrorism Database, except where otherwise noted.

No attacks using chlorine-enhanced IEDs occurred after June 2007. More than a year later, in July 2008, Iraqi police seized a truck loaded with explosives and chlorine tanks in Samarra.[14] Given the length of time separating the

Table 12.1. AQI chlorine attacks in Iraq, 2006–2007

Date	Delivery method	Location	Target type	Results
Oct. 21, 2006	Chlorine-enhanced suicide vehicle-borne improvised explosive device (VBIED)	Ramadi	Police facility	Three Iraqi police officers and 1 Iraqi civilian wounded by explosion. No chlorine-related casualties.[1]
Jan. 28, 2007	Chlorine-enhanced suicide VBIED	Ramadi	Police emergency response unit compound	Sixteen Iraqi police officers killed and 52 wounded by explosion. No chlorine-related casualties.
Feb. 20, 2007	Chlorine-enhanced suicide VBIED	Muham-mad Baqr	Civilian area	Nine Iraqi civilians killed by explosion. Estimated 150 people suffered symptoms of exposure to chlorine.
Feb. 20, 2007	Chlorine-enhanced suicide VBIED	Taji	Restaurant	Six Iraqi civilians killed by explosion. Estimated 130 people suffered symptoms of exposure to chlorine, of whom 2 later died.[2]
Feb. 21, 2007	Chlorine-enhanced suicide VBIED	Baghdad	Gas station	Two Iraqi civilians killed by explosion. Estimated 35 people suffered symptoms of exposure to chlorine.
March 16, 2007	Chlorine-enhanced suicide VBIED	Ramadi	Iraqi security forces checkpoint	One Coalition service member and 1 Iraqi civilian killed by explosion. Unknown number of people suffered exposure to chlorine.
March 16, 2007	Chlorine-enhanced suicide VBIED	Amiriya	Iraqi security forces checkpoint	At least 2 Iraqi police officers killed by explosion. Four other fatalities reported.[3] Estimated 100 people suffered symptoms of exposure to chlorine.
March 16, 2007	Suicide VBIED (dump truck containing a 200-gallon tank of chlorine)	Albu Issa	Near the home of Khamas al-Hasnawi, a leader of the Awakening movement	Two people killed and 6 injured by the explosion. Up to 250 people suffered symptoms of exposure to chlorine. This attack received the most media attention of any incident in the campaign.[4]
March 23, 2007	Chlorine-enhanced VBIED	Ramadi	Police station	Attack thwarted by police. Driver arrested. No casualties reported.

(continued)

Table 12.1. (*continued*)

Date	Delivery method	Location	Target type	Results
March 28, 2007	Two chlorine-enhanced VBIEDs	Fallujah	Government center	Both bombs detonated prematurely when fired upon by police. Fifteen Iraqi and Coalition soldiers wounded by explosions. Large number of people suffered symptoms of exposure to chlorine.
April 6, 2007	Chlorine-enhanced suicide VBIED	Ramadi	Iraqi police checkpoint	Under fire from police, the vehicle swerved into an apartment building, where it exploded. Between 12 and 35 Iraqi civilians were killed and 42 civilians and 1 police officer were wounded by the explosion. Between 40 and 50 people suffered symptoms of exposure to chlorine.
April 17, 2007	Nitric acid–enhanced VBIED	North of Baghdad	Joint U.S.-Iraqi security post	Truck overturned before reaching target. No casualties reported.[5]
April 30, 2007	Chlorine-enhanced VBIED	Ramadi	Al-Zawiya restaurant	Ten people killed and 10 injured by the explosion. Number of people suffering exposure to chlorine not reported.
May 17, 2007	Chlorine enhanced VBIED	Abu Sayda	Market	Sixty people were reported killed and 40 injured by explosion. Number suffering exposure to chlorine unknown.
May 20, 2007	Chlorine-enhanced VBIED	Ramadi	Iraqi police checkpoint	Explosive detonated prematurely when fired upon by police. No fatalities or injuries due to the explosion, though 11 people suffered symptoms of exposure to chlorine.[6]
June 3, 2007	Chlorine-enhanced VBIED	Diyala Province	Forward Operating Base Warhorse	No fatalities or injuries reported from the explosion, but 65 Coalition service members suffered symptoms of exposure to chlorine.

Table 12.1. *(continued)*

Date	Delivery method	Location	Target type	Results
June 13, 2007	Chlorine-enhanced VBIED	Khan Bani Sa'd, Diyala Province	Iraqi army base	One person was killed and 8 injured by the explosion. Unknown number suffered exposure to chlorine.[7]

[1] Jim Garamone, "Terrorists Using Chlorine Car Bombs to Intimidate Iraqis," *American Forces Press Service*, June 6, 2007.

[2] Baghdad Al-Iraqiya Television in Arabic, 1715 GMT, February 20, 2007.

[3] Kirk Semple, "Suicide Bombers Using Chlorine Gas Kill 2 and Sicken Hundreds in Western Iraq," *New York Times*, March 18, 2007.

[4] Semple, "Suicide Bombers"; Kim Gamel, "Chlorine-Laden Suicide Truck Bombs Strike Anbar Province, Sickening Hundreds," Associated Press, March 18, 2007.

[5] Baghdad Al-Sharqiyah Television in Arabic, 0800 GMT, April 17, 2007.

[6] Baghdad Al-Sharqiyah Television in Arabic, 1309 GMT, May 20, 2007.

[7] Baghdad Al-Sharqiyah Television in Arabic, June 13, 2007.

last incident from the 2006–7 chlorine campaign, and the impact of the Coalition's response to the campaign, it seems unlikely that the July 2008 incident involved AQI.

The total number of casualties caused by the chlorine campaign is difficult to quantify because of uncertainties and discrepancies in reporting. Open sources suggest an approximate total of 145 people were killed and 177 injured. This is a large figure to be sure, but a single attack with conventional explosives could cause loss of life on a similar scale. However, the total of individuals reportedly exposed to chlorine approaches eight hundred (of whom two are reported to have died), showing how the use of chlorine had a direct physical impact on a much greater number of people than were killed or injured by the explosions. The shock and outrage caused by the use of chlorine—which was even condemned by some jihadists[15]—shows how the psychological impact of the campaign spread much wider than the physical devastation. Homeland Security officials concerned that other jihadist groups would carry out similar strikes in the United States subjected the attacks to intense analysis.[16] By creating fears of copycat incidents outside Iraq, the chlorine campaign allowed AQI's theater of violence to reach audiences far beyond the limited area directly impacted by the attacks.[17] In this respect, the chlorine attacks constitute one of the most successful terrorist campaigns to have originated from war-torn Iraq.

COULD THE ATTACKERS BE DETERRED?

To the question "Can terrorists be deterred?" the literature offers three firm answers: yes, no, and it depends.[18] Some analysts contend that non-state actors (including terrorists) tend to employ a primarily rational strategic calculus and can therefore be influenced by threats common to interstate relations. Robert Pape is perhaps the strongest advocate of this position.[19] Other authorities take a more nuanced but still positive position, finding that while we cannot expect deterrence of terrorism to be robust and reliable in all cases, it is nevertheless sufficiently reliable to be an essential component of counterterrorism strategy. In other words, while deterrence is far from perfect, it is good enough, particularly for dissuading terrorists from orchestrating mass-casualty attacks and/or using WMD.[20] This assessment differs markedly from the requirements underpinning nuclear deterrence during the Cold War, when a single deterrent failure would have led to an unimaginable catastrophe. Where Cold War and counterterrorism deterrent strategies meet, however, is in their mutual emphasis concerning the efficacy of combining deterrence by threat of punishment with deterrence by denial.[21]

The opposite position is represented by Max Abrahms, who points to the dangers of assuming that terrorists act on the basis of a strategic logic mirroring that of sovereign states.[22] This does not mean that terrorists are irrational or suffer from severe mental health issues. Instead, from Abrahms's perspective most terrorists pursue clearly defined goals, but these goals stem from internal motivations that may be shared by adherents of an ideology or political movement or may be unique to a single group or individual (the "lone actor"). Those who act on ideological motivations may be less sensitive to calculations of material costs and benefits, including financial losses and casualties. Operational considerations are not unimportant, particularly for the leaders of jihadist groups, but they are secondary to the spiritual path of jihad.[23] Abrahms also finds that extremist groups tend to seek approval and admiration from like-minded extremists, suggesting that governments that the extremists consider inherently illegitimate can offer such groups few positive incentives apart from ideological conversion or capitulation. Some conclude that deterring al Qaeda by punishment is altogether impossible as a result.[24]

These analyses prompt the conclusion that leaders and operatives of jihadist organizations are not likely to be swayed by threats of punishment, though their operational plans may be susceptible to deterrence by denial.[25] The prevention of a planned attack on the Brooklyn Bridge by al Qaeda operative Iyman Faris, whose coded phrase "the weather is too hot" assessed both the security and damage resistance of his intended target, offers a textbook example of successful deterrence of terrorism by denial.[26]

Other experts conclude that while leaders and other committed "hardcore" members of jihadist organizations are not likely to be deterred from carrying out mass-casualty attacks, deterrence may dissuade their state sponsors, corporate enablers, and public supporters from making critical contributions that make such attacks possible. However, the civilian casualties involved in carrying out deterrent threats of punishment in counterterrorism would not only be morally problematic, but could quite possibly increase support for the very terrorists the retaliators are trying to deter.[27] Other deterrent dilemmas—such as uncertain attribution, (ir)rationality, communicating threats, and so on—are covered in greater detail elsewhere in this volume.

Differentiation between the motives of different entities involved in terrorism leads to the "it depends" position, well exemplified by a 2009 white paper prepared for the Secretary of Defense Task Force on DoD Nuclear Weapons Management.[28] The authors of the white paper distinguish between seven types of terrorist groups and argue that "religious fundamentalists" (in which they include al Qaeda) are least susceptible to deterrence logic. They contend, on the contrary, that deterrent threats might actually encourage such groups, who value martyrdom and/or seek to bring about an apocalypse, to launch attacks in order to pursue those very objectives. From this perspective, leaders and operatives of AQI are not likely to be swayed from using WMD, or indeed any other method of attack, by either threats or punitive actions.

Which perspective should this study adopt in order to assess the efficacy of deterrence in halting the chlorine attacks in Iraq? Because the focus of the chapter is the deterrence of CBRN use, rather than deterrence of terrorist attacks in general, a position similar to that adopted by Brad Roberts and by the Secretary of Defense Task Force seems most appropriate. Assuming that AQI was the perpetrator of the attacks, we may expect that deterrence by punishment was not likely to have persuaded the organization to refrain from using CBRN, but that deterrence by denial may have had the desired effect. As will become evident, Coalition forces responded to the chlorine attacks by intensifying their efforts to both apprehend or kill suspected AQI leaders and operatives (deterrence by punishment) and deprive AQI of the means to carry out

CBRN attacks (deterrence by denial). All other things being equal, if these actions prompted a decision by AQI to refrain from using chlorine or other chemicals, the cessation of these attacks might be construed as a success of deterrence. If, on the other hand, other factors, including side effects of Coalition activity, were responsible for halting the attacks, the case for successful deterrence must be regarded as unverified.

WAS DETERRENCE ATTEMPTED?

Coalition and Iraqi security forces quickly determined to halt the chlorine attacks by stepping up operations against AQI and attempting to restrict the supply of chlorine available to insurgents. These operations were undertaken as part of the new strategy for fighting the war in Iraq announced by President George W. Bush in January 2007. Most analysts date the actual implementation of the new strategy, popularly known as the "surge," with General David Petraeus's assumption of the command of Multi-National Force–Iraq on February 10 of that year.[29] A key component of the strategy was the Baghdad Security Plan, originally named Operation Fardh Al-Qanoon, or "Enforcing the Law."[30] Were these strategies and plans meant to deter AQI?

The question is difficult to answer, because the Coalition's response to the chlorine campaign straddled the analytical distinctions between deterrence and compellence and between deterrence and war fighting.[31] And from prospect theory, we find that individuals will accept greater risks to avoid losses, even of something recently gained, than they will be willing to accept the possibility of realizing equivalent gains.[32] In other words, both classical deterrence theory and prospect theory conclude that compelling an adversary to stop an attack, particularly if that attack seems to be succeeding, is more difficult than persuading the same adversary not to launch the attack in the first place. This was regarded as an important theoretical distinction, but had little practical influence on strategy.

The distinction between deterrence and war fighting, on the other hand, was critical (and controversial) in the development of U.S. nuclear doctrine and force posture during the Cold War. The main reason why the distinction became so important, however, was the objective of maintaining mutual deterrence once Soviet nuclear capabilities began to approach those of the United States in the 1960s. Before then, both the capability to launch a preemptive strike and to carry out a protracted nuclear conflict were considered conducive to the overall objective of preventing a nuclear strike on the United

States and its allies. Before the emergence of mutual assured destruction (MAD), war fighting was not viewed as either distinctive from or contradictory to deterrence for practical purposes.[33]

Therefore, while Cold War–era deterrence theory placed primary emphasis on deterring an all-out nuclear attack or a disarming first strike, it gave some thought to the problem of deterring escalation if a conflict began with a conventional offensive or limited nuclear strike. Both deterrence by punishment and deterrence by denial could be employed to dissuade an attacker from either horizontal escalation (spreading the conflict from one theater into another) or vertical escalation (moving from the use of conventional forces, to the limited use of WMD, to all-out nuclear war). This perspective saw little or no conflict between the conduct of military operations to defeat the adversary and the simultaneous use of threats of punishment and denial to dissuade escalation.

Coalition forces applied similar strategic logic in attempting to halt the use of chlorine-enhanced explosives by Iraqi insurgents. While the Coalition carried out offensive antiterrorist operations in an effort to defeat insurgent groups militarily, some operations were targeted specifically at reducing AQI's capability and will to use chemical weapons. As in almost all cases of counterterrorist strategy, mutual deterrence did not enter the picture at all. As far as the Coalition was concerned, the distinction between deterrence and compellence, and between deterrence and war fighting, made little difference. Intensified efforts to kill or apprehend AQI insurgents can therefore be regarded as communicating and carrying out threats of punishment, while making it more difficult for terrorists to acquire chlorine represents deterrence by denial. The Iraqi case therefore allows us to study how both forms of deterrence were attempted against a jihadist group that was vehemently demonstrating both its intention and capability to carry out attacks with chemical agents.

HOW WAS DETERRENCE ATTEMPTED?

While the chlorine attacks were certainly not the only reason why Coalition operations intensified in spring 2007, they quickly became a major focus of coalition efforts after the February 10 attacks in Mohammad Baqr and Taji. Coalition officials described the use of chlorine as an adaptive tactic that demonstrated insurgents' determination to defeat the new strategy and overcome political progress made through the Awakening movement.[34] Deterrence, both by denial and punishment, was an integral part of the Coalition response to the threat of chemical terrorism. This section highlights how Coalition operations attempted to dissuade AQI from using chlorine and degrade its ability to do so.

The heightened tempo of operations against AQI rapidly achieved significant success. U.S. and Iraqi forces captured two facilities described as "car bomb factories" in the Al Garma district of Anbar Province on February 21. This raid was the first operation that resulted in the seizure of chlorine containers likely intended for use in vehicle-borne IEDs (VBIEDs).[35] A few days later, an Iraqi official announced that an insurgent network that "specialized in booby-trapping vehicles with chlorine" was captured in Anbar Province. He added that "the Iraqi Government is planning to launch a large-scale attack on [Diyala Province] in the next few days to prevent terrorists from using these materials against citizens."[36] While Iraqi army troops subsequently seized a number of weapons caches,[37] no further captures of chlorine stockpiles were announced until March 21, when a major operation involving sixteen hundred Iraqi and Coalition troops uncovered containers of chlorine and nitric acid in two caches in Baghdad's Mansour district.[38]

Iraqi security forces achieved further success the following month with the capture of two suspects allegedly responsible for planning and building chlorine-enhanced IEDs in Anbar Province on April 11.[39] Provincial security forces then seized a small amount of chlorine in a weapons cache in Ramadi on April 15.[40] A short time later, on April 20, Coalition forces seized seven trucks loaded with chlorine near Al-Muahmudiyah, south of Baghdad.[41] On the same day, Muhammad Abdullah Abbas al-Issawi, alias Abu Abd al-Sattar and Abu Akram, was killed in an operation directed at "associates of a known senior leader" of AQI northwest of Baghdad.[42] Al-Issawi was the AQI "security emir" of eastern Anbar Province, a major weapons supplier to AQI and other insurgent forces, and was believed to have been closely linked to the chlorine campaign.[43] On April 30, Operation Iron Hammer uncovered a number of weapons caches, including one in the Jolan district of Fallujah that contained an unspecified (but probably small) amount of chlorine.[44]

Operations in May 2007 resulted in further seizures of materials for making chlorine-enhanced IEDs and captures of personnel believed to have been involved in the chlorine campaign. Coalition forces apprehended eight suspected terrorists allegedly involved in facilitating foreign fighters and an IED network known to use chlorine in its attacks in two raids north of Al Garma on May 2 and 3 as part of Operation Rat Trap.[45] One suspected terrorist allegedly involved in the chlorine attacks was killed, and two others captured, in an operation north of Al Garma on May 10.[46] Iraqi police uncovered eighty bottles of chlorine in the Al Kartan area of Anbar Province on May 12.[47] One or more weapons caches containing seven bags of chlorine powder were also seized by Iraqi security and Coalition military forces near Ramadi in the week prior to May 13.[48]

The most important success in stopping the chlorine campaign came on May 29, when Iraqi security forces in Mosul captured a "suspected key leader" of AQI "allegedly responsible for constructing both vehicle-borne and emplaced improvised explosive devices that contain chlorine gas."[49] This "key leader" was not named at the time, but he may have been Umar Wahdallah Dod al-Zangana, AQI's military emir of Baghdad, who was captured in 2007 and was described as the planner and perpetrator of chlorine attacks in the Iraqi capital.[50] Without further information about this individual and what he may have revealed about the chlorine attacks when interrogated, determining how valuable his capture was to Coalition efforts may be impossible. It should be noted, however, that Iraqi and Coalition forces began to uncover chlorine bomb materials at a more rapid pace after his capture. Iraqi security and Coalition forces seized two large stockpiles of chlorine within days of the capture. On June 2, an Iraqi police operation killed Muwaffaq al-Jughayfi, described as the "official in charge of the so-called Islamic State in Al-Fallujah," and uncovered four tons of chlorine and six containers of unspecified toxic materials during mopping-up operations.[51] A few days later, on June 6, an Iraqi jihadist website reported that security forces in Diyala seized thirty tons of chlorine and destroyed it in a "remote desert location."[52] As noted in the aforementioned attack chronology, two more chlorine VBIED attacks attributable to AQI were attempted after the unnamed leader was detained, but both came shortly after his capture and could well have been planned before he was apprehended.

Reports of captures of chlorine stockpiles and individuals suspected of involvement in the chlorine campaign dwindled in July 2007. On July 3, Coalition forces apprehended a suspected AQI operative near Al Asad who Coalition officials believed was involved in a March chlorine VBIED attack in Fallujah.[53] Marines from the Thirteenth Marine Expeditionary Unit found 250 kilograms of chlorine, approximately 6,000 kilos of nitric acid, and several tons of ammonium nitrate north of Al Garma on July 6.[54] No further seizures of chlorine were reported until March 2008, when a Baghdad resident led U.S.

soldiers to an arms cache in which four tanks of chlorine were found.[55] Iraqi army soldiers found two bottles of chlorine hidden in a schoolhouse in Sadr City, Baghdad, on May 24.[56] Soldiers of the Second Stryker Brigade Combat Team subsequently found two more chlorine tanks in Taji on July 5.[57] No further discoveries of chlorine caches were reported after this date.

The denial component of the Coalition's strategy against the chlorine campaign came with the enforcement of restrictions on the supply of chlorine to Iraqi water treatment facilities and other legitimate users. These restrictions were undoubtedly a major reason why chlorine became increasingly scarce in the country. The deterrent goal was to reduce the likelihood of successful attacks by denying AQI supplies of the chemical. Iraqi officials illustrated the need to cut off chlorine supplies in February 2007 by reporting insurgent efforts to steal the chemical, including one incident in Anbar Province where armed men not ascribed to any specific insurgent force stole 160 tons of chlorine from a convoy of trucks bound from Syria to Baghdad.[58] By September, however, restrictions on chlorine use for water treatment were blamed for a cholera epidemic. Iraqi Health Ministry officials reported on September 30 that two thousand Iraqis had caught the disease, thirteen of whom had died.[59] The epidemic continued into October, according to the Health Ministry, which mobilized local authorities, the Red Crescent, and other agencies to contain the disease.[60] Turkey, Iran, and other countries shipped chlorine to Iraq in response, with Turkish suppliers sending the chemical in tablet form to minimize its usefulness in IEDs.[61] While we may conclude that the supply restrictions certainly contributed to ending the chlorine campaign, the cholera outbreak serves as evidence of the cost and difficulty of attempting to prevent the use of common industrial and household chemicals as agents of opportunity for terrorist attacks.

The final blow against AQI's suspected use of chlorine IEDs came outside of Iraq. On July 28, 2008, Midhat Mursi al Sayid Umar, alias Abu Khabab al-Masri, was killed in a missile strike launched from an unmanned aerial vehicle in a Pakistani village in South Waziristan near the Afghan border.[62] Mursi, an Egyptian chemist, was widely regarded as al Qaeda's leading chemical weapons expert, believed to have masterminded the al Qaeda CBRN program known as al Zabadi ("Curdled Milk"), trained operatives in the use of chemical agents, and distributed information for making crude chemical and biological weapons.[63] He was allegedly responsible for using cyanide gas to kill dogs in al Qaeda experiments, which were uncovered in videotapes captured in 2002.[64] Mursi was on the FBI's list of Most Wanted Terrorists, but after he was erroneously reported killed in January 2006, the CIA admitted that a photo widely distributed as his likeness actually depicted Abu Hamza al-Masri, who used a similar alias.[65] An April 2007 report on a French website claimed that AQI insurgents received training in the use of chemical weapons in al Qaeda camps in Pakistan run by an Iraqi known as Abu al Marajel.[66] This report is uncorroborated, and in any case Mursi's demise came more than a year after the last attack in AQI's chlorine campaign. But if Mursi somehow encouraged or facilitated the chlorine attacks in Iraq, in the same way he allegedly promoted the use of crude and improvised chemical and biological agents by other al Qaeda operatives, his elimination may help explain why similar incidents expected in the United States and elsewhere did not materialize.

DID DETERRENCE SUCCEED OR FAIL?

In sum, a militant group (probably but not positively identified) starts using a chemical agent for reasons unknown, continues the campaign despite extensive and coordinated efforts to stop it, then forgoes using the agent some time after it becomes more difficult to acquire and shortly after a leader believed to be a key proponent of its use is apprehended. Given the scenario, is there room to assess whether or not deterrence succeeded or failed? Despite all the uncertainties surrounding the Iraqi chlorine case, there is.

Doing so requires recognizing that determining the success or failure of deterrence is often problematic in all but the most obvious cases. In early applications of deterrence theory, the criterion for success was deceptively easy to measure: if neither side launched its nuclear arsenal, deterrence succeeded for all practical purposes. Subsequent scholarship quickly realized that setting the standard for success was not that simple, however.[67] Could deterrence be regarded as successful if the purported attacker had little or no intention of attacking in the first place? Should each day on which no attack occurred be regarded as a separate success? As other authors in this volume discuss at greater length, the problem of setting clear standards for deterrence success has yet to be adequately resolved. The problem is compounded when decisions are made in secret and communicated clandestinely, in which case no evidence of the decision process or its outcome is available in open sources. Under these circumstances, which will almost always apply in the case of terrorist leadership, the analyst will have to infer decisions based on subsequent actions.

For deterrence by punishment to be regarded a success, a decision to refrain from taking a specified action must be observed (or inferred) and related
to the expected costs of the deterrent. To attribute a success in the case of deterrence by denial, decisions not to take an action (or cease taking it) must be
observed and related to the perceptions of lowered benefits. The criterion for
success in both cases is a decision based on cost-benefit analysis, and the burden of proof requires that the analyst show that such a decision likely took
place. In the case of the Iraqi chlorine campaign, the record indicates that no
such decision was made as a result of Coalition and Iraqi attempts at deterrence by punishment or denial.

Considering deterrence by punishment, the chlorine attacks clearly
stopped, so we can infer that AQI leaders made a decision to cease these attacks. If, however, the apprehension on May 29, 2007, of the "suspected key
leader" involved in the attacks was the principal reason for the cessation,
there is no reason to infer that the chlorine attacks stopped because decision
makers changed their minds. Instead, the leader with greatest responsibility
for the attacks was forcibly removed from the decision process, as were various other operatives suspected of carrying out the chlorine campaign. There
is no indication, then, that deterrence altered AQI's decision calculus. Analo-
gizing to the classical model of deterrence, if a leader of an enemy state is removed from power before taking an offensive action, or is killed after doing
so, we can consider the operations directed toward his removal to have
achieved their strategic goals of stopping or punishing the attack, but we cannot assign the episode a deterrent success. The same logic must apply to the
case of the chlorine attacks. In effect, the actions of Iraqi and Coalition forces
designed to punish AQI for using chlorine (and for perpetrating other acts of
terrorism) appear to have accomplished a "regime change" within the AQI
leadership. We may therefore credit the security forces with stopping the chlorine attacks, but not with deterring them by threats of punishment. This is
perfectly consistent with the expectation that terrorists motivated primarily
by a religious ideology that glorifies martyrdom are not likely to respond to
deterrence by punishment.

What about deterrence by denial? Here the determination is more difficult
to make. First, we cannot know what specific objectives AQI hoped to accomplish with its chlorine campaign. Without a clearer picture of why the insurgent group used chlorine-enhanced IEDs, among all the means available to
them, we cannot know if or when AQI leadership decided that the desired

effects were no longer being achieved, or whether any such decision resulted from Coalition actions. The case for successful deterrence based on diminished levels of effectiveness must therefore be regarded as not proven, and possibly as not provable.

Second, it is impossible to tell how well deterrence by denial actually denied AQI the capability to carry out chemical attacks. Coalition and Iraqi forces attempted to degrade AQI's ability to use chlorine by capturing chlorine stockpiles and by restricting the supply of chlorine available for illicit acquisition. Progress was made along both these lines, but chlorine was found in insurgent stockpiles more than a year after the chlorine attacks ceased, indicating that deterrence by denial was not completely successful. Chlorine could have become more difficult and dangerous to obtain, leading to a decision that using it in attacks was no longer cost-effective, but there is no reason to suspect that AQI made such a decision in June 2007.

If constructing and using chlorine-enhanced VBIEDs required a high level of specialized expertise possessed by only a few AQI operatives, it could be argued that operations intended to kill or capture individuals involved in the chlorine attacks constituted a form of deterrence by denial—specifically, denial of "know-how." However, as discussed earlier, the ease of obtaining chlorine and using it in a rudimentary fashion to enhance the effect of explosives is one reason why AQI may have chosen the gas as a chemical agent of opportunity. The result is that we cannot consider the strategy of targeting and apprehending personnel suspected of involvement in the chlorine attacks, tactically successful though it was, as an effective form of deterrence by denial.

With no compelling evidence to suggest that AQI decided the expected utility of the chlorine attacks had declined due to Coalition action, and some evidence to the contrary, we cannot conclude that deterrence by denial was successful in this case. This finding does not refute, however, the contention advanced by James Smith in his chapter that deterrence by denial of WMD terrorism is possible, because this conclusion is prompted by a lack of available evidence rather than a strong counterargument. Analysis of the AQI chlorine campaign highlights the fact that without firm knowledge of the specific terrorist objectives, it is very difficult to determine when deterrence by denial has succeeded.

WHAT LESSONS CAN BE LEARNED
FOR DETERRENCE IN PRACTICE?

Three lessons for deterring the use of CBRN weapons and materials by terrorists are evident from the conclusions drawn from this case study.

First, the Iraqi case clearly confirms that non-state actors are resistant, if not immune, to deterrence by punishment. The chlorine attacks compelled Coalition and Iraqi security forces to intensify their efforts against AQI, and these operations took a heavy toll on the organization. While these operations seriously degraded AQI's ability to conduct both conventional and CBRN terrorism, the damage they caused and the costs they imposed were insufficient to persuade AQI leaders to change their tactics. For its part, AQI was uninterested in weighing the benefits of using chlorine, which caused very few fatalities compared with conventional IEDs, against either the material costs of Coalition operations or the political costs in the form of opprobrium from their target audiences, including other jihadist organizations. This lesson is neither new nor counterintuitive, but the confirmation and substantiation of the limited utility of deterrence by punishment from the Iraqi case help drive the lesson home.

Second, given the life cycle of the chlorine attacks, efforts at deterrence by denial should concentrate on the weakest link within the kill chain. In the case of chlorine (a readily available agent of opportunity in widespread use for peaceful purposes), calculating the deterrent effect of restricting the chemical's supply on AQI's ability to use it for terrorist purposes is difficult. One might even make the uncharitable argument that restrictions on chlorine resulted in more deaths from cholera (thirteen) than by chlorine in the enhanced VBIED attacks (two, at the most). And yet, Coalition and Iraqi officials are not at fault for taking measures they thought were appropriate to counter what was perceived as a deadly innovation in insurgent tactics. Instead, the point is that where agents of opportunity are concerned, improving the security of facilities in which the agents are manufactured and used and safeguarding transportation links will in many cases be a more viable alternative than restricting supply. Conversely, for CBRN agents that are rare and difficult to produce, most especially nuclear materials, reductions in the amount of existing materials and restrictions on their use may be both efficient and effective in the long run.[68]

The final and most important lesson for deterrence generated by the Iraqi case study involves the critical role of AQI leaders who believed that CBRN weapons offered a legitimate and effective means for accomplishing their goals. The cessation of the attacks following the capture of key AQI leaders and the lack of subsequent CBRN use by al Qaeda operatives or affiliates indicate that the likelihood of CBRN terrorism can be significantly reduced by targeting leaders who have a particular interest in these materials. When efforts by terrorist organizations to acquire and/or develop CBRN capability are spearheaded by leaders like Midhat Mursi al Sayid Umar, who combine scientific expertise with a strong personal interest and fascination with these weapons, removing these leaders may be an extremely effective means of forestalling WMD attacks by those organizations. These key non-state leaders are akin to the state-based nuclear enthusiasts whom Peter Lavoy termed "nuclear mythmakers" who championed nuclear proliferation by inflating the value and hiding the costs of acquiring nuclear weapons.[69] Identifying CBRN advocates within terrorist groups will require painstaking and well-sourced intelligence, but the Iraqi chlorine attacks provide yet another illustration of why this can be crucial for preventing CBRN terrorism. Jacques Hymans's research on the psychology of proliferation, developed in the context of state leadership, raises the question of whether it may be possible to construct a psychological profile of individuals likely to advocate CBRN use.[70] The critical role of individual leaders brings us appropriately back to Jerrold Post's dictum that one cannot deter an adversary one does not understand. While there is much in this conclusion that is indisputable, the entire enterprise of criminal deterrence is based on the possibility of deterring unknown individuals sharing known characteristics from taking specific actions.[71] Deterring terrorists from using CBRN is a similar undertaking, and the Iraqi case emphasizes that even if psychological, ideological, and social factors make deterrence by punishment unlikely, deterrence by denial can still be an effective strategy if properly executed. The essential focus of deterrence on leaders, the decisions they make, and the values they have suggests that the promulgation of norms against the use of CBRN among current and potential leaders, operatives, and supporters of terrorist organizations may in the long term be the most effective strategy for deterring CBRN terrorism.[72] The tendency of extremists to seek approval from those they regard as cobelligerents in a moral and ideological struggle suggests that these norms must be propagated among extremists themselves, not just in the societies in which they operate.

WHAT LESSONS CAN BE LEARNED
FOR DETERRENCE THEORY?

These conclusions highlight the difficulties involved in determining whether and how terrorist organizations can be deterred. However, the methodological challenges described in this chapter are not categorically different from those associated with any other evaluation of deterrence. In this regard, the case of the Iraqi chlorine attacks offers both bad news and (relatively) good news for the deterrence theorist.

The bad news is that collecting and/or generating the data needed to rigorously measure the dependent variable in any study of deterrence is a notoriously difficult task. Few terrorist adversaries are likely to state clearly that they were deterred from taking violent action. Doing so would require admitting not only that they had violent intentions, but also that they were intimidated from carrying them out. The best the analyst can do, then, is to infer the success of deterrence over time, illustrated with somewhat greater clarity in particular incidents and episodes. In deterring terrorism, in rare cases, like the Faris plot in Brooklyn, intelligence intercepts may reveal both intentions and capabilities, but this information will seldom be disclosed in open sources. Even suspects apprehended and tried for terrorism will have strong incentives to lie about their specific intentions and decision processes, unless they decide to cooperate with the authorities to secure immunity or leniency in sentencing. Absent these unusual circumstances, the black box of decision making remains closed.

The relatively good news is that the Iraqi chlorine case provides a very rare example of deterrence attempted when both the intentions and the capability of terrorists to use CBRN were unambiguous. While the specific political and operational objectives of the chlorine attacks may never be known, AQI vehemently and violently demonstrated its ability and willingness to use toxic chemicals to enhance the effects of IEDs. Coalition and Iraqi forces responded by attempting to break their will to use chemical agents and by degrading their capability to do so. Their well-planned, effectively coordinated, and efficiently executed response degraded AQI's capability to use chlorine but had little effect on the insurgents' intentions and motivations until the critical figure in the organization's leadership was captured. These findings are consistent with the expectation that deterrence by punishment is not likely to dissuade religiously motivated terrorists and are not at variance with the contention that deterrence by denial may do so. We may therefore conclude that the case of the Iraqi chlorine campaign illustrates that theories of deterrence continue to offer sound strategic guidance in the post-9/11 era, despite the fact that adversarial decision-making processes are only partially and inconclusively understood.

NOTES

1. The Iraqi chlorine attacks have received surprisingly little scholarly attention. See Richard Weitz, Ibrahim Al-Marashi, and Khalid Hilal, "Chlorine as a Terrorist Weapon in Iraq," *WMD Insights*, May 2007; Marcus Binder and Michael Moodie, "Jihadists and Chemical Weapons," in *Jihadists and Weapons of Mass Destruction*, ed. Gary Ackerman and Jeremy Tamsett (Boca Raton, FL: CRC Press, 2009), 131–52.

2. Jamestown Foundation, "A New Chemical Arsenal for the Mujahadeen?" *Terrorism Focus* 2:17 (September 19, 2005).

3. Global Security Newswire, "Iraqi Insurgents Attempt 'Chemical Dirty Bombs,'" September 15, 2005.

4. For analysis of the organization, goals, and operations of al Qaeda in Iraq, see Kenneth Katzman, "Al Qaeda in Iraq: Assessment and Outside Links," Congressional Research Service Report for Congress RL32217, August 15, 2008.

5. Audio statement by Abu-Hamzah al-Muhajir, posted on Jihadist websites September 28, 2006.

6. Reuters, "U.S. Says Iraq Chlorine Bomb Factory Was al Qaeda's," February 24, 2007; *Al-Ittihad* (Baghdad), "Joint Iraqi-US Operations Result in Death of 'Scores' of Terrorists," February 25, 2007.

7. Andrew Tilghman, "The Myth of AQI," *Washington Monthly*, October 2007. Katzman also notes that Coalition forces may have overestimated AQI's activities. See Katzman, "Al Qaeda in Iraq."

8. Jerrold Post, "The Key Role of Psychological Operations in Countering Terrorism," in *Countering Terrorism and Insurgency in the 21st Century: International Perspectives*, vol. 1, *Strategic and Tactical Considerations*, ed. James Forrest (Boulder, CO: Praeger, 2007), 389.

9. Persons exposed to chlorine experience eye, nose, and throat irritations, and in high concentrations chlorine can cause burns, nausea, vomiting, and pulmonary edema. U.S. Centers for Disease Control and Prevention, "Emergency Preparedness: Facts About Chlorine," October 2, 2009.

10. Arpad Palfy, "Weapon System Selection and Mass-Casualty Outcomes," *Terrorism and Political Violence* 15:2 (2003): 81–95.

11. This expression was used by Environment Minister Nirmin Uthman, quoted in *Al-Adalah* (Baghdad), March 22, 2007, 1.

12. "OPCW Director-General Condemns Renewed Chemical Attacks in Iraq," Organization for the Prohibition of Chemical Weapons press release PR16 Rev. 1/2007, March 19, 2007.

13. "Secretary-General Strongly Condemns Terrorist Gas Attacks in Iraq," United Nations Department of Public Information press release SG/SM/10914/IK/564, March 19, 2007.

14. Dubai Al-Sharqiyah Television in Arabic, 1300 GMT, July 11, 2008.

15. "Writer Encourages Action to 'Heal the Rift' Between Jihadist Groups, Islamic State of Iraq," posting on jihadist website, April 6, 2007; interview with Muhammad Ayyah Al-Kubaysi, Al-Jazirah Satellite Television, 1812 GMT, May 24, 2007.

16. Chris Strohm, "Security Officials Seek Lessons from Iraq's Chlorine Attacks," *Congress Daily*, April 11, 2007.

17. Reuters, "Chlorine Bombs Raise Worries of U.S. Attack," March 23, 2007; Strohm, "Security Officials Seek Lessons"; and Charlie Savage, "Chlorine Attacks in Iraq Spur Warnings in US," *Boston Globe*, July 24, 2007.

18. See Jeffrey W. Knopf in this volume; Brad Roberts, "Deterrence and WMD Terrorism: Calibrating Its Potential Contributions to Risk Reduction," in Ackerman and Tamsett, *Jihadists and Weapons of Mass Destruction*, 259–84. For an excellent recent survey of deterrence theory in relation to twenty-first-century strategic issues, see T. V. Paul, Patrick M. Morgan, and James Wirtz, eds., *Complex Deterrence: Strategy in the Global Age* (Chicago: University of Chicago Press, 2009).

19. Robert Pape, *Dying to Win: The Strategic Logic of Suicide Terrorism* (New York: Random House, 2005).

20. Leading exemplars of this position include, among others, Paul Davis and Brian Jenkins, *Deterrence and Influence in Counterterrorism: A Component in the War on Al Qaeda* (Santa Monica, CA: RAND, 2002); Michael Quinlan, "Deterrence and Deterrability," *Contemporary Security Policy* 25:1 (2004); Robert Trager and Dessislava Zagorcheva, "Deterring Terrorism: It Can Be Done," *International Security* 30:3 (2005/6); John Stone, "Al Qaeda, Deterrence, and Weapons of Mass Destruction," *Studies in Conflict and Terrorism* 32:3 (2009); Wyn Q. Bowen, "Deterrence and Asymmetry: Non-state Actors and Mass Casualty Terrorism," *Contemporary Security Policy* 25:1 (2004): 54–70.

21. James Smith and Brent Talbot, "Terrorism and Deterrence by Denial," in *Terrorism and Homeland Security: Thinking Strategically About Policy*, ed. Paul Viotti, Michael Opheim, and Nicholas Bowen (Boca Raton, FL: CRC Press, 2008); 53–68; S. Paul Kapur, "Deterring Nuclear Terrorists," in Paul, Morgan, and Wirtz, *Complex Deterrence*, 109–32.

22. Max Abrahms, "What Terrorists Really Want: Terrorist Motives and Counterterrorism Strategy," *International Security* 32:4 (2008): 78–105.

23. Outstanding among the many efforts to analyze Islamism, jihad, and jihadism are Giles Kepel, *Jihad: The Trail of Political Islam* (New York: Belknap Press of Harvard University Press, 2003), Marc Sageman, *Understanding Terror Networks* (Philadelphia: University of Pennsylvania Press, 2004), and Fawaz Gerges, *The Far Enemy: Why Jihad Went Global*, 2nd ed. (Cambridge: Cambridge University Press, 2009).

24. James Van De Velde, "The Impossible Challenge of Deterring 'Nuclear Terrorism' by Al Qaeda," *Studies in Conflict and Terrorism* 33:8 (2010): 682–99.

25. Roberts, in "Deterrence and WMD Terrorism," offers this conclusion, which is consistent with the analysis by Jeffrey Bale in the same volume. See Jeffrey Bale, "Jihadist Ideology and Strategy and the Possible Employment of WMD," in Ackerman and Tamsett, *Jihadists and Weapons of Mass Destruction*, 3–60. For another viewpoint see William Browne III, "Constituency Constraints on Violence: Al-Qaeda and WMD," in *Globalization and WMD Proliferation: Terrorism, Transnational Networks, and International Security*, ed. James Russell and James Wirtz (New York: Routledge, 2007), 79–101.

26. Eric Lichtblau, "U.S. Cites Al Qaeda in Plan to Destroy Brooklyn Bridge," *New York Times*, June 20, 2003.

27. Uri Fisher, "Deterrence, Terrorism, and American Values," *Homeland Security Affairs* 3:1 (2007): 1–17.

28. Scott Helfstein et al., "Tradeoffs and Paradoxes: Terrorism, Deterrence, and Nuclear Weapons," white paper prepared for the Secretary of Defense Task Force on DoD Nuclear Weapons Management, *Studies in Conflict and Terrorism* 32:5 (2009): 776–801.

29. Kimberley Kagan, *The Surge: A Military History* (New York: Encounter, 2008).

30. "Baghdad Security Plan Officially Named 'Fardh al-Qanoon,'" Multi-National Force–Iraq press release A070217b, February 17, 2007.

31. Thomas Schelling, *The Strategy of Conflict* (Cambridge, MA: Harvard University Press, 1963), 195.

32. For a summary of developments in prospect theory see Rose McDermott, James Fowler, and Oleg Smirnov, "On the Evolutionary Origin of Prospect Theory Preferences," *Journal of Politics* 70:2 (2008): 335–50.

33. Outstanding among the many works analyzing these elements of U.S. strategy are David Miller, *The Cold War: A Military History* (New York: St. Martin's Press, 1998); Colin Gray, *The Second Nuclear Age* (Boulder, CO: Lynne Rienner, 1999); Lawrence Freedman, *The Evolution of Nuclear Strategy*, 3rd ed. (New York: Palgrave Macmillan, 2003); and David Coleman and Joseph Siracusa, *Real-World Nuclear Deterrence: The Making of International Strategy* (New York: Praeger, 2006).

34. "Iraqi Insurgents Employ Chlorine in Bomb Attacks," *New York Times*, February 21, 2007; Department of Defense news briefing with General Michael Barbero, March 20, 2007.

35. "Chlorine Cylinders Found in Iraqi Bomb-Making Factory: General," Agence France-Presse, February 22, 2007; Reuters, "U.S. Says Iraq Chlorine Bomb Factory Was al Qaeda's."

36. "Interior Ministry: We Discovered Complete Network for Booby-Trapping Cars with Chlorine," *Al-Bayan* (Baghdad), February 28, 2007.

37. "Second Large Cache in Three Days," Multi-National Corps–Iraq Public Affairs Office press release 20070303-08, March 3, 2007.

38. "Iraqi and Coalition Soldiers Begin Clearing Operations in the Mansour Security District," Multi-National Corps–Iraq Public Affairs Office press release 20070322-01, March 22, 2007.

39. "Iraqi Police Detain Suspects Involved in Chlorine IEDs," Multi-National Corps–Iraq Public Affairs Office press release 20070413-04, April 13, 2007.

40. "Provincial Security Forces Discover Weapons Cache," Multi-National Corps–Iraq Public Affairs Office press release 20070415-13, April 15, 2007.

41. Baghdad Al-Iraqiyah television broadcast, April 21, 2007.

42. "Al Qaeda in Iraq Security Emir Killed," Multi-National Force–Iraq press release A070425b, April 25, 2007.

43. Ibid.; Defense Department Special Briefing with General David Petraeus, Washington, DC, April 26, 2007.

44. "Operation 'The Iron Hammer' Results in Cache Find," Multi-National Corps–Iraq press release 20070504-10, May 4, 2007.

45. "11 Suspected Terrorists Detained," Multi-National Force–Iraq press release A070503b, May 3, 2007; Multi-National Force–Iraq press briefing with Major General William Caldwell IV, Baghdad, May 3, 2007.

46. "One Terrorist Killed, Bomb Making Materials Destroyed," Multi-National Corps–Iraq press release A070510b, May 10, 2007.

47. Baghdad Al-Iraqiyah television broadcast, May 12, 2007.

48. "Numerous Caches Found Near Ramadi," Multi-National Corps–Iraq press release 20070513-02, May 13, 2007.

49. "Iraqi Forces Detain Suspected Key Leader of al-Qaeda," Multi-National Corps–Iraq press release 20070601-02, June 1, 2007.

50. Press briefing by Rear Admiral Gregory Smith, Multi-National Force–Iraq Communication Division, Baghdad, January 20, 2008.

51. Baghdad Al-Iraqiyah television broadcast, June 2, 2007.

52. Iraqi News Network website, http://www.aliraqinews.com, June 6, 2007.

53. "3 Terrorists Killed, 29 Suspects Detained in Coalition Operations," Multi-National Force–Iraq press release A070703b, July 3, 2007.

54. "13th MEU Finds More Than 17 Metric Tons of Explosives," Multi-National Corps–Iraq press release 20070708-05, July 8, 2007.

55. "Local Resident Leads Coalition Forces to Weapons Caches (Baghdad)," Multi-National Corps–Iraq press release 20080319-02, March 18, 2008.

56. "IA Seize Weapons Cache at Schoolhouse in Sadr City," Multi-National Corps–Iraq press release 20080524-01, May 24, 2008.

57. "MND-B Soldiers Seize Cache in Taji," Multi-National Corps–Iraq press release 20080705-02, July 5, 2008.

58. "Security Official: Insurgents Obtain Chlorine Inside, Outside Iraq; Fears of Introducing Chemicals as Part of Equation of Violence in Iraq," *Al-Mashriq* (Baghdad), February 24, 2007.

59. Al-Jazirah satellite television broadcast, September 30, 2007.

60. Sa'idi Ghazalah, "Health Ministry Holds Some Services Ministries Responsible for Cholera Outbreak," *Al-Sabah* (Baghdad), October 7, 2007.

61. "Iran Sends Tons of Chlorine to Iraq," PressTV (Iran), September 9, 2007; *Anatolia* (Ankara), October 6, 2007.

62. Kathy Gannon, "Al-Qaida Said to Lose Key WMD Operative," Associated Press, September 8, 2008.

63. Bill Roggio, "Al Qa'ida Confirms WMD Expert Abu Khabab Killed in South Waziristan Strike," *Long War Journal*, August 3, 2008.

64. Julian Borger, "Al-Qaida Videos Show Poison Gas Tests," *Guardian*, August 20, 2002.

65. "Report: U.S. Used Wrong Terrorist Photo," United Press International, January 26, 2006.

66. "Baghdad: Al-Qa'ida's Chemical Attacks," Intelligence Online, April 6, 2007, accessed November 2010, http://www.intelligenceonline.com/political-intelligence/2007/04/06/al-qaeda-s-chemical-attacks,27624951-ART.

67. These dilemmas are discussed in Christopher Achen and Duncan Snidal, "Rational Deterrence Theory and Comparative Case Studies," *World Politics* 41:2 (1989); Richard Ned Lebow and Janice Gross Stein, "Deterrence: The Elusive Dependent Variable," *World Politics* 42:3 (1990).

68. This finding strengthens the argument in favor of eliminating highly enriched uranium in civilian use and for continuing to improve the security of nuclear weapons vulnerable to theft, reducing the number of such weapons, or eliminating them entirely. See among others, Matthew Bunn, *Securing the Bomb, 2008* (Cambridge, MA, and Washington, DC: Project on Managing the Atom, Harvard University, and Nuclear Threat Initiative, 2008); Christina Hansell, ed., *The Global Politics of Combating Nuclear Terrorism: A Supply-Side Approach* (London: Routledge, 2010).

69. Peter Lavoy, *Learning to Live with the Bomb: India, the United States, and the Myths of Nuclear Security* (New York: Palgrave Macmillan, 2007).

70. Jacques Hymans, *The Psychology of Nuclear Proliferation: Identity, Emotions, and Foreign Policy* (New York: Cambridge University Press, 2006).

71. The topic of criminal deterrence has produced a rich literature. See Sylvia Mendes, "Certainty, Severity, and Their Relative Deterrent Effects: Questioning the Implications of the Role of Risk in Criminal Deterrence Policy," *Policy Studies Journal* 32:1 (2004): 59–75. For an original perspective on applying criminal deterrence to prevent terrorist attacks, see James Kraska, "Torts and Terror: Rethinking Deterrence Models and Catastrophic Terrorist Attack," *American University International Law Review* 22:3 (2007): 361–91.

72. Norms of nonuse of CBRN have been widely researched in the case of state actors; see Nina Tannenwald, *The Nuclear Taboo: The United States and the Nonuse of Nuclear Weapons Since 1945* (New York: Cambridge University Press, 2007), and Maria Rost Rublee, *Nonproliferation Norms: Why States Choose Nuclear Restraint* (Athens: University of Georgia Press, 2009). Magnus Ranstorp and Magnus Normark include this approach in their suggestions for preventing CBRN attacks by terrorists in *Unconventional Weapons and International Terrorism: Challenges and New Approaches* (New York: Routledge, 2009), 47.

CONCLUSION

DETERRING TERRORISM
Moving Forward

Andreas Wenger and Alex Wilner

DETERRING TERRORISM will prove to be a challenge radically different from deterring the Soviet Union. During the Cold War, the political imperative to avoid all nuclear war produced a research agenda that was both theoretically fruitful and politically relevant. Deterrence theory provided policymakers with an abstract construction of a world in which the stability of the bipolar status quo was sustainable even in the absence of cooperation. But looking back, Thomas Schelling reminds us of how slow deterrence learning actually was during the Cold War, how long it took the United States and the Soviet Union to turn trust into "mutual deterrence," and how simple this bilateral relationship is compared with today's strategic environment.

In thinking about deterring conventional and WMD terrorism we are entering an unfamiliar and vastly more complicated terrain. Gone are the days of the Cold War when deterrence provided a unifying framework to study grand strategy. In the highly complex and dynamic international environment of the twenty-first century, policymakers, on top of civil wars and regional crises, deal with multiple actors, asymmetric relationships, and transnationally networked threats. Managing terrorism as one of these novel threats requires that we go beyond traditional deterrence theory and ask ourselves how deterrence, as one element of a broader toolbox, can contribute to countering this evolving threat.

In bringing together terrorism and deterrence experts, this volume seeks to assist the current process of renewed deterrence learning concerning contemporary, asymmetric threats. The theory and practice of deterring terrorism is still in its early days. Much of the research linking deterrence to terrorism has been policy-driven. Yet the theoretical logic of the assumed causal link between deterrent actions and deterrence outcomes is generally underspecified. Moreover, rigorous empirical evaluation of counterterrorism deterrence is in short supply. Thinking about the deterrence of terrorism requires that we reconsider Cold War deterrence and adapt its theoretical tenets to the context of today's novel challenges.

By combining theoretical and empirical research, the chapters in this volume shed light on how traditional and less-traditional theories of deterrence can be applied to counterterrorism. The various contributions offer preliminary assessments of specific cases, address the methodological challenges of empirically testing deterrence theory, and discuss the practical implications of all of this for effective counterterrorism. Taken together, the chapters allow us as editors to discuss the lessons derived from the volume and suggest avenues for further research. In keeping with the broader themes of the volume, we subdivide our concluding remarks into three pillars: theoretical lessons, methodological lessons, and practical lessons.

THEORETICAL LESSONS

The chapters of this book suggest that deterrence may contribute to the management of terrorism. Yet from a practical point of view it is quite clear that deterrence cannot be the focal point for counterterrorism. Deterrence is only one element of a broader influence strategy and therefore cannot serve as the overarching strategy for managing the relationship between states and terrorists. From a theoretical point of view, this means that the conceptual tenets of traditional deterrence do not provide an appropriate framework to study counterterrorism. Rather the theoretical prerequisites have to be readdressed in light of the characteristics of terrorism. The key challenge is to theorize the deterrent effects of a variety of manipulative engagements in the broader and highly dynamic context of a counterterrorism (or counterinsurgency) campaign.

THE LIMITS OF TRADITIONAL DETERRENCE THEORY

The "third wave" of deterrence research, Jeffrey W. Knopf reminds us in his contribution, criticized existing theory as abstract, static, and fundamentally apolitical. Terrorism and counterterrorism, by contrast, are concrete, dynamic, and highly political. The scope conditions of traditional deterrence theory are too narrow to provide an appropriate conceptual framework to study counterterrorism. Theorizing the link between deterrence and terrorism must start by recognizing three key contextual differences from the Cold War setting. First, the assumption of two similar, unified, and rational state actors does not apply in the context of deterring terrorism. Second, deterring terrorism cannot be conceptualized as a symmetric strategic interaction between status quo powers. And third, focusing on high conflict and threats of extreme punishment does not fit the challenge of a (conventional) terrorism campaign. These fundamental conceptual differences are discussed in greater detail below.

From an Interstate to a Non-state Relationship

First, traditional deterrence theory conceptualized deterrence as a process of interdependent decision making between two states or alliances with a similar power base and comparable strategic culture.[1] In reality, much of the Cold War debate about deterrence centered on the meaning of the changing nuclear and conventional balance of power and on the differences in strategic culture between East and West. Over time, however, the United States and the Soviet Union learned to accept nuclear parity and developed a mutual understanding of the fundamental parameters of their deterrent relationship. The theoretical assumption of two unified actors each with a rational decision calculus—while rightly criticized as a simplification of empirical reality due to the role of perceptions, cognitive biases, bureaucratic and domestic politics—did reflect the interests of both sides. Adversaries could guarantee centralized decision making, control over the escalation of violence, and uphold the state monopoly of force.

By contrast, a deterrence relationship between a state and a non-state terrorist adversary evolves in a context of huge power differentials and widely varying strategic cultures. The obvious material inferiority of a terrorist organization informs its strategic calculus, wherein terrorist attacks on civilians are understood as the only viable means of armed struggle. Values like status and honor are likely to have a very specific meaning in such a strategic context. Moreover, while we can assume that a state has a centrally organized authority and a decision-making cycle that can be manipulated, the same logic may not necessarily apply to a non-state actor engaged in terrorism. Terrorist groups are purposefully decentralized and build firebreaks within their organizational structures in order to carry out violence against much stronger opponents. By denying themselves centralized processes of decision making, they offer vastly different targets for states to manipulate. Depending on the type of group that engages in terrorism (for example, national versus transnational scope; cohesive structure versus loose network), a large variety of manipulative engagements may be appropriate. How should we conceptualize the deterrence process between state actors and a variety of violent non-state actors?

The unequal strategic relationship between a state actor and a non-state actor magnifies the challenges of correctly interpreting the motivations, capabilities, and strategic culture of the adversary. Designing, communicating, and understanding appropriate threats will be far more difficult to do than in a state-to-state setting. In interstate relations, deterrence is strengthened by the "common knowledge" shared between adversaries, something that is often lacking in deterring terrorism. States involved in a deterrent relationship, Janice Gross Stein explains, understand the parameters, political systems, and status quo inherent to that relationship. They have "codified practices and routines" and a mutual understanding of the "meaning of action" that is inherent to properly communicating and understanding deterrent messages.[2] In deterring terrorists, that strategic relationship does not often exist. State and non-state adversaries, like the United States and al Qaeda, do not share a common interpretation of the meaning of the other's behavior. And yet, at the regional level, familiarity between state and non-state opponents is much more common. From the case studies presented in this volume, it becomes apparent that over time and through repeated and close interaction, state and non-state adversaries do learn about the other sufficiently that they can at times construct a stable deterrent bargain. What lessons do these regional examples offer global conflicts?

From Symmetric to Asymmetric Conflict

Second, traditional deterrence theory conceptualized deterrence as a process of strategic interaction between similar actors with both common and conflicting interests. According to the theory's logic, deterrence involved a tradeoff between threats and incentives: adversaries can expect either retaliation (if they do not acquiesce to a threat) or inaction (if they do acquiesce to a threat). If a challenger expects to be attacked even if it complies with a threat, then deterrence loses all credibility and is impossible to pursue. In deterring state adversaries, both sides of a contest usually appreciate that a deterrent relationship will reflect the status quo. The theoretical assumption of a symmetric strategic interaction between two status quo powers—while much disputed in the early days of the Cold War when both sides perceived the other as "expansive" or "revisionist"—gained practical support by the mid-1960s once Moscow and Washington exchanged signals of mutual interest in the territorial and nuclear status quo, especially in Europe and Asia.[3]

In a symmetric deterrent relationship between states, the objective (upholding the status quo) and the strategy (deterring behavior with threats of punishment) are compatible. But in an asymmetric deterrent relationship between a state and a non-state adversary, there is a poor fit between the objective (targeting leaders for death and/or destroying the organization) and the strategy (using the deterrent effects of active punishment or denial within the context of an ongoing counterterrorism campaign). Both terrorism and deterrence share a common denominator: using fear as a strategy to manipulate an opponent's behavior. But in deterrence, fear is used to uphold a status quo; in terrorism, fear is used to change a status quo. In a symmetric deterrence setting, the defender manipulates fear through threats of potential force. The goal is to change the challenger's expectations about the defender's choices, dissuade an action, and reinforce the status quo. In an asymmetric deterrence setting, it is the challenger that manipulates fear through repeated use of force against civilians. The goal of such terrorist tactics is to change the defender's expectations about its own choices, instill a perception that deterrence is not possible, provoke (military and political) overreaction, and destabilize the status quo.

The incompatibility of the logic of terrorism and the logic of deterrence challenges us to theorize the interaction effects between the two seemingly contradictory, if at times mutually reinforcing, processes. How can states make sure that their deterrence attempts against terrorism are not part of the problem rather than the solution? At what point are states simply falling into the deterrence traps set out by their weaker adversaries? How should states evaluate the tactical deterrent effects of the active use of force as opposed to its potentially negative strategic effects? How much of an investment should states make into deterrence by denial? Conversely, under which conditions do the limited deterrent effects of active punishment or denial contribute positively to the management of terrorism and deny non-state actors their tactical and strategic goals? What is it that states will *not* do if terrorism is not used? Is there a politically and strategically acceptable status quo with terrorism? Building a mutually reassuring, status quo–oriented relationship with a terrorist organization may be difficult, if not impossible, to accept for most states. Given their current goals, for instance, would the United States and its allies be willing to accept al Qaeda's continued survival in exchange for a deterrent relationship? Are such bargains possible in the event of a WMD-capable terrorist organization? Do these calculations change at the regional level (between Israel and Hezbollah, for instance)?

From High Conflict to Low Conflict

Third, traditional deterrence theory conceptualized deterrence as a process involving threats of massive punishment in the context of high conflict. Threats of nuclear punishment against a limited set of military and civilian targets may not have always been credible, but they were effective, especially in conflicts of mutual existential interest and in cases where adversaries could not implement an effective denial strategy. From a Western point of view, the core problem of deterrence rested on how best to manipulate nuclear risks in order to deter a conventional attack on U.S. allies in Europe. Some theorists went a step further, arguing that in the event of a deterrence failure and a conventional war in Europe, the process of deterrence could be utilized within a nonnuclear war. Herein, the purpose of intrawar deterrence was to reestablish deterrence through the demonstrative or limited tactical use of nuclear weapons. In practice, most policymakers feared explosive escalation once the first nuclear weapon was used. But from a theoretical point of view, the coercive effect that could be gained from manipulating nuclear threats hinged on the assumption that the nuclear threshold and the geographic separation between the European and global theaters of war would provide a firebreak against the threat of excessive escalation.

By contrast, a deterrence relationship between a state and a terrorist organization evolves within the context of a low but already ongoing conflict. In the context of a conventional terrorism campaign, threats of massive punishment against cities and civilian populations have severe limits. This is why attention is focused on the deterrent value of more-targeted threats and use of force against particular elements within the terrorism system and, especially, on the utility of employing a variety of denial strategies targeting a broad set of terrorist objectives. From a theoretical point of view, this scenario epitomizes intrawar deterrence, in which the logic of deterrence is utilized within an ongoing conflict. The main purpose here is to either establish a deterrent relationship with a non-state adversary or to dissuade a geographic or substantive escalation of an ongoing terrorism campaign. Unlike in the Cold War setting, however, there is often no clear threshold or geographic separation between the already ongoing active counterterrorism campaign and threats or execution of further punishment.

DETERRING TERRORISM: MULTIPLE TARGETS AND DYNAMIC PROCESSES

From a theoretical point of view, traditional deterrence theory is challenged by two key insights from terrorism studies. The first is linked to the notion of disaggregating terrorism into its various parts and processes, thereby singling out the particular elements that are deterrable. The second stems from insight that conceptualizes terrorism and counterterrorism as inherently intertwined processes. Both are explored below.

Disaggregating Terrorists/Terrorism: Multiple Targets

While decomposing a terrorist adversary does highlight how specific sub-targets might be approached, it nonetheless works against the core logic of traditional deterrence as a strategy of controlled and coherent decision making between two unified actors. On the one hand, decomposition multiplies the type and nature of the targets to be deterred. This forces the analyst to far more carefully define what action by which actor is to be manipulated. On the other hand, decomposition also means that the intended deterrent effects on a particular element within the terrorist system may have unintended consequences on other elements within the very same system. There may be trade-offs between parallel deterrent and denial strategies that target various elements of the system and/or between threats and actions meant as deterrents and those used as part of a more comprehensive counterterrorism campaign.

Disaggregating terrorist organizations into their functional parts and identifying both conventional and WMD terrorism as intricate processes of multiple steps and stages reveal the specific targets against which deterrence might be successfully applied. Unlike interstate deterrence in which the target in question is usually another government (that is, political leaders and elites), in deterring terrorism, Paul Davis suggests in his chapter, the choice of target can range from the terrorist leader or foot soldier to the financial enabler or state sponsor, or, in terms of the terrorism process, from the acquisition of a particular weapon to its construction, placement, and use in theater.

The problem with broadening deterrence is that it muddies the theoretical meaning of the deterrent behavior and complicates the manner in which deterrence is put into action. By disaggregating a group engaged in terrorism, we have to identify which actors and processes are most susceptible to deterrence. Designing and communicating an effective deterrent to a specific target imbedded within a terrorist system will be a complicated task. How can we control for unintended side-effects on other elements within the system? What is the relationship between applications of deterrence and counterterrorism operations directed against the same sub-actor or process? And if we conceptualize counterterrorism as an influence campaign that integrates all versions of deterrence with other relevant instruments of coercive and non-coercive diplomacy, where do the conceptual boundaries of deterrence end? [4]

Importantly, different terrorist groups will offer diverging and varied deterrent and compellent options depending on the nature of the assets they value and on the idiosyncratic goals they seek. Groups fighting for independence or national autonomy, like those David Romano focuses on in his chapter, may value state-like assets such as sovereignty, political self-governance, and economic survival. But groups like al Qaeda that are transnationally organized and religiously (and politically) motivated will value other things, like strategic success, popular sympathy, religious legitimacy, and prestige. Still other groups, like the radical Marxist/socialist organizations active in Europe and North America during the Cold War (for example, the Red Army Faction, the Red Brigades, the Weather Underground, Action Directe) and modern right-wing extremists and supremacists, will strive for something else altogether. When we think about deterring terrorism, the group matters; the values, goals, and assets that are threatened will depend on the type and nature of the group and the specific actors and processes that characterize that group. And depending on these factors, different deterrent and compellent strategies that rely on both military and nonmilitary instruments will need to be applied. This goes well beyond the traditional notion of interstate deterrence by punishment and forces the analyst to redefine and broaden the conceptual meaning of deterrence in counterterrorism. All of this further complicates how and where deterrence will (and can) apply in counterterrorism.

Deterrence in Counterterrorism: Dynamic Processes

If we conceptualize counterterrorism as a reaction to an ongoing terrorism campaign, this means that we also have to understand deterrence as a process that aims at (re)establishing a deterrent relationship between a state and a non-state actor and/or dissuading a geographic or substantive escalation of an ongoing terrorism campaign. The difference between an act of terrorism and a campaign of terrorism is important because it suggests, in practical terms, the use of a different deterrent and, in theoretical terms, the investigation of a different unit of analysis.

In traditional deterrence theory, the focus was on deterrence as a static concept—on deterrence as the strategic outcome—for deterring an individual act of war or for deterring all major war. In deterring terrorism, the focus is on a variety of deterrent effects—on deterrence as a process at the tactical, operational, and strategic level—in the context of a dynamic response to an ongoing terrorism campaign. Traditional notions of strategic deterrence by way of territorial punishment may still hold some analytical and practical value if we think of deterring single acts of WMD terrorism. However, in deterring conventional terrorism campaigns, we need new conceptual tools that reflect the challenges of deterring an opponent with whom one is already engaged in conflict. In most cases, deterring terrorism involves intrawar deterrence. For analytical purposes, it makes sense to further distinguish between deterring a conventional terrorism campaign and deterring the nonconventional escalation of such a campaign.

DETERRING TERRORISM: GENERAL CHALLENGES
AND DIFFERENT CONTEXTS

As a result of thinking about terrorist organizations as disaggregated adversaries and of thinking about counterterrorism as a complex process, other theoretical challenges for deterring terrorism present themselves.

New Conceptual Tools: From Punishment to Denial

Deterrence works by influencing an adversary's cost-benefit calculus, by either adding additional costs on an action (punishment) or by diminishing the expected benefits of that action (denial). In thinking about deterring terrorism, the emphasis is often on denial strategies. For a variety of reasons offered by various authors in this volume, there is less room for punishment strategies. First, punishment is difficult to apply because of the asymmetry in power, capability, intent, goals, and motivation between state and non-state opponents. Second, the threat of massive punishment against communities that support terrorists in a context of low conflict is not credible and may be counterproductive. Third, targeted punishment involving the repeated use of limited force, rather than the use of threats, has at best an indirect deterrent effect at the tactical level. Fourth, punishment strategies rest on the premise that perpetrators are known, but with terrorism attribution is often difficult. And fifth, within the context of intrawar deterrence, challengers need to believe that defenders have the ability to credibly inflict further punishment.

Deterrence by denial is likely to be of greater value than deterrence by punishment in countering terrorism. At the tactical level, states can deny terrorists easy access to targets and weapons, increase the risk of operational failure, and impede day-to-day tactical successes. At the strategic level, terrorists can be denied state and societal support and, over the long term, the accomplishment of their overarching goals and objectives. Challenges remain, however. At the tactical level, there is the issue of the strategy's cost-effectiveness, since there are far too many potential targets to deny terrorists. And at the strategic level, support for terrorism may depend less on a defender's policies and actions and rather reflect the relationship between the terrorist organization and the local and regional communities. Likewise, further research is needed on mapping out how tactical denial relates to and affects strategic denial.

Communicating Multiple Threats to Multiple Targets

In deterring terrorism, the state's ability to communicate threats is undermined by organizational diffusion, fragmented decision making, and the limits of "common knowledge" between the challenger and the defender. Communicating deterrence in counterterrorism is especially tricky because it may often mean communicating multiple parallel threats to multiple targets. A broadened and more dynamic conception of deterrence requires that each specific aspect of a larger deterrence strategy be minutely tailored to the communicative task at hand—a complex and daunting task. In addition, the defender has to ensure that the individual deterrent messages do not inadvertently get into each other's way. Consider that a state communicating a threat of punishment in the event a specific target is attacked might simultaneously negate that threat by communicating that it has also taken measures to mitigate the effects a terrorist attack on the target in question will have. The threat of punishment stems from a desire (and hope) that the target will not be attacked, but the threat of mitigation is based on an expectation that the target *will* be attacked (and properly defended). The challenger, receiving both deterrent messages at once, might interpret the second as a form of weakness—evidence, in fact, that the defender itself questions its ability, commitment, and resolve to carry out the punishment.

Strategic Deterrence by Denial Built Bottom-Up:
Deterring Nuclear Terrorism

Deterring the acquisition and/or use of WMD weapons, especially nuclear weapons, may offer a case in which a deterrent effect can be built from the bottom up, through a combination of denial at the tactical and strategic levels and punishment at the operational level. James Smith in this volume argues that denial of WMD terrorism within an active campaign of terrorism and counterterrorism may be possible, if potential targets are hardened at the tactical level, capability is denied via threats of punishment against sponsors at the operational level, and the use of WMD is delegitimized at the strategic level. The net effect of deterrence by denial built from the bottom up may be an important part of combating WMD terrorism.

We need further research that maps out some of the theoretical puzzles and empirically identifies how strategic deterrence by denial built from the bottom up functions in practice. The acquisition and/or use of nuclear weapons by terrorists will imply the existence of a mature organizational structure and external facilitation by states. This suggests that targets exist that can be manipulated by a combination of denial and punishment strategies. But in terms of threatening state sponsors with punishment, what really counts is the denial-of-capability effect these threats will have on terrorists, who will be denied access to the materials and weapons they may want. While this gives the idea of deterrence some traction as an important conceptual pillar in preventing nuclear terrorism, the approach, as Martha Crenshaw illustrates in her chapter, is not well integrated into any overall strategic concept.

The following puzzles also have to be addressed in greater detail. First, the potential interactions between a denial-based deterrence of WMD terrorism and an active counterterrorism campaign against conventional terrorism are not clear. For instance, terrorist leaders targeted by the direct application of force may have greater incentive to acquire weapons of mass destruction for deterrent purposes. Conversely, the necessary technological capability and know-how may simply not be available. As Brian Michael Jenkins reminds us in this volume, a lot may depend on how terrorists acquire WMD (that is, theft/provision versus clandestine fabrication). In any event, relinquishing the option of nuclear terrorism may be easier for terrorists if states define an acceptable status quo with the group, a step that does not seem compatible with an active counterterrorism campaign aimed at the group's ultimate destruction.

Second, the interaction between denial attempts at the tactical and operational level and the delegitimization of WMD use at the strategic level is not well understood. If a defender uses threats of massive (nuclear) punishment against state sponsors at the operational level, this may undermine the credibility of its efforts to delegitimize WMD acquisition and use at the strategic level. Worse, it might reinforce a double standard and incentivize WMD acquisition. It is not clear how the denial effects at the tactical and operational level are linked to the denial of strategy at the strategic level. If the identity and ideology of a group cannot be shaped from the outside, then reluctance to acquire and use a nuclear weapon may indeed constitute a form of self-deterrence. In fact, Jenkins reiterates that there are many good reasons unrelated to the defender's denial strategy for believing that nuclear terrorism is unlikely.

Cumulative Deterrence: Deterring Conventional Terrorism

A scenario of ongoing conventional terrorism offers one context in which there appears to be little room for deterrence beyond the denial of easy targets. Theoretical debates continue, however, as to the deterrent effect of actively using force against terrorist adversaries. Several authors, including Stein, Crenshaw, Davis, and Shmuel Bar, investigate the notion of "cumulative deterrence"—the repeated use of force rather than the use of threats to produce deterrent outcomes. Bar, in his case study, suggests that Israel accomplished some sort of tactical deterrence through repeatedly employing force as punishment or defense as denial in its counterterrorism campaign against Palestinian terrorists. He argues that while Israel's policy of targeted killings was primarily intended to diminish the capability of various terrorist adversaries, the strategy also had a deterrent effect by producing an "atmosphere of fear and caution within leadership circles that translated into less terrorist activity" and eventually led to internal terrorist debates that favored unilateral cease-fires.

The main goal of Israel's proactive security measures was clearly the disruption of the Palestinian terrorist leadership. The deterrent effect, Bar argues, came as a corollary; the targeted killing campaign reduced the motivation of the recruiters and made leaders more cautious. At issue is whether the assumed behavioral change was a result of the eliminations (and their denial-of-capability effect) rather than a result of any increased deterrent leverage. Did the targeted killings change the decision calculus in planning further acts of terrorism, and, if so, how durable was this change? If coercive threats (both offensive and defensive) are pursued to the point that an opponent can no longer carry out an attack, then this is not deterrence per se, but military victory. The new equilibrium in the relationship between the state and the non-state actor must be based on more than the result of the active use of force, or deterrence has not been achieved.

The notion of cumulative deterrence as an unintended side-effect of the active and repeated use of force stretches the concept of deterrence as the manipulation of potential force and as a bargaining tactic that requires the active communication between two adversaries. More important, the limited deterrent effects at the tactical level may come at a strategic cost. Bar's analysis, for instance, reveals that in Israel's case, the removal of local terrorist leadership from Gaza and the West Bank unintentionally empowered terrorist leaders living outside Israel's immediate field of operation. And because Israel had less ability to influence these "external" leaders, it lost its ability to continue manipulating the behavior of the terrorist groups it faced. If cumulative deterrence results in a fragmented leadership and an antagonized community, it risks feeding the cycle of violence rather than contributing to the establishment of a more stable strategic relationship between a state and its terrorist adversaries.

Complex Denial Effects: Deterring WMD Escalation

Deterring a nonconventional WMD escalation of an ongoing conventional terrorism campaign may offer considerable room for the application of denial strategies. Yet the controlled application of a multifaceted denial attempt in the middle of an active counterterrorism campaign is a difficult endeavor involving complex trade-offs and huge communication challenges. Fred Wehling, in his case study, analyzes attempts by U.S. and Coalition forces in Iraq to halt the insurgent use of chemical agents (in this case, chlorine) in their improvised explosive devices. Coalition forces combined deterrence by punishment and denial, to dissuade horizontal and vertical terrorist escalation, with offensive antiterrorist operations to defeat the group militarily. Wehling's findings confirm that the combination of active military coercion and deterrence by punishment within the same operational setting is a difficult undertaking. Threats of punishment in counterterrorism may be undermined given ongoing antiterrorism operations, and non-state actors may be difficult to deter by punishment. A state actively at war with a terrorist organization may have trouble, for instance, credibly communicating a threat that hinges on additional punishments to those already being pursued as part of daily operations. Unlike intrawar deterrence during the Cold War, the defender cannot credibly threaten to increase the intensity of the force being used or threaten to expand the geographic scope of the operation.

The result of Coalition attempts to deny the insurgents access to the chemicals is also difficult to evaluate. Of interest—due to the multiuse character of chlorine—is the observed trade-off between denying insurgents access and denying the peaceful use of the chemical. The more widespread a material is, the more difficult it is to implement a denial strategy, and the higher the potential cost in terms of unintended side-effects on peaceful uses. Wehling concludes by suggesting that the abrupt stop of the chlorine bombing campaign was probably a result of the removal of key terrorist operatives. While this could be viewed as a denial-of-capability effect, he finds little evidence that the decision calculus of the group changed for any reason beyond the disruptive impact of force.

The value of denial and the limits of punishment strategies are further confirmed in Wyn Bowen and Jasper Pandza's chapter on the prevention of radiological terrorism. Their chapter reminds us that the more complex deterrence becomes in theory, the more complicated its use becomes in practice and the greater the odds of failure. The greater the number of activities that are included in the deterrent landscape, the more likely certain actions will negatively impact, confuse, and negate other deterrents. Consider, for instance, the concepts of *pre-event* and *post-event* deterrence by denial. Both concepts are internally consistent with the logic of deterrence and offer insight on influencing terrorist behavior: the former communicates an ability to impede a particular attack, while the latter communicates an ability to recover from a particular attack. In both cases, the goal is to communicate to terrorists that the state has the capabilities to deny them the anticipated benefits of an attack, thereby potentially manipulating their willingness to try. But pre-event denial and post-event denial also communicate contradictory messages to adversaries. The first hinges on the argument that the state has the means to ensure that certain attacks are doomed to fail, but the second, in communicating an ability to recuperate from an attack, assumes pre-event denial will fail and an attack will take place. Applying both concepts of deterrence simultaneously may negate the utility of both in practice. Moreover, deterrent messages to terrorists may undermine public resilience, either overselling the state's capabilities or stimulating public concern, fear, and panic.

MOVING DETERRENCE THEORY FORWARD

Theorizing the link between deterrence and terrorism can profit from a better understanding of the limited use of traditional deterrence in dealing with terrorist threats. Deterrence cannot serve as an overarching strategy to shape our response to terrorism, and traditional deterrence theory cannot serve as a unifying theory to study counterterrorism. In thinking about deterring terrorism, we have to conceptualize deterrence as one pillar of a counterterrorism strategy alongside other coercive and non-coercive influence pillars. The problem with building deterrence as one pillar of a multi-pillared counterterrorism strategy is that core deterrence concepts may negatively affect other pillars of the overarching strategy, and vice versa. We need more research that first identifies the conceptual boundaries of deterrence as one pillar of a comprehensive counterterrorism strategy, and then theorizes the interactions, trade-offs, and feedback loops among the different pillars while better integrating the intended deterrent effect into the overall strategy.

Disaggregating terrorism into its functional parts multiplies the type and nature of the targets and makes deterrence more complex. This means that a broader set of deterrence tools targets a wider spectrum of actors and processes at different tactical, operational, and strategic levels. But the greater the number (and variety) of deterrent activities a state pursues, the more likely certain deterrents will negate others. We need a better understanding of the combined effect of parallel deterrent attempts on the overall terrorism system, taking into account unintended side-effects as well as contradictory messages. Mapping the interaction effects between the processes of deterrence and terrorism is critical, given the inherent incompatibility of the logic of terrorism and the logic of traditional deterrence.

In deterring terrorism, the focus is on deterrence as a multifaceted process across several levels that—in the context of an ongoing counterterrorism campaign—(re)builds a deterrent equilibrium from the bottom up. Unlike in the Cold War setting, the operational boundaries are often diffuse, and there is no clear threshold regarding the level of threatened force. This makes it difficult to distinguish punishment and denial effects from more proactive military strategies. Threats of punishment against state sponsors and active use of force against terrorist leaders may amount to a denial-of-capability effect at the tactical and operational level, which may again be outweighed by a set of negative effects at the strategic level. We have to differentiate between conceptually distinct deterrent situations—deterring an act of WMD terrorism, deterring a conventional terrorism campaign, and deterring escalation within a conventional terrorism campaign—in order to increase the analytical value of our observations.

Finally, more research is needed on identifying how less-traditional notions of deterrence and compellence can be applied to counterterrorism. While this volume has taken important steps in refining how deterrence by punishment functions in counterterrorism and has greatly expanded the concept of deterrence by denial, much more work still needs to be done on exploring how persuasion, positive inducements, criminal justice, and delegitimization might also deter terrorism. As David Romano and Michael Cohen illustrate in their respective case studies, manipulating terrorists and their sponsors will often require a strategy that uses a complex set of influences that are neither purely punishment-based nor denial-based.

EMPIRICAL AND METHODOLOGICAL LESSONS

Not only is the theoretical logic of deterring terrorism underspecified, but the literature also lacks rigorous empirical research. As Knopf notes, qualitative and quantitative research on the subject of deterring terrorism is near nonexistent. To date, very few authors have applied deterrence theory toward specific historical events or terrorist case studies. In order to test and assess theoretical propositions, this will have to be remedied. To that end, different terrorist organizations (that vary in geographic scope, structure, ideological orientation, and so on) and specific conflicts and/or events will have to be evaluated in light of the deterrence literature. The four case studies presented in this volume offer a valuable and fascinating first contribution to empiricism. And yet, methodological constraints persist: causal relations are difficult to identify; data is hard to collect; and deterrence success (or failure) is difficult to define. Evidently, the underdeveloped theoretical logic of the underlying deterrent mechanisms and the conceptual imprecision of the postulated deterrent effects further contribute to these empirical challenges.

Causal Relations: Tracing Deterrent Effects Is Difficult

Identifying the causal links between deterrent actions and deterrence outcomes remains problematic. Tracing deterrence is a notoriously difficult task.

Doing so empirically requires information on a defender's objectives and motivations, on a challenger's intentions, and on the communicative relationship between the two (that is, whether a deterrent was issued by the latter and properly understood by the former). In testing deterrence theory in counterterrorism, these aspects are not always clear. Consider that states actively engaged in antiterrorism may be more concerned with defeating an adversary than with manipulating its behavior. If so, empirical evaluations of deterring terrorism may be difficult to distinguish from the effects of successful antiterrorism; the outcome of both is the same (that is, less or no terrorism).

The difference is subtle but important. An adversary who stops a particular action or behavior because it no longer has the ability to choose how it acts is not, strictly speaking, deterred but rather impeded or controlled (by brute force).[5] In the case study of the chlorine bombing campaign in Iraq, for instance, it is not apparent whether al Qaeda in Iraq (AQI) ceased these types of attack because it was motivated to change its behavior (deterrence and/or compellence), or because particular organizational elements within AQI were no longer able to effectively organize or carry out such attacks (organizational and leadership degradation). If AQI changed its behavior because particular advocates and facilitators of the chlorine attacks were removed from the organization, as appears likely, then it is theoretically problematic to suggest that coalition forces deterred rather than impeded the group from further carrying out such attacks.

While these empirical concerns are tied specifically to measuring the deterrent effect of punishment (for example, targeted killings) in counterterrorism, similar empirical difficulties are associated with measuring deterrence by denial as well. Israel's security barrier separating it from parts of the West Bank, for instance, might have had both a defensive effect on Palestinian terrorists (impeding access to Israeli targets) and a denial effect (decreasing terrorist motivation to carry out suicide attacks beyond the barrier). The latter might flow from the former—if terrorists are impeded from attacking they may be less willing to carry out attacks in the future—but defense and denial are nonetheless conceptually separate. Defense, in this case, is about taking away an adversary's behavioral option (you cannot attack here), while denial is about manipulating an adversary's decision making (you do not want to attack here). In this Israeli case, the distinction is not clear. Accordingly, there is a parallel between defense and brute force; both eliminate a particular behavior by targeting an adversary's *ability* to act, not by eliminating its *motivation* to act. Empirically separating defense and denial in order to test deterrence theory in counterterrorism is difficult because doing so relies on acquiring detailed assessments of an adversary's motivation, which is not often forthcoming.

Collecting Data: The Black Box of Terrorist Decision Making

Constructing robust case studies to evaluate deterring terrorism hinges on collecting and generating the proper data. This is a challenging task. Terrorist groups, by the nature of their organizational characteristics and the type of violence they employ, are clandestine organizations. Likewise, efforts to combat terrorists involve equally secret engagements. Little raw data on the motivations and expectations of challengers and defenders is available, except in the odd case, which not only complicates empirical evaluations more generally but also poses a challenge in the form of selection and sampling bias. Future empirical research on deterring terrorism will have to circumvent this deficiency with the development and use of novel data-collecting methodologies.

Defining Success: At What Level of Deterrence? At What Stage of the Terrorism Process? Against Which Actor?

It remains unclear how best to define deterrence success in counterterrorism. As suggested, deterring terrorism usually implies a broadened conception of deterrence applied against a variety of actors (for example, individual versus group action) and different levels of analysis (for example, tactical versus strategic deterrence). These multiple nodes of interaction complicate the manner in which we can measure deterrent successes. In traditional, state-based studies of deterrence, success is usually measured as a "nonevent"—a military confrontation that did not take place. In countering terrorism, on the other hand, a broadened conception of deterrence necessitates a multipronged form of assessment that may rest on a sliding scale of deterrence success. This will complicate empiricism. For instance, from the Israel–Fatah/Hamas case study, it is evident that, at times, Israeli action resulted in a degree of deterrent success at the individual, local, and tactical levels but proved near simultaneously unsuccessful at the group, regional, and strategic levels. Can deterrence both succeed at one level and fail on another at the same time? Is deterrence achieved if individual terrorists are manipulated but the organization they constitute is not? More research will be needed to clarify these issues.

PRACTICAL LESSONS

Simply thinking about deterring terrorism may provide important lessons that go beyond the manipulation of an adversary's behavior in practice. As important may be the specific mind-set that deterrence brings to a complex problem that is often approached too narrowly from the perspective of coercive military tactics. Thinking about deterring terrorism forces the policymaker to put himself into the mind of the non-state actor engaged in terrorism, absorb the logic of terrorism in its wider political context, acknowledge the unintended side-effects of his counterterrorism policies, face the trade-offs between alternative strategies, and consider the conditions of an acceptable status quo with a terrorist organization. Deterring terrorism not only provides practical lessons for more effectively countering terrorism, but expands the range of policy options available to decision makers

The chapters in this volume confirm that deterrence is relevant to countering terrorism and that it should not be relegated to the dustbin of history. Although deterrence cannot serve as an overarching strategy for counterterrorism, most authors seem to agree that it can contribute positively to the management of terrorist threats. The processes of deterrence carry value for the development and application of counterterrorism or counterinsurgency strategies. The manipulative potential inherent to deterrent processes can help states contain and delimit the terrorism threats they face. Several practical lessons for deterring terrorism are explored below.

Success at the Fringes Is Acceptable in Cases of Low and Asymmetric Conflict

Most authors argue that in deterring terrorism, success will come at the fringes of terrorist activity, limiting the type and ferocity of the violence terrorists are willing to inflict but not eliminating all threats of terrorism. From the case studies, it is clear that some states, under particular conditions, have had some limited success in coercing terrorist adversaries. Most of these successes came at the tactical and operational level and were of a temporary nature only—states were able to manipulate the level of terrorism they faced but unable to manipulate its occurrence altogether. In the context of low and asymmetric conflict, this may be "good enough" and certainly better than a horizontal or vertical escalation of terrorist violence. In this sense, success in counterterrorism is different from success in Cold War deterrence. During the Cold War, deterrence success between great powers meant the avoidance of all acts of (nuclear) war. Success at the fringes was possible in the case of regional extended deterrence, but repeated deterrence failure between the great powers would have resulted in direct military engagements and possible nuclear escalation. Today, in deterring terrorism, the stakes are lower and success is not an absolute necessity.

Deterring Terrorism Is More Complicated Than Deterring State Adversaries

The authors of this volume agree that deterring terrorism is a more complicated endeavor than deterring state adversaries. Applying deterrence to terrorism will be difficult to do well and consistently. It is about deterring multiple actors and processes at different levels in the context of an ongoing and dynamic terrorism and counterterrorism campaign. Deterrence is only one aspect of modern counterterrorism, a tool to use alongside other strategies. From the case studies, it is clear that successful deterrence was usually a result of utilizing a complex combination of strategies that mixed punishment with denial and at times included other influencing mechanisms, like positive inducements and political concessions. The lesson here is that no one tactic or strategy will suffice to deter terrorism. Instead, success is the result of constructing and applying the right series of multiple deterrent approaches; deterring terrorism is highly context specific. It matters if the deterrent effects are part of a narrow counterterrorism campaign that focuses exclusively on coercive mechanism or if they are part of a broader counterinsurgency campaign that also involves positive inducements.

Communicating Deterrent Threats to Terrorists Will Prove Difficult

The prerequisites of deterrence emphasize that a defender properly communicate a credible threat to a challenger in a way that is both clearly heard and properly understood. Deterrence cannot work if a defender's expectations and threats are improperly communicated (or lacking altogether) or if threats are poorly received or misunderstood by the challenger. In deterring terrorism, Frank Harvey and Alex Wilner explain in their chapter, these prerequisites of communication become problematic. Most individual terrorist leaders are loath to make their role in the organization (let alone their whereabouts) evident to state authorities. Unlike the world of diplomatic affairs, neither states nor terrorist groups can send attachés, staff, or personnel to the other to ensure a deterrent is properly communicated and received. The associated risk is that counterterrorism deterrent messages may be difficult to communicate clearly and that independent deterrent messages aimed at different elements of the same terrorist system may accidentally interfere with one another. The practical lesson here may be to keep the deterrence messages as simple and consistent as possible.

Deterring Terrorism Requires That States Be Exceptionally Familiar with Their Terrorist Adversaries

The application of deterrence to counterterrorism requires a detailed understanding of the non-state actor engaged in terrorism, so that different influencing mechanisms can be appropriately tailored and applied to a given situation. The prerequisites of deterrence will force states to learn as much as they can about their adversaries. What type of group do they face, and how is it organized? What are its values and goals? Information about the strategic culture of the terrorist organization is not only a precondition for designing and implementing tailored deterrent threats. Better understanding the adversary's motivation is also a prerequisite for putting the threat into proper perspective and not falling into the terrorist trap of militarily and politically overreacting. Cultural familiarity and geographic distance seem to matter in successfully deterring terrorism. From the case studies, it becomes apparent that the development of mutual understanding concerning the parameters shaping the state-terrorist relationship is more likely at the regional and local level. Processes of mutual learning are a precondition for the construction of a stable deterrent bargain—a fact that was borne out during the Cold War.[6]

WMD Acquisition Does Not Necessarily Lead to WMD Use

Thinking about deterring WMD terrorism forces the analyst to ask how non-state actors engaging in WMD terrorism may think about these weapons. Some authors maintain that though terrorists are unlikely to achieve nuclear capabilities, even if they do, acquisition may not necessarily lead to nuclear use. This contradicts commonly held assumptions, but the decision to use nuclear weapons may rest on a more complicated series of equations than is usually appreciated. The manner in which terrorists acquire such weapons (by donation, theft, or autonomous development) may influence their decisions over what to do next. The very acquisition of nuclear capabilities may force some terrorists to think about these weapons' use, value, and efficacy. Likewise, some terrorists may have self-restraints dictating what action is and is not considered legitimate. In all cases, such calculations leave room for deterrence. Conversely, if nuclear-weapons states want to delegitimize WMD use, they may have to carefully consider the deterrent signals they send to non-state actors and their (potential) state sponsors with their own nuclear arsenals.

Denial Is Less Prone Than Punishment to Have Unintended Side-Effects

Most authors agree that deterrence by denial is likely to be of greater value than deterrence by punishment in counterterrorism. Denial strategies are also less intrusive than punishment strategies that involve the active use of force, and they are less likely to have negative unintended side-effects at the strategic level. They are a more appropriate hedge against low-probability/ high-impact WMD attacks. Unlike threats and use of punishment, denial is both more readily distinguishable from and more compatible with an ongoing military counterterrorism campaign, especially concerning the denial-of-capability effect that results from the use of force. Punishment is most credible when the perpetrator is known and the intensity of the threat and the targeted operational theater are distinguishable from the ongoing counterterrorism campaign. For example, given that the United States seeks to destroy al Qaeda, how much more punishment can it credibly threaten? And yet, under different circumstances, these communicative restraints may be less evident. In its current relations with Hamas and Hezbollah, for instance, Israel can conceivably communicate a threat to punish both organizations with a military escalation against Gaza and Lebanon. This would not have been the case in years past when Israel controlled Gaza and occupied southern Lebanon, a circumstance under which Israel presumably did all it could to disrupt and punish the organizations active in the territory under its control.

Disrupted, Fragmented, Externalized Terrorist Leaders Are Less Amenable to Deterrence

Deterrence as a bargaining strategy presupposes coherent decision making on the side of the challenger. Non-state actors engaging in terrorism are not irrational; their organizations have strategic goals, and their leaders are, in principle, deterrable. Yet success in influencing such groups depends on their sovereignty (territorial versus nonterritorial) and their control over the level of violence. The case studies remind us that disrupted, fragmented, and externalized leaders are less amenable to deterrence. In thinking about applying deterrence to terrorism, states need to consider the trade-offs between short-term tactical benefits of an active military campaign and the unintended side-effect of losing manipulative leverage over the group's future behavior.

Deterrent Bargains Will Require That States Think About Acceptable Status Quos

Deterrence in practice is a bargaining tactic that requires issuing threats while offering opponents an alternative way to behave. Thinking about a stable deterrent bargain signals that the elimination of the adversary is not a necessary condition for the security of the defender. The challenger may eventually change its behavior, allowing for the development of a political solution. Yet defining an acceptable status quo with a group that purposefully uses indiscriminate violence against civilians involves high domestic costs and might simply not be acceptable. Since 9/11, for instance, the United States has pursued and communicated a strategy of destroying al Qaeda and its proxy and allied organizations. While there is practical importance in pursuing this strategic goal, carrying it out also contradicts and negates the feasibility of credibly communicating and constructing an alternative, deterrent-based relationship with the organization. To paraphrase Crenshaw's argument, the twin aims of destroying and deterring a single opponent are incompatible. If al Qaeda is right to assume that the United States and its allies are seeking its annihilation, there may be little reason for it to credibly believe that a deterrent relationship, in which it is allowed to survive, is ever feasible. And while Jenkins and Davis suggest that destroying al Qaeda now may deter other groups later, this only further binds the utility of deterrence in counterterrorism to particular engagements while leaving out its role in countering what is usually deemed the most prominent and dangerous transnational terrorist group.

CONCLUSIONS

Deterrence theory has come a long way over the decades. Its role and importance in managing threats and influencing global interactions have waxed and waned. With the end of the Cold War and especially following al Qaeda's 2001 attack on the United States, the theory and practice of deterrence reached a nadir. The threat of nuclear war between the great powers declined dramatically, and the emerging threat of mass-casualty terrorism seemed to negate the very logic of deterrence. Against this backdrop, the prospect of deterring terrorism seemed difficult, if not impossible. This volume offers a more nuanced and critical assessment of these claims. By advancing a three-part research agenda that focuses on the theory, practice, and empiricism of deterring terrorism, we offer academics and policymakers a rigorously updated assessment of the strengths and weaknesses of applying deterrence to counterterrorism. As we summarize here, more research is surely needed, but the thoughtful observations offered in these various chapters go a long way in advancing our thinking about deterring terrorism. We are reminded, once again, of Schelling's opening observation: deterrence learning during the Cold War was "scandalously slow." And like Schelling, we, too, hope that learning how to deter terrorism will prove a smoother and more expeditious endeavor. This volume, in generating insight on the theory and practice of deterring terrorism, is an attempt to get that process started.

NOTES

1. Thomas Schelling, *The Strategy of Conflict* (Cambridge, MA: Harvard University Press, 1960); Thomas Schelling, *Arms and Influence* (New Haven, CT: Yale University Press, 1966).

2. See Janice Gross Stein, "Rational Deterrence Against 'Irrational' Adversaries? No Common Knowledge," in *Complex Deterrence: Strategy in the Global Age*, eds. T. V. Paul, Patrick Morgan, and James Wirtz, (Chicago: University of Chicago Press, 2009).

3. Andreas Wenger, "Kennedy, Chruschtschow und das gemeinsame Interesse der Supermächte am Status quo in Europa," *Vierteljahrshefte für Zeitgeschichte* 46:1 (1989).

4. Alexander George, "The Need for Influence Theory and Actor-Specific Behavioral Models of Adversaries," in *Know Thy Enemy: Profiles of Adversary Leaders and Their Strategic Cultures*, ed. Barry Schneider and Jerrold Post (Maxwell Air Force Base, AL: Air War College, 2003); Alexander George and William Simons, eds., *The Limits of Coercive Diplomacy*, 2nd ed. (Boulder, CO: Westview Press, 1994).

5. Lawrence Freedman, *Deterrence* (Cambridge, UK: Polity Press, 2004), 26.

6. Andreas Wenger, *Living with Peril: Eisenhower, Kennedy, and Nuclear Weapons* (Lanham, MD: Rowman & Littlefield, 1997).

INDEX

Page numbers in italics refer to figures or tables.